FROM THE PACIFIC TO LA PAZ

The Antofagasta (Chili) and Bolivia Railway Company 1888–1988

FROM THE PACIFIC TO LA PAZ

The Antofagasta (Chili) and Bolivia Railway Company 1888–1988

Harold Blakemore

Antofagasta Holdings PLC
Lester Crook Academic Publishing

Antofagasta Holdings PLC, Park House, 16 Finsbury Circus,
London EC2M 7AH

Lester Crook Academic Publishing
London House, 271–273 King Street, Hammersmith,
London W6 9LZ

© Harold Blakemore 1990

All rights reserved; no part of this publication may be reproduced, stored in a retrieval system, or transmitted in any form, or by any means, electronic, mechanical, photocopying, recording, or otherwise without the prior written permission of the Publishers.

First published 1990

British Library Cataloguing in Publication Data:

Blakemore, Harold, *1930* –
From the Pacific to La Paz: the Antofagasta (Chili) and Bolivia Railway Company 1888–1988.
1. Bolivia. Railway services, history
I. Title
385.0984

ISBN 1 – 870915 – 09 – 7

Set in Bembo by Action Typesetting, Gloucester

Printed by Butler and Tanner, Frome

CONTENTS

Preface

The invitation by the Board of Antofagasta Holdings to write the centenary history of the Antofagasta Railway was a challenge in line with my long-standing interest in the history of Chile's desert north and particularly in the role played in its economic evolution by foreign, and notably British, capital and enterprise. I was, therefore, delighted to accept though I was not then fully aware what a task it would be in the light of the vast amount and value of company's archival resources. In the writing of this book, I have been given much asssistance and support, and it is pleasant to record here my gratitude to those who have helped me most while, of course, I alone take full responsibility for the final product.

I owe a particular debt to my research assistant, Dr Andrew Barnard, who has borne the brunt of devilling through the great mass of raw material to give me the refined ore from which to fashion this book. Earlier research was done by two Chilean colleagues, Dr Luis Ortega and Leonardo León and, in Chile itself, Pedro Melo and Ignacio Munoz played a similar part in the later stages. My friend, Dr Ricardo Couyoumdjian of the Catholic University in Santiago, has given me constant encouragement and helpful advice throughout. But I am most indebted to Andrew Barnard and he ought to be described as co-author of the work. I am also grateful to Mr George Craig, who not only supplied me with copies of his own copious notes on the history of the railway but also gave me the benefit of his long experience as an engineer with it, and to Lt-Col. A. E. Heskett, son of a long-serving manager, the redoubtable 'Don Arturo', for the memoirs of his boyhood days in Bolivia and Chile. These were valuable supplements to the very rich archive of the company on which the book is based.

From the beginning, Dr Barnard and I have had close co-operation from the staff of the London office of Antofagasta Holdings, and from the Santiago and Antofagasta offices, who have supplied valuable material, including photographs. The Chairman, Mr Andrónico Luksic, also has taken a personal interest in the enterprise.

Andrew Barnard and Alistair Hennessy critically surveyed the entire text, and I am also grateful, for helpful comments on the early chapters, to George Craig, Dick Harrison, Hugh Holley and R. A. Humphreys. Andrew Henderson, whose family connection with the company as consulting engineers goes back to the beginning, under the style of James Livesey and Son from 1885 to 1891; Livesey, Son and Henderson from 1891 to 1932; Livesey and Henderson from 1932 to 1973; Henderson, Hughes and Busby from 1973 to 1980; Henderson, Busby International from 1980 to 1986; and from 1986, as Kennedy, Henderson Ltd., also gave valuable advice. David Fox of Manchester University and Valerie Fifer, formerly of Goldsmiths' College, University of London, gave important bibliographical assistance on Bolivia. Mel Turner and Ray Ellis, two Australian historians of narrow gauge railways, provided Appendix I, and I am indebted to them and to Mike Swift of the Narrow Gauge Railways Society for permission to use this material. Many of the illustrations come from the company archives, but Ian Thomson of CEPALC provided recondite information and valuable illustrations; as did George Craig; Arthur Heskett, and Dr Sheila Sherwood of the Orient Express.

The book itself is, perhaps, much less the history of the railway than of the people who ran it, and I have tried to portray the problems of the enterprise from the standpoint of those who had to face them – chairmen and members of boards, managing directors, company secretaries, general managers and their staffs in Chile and Bolivia, and senior management and staff in the London office, as well as *empleados* and *obreros* – all confronting the operational issues such a business entailed, and including the wider national context in which it worked. To write a comprehensive history of the FCAB would take far more than one book and, as it is, the writer is as conscious of what has been left out as he is of what is included. His intention was to write a readable story of a remarkable overseas British mercantile operation: it is for the reader to decide how far he has succeeded.

Harold Blakemore
London, December, 1989

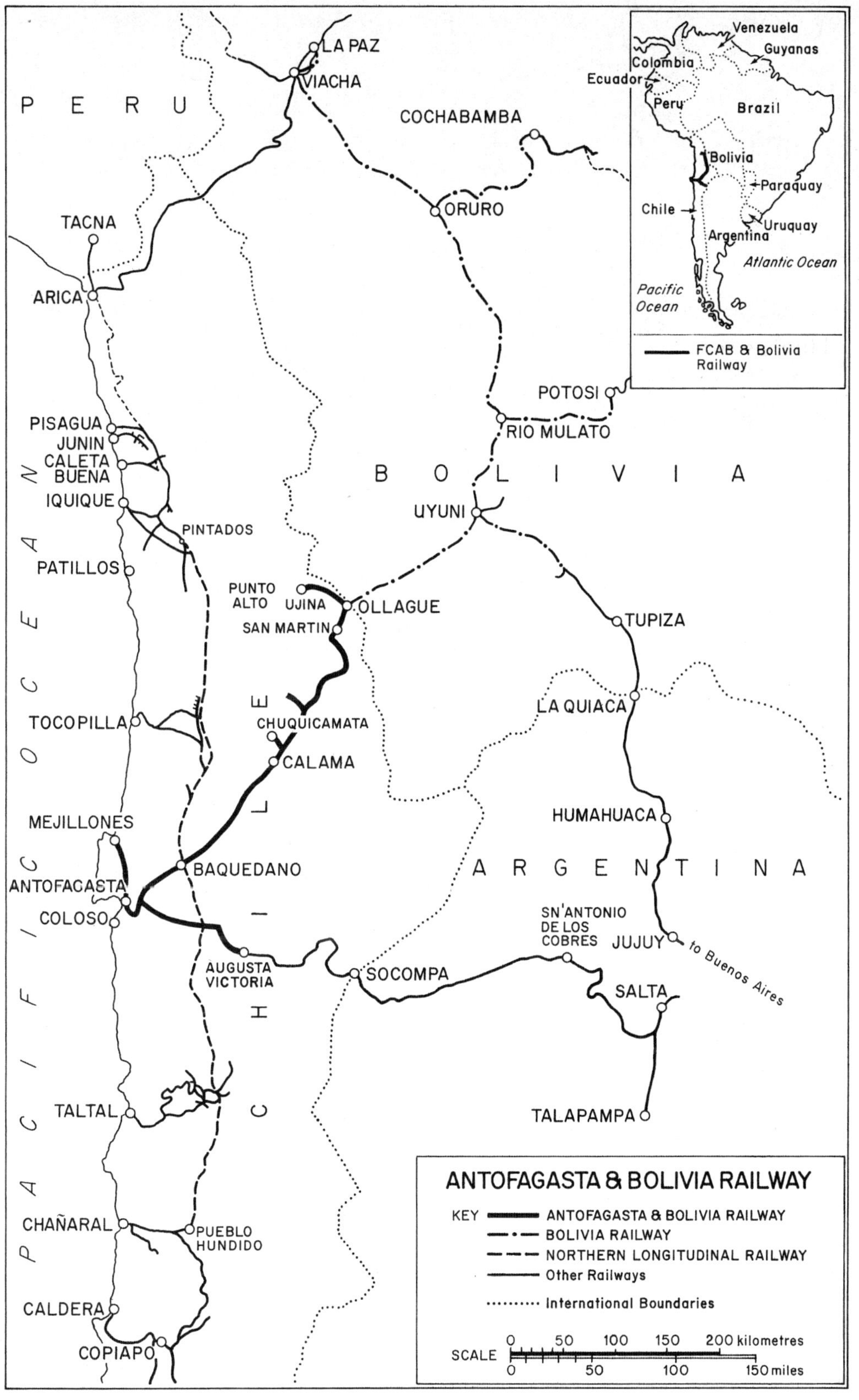

ANTOFAGASTA & BOLIVIA RAILWAY
KEY
ANTOFAGASTA & BOLIVIA RAILWAY
BOLIVIA RAILWAY
NORTHERN LONGITUDINAL RAILWAY
Other Railways
International Boundaries
SCALE
0 50 100 150 200 kilometres
0 50 100 150 miles
PERU
BOLIVIA
CHILE
ARGENTINA
PACIFIC OCEAN
LA PAZ
VIACHA
COCHABAMBA
ORURO
TACNA
ARICA
POTOSI
RIO MULATO
PISAGUA
JUNIN
CALETA BUENA
IQUIQUE
PINTADOS
UYUNI
PATILLOS
PUNTO ALTO
UJINA
OLLAGUE
SAN MARTIN
TUPIZA
LA QUIACA
TOCOPILLA
CHUQUICAMATA
CALAMA
HUMAHUACA
MEJILLONES
BAQUEDANO
ANTOFAGASTA
COLOSO
SN'ANTONIO DE LOS COBRES
JUJUY
to Buenos Aires
AUGUSTA VICTORIA
SOCOMPA
SALTA
TALTAL
TALAPAMPA
CHAÑARAL
PUEBLO HUNDIDO
CALDERA
COPIAPO
Venezuela
Guyanas
Colombia
Ecuador
Peru
Brazil
Bolivia
Paraguay
Chile
Uruguay
Argentina
Atlantic Ocean
Pacific Ocean
FCAB & Bolivia Railway

1 THE BEGINNINGS: LAND, TIME AND MEN

The geographical scene: landscape and climate

Landscape

The railway which was eventually to link the Pacific port of Antofagasta with Bolivia's largest city, La Paz, and also become the main line of a network totalling over 2,800 kilometres, had to traverse a forbidding and dramatic landscape. Today, the main line runs from the coast broadly in a north-easterly direction for rather more than half its length before curving north and north-west across the high plateau (*altiplano*) of Bolivia. So doing, it first cuts across the three basic geographical divisions which, running from north to south, characterize the physiography of Chile.

First, in the west, behind a very narrow shoreline, lies a fragmented range of coastal mountains, with an average height of some 1,000 metres, overhanging the few coastal towns such as Antofagasta, Mejillones, Tocopilla and Taltal, which stand on wave-cut terraces hammered by the ocean swells. Inland, behind these barren heights, the second major longitudinal feature is the great central plateau which stretches to the foothills of the high Andean mountain range in the east, some 250 kilometres from the coast. This is the huge hot desert of the Atacama, 750 kilometres in length, the world's driest region, a vast space of naked rock and sand, and for the most part without vegetation, but not without beauty or wealth. Seen from the air, it looks entirely barren and is mostly brown in colour: at the surface, however, while that monochrome persists throughout the day, as the sun declines and late afternoon winds stir up great clouds of dust, the filtered light bathes the landscape in a kaleidoscope of colour, from bright yellow to violet and then to various shades of purple, before night falls. Though the desert may seem worthless, it contains some of the world's richest deposits of minerals, the exploitation of which – first nitrates, then copper – has been the major prop of the Chilean economy for over a hundred years, and the economic justification, in part, for the building of the railway itself.

From north to south, only one quasi-permanent river crosses the Atacama, the Loa which, rising in the Bolivian Andes, pursues an extraordinarily tortuous course to the Pacific, north of Tocopilla. Other rivers peter out in the desert or run into large salt basins (*salares*), created when volcanic flows in the past cut off drainage outlets. But intermittent streams have cut deep, gorge-like valleys (*quebradas*) into the land surface, giving it, from the air, a fissured, corrugated appearance.

On the eastern side of the desert, in the lee of the first high range of the western Andes, the water-supply has, throughout history, been more secure, owing to run-off streams and rivers, fed by the melting snows of the lofty peaks. Here, oasis towns and villages have survived for centuries, towns such as Calama and San Pedro de Atacama, and historic villages such as Chiu-chiu, Toconao and Ayquina with their old colonial churches and, in some cases, distinctive annual *fiestas* which reflect not only their Spanish Catholic origins but also native Indian roots. Such settlements were based on agriculture, though most lie over 2,000 metres above sea-level. Within 50 kilometres to the east of Calama, however, the land rises steeply to over 3,000 metres as the real mountains are reached.

The western range of the Andes mountains (the *cordillera*) is the third longitudinal band of the Chilean landscape. In many respects, it can equally be regarded as the south-western extension of the Bolivian and Peruvian *altiplano*, known in Chile as the Puna de Atacama, a sterile elevated plateau ranging in height from over 3000 metres to 5,000 metres but buttressed on both sides by heights reaching, at their highest, over 6,000 metres. It is between these peaks and mostly along the *altiplano* that the main line runs in its Bolivian section to La Paz, crossing *en route* several large and impressive *salares*. In fact, however, the highest point on the line is at Ascotán on the Chilean side of the Andes, with an elevation of just under 4,000 metres. The scenery, especially for the lowland dweller, is breathtaking – snow-covered mountains, huge dry basins, but also lakes of which the most impressive is Lake Poopó, along the eastern side of which the railway runs.

Such, in brief, is the varied environment with which the railway builders had to contend, and it posed its own problems of construction and maintenance. But landscape was not the only challenge: climate, too, was a significant factor.

Climate

The most striking climatic characteristic of so much of the terrain over which the railway was to run is its complete lack of regular rainfall. The Atacama includes places where no rain has ever been recorded and throughout time and, in the towns on the coast especially, the assumption that no rain would fall determined such things as the major forms of house construction – wood and mud-bricks. On the coast, there is a higher relative humidity than inland, and more uniform seasons and diurnal temperatures. North of Antofagasta the coast has the phenomenon known to Chileans as the *camanchaca* and to Peruvians as the *garúa*, a kind of grey 'Scottish mist', formed as follows: along the Pacific coast from south to north runs the cool Humboldt current and over it and over the upswelling cold waters between the current and the land fog banks form which drift inland on the onshore breeze. But 'the prevailing temperature inversion prevents vertical air movement and the formation of [actual] precipitation'.[1] Indeed, while Antofagasta has its fogs in its winter season, on many days of the year the traveller there may stand on the shore and, looking south, see cloudless blue sky while, to the north, white clouds form. But, while the average annual rainfall at Antofagasta is no more than 9mm, from time to time, when the northward run of the Humboldt current falls short of its accustomed course, mist becomes rain, and heavy rain at that. In June 1911, for example, 'rain fell at Antofagasta in the early morning; it was accompanied with a violent thunderstorm that caused great alarm among the people, so rare is such a phenomenon on the coast'.[2]

Such rains, so unexpected and against all assumptions, can do immense damage. And there is no regularity, and hence predictability, in their occurrence. For the railway, the rains of 1911 were not so bad: as the sub-manager at Antofagasta reported to London, '. . . a heavy thunderstorm passed over Antofagasta, followed by (for this part of the world) heavy rain, but fortunately no damage was done to Cos. *(sic)* property, apart from leakages through the roofs of some of the houses'.[3] Twenty years later, one of his successors had a different tale to tell: 'We regret to inform you that, as a result of exceptionally heavy and prolonged rains which commenced to fall at an early hour on the 20th instant, our lines were cut in several places with the consequence that all trains had to be suspended . . .'[4] A week later, he spelled out the facts: 'It was immediately necessary for us to suspend all trains on the sections Antofagasta/Mejillones, Antofagasta/Baquedano and on the Aguas Blancas Railway . . . we were able to run the International train from La Paz on the 20th instant as far as Baquedano . . .'[5] The cost of repairs, not inconsiderable in those days, came to £2,959.[6]

Behind the coastal *cordillera*, in the desert proper, such vagaries of climate are more infrequent, though they do occur. Here, the key factor is temperature not precipitation, and the range, from day to night, is among the most extreme in the world. Between the coast and Calama, it can be as much as 20°C, higher than that for either the Sahara and Gobi deserts. Only very infrequently does the weather pattern in the high Andes to the east, notably precipitation, invade the desert below the 3,000 metre mark. But, when it does, the effects are dramatic.

The snow-line in the western *cordillera* of the Andes lies at approximately 4,400 metres, above which, particularly in the Bolivian summer rainy season (often miscalled by foreigners 'the Bolivian winter'), rain, hail, sleet and snow fall most years between January and March. And again, as on the coast, climatic behaviour is not entirely regular. While generally, the heavy precipitation is confined to the highlands, in particular years it pushes into the desert itself, affecting the Chilean section of the line as well as the Bolivian. A classic year was 1953, and the report of the resident engineer at that time, George W. Craig, is worth quoting at some length.

> The first heavy rains of Friday March 6th commenced about 3pm and continued until 7pm. It rained heavily in Calama and Chuquicamata, but in the San Pedro-Polapi area the rain was of a torrential nature. Reports ... began to arrive about 10pm and indicated severe damage to the high embankment over the Loa culvert in Km.306.500 and another high embankment in Km.307.600 completely destroyed ... The writer and the District Engineer, Calama, inspected the affected area early the following morning ... some 900 cubic [metres] were washed away, and the track left suspended in the air for some 10 metres. In Km.307.600 the embankment was washed away over a distance of 55 metres and required a calculated filling of 330 cubic metres ... At 6pm (on March 7th) torrential rain and heavy thunderstorms broke directly over Km.306 and the Abra hills ... All work was suspended ... That night the rains extended as far south as Sierra Gorda ...[7]

It should be noted that Sierra Gorda, in the Atacama desert, is a mere 100 kilometres as the crow flies from the Pacific coast, much less than half the distance from where the storms began. While it is true that, as Craig puts it: 'the storm was unprecedented, both in duration and severity, and nothing of its nature has been known in living memory'[8], others less dramatic occurred both before and since, interrupting traffic and necessitating urgent repairs. In 1953, traffic on the main line was affected for a week, and some repairs had to be temporary simply to restore working lines until more durable repairs could take place.

In the *cordillera* – Chilean and Bolivian – snow was, if not a frequent, at least an annual, hazard, requiring the use of snow-ploughs, as well as locomotives equipped with special blades (*trompas*), not unlike cowcatchers in the American west, to deal with the lesser drifts. Nonetheless, arriving at stations above the snow-line, 'it was often to find the station building completely buried, with just a wisp of smoke arising through the snow from a fire inside the building, the station-master and his family living quite happily inside'.[9]

Hence, climate, like landscape, was and is an important factor in the evolution of the Antofagasta-Bolivia railway. But, of course, environmental issues were not the only ones to be faced in the construction and operation of the lines.

Railway building in the region: general problems

According to H.T. Booker who, during his remarkable career as a railway engineer, worked for the Central Railway of Peru, 'no other line in the world can compare with the Central of Peru. The Chilean section of the Antofagasta-Bolivia was "duck soup" in comparison!'[10] He was referring solely to the actual construction problems of the two lines, but *any* comparison with the Central of Peru is invidious in that respect, scaling as it does the high Peruvian *cordillera*, though the world's highest rail summit, at about 4,800 metres was actually on the Collahuasi branch-line of the Antofagasta Railway at Punto Alto until December 1958 when the track was lifted. Moreover, Booker's statement was confined to the Chilean section of the Antofagasta-Bolivia railway which, once it crossed the coastal range, had a comparatively easy climb to the Andes across the Atacama desert. Nevertheless, while, in comparison with other Andean railways, 'the Antofagasta railway [was] built quickly, cheaply, and efficiently',[11] it had precisely similar problems as others in its creation, construction and continuance. The purely engineering problems were not so acute as elsewhere (though maintenance was a different matter) for by the time the railway was being constructed, highland construction had advanced tremendously since the days of Richard Trevithick and George Stephenson, both of whom were interested in railway possibilities in South America in the first half of the nineteenth century, not least in Chile and Peru. But both pioneers came too early in terms of technology tackling topography. By the 1870s and 1880s, however, the accumulated experience of railway building in Alpine Europe, India and the North American Rockies, had taught many lessons, and, by that time also rails, rolling stock, and other machinery for operating mountain railways had been developed sufficiently for undertakings in the Andes.

Purely technical problems in railway building, however, are broadly universal where physical environments are alike. Other problems are not. These include the financing of particular projects and their likely profitability, the provision of labour to construct and maintain plant, and the accessibility to appropriate technology. Such problems have additional dimensions for railway companies operating in foreign settings, not least since they also involve the governments themselves.

In Latin America, after the destructive wars of independence in the first quarter of the nineteenth century, all the infant republics lacked the necessary tools for building their economies. The wars had been expensive and the economies had been disrupted; much Spanish capital had flown home, and a lot of domestic capital was tied up in land. Secondly, the new states lacked the technical skills to create the infrastructure of better communications, ports and other public works, owing partly to colonial educational traditions in which attention to practical matters had taken second place to what were regarded as more gentlemanly pursuits. There were, of course, exceptions to these generalizations but they tended to prove the rule. Consequently, to supply the needs of finance and expertise, the more enlightened of the new leaders looked abroad, and notably to Great Britain where the industrial revolution was moving into top gear. This is not the place to re-tell the economic history of nineteenth-century Latin America, nor the vicissitudes of the many foreign entrepreneurs, bankers and traders who saw in Latin America tremendous challenges and opportunities for doing good business: suffice to say that, with more settled political conditions in many countries from mid-century, the economic nexus between Latin America and the industrializing countries of Western Europe and the United States increasingly developed. It was fuelled, of course, by growing external demand for the continent's raw materials – foodstuffs for rising populations in the more developed world, minerals to feed the burgeoning industries, and other commodities demanded by new technology.

In this process, 'investment in railways . . . was the key . . . the coffee of São Paulo, the wheat and cattle of the River Plate, the minerals of Mexico, and the nitrates and copper of Chile were moved to the seaports along railway lines partly or wholly financed by British capital'.[12] And the necessary complements to finance were engineering skill and technical experience, and the labour force to build the lines.

With the FCAB, the first two elements came mainly, though not entirely, from abroad, labour from home, a common characteristic of railway building in Latin America. Capital investment as the railway was extended was always forthcoming, based, obviously, on shareholders' assumptions of reasonable profits. But, as with most railways in the region, the problems would depend upon market conditions for the freight carried. To this extent, the FCAB would always be, to a certain degree, dependent upon world economic factors over which it could have no control, notably prices of the commodities it carried out for which demand was to prove highly elastic. This was true of Bolivian silver and tin, as it was for Chilean nitrates and copper. The profitability of the line, therefore, was not simply a matter of good management and amicable relations with host governments. External shocks, such as the two world wars, and world economic recession, particularly in the late 1920s and early 1930s, had a dramatic effect, often a sudden one, on the company's prospects.

The provision of adequate direction and management was not so difficult, given Britain's depth of experience by the mid-nineteenth century, and the foremost position she occupied in the world economy and in technological development, partly a reflection of an educational system in which mechanics and engineers were coming to be regarded not simply as labourers, but as men of ingenuity and vision. And, throughout its history, the FCAB seems to have been singularly fortunate, not only in the quality of such men who served it but also in their long-standing loyalty to the company they had joined. Inevitably, there were some misfits who, through lack of competence or personality, failed to make the grade. But they were few and far between. Most were highly motivated, well-trained, and pragmatic enough to deal with both technical and human problems. Invidious though it may be to give examples, two will reinforce the point.

A.E. Heskett joined the company on an initial three-year contract in 1906, arriving in Antofagasta as an engineer in November, at the age of 25 and at a salary of £300 a year. He was successively in charge of various sections of the line, becoming Assistant Resident Engineer in 1911, Acting Resident Engineer in 1914, Resident Engineer in 1915, and General Manager of the Bolivian section in 1921. He became General Manager of the Chilean section of 1929, at a salary of £4,000 plus £500 entertainment allowance. He retired at the end of September 1947, after forty-one years of service.[13]

G.W. Craig arrived in Antofagasta, aged twenty-four, in August 1925, as an assistant sectional engineer on a salary of £300. He progressed from being engineer for the Calama section in 1930, to assistant to the Resident Engineer in 1946, Resident Engineer in 1948 and retired early in February, 1962, with thirty-seven years' service to his credit.[14] And such remarkable continuity of service by those who actually ran the railway on the ground was paralleled by the tenure of office of many of those who directed it from abroad.

As with all other foreign-built Latin American railways, senior staff were always expatriate until recent times though at middle management levels the local-born who had acquired the necessary skills were not uncommon; as a widely-travelled observer noted in 1922:

> Englishmen who travel or reside in Latin American countries are generally men not falling below a certain standard of education, and if not always of

> independent means, they have come as representatives of wealthy firms, companies or syndicates. They are managers of branch houses, engineers, travellers, sportsmen, financiers . . . [15]

Consequently, though the lines of the FCAB were planned and directed by foreigners, they were built, and to a large extent manned, by local labour, at least at the lower levels. In this respect, the company was assisted by one feature of nineteenth-century Chile which was much less marked in other states where massive foreign immigration did not occur as it did in southern Brazil, Argentina and Uruguay. This was internal and external migration, when new economic opportunities opened up. Thus the gold bonanza in California in 1849 attracted large numbers of Chilean labourers. The traditional system of labour on the land, known as *inquilinaje*, was not so restrictive of individual movement as were similar systems in other countries. During the nineteenth century, for example, landowners in the central valley frequently complained of labour shortages as their hands left the estates to build public works, including railways. And the nitrate industry – the bastion of the Chilean economy from, roughly, 1880 to 1920 – would not have developed as it did without sucking in labour from the south to the north.

Such migrant labourers laid the lines and maintained them. And the *roto*, the Chilean labourer, had a reputation for durability: 'as tough and capable of prolonged fatigue on the poorest of food as the admirable little horse he bestrides'.[16] 'I have seen', said another traveller, '*rotos* carrying bags of nitrate, each weighing 300 pounds all day, and tossing them about like bags of feathers. Four of them will lift a piano and trot off with it, and at the mines peons may be seen carrying bags of ore, each weighing 150 pounds, up the notched sticks that serve as ladders, all day long.'[17]

With that combination of foreign finance and technical expertise, and with native labour, the railway lines were laid. But all of them had specific, as well as general, problems to confront, none more severe than the FCAB.

Running, as it did, for much of its length across the most barren desert in the world, the FCAB had, as few other railways anywhere, the problem of water supply. This was not simply a matter of filling the boilers of railway engines in the age of steam; it also concerned the industries and the communities the railway served. On the coast, at the outset, desalination plants and condensers appeared by the late 1870s; inland, artesian wells were bored for the nitrate works. But, as the port of Antofagasta developed, and as demand for water grew, the FCAB and, indeed, its predecessors, had to tap more secure resources. Such was the river Loa: by a series of concessions to use its water, and that of its tributaries, the FCAB became the major supplier of water to the desert region as well as to Antofagasta itself. Later, springs nearer the Andes would be tapped, and pipe-lines laid. In respect of water supply in desert regions, the FCAB was more than a railway.

The historical setting: Chile and Bolivia

Chile

Throughout its history, the FCAB operated as a foreign company in alien environments, and it had to come to terms with them. Yet, in that context, it had the great advantage that it was not a newcomer so much as an inheritor of what had gone before. The two countries in which the company was to operate shared, of course, much of a common historical experience as legatees of the Spanish empire in America. Yet, for neighbouring countries with that inheritance, both throughout the long colonial period and after independence in the early nineteenth century, the differences between them were many and profound.

Geography was a major factor in shaping their distinctive evolution. When Chile declared its independence, it was about one-third of its present size, and its frontiers were remarkably natural. The new republic consisted of a compact block of territory, some 960 kilometres long but nowhere more than 160 kilometres wide, its western limit the Pacific shoreline, its eastern boundary the Andean *cordillera*. At the southern end of the fertile central valley – the core of the country – the river Bío-Bío was the dividing line between Spanish and Indian territory, though beyond that limit stood a few small towns, such as Valdivia and Osorno, founded as sea-borne settlements and to a great extent dependent on maritime links for their survival. Even further south, virtually on the edge of the Antarctic continent, Punta Arenas, founded in 1849, asserted Chile's claim to control the straits of Magellan, of vital strategic and commercial significance. The northern frontier was much less well-defined though hardly less natural, corresponding to the transitional zone between the northern part of the central valley and the immense Atacama desert.

Within these confines, the Kingdom of Chile, as it was called in the colonial period, developed specific characteristics that gave their stamp to the independent nation. One was racial structure. The most populous of the native Indian tribes, the Araucanians, lived in the dense forest region south of the Bío-Bío which was, in effect, a military frontier until the pacification of the Indians in the 1880s. The Indians of the central valley had, by the beginning of the nineteenth century, been virtually assimilated, so that a two-tiered racial structure existed: whites and *mestizos* – the product of white and Indian fusion. Thus, unlike most other Spanish American states, Chile avoided the complications of a more complex mixture of races.

In part the mirror of this racial picture, Chilean society was also clearly defined. It had evolved as essentially an agrarian society, in which a close-knit landholding white oligarchy dominated the national life, while the great mass of the mostly illiterate *mestizo* poor laboured on the oligarch's estates and ministered to his needs. The Chilean upper class was remarkably homogeneous, its members interrelated through marriage, and its solidarity was little affected by different economic interests, or by ideological divisions, such as attitudes to the Church and forms of government. From independence, under the realistic constitution of 1833, Chile was a highly centralized state, run from Santiago, and attempts to assert regional autonomy from time to time, as in 1851 and 1859, failed completely. The oligarchy and certain key figures in the formation of the republic such as Diego Portales (1793–1837) implanted in Chile a firm tradition of constitutional government of an authoritarian but impersonal kind, and in which the common Spanish American experiences of militarism and arbitrary dictatorship did not occur. The transfer of government from one president to another, with few exceptions, was smooth and orderly, and while elections were subject to abuses, and not least by sitting governments, the comparative stability of Chile in Spanish America had, by the 1880s, earned it the accolade of 'the England of South America'.

Another reason for that recognition was the economic development of the republic. Stable government and enlightened leadership enabled Chile to capitalize on its considerable resources, agricultural and mineral, in an expanding world economy, and trade was the motor of its development. While there were periods of recession, notably in the 1850s and 1870s, overall there was steady growth. Exports of agricultural produce from the central valley, notably wheat, and of minerals – copper and silver – from the northern regions enabled Chile to increase the value of its external trade ten-fold between 1825 and 1875. From the 1840s to the 1870s government revenues exceeded expenditure, and – further testimony of the country's probity and growing international reputation – unlike most of her neighbours, Chile promptly met her obligations on her foreign debt.

Such development permitted the growth of a broader infrastructure, social as well as economic. The educational system expanded, though as yet, it did not touch that 80 per cent of Chileans who, up to the 1870s, lived in the countryside. But government steadily increased the proportion of expenditure on public works such as roads, bridges and ports, and, with economic expansion, institutions such as banks and joint stock companies developed. The first law governing the latter's operations was passed in 1854: by 1875, 159 such companies had been established, of which no fewer than 77 were in mining, 24 in transport and communications and 21 in finance. The predominance of mining enterprises reflected the rapid expansion of what is still Chile's most important natural resource – copper. Between the 1840s and the 1870s, Chile was the world's major producer, and the world standard for the metal was 'Chile bars', a title only dropped in the 1880s, as North American and Spanish competition pushed Chile into third place as a world producer.

Vital to all these developments were, of course, communications, notably railways, and mining expansion was a major stimulus to their construction. Though Chile's first railway was South America's third – preceded only by short lines in Peru and in British Guiana – it was, when opened to traffic in December 1851, the most substantial, linking the northern port of Caldera with the rich mining district of Copiapó on the fringe of the Atacama. Over 400 kilometres long, the line stimulated not only the expansion of mining in the region but also the agricultural regions further south in the provision of foodstuffs to the north. Its constructor was the remarkable American engineer, William Wheelwright (1798–1873), a key pioneer in engineering works in South America, active not only in Chile but also in Argentina, Peru and Ecuador. And remarkable Wheelwright certainly was: it was he who, inspired by a vision to build a line linking Chile on the Pacific with Argentina on the Atlantic, secured from the Chilean government in 1849 a concession to build a line linking Valparaiso to Santiago, across the *cordillera de la costa*. Unfortunately, he could not raise the funds, so in 1851, the government itself, in association with various Chilean capitalists, agreed to finance the line which was begun in 1852. Financial constraints made progress slow and in 1858 the government contracted a foreign loan. The line was completed in 1863, much of the work undertaken by another American pioneer of railway building in Spanish America, Henry Meiggs (1811–77), active on other lines in Chile but chiefly remembered for his extraordinary engineering feats in Peru.

Wheelwright himself had other roles to play in developing Chilean communications. It was he who persuaded British investors to found, in 1835, the Pacific Steam Navigation Company, based in Liverpool, which by 1840, had paddle-steamers operating along the Pacific coast and, from 1868, ran a line of steamer ships between Liverpool and Valparaiso via the straits of Magellan. It was also Wheelwright who joined Valparaiso to Santiago by telegraph in 1851–52, initiating a national network which, by 1876, embraced 48 towns through over 2,500 kilometres of cable.

The railway developments of the 1850s and 1860s set the pattern for future growth, a combination of public and private enterprise. The state's assumption of a prominent role in the Valparaiso-Santiago line logically implied that successive governments should – as they did – recognize that, given Chile's extraordinary shape, a basic national objective must be to bind the outlying provinces to the core through a predominantly state-run rail network. Though many of the sections of the main line from north to south, together with lateral branches, were originally constructed by private companies under government concessions, primarily to promote economic development, such as agriculture and coal in the south and mineral resources in the north, government pursued a fairly consistent policy of buying out. From the 1850s, a long central trunk line was constructed which, to the south of Santiago at the country's heart, had reached Puerto Montt (1079 kilometres) by 1913, and, to the north, Iquique on the coast of the Atacama desert (1200 kilometres) by 1929. At the same time government consolidated its hold on sections which had been built by private enterprise. Hence, it acquired the Chañaral Railway in 1888, the railway from Coquimbo to La Serena and Ovalle in 1895, the line from Ovalle to Tongoi in 1901, and the Copiapó Railway itself in 1911, all originally privately owned. By 1914, the Chilean state owned and ran about 60 per cent of the total system of over 8,500 kilometres. But many of the initiatives for what, by then, was one of the best railway systems in Latin America had come from the private sector.

Chile's attitudes to foreign capital and enterprise were another factor in its nineteenth-century reputation. Almost from the time of independence, governments pursued a policy of 'the open door' to foreign capital and enterprise: as it was said in 1880, 'welcoming such impulse as these foreigners gave to the trade and industry of the country, harbouring no envy or jealousy of the fortune these came to accumulate.'[18] A Wheelwright or a Meiggs who had technical skill and the capacity to raise capital for development was recognized as a co-partner in development, and the government's liberal attitude towards that contribution was little influenced by nationalist sentiment. Among those foreigners, the British predominated. 'The workshop of the world', Great Britain, was, throughout the century, Chile's chief trading partner: by 1860, Britain supplied 33 per cent of Chilean imports, and took over 50 per cent of Chilean exports – notably minerals and wheat – while, by 1875 Britain imported 60 per cent of Chilean exports and provided 40 per cent of Chilean imports, chiefly manufactured goods. A dozen British merchant houses were established in Valparaiso by the early 1820s, pre-eminent among them was Antony Gibbs and Sons, to be joined later in the century by such firms as Williamson, Balfour, and Duncan Fox. Although, like most great ports, Valparaiso had a cosmopolitan character, the British came to occupy first place in the foreign community, so much so that a visitor from the United States in 1888 declared:

> Trade is practically controlled by Englishmen, all commercial transactions are calculated in pounds sterling, the English language is almost exclusively spoken upon the street and in the shops, an English paper is printed there, English goods are almost exclusively sold, and this city is no more than an English colony.[19]

There was a certain exaggeration in this, but not much.

A number of the commercial houses were engaged in other economic activities such as mining in the north and milling in the agricultural south, and their capital and enterprise were very evident by the 1870s. They were also, necessarily, involved in finance. And, of course, they took their culture with them, not least in education and sport. Finally, one other significant aspect of the Anglo-Chilean connection lay in the intermarriage of British men and Chilean women, from the earliest years of the nineteenth century; these relationships gave rise to the Anglo-Chilean families whose role in Chilean history was to be so considerable and whose names recur throughout the history of the republic – Edwards, Lyon, Blest, Ross and Walker, to name but a few. They are recorded, as are the prominent British entrepreneurs who played such a significant role in Chilean development. Hundreds of others are unremembered – copper miners, many from Cornwall, engineers and engine drivers, mechanics, artisans and clerks – though their contribution, in technical skill was hardly less significant.

Such, in brief, were the origins and development of British enterprise in Chile, a country in which that enterprise was to be further employed in the decades to come.

Bolivia

The geographical, racial and political advantages enjoyed by independent Chile were not present in Bolivia. Although at the time of independence in 1825, Bolivia had a Pacific coastline in that part of the Atacama between the rivers Loa and Salado, it was still one of the two most isolated countries in South America – the other was Paraguay – and its frontiers were very ill-defined. Known in colonial times as Upper Peru, its territory had a highly varied physical character, ranging from the high Andes in the west to the sprawling low-lying zones of rain-forest, swamp and grasslands in the north and east. Few countries in the world confronted more formidable problems of creating unity and centralized government and, in contrast with Chile, geography did nothing to help solve the problems of national organization. One consequence was a stronger sense of regionalism in Bolivia than in Chile, and this had not a little to do with Bolivia's much more turbulent history.

Racially, too, Bolivia had a more complex character. At independence, its population was about 1,100,000 – about twice that of Chile – but there were three races, not two as in Chile. Indians were the majority, some 800,000 compared with 200,000 white Spaniards and Spanish born in America (creoles), and about 100,000 *mestizos*. Naturally, the whites constituted the nation, such as it was. A contemporary observer wrote:

> Public feeling may be said to be exclusively confined in Bolivia to the white or creole population, since the aborigines who have scarcely enjoyed a political existence heretofore, cannot be supposed to possess any other feeling beyond that which regards their immediate interests.[20]

Consequently, and here there is a comparison rather than a contrast with Chile, the Indians in Bolivia occupied a social position akin to that of *mestizos* in Chile itself, though very different in its characteristics. They were passive elements in the country's evolution, political and economic. But, whereas in Chile, the *mestizos* were bound to the great estates of the landowners, in Bolivia the Indian communities retained their own lands, in communal ownership, until much later in the century. Either way, the monopoly of social, political and economic power rested with the mineowners, merchants, landowners and military.

Unlike the tradition of impersonal government established in Chile from the 1830s, Bolivia's political evolution to the 1880s was marked by a succession of *caudillos*, autocratic military leaders, some enlightened, others little short of barbaric. Their rule was often challenged by other *caudillos*, and most were replaced by force. 'It has been estimated that in the decade between 1840 and 1849 alone there occurred in Bolivia sixty-five attempted coups d'etat'.[21] It is impossible to say precisely how far political instability affected economic development, though there is abundant contemporary opinion to suggest it deterred foreign investment to a certain degree. A higher level of stability obtained after 1880 by which time the motor of the economy – enormous mineral wealth – had already become the main attraction to nationals and foreigners alike.

Throughout the colonial period, from the discovery in 1545 of the fabulous silver mine of Potosí, what became Bolivia had been famous for its mineral wealth. Pentland[22] estimated that from that date to 1800 over £3bn worth of silver (at then current prices) had been produced – 46,000 tons of pure silver. But the independence period brought stagnation: the wars disrupted production and created a flight of Spanish capital; mines were flooded, their tunnels collapsed, requiring sizeable capital resources to resuscitate them. Bolivian mining went into recession until the 1850s. Recovery then began as a new mining elite emerged, landowners and commercial men, mostly from Cochabamba, who bought out the smaller mine-owners and rehabilitated the mines with modern technology. Prominent among them was Aniceto Arce, a later President of Bolivian (1888–92) and head of the Huanchaca Company, whose involvement in mining is closely related to the history of the FCAB.

The Huanchaca Mining Company had been founded in 1832 but, such were the costs of restoring the mines that, after twenty-four years' operation, shareholders had received no dividends. In 1856, Arce acquired the controlling interest and began to turn the company round, and modest profits were made. Capital, however, was still in too short supply to expand operations, notably in refining capacity and better communications.

To solve this problem, Arce turned to Chile where considerable economic progress had been made by the 1870s and sizeable fortunes created, not least in mining. The key person he contacted was a leading Chilean politician and businessman, Melchor Concha y Toro, a former Minister of Finance, who, with other prominent Chilean capitalists, visited Bolivia in 1872 to survey the Huanchaca properties in Pulacayo. Negotiations resulted, in 1873, in the foundation of the Bolivian Huanchaca Company, in which Arce held a third of the shares, the Chileans, for the most part, the rest. Thereafter, the company prospered, and further reorganization in 1877 permitted an influx of European capital, British, French and German.

Such capital, along with Chilean, had already long been active in the exploitation of the mineral resources of the Bolivian littoral in the Atacama desert, and that development was to exercise a decisive influence on the relations between Bolivia and Chile in the late 1870s.

Antecedents and precursors to 1888

In the history of relations between Chile and Bolivia almost from independence to the present day the crucial issue has been the demarcation of common frontiers. The Bolivian claim to a Pacific coastline had been underlined by 'the Liberator', Simón Bolívar himself, who had designated the tiny port of Cobija, at 22° 32′ S, as Bolivia's outlet to that ocean. During the late 1820s and early 1830s, failing to negotiate with Peru for the cession of the well-watered port of Arica further north, much more accessible to the Bolivian centres of population in the highlands, successive governments sought to develop Cobija. But, as a British observer remarked: 'it is a benighted spot separated by an immense desert of sand from the inhabited part of the country'.[23] Its water supply was precarious and it was almost 1,000 kilometres from the high plateau where most Bolivians lived, three times as distant as Arica.

In short, as Bolivia's Pacific port it was economically unviable. Hence, Arica assumed that role.

Cobija's failure emphasized Bolivia's problem in making effective her claim to part of the Atacama; and that claim came under further attack with the discovery of mineral deposits there from the 1840s. It was guano, the rich natural fertilizer formed over time from the droppings of countless millions of sea-birds, that first attracted attention. Peru's exploitation of her own vast deposits on the mainland in the province of Tarapacá and, more particularly, on the Chincha islands, was already, by the 1840s, providing more than two-thirds of the state revenue, and exciting the interest of Chile in the Atacama. In 1842, a Chilean expedition went up the coast to Mejillones (23° 2′ S.), and discovered rich deposits. This led President Manuel Bulnes to claim that latitude as Chile's northern boundary, and Bolivian protests for the next two decades were to no avail. However, in the immediate aftermath of the war of 1866 between Spain on the one hand and Peru, Chile, Bolivia and Ecuador on the other – the last attempt by the former colonial power to reassert itself on the Pacific coast – conciliation prevailed. The treaty between Chile and Bolivia in 1866 established their desert frontier at 24° S. but also stipulated that between latitudes 23° and 25° S. the proceeds of mineral wealth should be shared equally between them. But, in terms of physical control, Chile had it all her own way. The remoteness of La Paz from the coast and the physical obstacles in getting from one to the other contrasted with Chile's maritime advantage, an ease of access which made the Chilean presence in the shared zone predominant. And, in Bolivian Atacama, it was to grow rapidly.

In 1860, when nitrate was beginning to overtake guano in the world market for natural fertilizers, and had long been exploited in Peruvian Tarapacá, the Chilean José Santos Ossa discovered rich deposits of nitrate at Salar del Carmen, north of the Chilean official boundary and in the hinterland of the tiny port of La Chimba. Together with another Chilean entrepreneur, Francisco Puelma, he finally secured, in 1866, a Bolivian government concession to exploit the deposits. On the basis of this concession, the partners looked for additional capital, to found, in 1868, the *Sociedad Exploradora del Distrito de Atacama*. That same year, the despotic ruler of Bolivia, Mariano Melgarejo, granted additional privileges to the original concession. In addition to the cession of five square leagues of nitrate grounds in the desert, and four more near La Chimba for agricultural purposes, he now gave the company the monopoly of nitrate extraction and shipment from Bolivian Atacama, the right to build a cart road to the deposits from La Chimba, now called Antofagasta, a league of land on either side of the road, and the right to build a railway in due course. For its part, the company paid a licence fee, undertook to build a mole at Antofagasta for state use, provide water-posts and accommodation for travellers, and maintain eight carts on the road. All this property would revert to the state after fifteen years but, if a railway were built, the monopoly would last for forty years and the concession for another forty, after which the state would assume ownership.

But, however valuable the concession, the partners did not have sufficient capital to exploit it. Virtually no infrastructure existed and, when it was created, the costs of extracting and refining the nitrate would have to compete with the now rapidly-expanding fields in Peruvian Tarapacá. There, a large amount of British capital and enterprise was involved, not least that of the House of Gibbs. Ossa and Puelma, therefore, turned to one of Chile's richest men, Agustín Edwards Ossandon, son of George Edwards, a British doctor who had arrived in Valparaiso in 1807 – before the Spaniards left – married into a prominent local family, and began a dynasty whose prominent role in Chilean public life has lasted to the present day. Don Agustín had made his money in mining and banking, which had brought him into contact with a number of prominent British business houses in Chile. They, after all, had capital to invest and, more importantly, long experience not only of nitrate extraction but also of the export markets. Pre-eminent here was Gibbs and, in March, 1869, that House, prompted by Edwards, joined forces with him, Puelma, Ossa, Jorge Smith – an old nitrate 'hand' – and Melbourne Clark, another important British nitrate capitalist. The company was registered as Melbourne Clark and Co., though Gibbs had the largest share-holding and assumed the dominant managerial role. The Chileans held 56.6 per cent of the shares, the British 43.4 per cent.

Work went forward rapidly. The *oficina* (nitrate works) of Salar del Carmen was established by British engineers by the end of 1869; two moles – one for the Bolivian state, one for the company – were constructed at Antofagasta, and a cart road with water posts was laid down. Antofagasta itself was officially 'founded' by the Bolivian government on 22 October 1868, but its growth was slow until, in 1870, rich silver deposits were discovered at Caracoles, some 200 kilometres from the coast, south-west of the oasis of Calama. Caracoles became a vast mining-camp, in which Chileans predominated, though it was officially Bolivian territory, and Antofagasta was its natural port. At the same time, Melbourne Clark & Co., now managed by a Gibbs' nominee, George Hicks, discovered new nitrate deposits at Salinas, 128 kilometres from Antofagasta, and sought to exploit them. The idea of building a railway gained impetus from these events.

In 1872, Melbourne Clark & Co. was reconstituted, and registered as a new company: the *Compañia de Salitres y Ferrocarril de Antofagasta* (the Antofagasta Nitrate and Railway Co.). Smith had died in 1870,

Clark had played no active part, Ossa was losing interest, so the new company's original shareholders were Gibbs, Edwards and Puelma, the latter two with 848 shares each, the former with 804, in a total capitalization of some £460,000. But, significantly as it turned out, during the 1870s re-issue of shares took place, some being acquired by important Chileans, including ministers and congressmen.

The extensive concessions originally granted by Melgarejo – including freedom from taxation of any kind – enabled the company to compete effectively with Tarapacá. But, early in 1872, after the overthrow of the dictator, the Bolivian Constituent Assembly annulled all the concessions he had made, and both the company and the Chilean government protested. After lengthy negotiations, the company's rights were re-affirmed and, indeed, recognized in a treaty between Chile and Bolivia in August 1874. This established the common boundary at the 24th parallel, reduced Chile's claim to receipts from the 'shared zone', but also included a guarantee that for twenty-five years Bolivia would not raise taxes on Chilean interests and exports. Meanwhile, Bolivia, alarmed at the rapid increase of Chilean economic interests, as well as population, in her desert territory, signed in February 1873, a defensive treaty with Peru to guarantee each other's independence, territory and sovereignty against external threat, meaning Chile. This so-called 'secret' treaty was well-known in Santiago within months. Both countries had grounds for apprehension at Chilean encroachment: by 1875, 10,000 Chileans were active in Peruvian Tarapacá, and British and Chilean capital were predominant in the nitrate industry. The same was true of the Bolivian Atacama: with the development of nitrates and the silver of Caracoles, by the mid-1870s over 90 per cent of the population of Antofagasta was Chilean.

Some impetus had been given to this development by the increased operations of the Antofagasta Nitrate and Railway Co. By 1 December 1873, it had built the railway line between the port and the *oficina* of Salar del Carmen, of 2ft 6in gauge. In 1877, the line was extended to Carmen Alto, 127 kilometres from Antofagasta and, in 1878 to Salinas (128 kilometres). At that time, the nitrate raw material (*caliche*) was transported to Antofagasta for elaboration and there, too, the company had built condensers and a desalination plant, both to process the raw material and provide water for the port. In the 1870s the company prospered but towards the end of the decade, international developments threatened its existence.

On 14 February 1878 the Bolivian government of Hilarión Daza unilaterally, and in clear contravention of the 1874 treaty, imposed a tax of 10 cents per *quintal* (about 100 lb) of nitrate exported from the 23° – 24° zone and, indeed, made it retroactive to the date of the treaty. If permitted, this measure would seriously undercut the company's competitive position with the nitrate of Tarapacá, since it was the tax concessions which made it viable. The Chilean government's aid was invoked, and Santiago protested to La Paz, suggesting arbitration since a protocol to the treaty, signed in 1875, allowed for that. Negotiations dragged on but got nowhere; the company's manager at Antofagasta, the redoubtable and pugnacious George Hicks, flatly refused to pay the 90,000 Bolivian pesos demanded and finally, the Bolivian prefect at Antofagasta, Severino Zapata, ordered the embargo of the company's property on 11 January 1879 and the arrest of Hicks. The latter had so annoyed the authorities on a variety of issues that, as he himself put it:

> All the authorities are exasperated with the company and it is virtually impossible to approach them; have no doubt that they will put every possible obstacle in our path.[24]

They were probably even more annoyed that they could not arrest him for he prudently took refuge on the Chilean ironclad, *Blanco Encalada*, which had fortunately arrived at Antofagasta a little before. Events then moved fast: on 1 February, a Bolivian decree cancelled the company's nitrate concessions, and another ordered the auction of the company's property to pay the tax. The date fixed was 14 February 1879.

Meanwhile, however, in Chile, the company's shareholders had not been idle, and they included, as noted, a fair number of prominent public men. A campaign of support was mounted in the press, emphasizing the sanctity of treaty rights, and counting those important Chileans whose economic interests lay in Bolivia, notably Melchor Concha y Toro, by then president of the Huanchaca Company. The Antofagasta Company won the day, and further pressure was applied to the rather diffident President of the Republic, José Anibal Pinto. Bolivia received a final ultimatum: arbitration or force. Daza, knowing of the 'secret' treaty with Peru, refused arbitration. On the date fixed for the auction, two Chilean ironclads, recently built at Hull, the *Cochrane* and the *O'Higgins*, disembarked troops at Antofagasta who quickly took possession of the port. The first salvo had been fired in the War of the Pacific, though none of the combatants was ready for it.

The Peruvian government of President Manuel Prado was appalled at the turn of events and desperately sought to avoid, through negotiations, its obligation to Bolivia in the treaty of 1873. Profligate borrowing – largely to build railways in the 1870s – had bankrupted the country, and it had reneged on its external debt in 1876. A year before, in a desperate attempt to raise revenue, it had nationalized the predominantly foreign-owned nitrate industry of Tarapacá. The Bolivian government, isolated from its Atacama littoral, was quite impotent to resist Chilean encroachment in the desert after the seizure of Antofagasta. As for Chile, though the economy was weakened by the acute economic depression of the second half of the 1870s and though the country was riddled by factional political strife, she still had assets her adversaries did not: 'greater national coherence and traditions of settled government'.[25] She officially declared war on Bolivia and Peru on 5 April 1879.

In the war itself, Chilean naval strength, after early vicissitudes, proved decisive, especially after the capture of the Peruvian ironclad *Huáscar* in October. By that time, Bolivia's participation had been reduced to nullity, and Chile turned to Peru. An expeditionary force of some 12,000 men invaded Tarapacá and forced the Peruvian army to fall back on Tacna and Arica where, after two bloody battles in May and June 1880, Chile controlled the entire desert littoral. Forced on by public opinion, a sea-borne expeditionary force of 26,000 troops landed on the Peruvian coast near the capital, Lima, and after two fierce battles at Chorillos and Miraflores in January 1881, seized and sacked Lima. Though sporadic resistance continued for two more years in the Peruvian hinterland, the war was effectively over, and Chile had won it decisively.

The terms of peace were harsh. By the Treaty of Ancón 1883, Peru was obliged to cede to Chile in perpetuity the rich nitrate province of Tarapacá and the possession of Tacna and Arica for ten years, after which a plebiscite would decide final sovereignty. A separate truce with Bolivia in April 1884, left Atacama in Chilean hands, though a final peace settlement, confirming her ownership, came only in 1904.

The war increased Chilean national territory by about a third; it secured her the vast nitrate deposits of the north which were to account for nearly a half of government revenue for the next forty years, and it enhanced both national pride and Chile's international reputation. For the Antofagasta Nitrate and Railway Company, it seemed that its rights against Bolivia had been vindicated and that its future was assured. As it turned out, it was not quite so simple as that.

The Peruvian 'nationalization' of nitrate in Tarapacá had taken the form of bond issued to the nitrate producers, redeemable by the government within two years and paying an annual interest of 8 per cent. The bonds were made payable to bearer, and the Peruvian government expected to redeem them by raising a loan of £7m abroad. This, however, it could not do and, as the war went on, the nitrate bonds fell rapidly in price. 'In these circumstances, a number of speculators bought up large quantities of the depreciated bonds which would, in effect, be the title-deeds to the nitrate grounds if Chile were to return the industry to private ownership'.[26]

This is precisely what happened. Two Chilean government commissions in 1880 and 1881 recommended the return of the nitrate industry to private hands, and the speculators made a killing. Prominent among them were John Thomas North, 'the Nitrate King' (1842–1896) and Robert Harvey (1847–1930) whose name will recur in this narrative. They spearheaded the formation of British joint-stock companies in nitrate in the 1880s, so that, by 1890 the British owned 70 per cent of the industry's assets. But the focus of activity was Tarapacá, not Antofagasta. The railway linking the richest nitrate fields in Tarapacá with the coast had been built between 1868 and 1875; the *oficinas* were well-established and run largely by British engineers abreast of the latest technological developments, and the ability of their owners to raise capital easily had been proved by the stock-exchange boom of the 1880s. The nitrate deposits in Atacama were of lower grade than those in Tarapacá; the lack of refining capacity in the Atacama *oficinas* put production costs there significantly higher than in Tarapacá, and, in fact, they could only compete with Tarapacá if their tax-free concessions survived. The company's fortunes were closely linked to that assumption.

It proved to be mistaken. During the war, the profits of the Antofagasta Nitrate and Railway Company had risen dramatically with the early Chilean occupation of Bolivian Atacama and the uncertainty surrounding Tarapacá. The company was a tempting target for taxation by a nation at war and, in fact, during 1880, various proposals for taxation went before the Chilean Congress. The close relations of the company's directors with prominent members of the Chilean elite blunted the worst suggestions and a tax was imposed which, though it ate into profits, was not crippling. Not long afterwards however, a proposal was mooted to impose a uniform tax on nitrate shipments from both Tarapacá and Antofagasta. This was a much more serious threat to the company's profitability, given the resurgence of the industry in Tarapacá and its comparative economic advantages. The bill was passed not least through the advocacy of Melchor Concha y Toro and his brother-in-law, Francisco Subercaseaux, who had substantial interests in Tarapacá. The effect was a rapid fall in profits, from 1,776,634 pesos in 1880 to a loss on nitrate traffic of 148,625 pesos in 1883, only partially offset by a profit of 134,871 pesos on freight carried to the mines.

In these circumstances, the Gibbs House, which had already decided that its basic interests lay in Tarapacá rather than Antofagasta, reduced its holding, and hence ceased to be a capital source for the company. In 1883, the company, having fought long and fruitlessly against the violation of its privilege of no taxation, took another tack to re-coup its losses and recover its prosperity. This was to concentrate on the railway rather than the *oficinas* and here 'economic interests were to make for strange bedfellows'.[27] For, whereas Concha y Toro and other Chilean capitalists interested in the nitrate of Tarapacá were quite prepared to harm the Antofagasta company through a uniform tax, they had a more substantial stake in mining in Bolivia. Consequently, when in 1883, the company petitioned the Chilean government to extend its line to Ollagüe on the re-drawn Chilean-Bolivian frontier, it got that political support it had lacked on the taxation issue. Under its previous concessions, the company had constructed further extensions: to Central (131 kilometres from Antofagasta) in 1882, and to Pampa Alta, later called Unión (150 kilometres) in 1883. All these were, of course, of 2′ 6″ gauge and the standard rail-weight was 36lb a yard. The extension to Ollagüe would mean extending the line from Pampa Alta a further 291 kilometres and involve a sizeable investment. Hence, in its petition the company requested a state guarantee of 6 per cent interest *per annum* on the capital invested on the extension, the exclusive privilege of construction, and free importation of necessary equipment, as well as freedom from duties on mineral exports.

The Chilean law of 17 January 1884 conceding the core of these requests – but with some reservations – went through Congress mainly because of the powerful political friends the company had in Santiago: indeed, no fewer than fifteen holders of stock were either deputies or senators. They included not only Concha y Toro, but his friend, the remarkable Ramón Barros Luco (1835–1919) a highly prominent politician who, at the age of seventy-five, became president of the republic in 1910. With such advocates, seeking to protect and, indeed, enlarge, their economic interests, the passage of the bill was almost a formality.

The state guarantee of 6 per cent under this new law was to run for twenty years; and a privileged zone of 75 kilometres for the same period meant that no other concession for a line to the Bolivian frontier could be granted, though other lines not going there might be built. Materials for construction and operation were duty free, as were mineral exports not exceeding 6,000 pesos for each kilometre of line. The guarantee was restricted to 3,472,000 pesos (about £1,320,000 at the prevailing exchange rate), and detailed rules were laid down relating to profits, tariffs and governmental use of the railway, such as half-fare for public officials travelling on state business and 50 per cent of the normal tariff for the carriage of government goods. Finally, the concession would lapse if 200 kilometres of line had not been laid down and brought into service within five years.

The prominent Chilean investors in Bolivian mining – and notably in the Huanchaca Company – had lobbied for the concession to serve their own interests. By that time, it had become imperative for Huanchaca, in expanding its extraction of ore for shipment to the Pacific ports, to have a cheaper and more efficient means of bulk transport than the traditional one of pack animals and carts on tortuous roads and trails. It has been calculated that the average monthly exports of the Huanchaca Company between 1889 and 1899 would have required by these means either 60,000 llamas or almost 30,000 mules to carry the ore to Antofagasta, a journey of some twenty-five days. 'Such a number of pack animals was very large, considering that the biggest transport company ... serving between Arica and Oruro boasted no more than 5,000 llamas ... The railroad was, then, the only possible solution'.[28]

There was, therefore, a natural alliance of interests between the Huanchaca Company and the Antofagasta Company, and it was spelled out in an agreement between them made on 28 May 1885, based on the latter's new railway concession. By the agreement, both companies declared their aim of extending the railway line to the frontier at Ollagüe, to the mines at Pulucayo near to Uyuni and, indeed, beyond if appropriate concessions could be obtained from the Bolivian government. The Antofagasta Company's obligation to this joint venture was the existing line, and its own mole and water condenser at Antofagasta, whereas Huanchaca agreed to invest 2,600,000 pesos (equivalent to the valuation of the existing Antofagasta properties) and, that amount expended, the partners were to share future profits and losses. A tariff structure was agreed, Huanchaca paying less than other users, and they also undertook to provide in equal parts any further capital required for construction. Management was vested in a board of four – two from each company – meeting regularly in Valparaiso. It was also stipulated that, once the line had reached the Bolivian border, a new company would be formed.

The construction work continued in the next few years. By 1886, the line had reached the oasis town of Calama, 238 kilometres from Antofagasta, and the frontier at Ollagüe (435 kilometres) the following year. Further expansion into Bolivia would require the approval of that country's government and, by that time also other economic considerations had begun to change the picture. Apart from the fact that the two companies' relations turned out to be less than cordial, it was these economic circumstances which led the Antofagasta Company to turn once again to nitrate for its profits, rather than to the railway.

The uniform export tax on nitrate shipments imposed by the Chilean government in the early 1880s had benefitted Tarapacá and disadvantaged Antofagasta, as we have seen. At that time world demand for the fertilizer was high, and a new refining process – the Shanks method of lixiviation, named after the English chemist who invented it – promised still higher output at lower cost. But the market was not sufficiently elastic. Consequently, a glut of production ensued, and prices and profits fell. To sustain both, in 1884 producers resorted to a device which would be repeated from time to time: a combination whereby fixed production quotas were allocated to each producer until supply and demand returned to balance. It lasted two years but one of its effects was to give companies like Antofagasta financial stability with their fair share of the market. The loss of nearly 150,000 pesos on nitrate in 1883 became a profit of about 600,000 pesos in 1886. A second factor in the company's renewed interest in nitrate was its close relations with European capital and more cost-effective technology. In short, the company was again competitive.

In these circumstances, the Antofagasta Company divested itself of its railway interest to concentrate on nitrate. On 3 March 1887, it sold the railway to the Huanchaca Company for 3,000,000 pesos, while maintaining its privilege of lower tariffs than those charged to others for traffic in its goods. The Huanchaca Company was to form a railway company, raise a loan in London of £1,770,000 to take the line further into Bolivia, issuing bearer bonds at 7 per cent for that purpose, and the sale and arrangements were approved by the Chilean government on 26 March.

A leading role in these transactions was played by the Bolivian mining magnate and later president of his republic, Aniceto Arce, who saw the future of Bolivia in a close relationship with foreign capital to exploit its resources, and in improved communications, notably railways, to develop the country. With his interests in Huanchaca and other mining companies, in which a good deal of foreign capital had been invested, and with his conviction that the rail link to Antofagasta was vital to their growth, he was often the target of domestic criticism, accused of being both an agent of Chilean encroachment on Bolivia and of economic imperialism. His past history reinforced such attitudes: as Vice-President of Bolivia when the War of the Pacific broke out, he had consistently argued against it, and sought a direct settlement with Chile. However, as the head of one of three great mining families which, in many respects, ran the republic – Arce, Aramayo and Pacheco – he could survive these attacks, though there was often fierce opposition in Congress to his economic plans. In 1886, for example, when the Huanchaca Company sought a concession to extend the Uyuni railway to Oruro and La Paz, on condition of a government guarantee of 6 per cent return on invested capital, the proposal was strongly attacked by his political opponents. A similar situation obtained when he proposed the extension of the Antofagasta railway from Pampa Alto not only to Huanchaca but, indeed, to La Paz, though in 1888 the Huanchaca Company was able to build 45 kilometres of the line linking Uyuni and Huanchaca itself. And despite adverse criticism of the conflict of political and economic interests he was alleged to represent, he was elected President of the Republic in 1888 for a four-year term.

Though, as President, Arce, the leader of the Conservative Party, had a turbulent political situation to face, including armed insurrections by the opposition Liberal Party, his term was one of the most dynamic in the history of Bolivian economic development. He had a positive mania for railway construction, and his rule witnessed the rapid extension of that part of the Bolivian network which subsequently became part of the FCAB, in whose creation he was, in fact, a key figure.

Notes

1. Harold Blakemore, 'Chile' in Harold Blakemore and Clifford T. Smith, eds. *Latin America: Geographical Perspectives* 2nd edn. Methuen, London, 1983, p. 463.
2. Isiah Bowman, *Desert Trails of Atacama* (American Geographical Society, Spacial Publications No. 5, 1924, New York), p. 42.
3. Sub-general manager to secretary, Antofagasta, 30 June 1911. Letter No. 352. (London: Archive of the Antofagasta (Chili) and Bolivia Railway Co.)
4. Acting general manager to secretary, Antofagasta, 22 August 1930, Letter No. 278.
5. *Ibid.*, Antofagasta, 29 August 1930. Letter No. 279.
6. *Ibid.*, Antofagasta, 17 October 1930. Letter No. 286.
7. Resident Engineer's Report on Summer Rains, Antofagasta, 25 March 1953. I am indebted to Mr Craig for a copy of this report, and for much other valuable information.
8. *Ibid.*
9. Personal communication, G.W. Craig to the author, September 1986.
10. Brian Fawcett, *Railways of the Andes*, George Allen and Unwin Ltd., London, 1963, p. 47.
11. Rory Miller, 'Transferring Techniques: Railway Building and Management on the West Coast of South America', in Rory Miller and Henry Finch, *Technology Transfer and Economic Development in Latin America, 1850–1930,* University of Liverpool: Institute of Latin American Studies, Working Paper 7, 1986, p. 8.
12. David Joslin, *A Century of Banking in Latin America, to commemorate the centenary in 1962 of the Bank of London & South America Limited,* Oxford University Press, London, 1963, p.101.
13. A.E. Heskett Employment Card, FCAB Archive.
14. G.W. Craig Employment Card, FCAB Archive.
15. C.R. Enock, *The Republics of Central and South America*, London, 1922, p. 497.
16. W. Anderson Smith, *Temperate Chile: A Progressive Spain*, London, 1899, p. 37.
17. Frank G. Carpenter, *South America: Social, Industrial and Political*, New York, 1900, p. 240.
18. *The Times*, 26 April 1880.
19. W.E. Curtis, *Capitals of Spanish America*, New York, 1888, p. 454.

20. J.P. Pentland, *Report on Bolivia*, 1827, ed. and with an intro. by J. Valerie Fifer, London: Royal Historical Society, *Camden Miscellany*, XXV, 1974, p. 260.
21. Heraçlio Bonilla, 'Peru and Bolivia from Independence to the War of the Pacific', in Leslie Bethell (ed.), *The Cambridge History of Latin America*, Vol. III, Cambridge University Press, 1985, p. 572.
22. Pentland, op. cit. p. 205
23. C. Masterton to J. Bidwell, Chuquisaca, 10 August 1843. London: Public Records Office, Foreign Office Archives, Bolivia (F.O.11), Vol. 1. Cited by J. Valerie Fifer, *Bolivia: Land, Location, and Politics since 1825*, Cambridge University Press, 1972, p. 48, n.1.
24. Hicks to Evaristo Soublette (general manager at Valparaiso), Antofagasta, 10 December 1878. In a typescript collection of letters from the archives of the Anglo-Lautaro Company, compiled by Arturo Fuenzalida, known as 'Guerra del Pacífico. Cartas', in my possession. My translation from the Spanish. A selection of this correspondence, including this letter, has been published by Manuel Ravest Mora, *La Compañiá Salitrera y la ocupacióñ de Antofagasta, 1878–1879,* Santiago Editorial André Bello, 1983.
25. Simon Collier, 'Chile from Independence to the War of the Pacific', in Leslie Bethell (ed.), *The Cambridge History of Latin America*, Vol. II, Cambridge University Press, 1985, p. 612.
26. Harold Blakemore, *British Nitrates and Chilean Politics, 1886–1896: Balmaceda and North*, Athlone Press, London, 1974, p. 21.
27. Thomas F. O'Brien, 'The Antofagasta Company: a Case Study of Peripheral Capitalism', *Hispanic American Historical Review*, Vol. 60, No. 1, Feb. 1980, p. 24. I have relied heavily on this article for this section.
28. Antonio Mitre, 'The Economic and Social Structure of Silver Mining in XIX Century Bolivia', Unpublished Ph.D. thesis, Columbia University, 1977, p. 234.

2
YEARS OF EXPANSION, 1888–1914

Foundation of the FCAB and the Huanchaca Phase 1888–1904

Early in 1889, the London press announced that:

> Messrs Frederick Huth and Co. and J. Henry Schröder and Co . . . are authorized by the Antofagasta (Chili) and Bolivia Railway Company (Limited) to invite subscriptions for £1,150,000, or 11,500 shares, at par, part of the capital of £1,450,000, in 14,500 shares of £100 each . . . for the purpose of acquiring from the Compañía Huanchaca de Bolivia the concessions granted by the Governments of Chili and Bolivia for the construction and working of railways and telegraphs from the port of Antofagasta . . . to Huanchaca . . . including the privilege . . . of establishing waterworks for the supply of the railway and the district it serves, including . . . Antofagasta . . . [1]

The basis of this public launching of the company was two agreements made between the FCAB and Huanchaca on 28 November 1888, relating to the concessions obtained, and installations built and under construction. In one sense, that date may be regarded as the birthday of the FCAB, though Chilean government approval of the sale came on 2 April 1889, after Bolivia had ratified it on 8 December 1888.

The first *convenio* related to the sale by Huanchaca of all its concessions and properties relating to the lines and water supply, including works in progress which Huanchaca was to complete. These were basically the extension of the line to the station of Huanchaca itself and waterworks supplied by the river Loa, the line to be finished in two years, the waterworks within three from 1 October 1888. By the second agreement the FCAB as owner was to lease back to the Huanchaca Company for a period of fifteen years all the properties it was buying, that is until 31 December 1903. Both agreements were, inevitably, somewhat elaborate but only the salient features call for comment here.

On the sale price, of the sum to be paid by the FCAB, £850,000 represented the already fully-operating line between Antofagasta and the Bolivian frontier: £300,000 the Bolivian section, and £300,000 the water undertakings. The Huanchaca Company undertook not only to pay all legal and documentation fees but also for the services of the consulting engineers to be contracted by the FCAB. The latter's directors chose wisely and well in selecting for this purpose the firm of James Livesey and Son, founded by James Livesey in 1862 and already with a reputation in Latin America.

In addition to the purchase price, the FCAB assumed responsibility for a loan of £660,000 at 5 per cent interest contracted by the Huanchaca Company for the extension of lines into Bolivia and hypothecated on the Chilean section. This loan had the back-up of the Chilean guarantee of 6 per cent interest for twenty years from the law of 1884, already mentioned but, in fact, it never proved necessary to invoke that guarantee. If the Huanchaca Company redeemed the mortgage, the FCAB was to pay the latter £36,000 annually for eighty years or, alternatively, Huanchaca might take FCAB debenture stock to that amount year by year. Other clauses in the agreement related to tariffs, operations, representations of both companies and, if it should prove necessary in case of disputes over interpretation, arbitration procedures. Interestingly enough, the Huanchaca Company also undertook to pay the FCAB £10,000 for administration in London.

The *lease* agreement meticulously spelt out the terms of Huanchaca's obligations and the rights of the FCAB. On the financial side, the former would receive 60 per cent of gross receipts for the period to 31 December 1893 – five years – and 55 per cent for a further ten years, after which the FCAB would assume all the workings as owner. Similar clauses to those in the sale agreement related to operations, representation and arbitration.

Both documents were signed in London, for the FCAB by a director, Richard H. Glyn and the Acting Secretary, James E. Davies, and for Huanchaca by its then President, Melchor Concha y Toro. His name has already appeared in this narrative, and his very close connection with the Bolivian *minero*, and by this time President of his country, Aniceto Arce, was to continue to be valuable to British railway interests in their part of South America, and not least the newly-formed FCAB.

That company was actually incorporated on 27 November 1888, the day before the agreements with Huanchaca were signed. But, clearly –

though there is little actual documentation on the preceding period – a good deal of preparation had gone into the launching of the company. Indeed, it must be assumed that those who founded it had long been in contact with the Huanchaca Company, possibly from early 1887 when the Antofagasta Company had sold its railway and other rights to Huanchaca. From its very beginnings, however, the FCAB seems to have been fortunate in the standing and expertise of those who directed it, as well as for the continuity of their service.

The first board of directors consisted of E.M. Underdown QC, R.H. Glyn, Sir Lepel Henry Griffin KCSI, and W.A. Michael. Underdown, a distinguished lawyer, was also prominent in business as chairman of several companies and leader of a number of commercial missions, for example, to Spain and Cuba. He served on the board of the FCAB from 1888 to 1912 and was chairman from the beginning until 1907 – almost twenty years. Glyn was also a prominent businessman, among other things chairman of the London board of the Bank of New Zealand: he was a director of the FCAB from 1888 to 1913. Griffin had an extraordinary diplomatic career, notably in India, Persia and China, and his business interests, as chairman of several companies, reflected that fact. He also wrote several books on oriental affairs, and was a director of the FCAB from 1888 until his death in 1908. Michael has gone unrecorded in standard reference works but he seems to have been an engineer and he sat on the board for fifteen years, from 1888 to 1903. Obviously, in any company longevity of service alone is not necessarily a guarantee of capacity though, if shareholders are not satisfied, directors rarely get re-elected. In that respect, the first team in the FCAB set a standard of performance and service which became almost a tradition, as the following selective examples illustrate.

The Hon. Charles Napier Lawrence succeeded Underdown as chairman. He was the second son of Lord Lawrence of the Punjab who was ennobled for his role in the Indian Mutiny, but he secured his own title as Lord Lawrence of Kingsgate in 1923, not in his father's footsteps but as a major figure in railway enterprise in the United Kingdom: 'his common sense, clear judgment, and charm and courtesy of manner made him an admirable chairman of a large board [that of the London, Midland and Scottish Railway] ... and testified to his powers as financier, negotiator and administrator'.[2] Those qualities also served the FCAB well: he joined the board in July 1907, and left it only when he died on 7 December 1927, having been chairman for eighteen years.

Robert Harvey (Sir Robert from 1901) was a director of the FCAB from March 1908 until October 1926. And he, much more than most, had long, direct experience of the west coast of South America, having first gone there as a fitter in 1869, working in nitrate *oficinas* for many years and becoming Inspector-General of Nitrate for the Peruvian government in 1876. He was the key partner of John Thomas North, 'the Nitrate King' in the rapid expansion of British interests in the nitrate industry of Tarapacá – including railways – after the War of the Pacific. He became a director of the Bank of Tarapacá and London, a major constituent of what became the Bank of London and South America, in 1894, six years after its foundation, and was its chairman until 1918. None knew better the nitrate industry and the local and national environment, and his recruitment to the board of the FCAB in 1908 showed quite clearly that the other directors knew exactly what they were about.

Bernard Greenwell (Sir Bernard from 1906) was a director of the FCAB from 1905 to 1939. His interests were in stock-broking, the electricity industry and agriculture, and he brought that wide experience to the company for over half his life. More in the mold of Robert Harvey was A.H.A. Knox Little, a director from 1912 to 1921. An engineer, he was active in railway construction in Argentina and Brazil, and spoke both Spanish and Portuguese fluently. What was said at his death showed the company's appreciation and his association with the FCAB:

> Anyone acquainted with the way in which British enterprises in foreign countries are conducted from London knows that the directors, though usually well-versed in finance, often know nothing of the technical side of the businesses which they are supposed to direct ... Lack of technical and local knowledge is an obvious source of weakness ... The difficulty of finding someone to fill the vacancy created by Mr Knox Little's untimely death will, we hope, bring home to the boards of British companies operating abroad the importance of ... men who have gained actual experience in the country in which their concerns operate.[3]

That lesson the FCAB never had to learn. Moreover, the company never lacked financial acumen on its board. The classic example here is, in fact, the longest-serving director, Henry F. Tiarks. He joined the board in October, 1926, and remained with it until the end of 1967, a span of over forty years. His close association with the banking family and firm of Schröder, whose board he also joined in 1926, paralleled the relationship between the FCAB and that financial house. Similarly, Robert John Hose, who sat on the board from 1921 to 1935, was a major architect in the creation of the Anglo-South American Bank, forerunner of the Bank of London and South America, a man who 'combined a considerable measure of conservatism in the detailed conduct of business with great imagination and daring in taking strategic decisions'.[4]

At the managerial and administrative level, the FCAB also attracted, and retained, outstanding personnel. Though he did not have a high public profile and, indeed, is not even mentioned in any standard work of reference, A.W. Bolden is the classic example. He was appointed secretary of the FCAB in 1907 but in 1917, as the chairman put it, 'in order more correctly to describe that gentleman's duties', he was designated London Manager and Secretary.[5] A year later, he was elected to the board and, though he ceased to be secretary in 1929, continued to serve on it as managing director until his death in 1941. He actually died in harness, at a meeting of the Staines, Laleham and Stanwell War Weapons Week when the fatal seizure occurred. In the thirty-four years he served the company, he exercised a powerful influence in its fortunes. Again, his successor as secretary, Charles Cowley, who had joined the FCAB in 1906, was appointed to that post in 1929, joined the board in 1941 and remained there until 1954.

Many other examples could be cited of both length of service and expertise in the running of the FCAB. The point of this apparent digression from its history is to emphasize its success in recruiting loyal and experienced servants throughout, a characteristic which has survived changes of both circumstances and name.

The first board, with Underdown as chairman, established those traditions. It also guided the FCAB successfully through its formative years. In the first phase, as noted, from 1888 to 1904, the onus of running the lines, the telegraph and the waterworks fell on the Huanchaca Company which, though based on Bolivian mineral resources, was registered in Valparaiso, underlining the role of Chilean capitalists in its operations. The relationship between the two companies – the FCAB as owner, and the Huanchaca as lessee – seems to have been, in general, cordial enough, though there were occasional points of friction. The elaboration of the agreements between them, made in 1888, took place in 1889, through direct negotiation. Underdown had several meetings with M. Nicolás Peró, the Paris agent of the Huanchaca Company in Paris, and subsequently reported that he had

> . . . fully discussed with him the respective positions which this company as owner, and the Huanchaca Co. as worker of the railways and works should occupy, and that Mr. Peró had stated the view . . . that that Co. should . . . act as working manager of the Railway and Waterworks on account of this Company and not as holding an independent position as a working Railway Co.[6]

Overall control thus rested with the board of the FCAB, which approved tariffs and contracts; expenditure on new works, including the extension of lines, and the expansion of the waterworks. The Huanchaca Company ran the enterprises and was obligated to keep all the installations in good repair, as well as ensuring that the agents of the FCAB were fully informed of the financial aspects of the business and that the latter's share of the revenue produced was paid promptly and regularly through the banking house of Schröder. To ensure that these obligations were discharged, and to exercise a degree of local control, the board appointed both a resident engineer in Chile – usually selected by Livesey – and local agents, the first of whom were 'Messrs Welbrock and Walbaum, both resident in and of the commerce of Valparaiso' with

> general powers to represent this Company in the Republics of Chile and Bolivia . . . and to take in the name and representation of this Company all steps judicial, extrajudicial, commercial or official, necessary or convenient for the due execution of such general and special powers. To appear before tribunals of all kinds, consent to arbitrations, with faculty of substitution and new appointments in the whole or in part of these powers so conferred.[7]

But other legal representatives were also retained in both Chile and Bolivia, in the former a relative of Melchor Concha y Toro, Carlos Concha.

The resident engineer, however, was invariably British, the first being William Murray who was engaged early in 1889 at a salary of £900 a year. His role and, of course, that of his successors, was crucial in the effective implementation of the agreements with Huanchaca, particularly since the latter had the obligation to complete the lines in Bolivia for which the pliant government of José Aramayo had granted concessions in 1887. Murray inspected the lines, and the board of the FCAB required his approval of standards of construction before paying Huanchaca. In November 1889, for example, he recommended that £10,000 be held back since, while the line from Julaca (505 kilometres from Antofagasta) to Uyuni (610 kilometres) in Bolivia had been laid, some of the bridges were not up to his requirements. Murray set standards of performance as resident engineer, advising the board on matters ranging from track maintenance to tariffs, which most of his successors were to follow, another tradition of the FCAB which was begun at its birth.

Under the Huanchaca lease construction work continued, to Uyuni by the end of November 1889, and to Oruro (924 kilometres) by mid-May 1892. It was entirely appropriate that the inauguration of this latest section was marked by the presence of President Aniceto Arce who drove a gold spike into the last rail length. For him, it was the realization of another dream in the building of Bolivia, though the dream must sometimes have seemed more like a nightmare, given the political opposition to his grand designs. His approval of the FCAB-Huanchaca accords had aroused the wrath of his enemies: as one newspaper of La Paz put it:

> The machines which have penetrated to the Plaza of Oruro bear the inscription RAILWAY FROM ANTOFAGASTA TO BOLIVIA which is

> the same as saying that Chile owns Bolivia and that the potentate of Antofagasta and Huanchaca is the protagonist of this drama.[8]

Arce's own vision was completely different. Earlier he had written:

> I believe in peace and the desire to see lines cross our barren *altiplano*, our bramble patches, our unsettled areas, our lonely landscapes and our tortuous roads – to see them all overcome by the joint action of work and capital.[9]

The results of that philosophy of international economic co-operation – which the FCAB represented – were almost immediately apparent. The extension of the railway to Oruro, and with a spur to the main Huanchaca mining properties at Pulacayo, resulted in a dramatic increase in silver ore shipments to Antofagasta: indeed, compared with the period 1882–88, they increased by no less than 86 per cent in the period 1889–95. For the Huanchaca Company, the reduced costs of transportation the railway brought were reflected in a virtual doubling of profits in 1889 over 1888. Nor was that all – as the same source spells out: 'at the same time that the railroad prolonged the duration of the silver boom, it also initiated the era of tin'.[10] Bolivia possessed that commodity in abundance and the international tin market was then expanding rapidly as a result of increasing demand, not least for canning in the industrialized world. The railway was the key to the rapid growth of tin mining in Bolivia, the ore being carried to Antofagasta and smelted abroad, largely in Great Britain. By 1900, some 10,000 tonnes of ore were being produced, precisely when silver mining had gone into eclipse, and new mining magnates, such as Simón Patiño, began to emerge.

This dramatic economic development had a marked impact on the port of Antofagasta, not only in terms of exports, but also of imports, since, obviously, the railway increasingly carried commodities upcountry into Bolivia as well as down. The value of imports through Antofagasta increased almost four-fold between 1890 and 1894, to over 3 million pesos, as the port consolidated its crucial position in the Bolivian economy as a whole. A basic reason for this was the lack of transport networks within Bolivia, so that even nationally-produced foodstuffs such as flour and sugar could not compete with imports since they were not competitive in transport costs. Similarly, manufactured goods, such as textiles made abroad had a cost advantage over locally-produced articles.

Some Bolivian nationalist historians have argued that these developments, and Bolivia's dependence, through the railway, on Antofagasta were negative factors in the country's development. But this is a simplistic view. The extension of the line to Oruro coincided with the beginnings of the first tin boom from which Bolivia would have profited little but for the existence of the railway. Moreover, alternative and economical transport for bulk carriage of tin exports did not then exist. The railway from the Pacific port of Arica to La Paz, constructed by Chile for Bolivia as part of the final peace terms after the War of the Pacific and though only a third of the length of the Antofagasta line, was not begun until 1906 and completed only in 1913. Moreover, its construction and maintenance presented far more severe problems than those of the other line because of far steeper gradients and much sharper curves, and it included a rack section 41 kilometres long with a gradient of 6 per cent. Consequently, even when built, it could not compete with the Antofagasta line. The same was true of the only other possible route. Henry Meiggs had built a railway from the Peruvian port of Mollendo to the town of Puno on the western edge of Lake Titicaca in the early 1870s. In that decade steamers ferried goods across the lake to the Bolivian town of Puerto Pérez on its south-eastern shore: the freight was then carried by wagon to La Paz, some 65 kilometres away. This cumbersome passage was only partly improved by the opening of a railway from La Paz to Guaqui at the southern end of Lake Titicaca, since the loading and unloading of goods for the steamers still took a lot of time. Bulk freight, such as tin, was out of the question. Hence, Antofagasta, though much further as the crow flies from the Bolivian mining centres than either Arica or Mollendo, easily established its predominance for the Bolivian traffic. The extension of the railway from that port to Oruro, in the heart of Bolivian mining country, in 1892 came at precisely the right moment for the FCAB and the Huanchaca Company.

For the latter, the concession for that part of the line included a branch from Uyuni to its principal mine at Pulacayo which was opened on 25 November 1889, and enabled the company, through cheaper transport costs, to exploit its low grade ores. Consequently, its gross and net income reached their highest levels in 1893 and 1894, and dividends recovered almost to the levels they had reached in 1889 and 1890 at the height of the silver boom. The FCAB's share of profits from the lease agreement came to £107,862 in 1890, £117,538 in 1892 and £134,581 in 1894. At the annual general meeting in 1894, the chairman reported that:

> Ores and bar silver from Huanchaca had increased by more than 100 per cent in 1893 compared with 1892; up traffic had increased by 22 per cent; the ores from the Chilian mines were about the same ... If their revenue had not increased in the same proportion it arose from circumstances beyond their control – the price of silver and the condition of the exchange ...[11]

He thus underlined two of the imponderables in the company's profitability: world market prices for the chief commodities the railway carried and fluctuating exchange rates between Latin American currencies and the pound sterling. And imponderables they would remain.

Although, under the eagle eye of William Murray, the Huanchaca Company was responsible for building and maintaining the Bolivian extensions to the line, the FCAB – as owner – had to pay for them. Thus, in 1890, the second annual general meeting approved a resolution to raise the capital by £850,000 in connection with the extension to Oruro, though, in fact, the issue was not made until November 1892, five months after the line was opened. At the AGM in June 1894, the chairman reported that:

> . . . they had been urged to continue the line from Oruro to La Paz . . . they had thought it their duty to have this route surveyed and examined, because La Paz was capable of being brought into communication with the coast by Peru. They did not, however, yet contemplate taking any steps to prolong the line; indeed, they did not contemplate any further capital expenditure whatever at present.[12]

He did, nevertheless, refer to the possibility of branch lines being built to tap both the silver mines of Bolivia and the nitrate fields of Chile which as yet had no rail links to the main line, and indicated that the company had had the prescience to survey the areas. Some extensions, however, were built before the expiry of the Huanchaca lease, though the major ones came later.

Meanwhile, relations between the two companies were cordial enough and, indeed, in many respects were quite close. When, in 1891, for example, Huanchaca decided to set up an agency in London, the offices of the FCAB at 57½ Old Broad Street and the officers of that company – at the time, the secretary, an accountant and a clerk – were used for that purpose at a rental of £100 a year and payment for office work undertaken for Huanchaca. Underdown, in fact, became president of the agency, and its secretary was the secretary of the FCAB. In addition, Huanchaca nominated its French agent, Peró, who had the power to propose additional members.

So far as payments made by Huanchaca under the lease agreement were concerned, these came quarterly and regularly through Schröder, except for one period when Huanchaca were in financial difficulties. That company went through a depressing time in 1896–97, owing to a combination of a fall in silver prices and the flooding of its mines at Pulacayo. In those two years, 'for the first time in 23 years, the company's balance showed a deficit of 833,492 and 1,281,818 pesos respectively.'[13] That was undoubtedly the reason why, in late March, 1897, the FCAB received a telegram from Huanchaca:

> In consequence of Chile Bank stopping suddenly Company's credit, and unforeseen delays completion pumps, there is reason to fear we shall not be

> able meet coupon 31st March punctually. Hope remit by telegraph £10,000 on account, remitting balance April, May. We are very sorry. We are making every effort.[14]

Every effort, the FCAB pressed them to make, and emergency arrangements were made for payment by Huanchaca through Schröder: the board heard with satisfaction within a fortnight that the full amount due – £33,000 – had been received. This incident and another in May, concerning the cancellation by Huanchaca of an order in France for iron sole plates for sleepers and an earlier difference of opinion on who should pay what for them, led the FCAB to tighten up its overall control.

The original local agents were replaced by the long-standing Valparaiso firm of Vorwerk and Co., and the terms of the power of attorney were strengthened, appointing them

> ... to represent this Company in the Republics of Chili and Bolivia and especially for the following purpose, viz.:- To watch over and ensure the carrying into effect of the provisions and stipulations of the Contracts of Working ... between this Company and the Compañía Huanchaca de Bolivia, taking care that the aforesaid Cia ... complies with and executes all the stipulations of the said Contracts ...[15]

Tougher tones were soon needed for Huanchaca which, also in May, asked the board for a loan, raising fears that, with an AGM pending, the coupon due on 1 July would not be forthcoming. The following cable was sent:

> No loan here possible without Mortgage on all your assets. Do your utmost raise temporary loan there to avoid any default which would be most disastrous to present position and future credit. We beg to draw particular attention to fact our proportion of receipts not applicable to your Company's purposes ...[16]

The AGM was postponed to July, by which time the board had been reassured, but rumours had flown and at the meeting the very persuasive chairman, Underdown, felt obliged to scotch them:

> In reply to remarks made in the money article of one of the newspapers [he was reported as saying] they [the directors] pointed out that the position of matters with regard to Huanchaca had had the most earnest attention ... as no default had occurred, and the general meeting of the Huanchaca Company was taking place that very day in Valparaiso, it was thought that any public statement would be premature.[17]

Huanchaca eventually resolved its financial problems, largely through, first, loans from Schröder and, second, in 1899–1900, by agreements with the powerful New York firm of Guggenheim and Sons for the latter to invest in its undertakings. That story is not part of this one: suffice to say that, according to the records, between 1897 and 1904, when its lease from the FCAB expired, Huanchaca fulfilled its obligations on payments though there were sometimes other points of friction, largely on the fixing of freight and water tariffs.

At the time of the crisis of 1897, the board of the FCAB learned that Huanchaca, without consultation, had changed tariffs for up-carriage of coal, iron and timber, and felt it important to remonstrate. Seven months later, a similar infraction occurred when Huanchaca unilaterally raised tariffs on the Bolivian line, and the board sent an admonishing cable: 'Surprised at increase in Bolivian tariff without our approval. Await explanation'.[18] Dissatisfied with the explanation, the FCAB protested again in March but in April apparently compromised in the following words: '. . . Without prejudice terms the Working Agreement, we give you authority make concessions, agreements, without our previous assent, if you consider it necessary develop traffic . . .'.[19]

The same pragmatism over disagreements was also evident on water. Though income from that source only began in 1892 and, throughout the decade, was only a small proportion of total receipts (less than £3,000 out of £131,000 in 1894, and £5,815 out of £183,924 in 1897), the board was well aware of its quasi-monopoly position as a supplier of water in the arid regions its railways crossed, and jealously guarded its current interests and future prospects. Thus, when in 1899, the Huanchaca Company proposed to ask the Chilean government for a subsidy to extend pipes to the recently-discovered Polapi springs in the lee of the Andes, 25 kilometres from San Pedro de Atacama in return for a lower tariff on the existing rates related to the earlier concessions on the rivers Loa and San Pedro, it was brusquely informed by cable:

> Board is much opposed to the proposition reduce price water. We beg draw your particular attention to fact, this Company owner waterworks. Our approval necessary any alteration . . .[20]

As it happened, the Chilean government declined to accept the proposed rates but, some months later, a concession was granted to the Huanchaca Company for twenty-five years, and the FCAB agreed to pay part of the costs of construction. The terms were elaborated by a government decree in November 1901: this imposed on the concessionaire the obligation to supply, free of charge, water for state railways, educational and benevolent institutions, barracks, and other state establishments, as well as prohibiting the transfer of the concession without government permission. That leave was granted in May 1902, and the FCAB secured the concession in its own right. In the same period, 1901–02, the company agreed to supply Calama with free water, subject to reduction if the railway needed it, and also the municipality of Antofagasta up to 100 cubic metres a day for public consumption.

Such disagreements with Huanchaca caused little reaction among shareholders at meetings, and Underdown successfully played down their fears. At an extraordinary meeting on 24 March 1898, for example, he asserted that the flooding of the Huanchaca Company's mines had been greatly exaggerated, that the company, as guarantor to the FCAB, was in a fundamentally sound position and that, moreover, while Huanchaca was the most important single user of the railway, it was far from being the only one. At the end of the meeting, a resolution was easily passed that 'the board should be supported in their efforts to continue their friendly relations with the present judicious . . . administration of the Huanchaca Company, while insisting upon the fulfilment of the engagements of the working contracts'.[21] From then to the end of the 'Huanchaca phase' on 31 December 1903, and assisted by the recovery of that company's fortunes, that confidence remained, and relations between the two companies were amicable enough.

Long before the FCAB commenced working the installations in Chile and Bolivia at the beginning of 1904, the board had been preparing for the change. Indeed, a feature of all the chairman's speeches at annual general and extraordinary meetings from 1897 – six years before the lease expired – was to remind shareholders of that fact. And, in appraising future prospects, he reported, from time to time, on preliminary negotiations with, for example, owners of nitrate works for the building of branch lines. Apart from those lines already mentioned, another was constructed under the management of Huanchaca. This was from the main line just north-east of Calama to the copper-mining district of Chuquicamata, which was subsequently to prove of the greatest importance to the FCAB. The original concession by the Chilean government had been granted to a Mr Norman A. Walker in July 1900, but Huanchaca built the line, advancing the funds at 8 per cent interest, the advance to be repaid within two years. Agreement was made in August for Huanchaca to work the line for 60 per cent of the gross receipts and take an option to purchase it. These arrangements were modified, the option to purchase being set at six months within two years of the completion of the line, with Walker receiving 25 per cent of the gross receipts for three years as compensation. In January 1902, however, the FCAB bought the line from Huanchaca for £12,500, and assumed the obligation to Walker, though Huanchaca continued to work it until 1904. It was only 10 kilometres long, but the chairman's statement at the AGM in 1902 that 'the directors regarded the purchase as a very satisfactory one'[22] could not anticipate that, from the 1920s, Chuquicamata was to grow into the world's largest open-cast copper mine, a major prop of the Chilean economy, and the source of a huge traffic for the FCAB. 'Very satisfactory' proved an understatement.

During the time of the Huanchaca lease, the financial structure of the FCAB had been changed considerably. The 5 per cent first mortgage bonds of £660,000 issued by Schröder in 1887, and assumed by the FCAB in its contract with Huanchaca, were redeemed by early 1892. As noted, in 1890 it was resolved to increase the capital by £850,000, and the issue of 4 per cent debenture stock to that amount took place between June 1890 and January 1892. A further issue of £150,000 was authorized by an extraordinary general meeting on 6 December 1900, again as 4 per cent debenture stock:

> . . . mainly to provide the company with funds required under an agreement recently arrived at with the Huanchaca Company in anticipation of the approaching termination of the working agreement with that company, to repay them the amount agreed on in respect of new works executed by them during the past 12 years, and also to defray the expense of new rolling stock, which the increased traffic of the railway renders necessary.[23]

That stock was all taken up by September 1901, and the proceeds expended by June 1902: at the same time Huanchaca was advised not to begin any new works during the period of the lease. Before this, in 1900, acting on the advice of W. Greenwell and Co., a firm which had joined Schröder and F. Huth and Co. as financial consultants, the company had converted the existing ordinary stock into preferred and deferred ordinary stock, holders being able to split their holdings into equal amounts of the two stocks only between 1 January and 23 March each year. Such conversions averaged £300,000 between 1900 and 1904.

Events moved fast in the final year of the lease. In March, a final protocol on the handover was signed between Huanchaca and the FCAB, and the latter started to make appointments for its own running of the works. Murray was confirmed as resident engineer, though, for reasons unknown, he left the company's service less than a year later, and was replaced by F.J. Cochrane; R. Henderson was appointed traffic manager in May, Harry Usher as General Manager in August (at a salary of £1,800 a year), and an assistant engineer (B. Smith), a chief storekeeper (E.F. Banner) and a bookkeeper (H. Warren) were also appointed. It is interesting to note that both Cochrane and Warren had previous experience of Uruguayan railways. The firm of Vorwerk in Valparaiso were retained as local agents in Chile. At the same time, orders were placed for material, particularly coal and sleepers; contingency arrangements for possible loans from Schröder, if necessary, were arranged; and, in short, very little was left to chance. To ensure that nothing was, the directors sent one of their number, Alfred Frewin, to Chile to supervise the transfer arrangements for a fee of £1,000. He was accompanied, in November, 1903, by the secretary, H.D. Greville.

By 1 January 1904, all the technicalities had been sorted out. Much more than that, however, the company had planned for its new future. Reporting on the results for 1903 in May 1904, the chairman indicated that:

> The province of Antofagasta was being very largely developed; the company must be in a position to assist in that development, and they must not allow mining centres at reasonable distances from their line to be connected with rival enterprises ... A branch was to be built to a place called Conchi, and there was to be a branch to another mining district called Collahuasi; and extensions to the company's premises and purchases of land would also have to be made ... The existing line would also be put into thoroughly good order ...[24]

As events were to prove, these comparatively modest objectives were soon to be achieved. But they paled into insignificance in the light of other developments in the next decade, when the economic fortunes of the FCAB became even more closely interlinked with those of the countries in which it operated.

Nitrates and network growth, 1904–1914

The ten years between the commencement of working its properties by the FCAB and the outbreak of the First World War were among the most profitable in the history of the company, due largely to the expansion of the Chilean economy in that period, and notably to the impressive growth of the nitrate industry. No less important, of course, was the company's capacity to take advantage of the new opportunities the situation offered to extend the network of lines, augment water supplies, renovate the older permanent way and rolling stock, keep abreast of advances in railway technology and, not least, demonstrate its significance as a lifeline in both the regional and the national economy.

Nitrate was essentially the initial spur. And, boring though statistics may sometimes be, they illustrate graphically how rapidly the industry expanded in the decade. Throughout the entire nitrate region of the Atacama desert, principally the provinces of Tarapacá and Antofagasta, there was a bonanza as the following table illustrates:

TABLE 1. Nitrate, 1904–1914

Date	No. of Oficinas	Employees	Production (1,000 tonnes)	Exports (1,000 tonnes)
1904	76	c.25,000	1,559	1,498
1905	90	30,600	1,854	1,649
1906	96	c.34,000	1,822	1,727
1907	110	39,700	1,846	1,653
1908	113	40,800	1,970	2,050
1909	102	37,800	2,110	2,133
1910	102	43,500	2,465	2,333
1911	107	43,900	2,421	2,445
1912	118	47,800	2,585	2,490
1913	127	53,200	2,772	2,735
1914	137	44,000	2,463	1,846*

Sources: Michael Montéon, *Chile in the Nitrate Era: the Evolution of Economic Dependence, 1880–1930*, University of Wisconsin Press, Madison, 1982, p. 70; Leopoldo Castedo, *Resumen de la Historia de Chile, 1891–1925* Editorial Zig-Zag, 1982 Santiago, pp. 362, 614.

The fall in exports in 1914 is attributable to shipping disruption in the last few months of the year, after the war had broken out.

For the Chilean government, the growth of the industry was of the greatest significance: export taxes on nitrate accounted for 47.99 per cent of ordinary revenue in 1905 and 51.32 per cent in 1910. Though that proportion fell in 1914, due to the initial impact of the war, a year later it was up to 60.16 per cent. In these same years, nitrate accounted for 78 per cent, 79 per cent and 76 per cent of the total value of Chilean exports.

It was increased world demand for nitrate both as a fertilizer and as a component in explosives which fuelled these developments. That market naturally fluctuated but between 1904 and 1914 it was on a rising curve and, for the FCAB, the boom could not have come at a better time. For, whereas, for reasons indicated in Chapter 1, the former Peruvian province of Tarapacá had dominated the nitrate industry since the 1870s, in a period of rapidly rising world demand its comparative cost advantages over Antofagasta were now less significant. Moreover, the newer *oficinas* in the latter province had taken advantage of the latest technology and, in the main, now had superior infrastructure in terms of transport and shipment. In fact, during the first twenty years of this century Antofagasta replaced Tarapacá as Chile's principal nitrate province, and the port of Antofagasta took over from Iquique in Tarapacá as Chile's chief entrepôt for the desert regions. As an outstanding traveller noted in the early 1920s:

> In 1899 Iquique's revenues from import and export trade amounted to over seven times as much as those of Antofagasta; in 1912 they were practically identical; and in 1915 revenues from nitrate alone were half as great again for

> Antofagasta as for Iquique ... Iquique had over 40,000 people in 1907; reduced to 37,421 in 1920. In 1907 Antofagasta had 32,496; increased to 51,531 in 1920.[25]

Nor was it, of course, nitrate alone which accounted for Antofagasta's booming exports: the period also marked the first stage of the Bolivian tin bonanza, and Antofagasta was now already clearly Bolivia's principal outlet to the world market.

In this context, the FCAB had tremendous opportunities to re-inforce and extend its existing interests, and it did not hesitate to seize them.

The new management team on the ground, nominated largely by Frewin with some assistance from the consulting engineers (now Livesey, Son and Henderson), had its hands full in its first year of operation. In the first place, it appeared that the upkeep of the installations had been somewhat neglected. The general manager hoped, in March 1904, that new points and crossing were on the way since 'the engineer reports that some of the points and crossings on the Chilian section are in a dangerous condition, and we have none to replace them'.[26] A little later, regarding water, he reported that 'the Huanchaca Co. left the tanks at San Pedro in a very dirty condition, and we had to clean both of them out and do some small repairs'.[27] Similarly, the Bolivian line had been neglected:

> The condition of things in the Bolivian Section of the permanent way Department continues to be very unsatisfactory. The line between Uyuni and Oruro is in bad shape and there is no discipline among the men. It is most important with a large number of wooden bridges in this section that we have a really good man in charge ...[28]

Consequently, he sacked the incumbent engineer and appointed one who was 'highly recommended'.

Such technical matters, of course, required constant attention, and Usher, the General Manager, certainly gave it, as the following letter indicates:

> I am sorry to say [he wrote in his own hand] that the working of the traffic Department of the Bolivian section, which we placed under Mr. Henderson's charge, has not been at all satisfactory. I have several times addressed Mr Henderson's attention to it but notwithstanding this on my last journey I discovered a particularly discreditable state of affairs at Uyuni. I have therefore had to take up the matter very strongly with him and insist upon his going over the section more regularly and exercising a closer supervision.[29]

These kinds of distractions he could well have done without, given so much pending business, namely contracts with users, concessions for further developments and relations with government, both local and national. All three aspects of the work to expand the company's interests were naturally intertwined, and there was a good deal in train when he and his colleagues took over. Every contract with potential users and the renewal of contracts with existing customers took a good deal of time, and negotiations were a major part of the general manager's business. This was increasingly so as the nitrate fields of Antofagasta were rapidly opened up. 'Whereas in 1903 there was but a single nitrate *oficina* on the Antofagasta *pampa*, five years later twenty were working or in course of construction'.[30] And almost all of them relied on the FCAB to carry the nitrate to the coast for shipment. Terms were arranged with individual customers and it appears that the manager tried to establish as uniform a structure as possible. However, for particular reasons, this was not always so, and it seems obvious that customers consulted one another in order to get optimum tariff rates. Thus, in February 1904, the representative of the Borax Consolidated Co., Mr Lesser

> . . . laid stress upon the fact of his Co. insisting upon the same terms as those given to Carrasco and Zanelli [nitrate producers]. The rates submitted . . . were based on a yearly haulage of 22,000 tons . . . but Mr Lesser having told me that the quantity would be considerably increased this year, I saw in this a way to meet them without lowering the rates previously quoted by us, by raising the minimum quantity to be guaranteed to 28,000 tons . . .[31]

The head office of Borax in London rejected the terms and asked for a further reduction and Usher wrote:

> This I told Mr Lesser I would not make, nor could I think of recommending it to my Directors, as we had in my opinion already quoted more favourable terms than the traffic warranted.[32]

Lesser then threatened both to take legal proceedings against the FCAB – but did not spell them out – and to shut down the company's mine at Cebollar, but Usher stood firm in discussions 'extending over several days' and the contract was finally signed, largely on his terms.

This particular example of a freight contract illustrates not only how time-consuming the process could be but also how much the FCAB had to rely on the local manager's judgement. And the correspondence over the period relating to freight contracts is voluminous. Whenever possible, however, new contracts were based on existing ones: this worked more smoothly with the new nitrate *oficinas*. In April 1904, for example, a new customer whose firm intended setting up a new *oficina* was simply given 'a proforma contract on the same lines as that signed by Inglis Lomax and Co.'[33] The contract was duly signed three months later, five months before the *oficina* was due to start working. Similarly, almost exactly a year later, four new contracts were made for the carriage of nitrate, all in identical terms, as were eight contracts signed at the same time relating to water supply.

Obviously, contracts for carriage depended largely on concessions to build lines. While many new *oficinas* in Antofagasta lay near the main line, the nitrate boom opened up more distant ones, requiring cost-effective transport. Long before the FCAB started working the lines on its own account, it had investigated certain possibilities, and it now had to pursue them. Some transactions were comparatively easy, others complicated and protracted owing not least to competition from others.

The branch line from Conchi to Conchi Viejo presented few problems. Conchi (300 kilometres) lay on the main line, some 13 kilometres south-west of San Pedro, Conchi Viejo 19 kilometres north-west of Conchi itself. In July, 1903 a concession had been granted to the *Sociedad de Minas y Fundición de Calama* which transferred it to the FCAB, the transfer being approved by the Chilean government at the end of September 1904. The line was opened to traffic early in 1906, construction work having been delayed 'principally owing to the illness of the Contractor' after 13 kilometres had been opened in mid-1905.[34] Similarly, despite certain temporary tremors, the line to Collahuasi, a rich copper-mining district, was built between 1904 and 1908. The take-off point from the main line was at Ollagüe (441 kilometres) and the final length constructed was nearly 95 kilometres. The general manager worked hard to get the concession, since there was both a competitive and international dimension to it. As he reported in April, 1904:

> I think we ought to apply for the concession to build this line without delay. From what I have heard in several quarters there is considerable agitation to build a line to connect with the Iquique lines, and if such connections were made it might in the future mean a further extension of the Iquique Collahuasi line to Bolivia.[35]

That, of course, he had to prevent, and he did. After one or two further hiccoughs, but with the backing of several freight contracts already signed by several mining companies, he was able to report in August that the concession had been granted. The line opened to traffic on 1 April 1908.

Mejillones

With other concessions, it was more difficult. By 1903, it was obvious that the port of Antofagasta was becoming incapable of handling the increased traffic, and private and public attention turned to the port of

Mejillones, some 50 kilometres north of Antofagasta in a direct line, 'the finest natural harbour in Chile'.[36] Moreover, its hinterland contained some very rich nitrate deposits, especially at Boquete, south-east of the bay. In 1901, a certain Emilio Claro had obtained a concession to link Mejillones and Boquete by rail, but he was willing to transfer his rights to the FCAB. Unfortunately for the latter, others were also interested in what promised, when built, to be a highly profitable line. Several put in bids, the most serious and powerful coming from a Chilean group, as the general manager reported in May 1904:

> The Pinkas-Puelma Syndicate, at whose back are Carrasco & Zanelli [Italian nitrate producers], have powerful influence just at present in Santiago, and they are making every effort to secure the concession for the Boquete to Mejillones line and branches ... A factor in their favour is that Señor Huet, the Railway Commissioner, has reported favourably on their scheme ...[37]

But they were not the only ones:

> In addition there is one of Mr Lawson, an American said to represent large American interests. The latter has considerable influence with Sr Valdes Cuevas, the present Minister (*sic*) de Industria, and before leaving Santiago ... Mr Lawson had a long interview with the President ... I heard on good authority that he was very pleased with the Boquete properties, and intended closing with Carrasco and Zanelli if he could arrange that the concession ... were passed to him with the properties[38]

As it happened, that deal did not materialize, and the Pinkas group remained the most serious threat. Usher was in favour of seeking in the first instance only the building of a line from Boquete to the main line, since the opening of new ports, such as Mejillones, was a complicated matter under Chilean legislation and, in any case, the board in London was also cautious in view of the expenditure likely to be involved for the entire scheme. But he, too, had his friends in Chile:

> The appointment of Sr Avalos as Minister (*sic*) of Industria [he wrote a week later] places us in a much better position ... He is undoubtedly against the Pinkas ... and as far as I can judge he will favour us in the granting of any new concessions. The Intendant [of Antofagasta], whose father is now Minister of Justice, is very much in our favour and has written previously to the president urging the justice of giving the development of the Province to this Company ...[39]

Though the intendant and Usher disagreed on when the future port of Mejillones should be inaugurated, they were at one in believing that the FCAB should get the concession. And get it, it did. A decree of October 1904 granted the FCAB the right to build and own a line from Mejillones to the main line, imposing obligations on the company, *inter alia* to build a mole at the port, available without charge to state vessels; free water for state establishments; the sale of water to others on fixed terms, and a rebate of 50 per cent for the carriage of state personnel and freight. Subsequent decrees in 1905, 1906 and 1907, refined and extended the original terms. Interestingly enough, an obligation imposed on the FCAB by decree of September 1906 to build other moles was invalidated in December in return for the FCAB undertaking to spend a minimum of 200,000 pesos to build a hospital. *Force majeure* or not, the contribution of the company to regional services and amenities was quite considerable.

The branch from Mejillones to the main line was opened to traffic in 1907, the take-off point from the latter being at Prat station (59 kilometres) and the length of the branch being 77 kilometres. It was not an easy line to build, heavy grades and sharp curves being a feature of the first 16 kilometres from Prat. Subsequently, the FCAB, by concession in 1911, built another line from Antofagasta and the Pampa station on the Mejillones branch of 41½ kilometres, Pampa being 28 kilometres from Mejillones.

Usher had every reason to be pleased, and was clearly very relieved, about the Mejillones transaction. He wrote:

> I feel sure the Company will have reason to congratulate itself in the course of a few years, not only that permission has been obtained to connect with ... the harbour ... but also that it was obtained in time to have an extra outlet for the increased traffic before the end of 1906.[40]

He was no less gratified to report, a little earlier, after a meeting with the Head of State:

> The Board will be pleased to hear that both the President of the Republic and his advisers are well disposed towards the Company, and several times during my stay in Santiago I heard satisfaction expressed by influential people that the Railway had passed into the English Company's hands ...[41]

And he added, with a certain glee, that he had been able to convince the President that the arguments of Pinkas that the FCAB had raised tariffs since taking over the lines were completely unfounded. The old Anglo-Chilean connection did, indeed, seem to be in a healthy state.

During the decade under review, the FCAB increased its Chilean network, mainly through the building of branch lines to new *oficinas* but it would be tedious here to present a catalogue. The case of Mejillones is a significant example, however, not only in indicating the rapid growth of the regional economy but also the responsibility that fell on the local senior staff to safeguard and extend the company's interests. It also indicates quite clearly the need for them to have good relations with both local and national people of importance in order to do that. Two other railway issues, however, were significant in this period, both as illustrative examples of the FCAB's policies and of the company's acute awareness of opportunities to be taken.

Aguas Blancas

A short distance south from the port of Antofagasta lay the much smaller port of Caleta Coloso. Its hinterland south-east contained some of the richest nitrate deposits in the province, notably in the canton of Aguas Blancas, which had been exploited since the 1870s. By the turn of the century, the leading entrepreneurs in the district were two Chileans, Matías Granja and Baltazar Domínguez, but the latter died in 1901, and Granja bought out the holdings of his relatives in their joint company. Granja was an outstanding businessman, of whom it was said:

> After Mr. North, the great English industrialist, and Don Oscar Salbach, our compatriot, in Tarapacá, it can be said that he is one of the leading standard-bearers to push forward the nitrate industry ...[42]

In 1898–99, Granja and Domínguez had secured from the Chilean government a concession to build a railway line, some 100 kilometres long, to link their *oficinas* at Aguas Blancas to the coast in the vicinity of Antofagasta. In fact, Coloso, 10 kilometres south of that port was chosen as the coastal terminus, and the line was built and opened to traffic in October, 1902, under the management of a former employee of the FCAB, Arnold Reid. That line gave new life to the region as nitrate shipments grew rapidly, feeder lines from a number of *oficinas* were built to the main line, and port installations were constructed. With this development, the municipality of Antofagasta began to show a keen interest in the construction of a branch line from the Aguas Santa Blancas railway direct to that port itself, in order to get a share of the traffic and hence of the profits. This was projected to run from a point 8 kilometres north of Coloso to Antofagasta, running parallel with the FCAB's main line. Naturally, that company was also an interested party. Usher noted in 1904:

> If we built the Boquete and Aguas Blancas branches ... we should, in my opinion, in addition to largely increasing our traffic at remunerative rates, do away with all prospect of serious competition ... I consider we ought to think of these branches as extensions of our general system. The opening of Coloso port lost us the traffic of Granja's oficina 'Pepita' ... [43]

A survey of the board minutes for the next few years indicates that the directors shared these views, and the issue of the proposed extension to

Antofagasta took up a good deal of time, largely because Granja himself was not in favour of it. After all, he had the monopoly of the increasing traffic through Coloso, and feared to lose it if the extension were built. But he was in a difficult position since the original concession for the Aguas Blancas line had stipulated Antofagasta as the terminus, and he had departed from it. There followed an extraordinary succession of events, marked by frequent debates in the Antofagasta municipal council, pressure on the Granja company to build the line, but also strong resistance from local interests to its proposed route since that involved the cession of land. These issues also involved the Chilean government whose permission was necessary for what would be virtually a new railway concession. Granja himself bowed to the inevitable and petitioned for a concession to build the line which was finally granted by the Ministry of Industry and Public Works in October 1905. Seven months later, Matías Granja died at the age of sixty-six, having left a will which divided his property among fifteen heirs. In August 1906, one month after the death of Don Matías, the inheritors agreed to liquidate Granja and Company, but the process was a very long and tortuous one, partly because of the difficult relations between individuals, but more because of the sizeable debts it was discovered Granja had not discharged. Eventually, at the end of 1907, the Banco de Chile, acting for the Chilean government itself, granted to the Granja heirs a loan of £500,000, guaranteed by the Granja holdings, including Coloso, the Aguas Blancas railway, and several *oficinas*. This was to be re-paid within six months.

The transaction eventually caused a great public and political scandal, with fierce criticism of the government by its opponents in Congress, and a plethora of press comment. The government's argument that it had stepped in because of the dangerous consequences of the collapse of the Granja interests to the regional and national economy was countered by arguments that it was improper and unconstitutional for government to intervene, coupled with suggestions that corruption had come in. It was obvious that the only solution was the disposal of the Granja properties. And several parties were interested.

The position of the FCAB has already been spelled out, and its board had long been working to make a strong bid. Early in 1908, one of the directors, Sir Bernard Greenwell, had cabled from Chile that £700,000 in bearer obligations would probably be enough: he was instructed to 'discuss thoroughly prospect and value property on spot, quality nitrates doubted.'[44] Reassured, the board went on planning, agreeing in March that Schröders should act as agents to purchase the properties for up to £800,000 at 2 per cent commission. But there were threats. In August, it was reported that:

> Sr. García de la Huerta (one of their lawyers) sends me cuttings from the 'El Ferrocarrill' (*sic*) of Santiago ... in which Sr. Gonzalo Bulnes writes

> advocating the purchase by the State of the Aguas Blancas Railway, in order to secure low freights . . . frequent allusions are made to this Company – many of them unfavourable. Sr. Bulnes fears that should this company be allowed to purchase the Aguas Blancas Railway and thus acquire the port of Coloso, a monopoly will be established . . .[45]

Bulnes was a prominent public figure, son of a former president of Chile and national hero, Manuel Bulnes (1799–1866), and himself subsequently the author of the standard Chilean work on the War of the Pacific.

Circumspection, therefore, was required in the acquisition of the Aguas Blancas railway, and circumspect the directors of the FCAB certainly were. Later in 1908, a syndicate was formed in London to purchase the Granja properties in which Sir Robert Harvey, who had recently joined the board of the FCAB, was prominent: he 'declared his interest' and did not vote at meetings when Aguas Blancas came up, but there is little doubt that he played a leading part in subsequent events. The Aguas Blancas syndicate offered to act as agents for the FCAB eventually to acquire the railway for £680,000 at 5 per cent commission plus expenses, together with the other Granja interests for a total of £750,000. In fact, however, the agent for the syndicate itself was the powerful American firm of W.R. Grace and Co., and it was to that company – with long experience of the west coast of South America – that the Chilean government transferred the railway in December 1908. Though it had always been the intention of the FCAB to acquire the line, the directors still acted prudently: on 1 December, the board agreed 'that no steps be taken for bringing the acquisition of this railway etc. to the knowledge of the proprietors until receipts of further advice.'[46] The general manager of the FCAB in Antofagasta W.H. Robinson was himself only partly in the know. As he wrote in mid-December:

> Up to the time of writing . . . outside the parties interested nobody has an inkling of the fact that the Aguas Blancas Railway will be acquired by us. The transfer has been duly effected by Messrs. Grace and Co.'s representative, and yesterday their Mr Chandler called and showed me the private telegram he had received . . . I explained . . . that I did not know exactly what the position was; whether to take the line over immediately and whether it is to be run as a separate company or to form part of our existing system.
>
> Of course, I am in the dark as to the way in which the Board proposes to run the Aguas Blancas line. If it is to be treated as a branch of our main line and to divert the traffic, which at present goes to and from Coloso, to Antofagasta, it should prove a good feeder and produce good results. On the other hand, if it is intended to keep Coloso open and have all the stores etc. and heavy shops expenses, it will not be so remunerative . . .[47]

Such decisions had not yet been announced, since the legal and financial transactions involved in the acquisition were somewhat tortuous, and preoccupied the board in late 1908 and early 1909. However, in December 1908, Grace having purchased the Granja interests, there was founded and registered in Santiago, the Aguas Blancas Railway Company. Grace held 90,000 shares, with six individuals – two of them Chilean – with holdings of 1,000 to 2,000 shares. The actual transfer of the property to Grace took place early in January 1909, and on 11 January, President Pedro Montt – himself an enthusiast for railway building in Chile – signed the decree which recognized the company, approving its statutes. Thereafter, and by the beginning of February, the FCAB had acquired the shares, which were registered in Santiago in the individual names of the directors, and assumed the management of the company. For its pains the House of Grace received £5,250 and a contract as the company's agent for the purchase of all materials from the USA on a commission of 2½ per cent. The legal advisers to the FCAB in Chile were also handsomely rewarded, the two principals receiving gratuities of £3,750 each.

For the parent company, the acquisition of the Aguas Blancas railway and the port of Coloso was a considerable coup: as the chairman reported to the shareholders at the AGM in June, 1909:

> ... we have obtained a very good bargain and one which should prove of very valuable interest to us. It not only rounds off our property on the coast, and gives us another port, but we hope effectually does away with much danger of competition in the particular nitrate zone we serve.[48]

To effect the purchase, the Aguas Blancas Company issued £900,000 of 4½ per cent debenture stock, the principal and interest being guaranteed by the FCAB. From the middle of 1909, the Aguas Blancas line was worked as an integral part of the main system for economic reasons, for example, since the FCAB's principal workshop was at Mejillones, from that year on the Coloso workshops were gradually closed down and the machinery taken to Mejillones. But, because of the way in which Aguas Blancas had been acquired, it had technically to be kept distinct from the main operation, and while coming under the management at Antofagasta, separate accounts had to be kept. Similarly, as a Chilean-registered company, its official address was in Santiago (and later Antofagasta) and its board had two councils, one in Chile and the other in London. Although, on 28 February 1911, the two companies signed a contract whereby the FCAB took a thirty-three-year lease of all the Aguas Blancas properties, backdated to 23 November 1908, these arrangements remained in force and, as events were to prove, could be a nuisance to the FCAB with both central and local Chilean officials on such matters as taxation and tariffs. For the moment, however, the parent company had every reason to be pleased as, in largely booming conditions for nitrate down to the First World War, Aguas Blancas proved a profitable undertaking.

Bolivian railways

Busy as the board and its employees were with extensions to the Chilean network in the first decade of the century, the Bolivian sphere of operations was far from being neglected. Here, quite fortuitous circumstances helped. The extraordinarily diverse physical landscape of Bolivia, allied to poor communications, meant that in the outlying regions of the country, far from La Paz, the government's control was weak. This was strikingly true in the northern Amazonian territory of Acre which, in the last two decades of the nineteenth century, became the scene of a huge rubber bonanza, fuelled not least by the growth of road transport in the developed world and, from the late 1880s, the introduction of rubber tyres for bicycles and cars. Some Bolivians made immense fortunes, notably Nicolás Suárez (1851–1940), but, given the indeterminate nature of the frontier between Bolivia and Brazil, the boom led to a massive influx of Brazilians into Acre, whose numbers were reckoned at over 60,000 in 1900.

Such were the circumstances which brought the two countries to the verge of outright war, after a whole series of disputes about boundaries, customs duties, and settlers, the Brazilians in Acre declaring virtual independence in 1902. The complicated story need not be detailed here: suffice to say that Brazilian superiority forced Bolivia to conclude, in November, 1903, the treaty of Petrópolis, whereby the boundary was delimited, Bolivia ceding the Acre territory to Brazil – some 191,000 square kilometres. In return, however, Brazil agreed to indemnify Bolivia to the tune of £2 million. It was that windfall that Bolivia used to expand its railway network, in alliance with foreign capital and enterprise, and it was to provide the FCAB with the opportunity to enlarge its Bolivian interests.

It was also fortunate for foreign interests that two presidents who governed Bolivia in the period – José Manuel Pando (1899–1904) and Ismael Montés (1904–1909: 1913–1917) – were both staunch believers in laissez-faire, and in the key role of foreign capital in their country's development. Both, too, like Aniceto Arce before them, saw in railway construction a vital means not only to unite the country more effectively but also to secure more efficient routes for the export of its mineral wealth.

By contract dated 22 May 1906, made on the one hand by the Bolivian government and, on the other, by Messrs. Speyer and Co. and the National City Bank of New York, Speyer agreed to set up a company to build and run a railway system in Bolivia within ten years, a period later extended by two years later to 1918. Under what came to be called 'the Speyer contract', the lines to be built were as follows: Oruro to Viacha (207 kilometres); Oruro to Cochabamba (211 kilometres); Oruro to Potosí (352 kilometres); Potosí to Tupiza (280 kilometres); Uyuni to Potosí (280 kilometres), La Paz to Puerto Pando (124 kilometres) with a number of branch lines to other places. (See map p. ix) The Bolivian concession would be the basis of a company which would expend £5,500,000 in construction and equipment, and that organization, the Bolivia Railway Co. was incorporated under the laws of Connecticut in February, 1907.

By the terms of the concession, the company was allowed duty-free importation of all construction and operating material for 30 years, and the gauge was to be one metre. Funds were to come from the issue of £3,750,000 5 per cent First Mortgage Bonds, maturing on 1 January 1927, the interest on which was guaranteed by the Bolivian government. The issue was purchased by the underwriters of the company at 80 per cent of its face value, producing £3,000,000, and the Bolivian government, apart from its guarantee on the First Mortgage Bonds, agreed to find 40 per cent of construction and equipment costs on the security of Second Debenture (Income) Bonds, not exceeding £2,500,000, in effect the income from the Acre transaction with Brazil. The government, then, received £2,500,000, 5 per cent second-mortgage, non-cumulative bonds, due on 1 January 1932.

Given its already extensive interests in Bolivia, the FCAB was naturally highly interested in these developments. As the chairman, E.M. Underdown KC, reported to the nineteenth ordinary annual general meeting in 1907, the directors:

> . . . took the very greatest interest in Bolivia, where a very extensive system of railways was in contemplation. The directors considered that the company had a moral right . . . to carry out those railways under the terms of the company's general concession, but they had no desire to enlarge their system unreasonably or to go into part of Bolivia which did not form what might be considered their own zone . . . the directors hoped that a reasonable view would be taken by the Government [of Bolivia] and by those interested in the projected lines, and that they would be able to make arrangements which would be mutually advantageous . . . there was no reason why the systems of railways which it was assumed were about to be constructed in Bolivia under a concession given to Messrs. Speyer and Co. should really cause this company any anxiety . . . in these matters emnity was no use; friendly arrangements were very much better . . .[49]

'Friendly arrangements', on the whole, had existed with the Bolivian government from the time the Huanchaca lease expired at the end of 1903, and the FCAB took over the working of the line, with its branches, from Antofagasta to Oruro. There were occasional hiccoughs, mostly over the annual bargaining on freight tariffs, though here, as occasion demanded, the FCAB was very cooperative in granting rebates. Thus, the general manager reported in 1904:

> I enclose a letter from President Pando, in which he asks that a rebate should be conceded on imported hay on account of the bad harvest in Oruro district. As the tariffs had now been definitely approved, I considered it advisable to grant this, and enclose letter of my reply giving a rebate of 25% on the Chilean section and 60% on the Bolivian section. I enclose the President's letter of thanks.[50]

Local officials could also be troublesome. Later that year, the government inspector in Oruro, a certain Señor Lora, who had, said the manager, 'waged open war upon us ever since we took the railway', and 'canvassed against us amongst the Deputies and mineowners and merchants of Oruro, written bitter articles against us in a local paper, and . . . has even tried to stir up trouble among the employees on the Bolivian section', provoked the manager, on the advice of the Bolivian legal adviser, to address a formal letter of protest to government. Lora was asked to resign, refused and was dismissed as was the sub-prefect at Uyuni for similar activities, because 'the President and at any rate one or two of his Ministers are men of broad views who are anxious not to hostilise [sic] foreign capitalists'.[51]

Such relations stood the FCAB in good stead in what followed. After negotiations with representatives of the Bolivia Railway Company in September 1908, by which time that company had completed the Oruro-Viacha line, on 19 October the two companies entered into contract for the FCAB to acquire one-half of the First Mortgage Bonds of the Bolivia Railway Company (£1,875,000), together with a controlling interest in its common stock (76 per cent), a total cost of £2,095,000. The agreement entailed the construction by the FCAB of the lines in the Speyer contract and, when built, their lease to the FCAB for ninety-nine years, that is, until 31 December 2,007. Among the other clauses was one obliging the FCAB to build not only the new lines at one metre gauge but also to convert its own Uyuni-Potosí line from 2 feet 6 inches to that standard width. Secondly, the Speyer Contract was to be amended, eliminating the obligation to build the lines Oruro-Potosí, Potosí-Tupiza and Uyuni-Potosí, but to add to the original list lines from Uyuni to Tupiza, and from Rio Mulato to Potosí. Under the lease, the FCAB was committed to paying the Bolivia company a rental of 25 per cent of the gross receipts of each line opened for five years, rising to 30 per cent of the next five, 35 per cent for the next five, and 40 per cent of gross receipts for the remainder of the ninety-nine-year period. There were a number of other detailed clauses but the gist of the agreement was aptly summed up by the chairman of the board in December 1908: 'the agreement ... will give your Company the complete control of the Bolivia Railway Company'.[52] Or, as a modern scholar puts it: 'Although the two were run as separate companies, one in New York and one in London, their boards of directors were almost identical and the distinction between them was a technical one'.[53]

The acquisition of the Bolivia Railway Co. was, in fact, a master stroke, comparable with the transactions over Mejillones and Aguas Blancas on the Chilean side of the Andes. All three enabled the FCAB to head off what might have proved serious competition for traffic, and establish a dominant position as the major carrier of not only Chilean nitrate, copper, borax and other minerals for shipment abroad but also Bolivian silver and tin, respectively the two countries' major exports. They also ensured for the company the predominant role in the transport, through Antofagasta, of up-traffic – material, machinery, foodstuffs, fuel – to the burgeoning economies of both Chile and Bolivia.

The threat of competition was certainly real. When the Speyer contract was signed, the general manager thought it 'a menace to this Company which should certainly control the southern cone of Bolivia'.[54] The Bolivia railway transaction obviated that threat but it was not the only one. Another might have come from the Peruvian Corporation which owned the Southern Peruvian Railways, including the line from the port of Mollendo to Puno, north-west of La Paz, and which subsequently bought from the Bolivian government the line from Guaqui to La Paz, built between 1900 and 1905. Though Puno and Guaqui were separated by the waters of Lake Titicaca, the corporation more than once sought to interest the Bolivians in using the Guaqui and Mollendo lines by employing steamers to tranship traffic between them, since this put La Paz only four days' travel time from the Pacific, somewhat less than the Antofagasta line, as the final link from there to the Bolivian capital was not opened until 1917. There was also another cloud on the horizon. In 1904, Chile and Bolivia signed the definitive peace treaty on the War of the Pacific: one of its provisions was the construction by Chile of a railway from Arica to La Paz, the Bolivian section to be handed to Bolivia fifteen years after completion; another was free transit in perpetuity for Bolivian commerce across Chilean territory. Given the fact that Antofagasta is roughly two-and-a-half times more distant from La Paz than is Arica, the proposed railway might well compete with the FCAB for the Bolivian traffic. And in Chile itself, another threat was emerging. Like his Bolivian counterparts, President

Pedro Montt (1906–10) was a passionate advocate of railway construction: and the two projects adumbrated – one partly begun – during his administration were the extension of the largely state-owned great central trunk line into the Atacama and a line linking Antofagasta with Salta in north-west Argentina. When the former was first proposed officially, the general manager was apprehensive:

> ... if this line is constructed [he wrote] and there seems to be every probability of this being done within the next few years, it is likely to be a menace to this Company by cutting rates and so drawing traffic from this Company or causing us serious prejudice by compelling us to reduce our tariffs ...[55]

How the FCAB dealt with that challenge and the others will be seen in due course. Down to the First World War, however, such competitive threats were not significant: the Peruvian Corporation's attempts to divert traffic from Bolivia were hampered by several factors. First, Bolivian exports were primarily metal ores or the refined products, that is, bulk traffic, and the land gap between their lines presented serious and costly transhipments. Second, the lines had far more steep grades and sharp curves than those of the FCAB. The Arica-La Paz line was not opened until May 1913 and the inauguration gave the general manager of the FCAB a good deal of amusement and a splendid opportunity for enhancing FCAB's image:

> The inauguration was not altogether a success ... as, due to the bad state of the Locomotives, the Bolivian Committee, which left La Paz on the 11th (Sunday), took two days to make the trip, and another two days on the return journey, so that they were four nights without sleep. The Chilean delegates arrived in La Paz at half-past five on the Thursday morning, having been up for two consecutive nights and were then without their luggage, which did not arrive until the evening of the 15th and all the festivities that had been prepared for them were consequently postponed until the Friday ... If the trip over the Arica/La Paz system was a fiasco the same cannot be said of their return over this Company's system. Arrangements were made for ... a train comprised of a dining car, two first coaches and a brakevan ... The dining car was beautifully decorated and each meal was a banquet, to the delight of our guests who showered congratulations on the Railway Company. We went so far as to have hot baths ready for them on their arrival here ... prior to their departure ...[56]

Since the Chilean delegation to La Paz included three ministers, with whom the manager had long conversations on matters affecting the railway, this was clearly a master-stroke of public relations. And, though he did not mention this, the fact that the train had sleeping accommodation, which the FCAB had provided for many years, must also have been appreciated. There was, it seemed, little to fear on competition from the new line.

As for the northern section of the Longitudinal Railway, authorized in 1908, it was planned to link the main Chilean metre gauge system from La Ligua to Arica, and its *raison d'être* was much less commercial than strategic – to bind the desert provinces more closely to Santiago. Some modifications were made to the original plans but, finally, in 1909–10, after complicated negotiations involving many parties, the Chilean government accepted the proposals of a British syndicate, under the umbrella name of the Chilean Northern Railway Company, to build and run the line from Pueblo Hundido in the south to Pintados, south-east of Iquique, and crossing the FCAB's main line at Baquedano. The line opened in 1913 but was a loss-maker from the start and in 1919 the owners approached the FCAB with a view to the latter taking over its operation. This was agreed with government approval, and with the clear understanding by the board of the FCAB that the line was not likely to be very profitable: its aim in acquiring it was essentially defensive, namely to prevent the prospect that, in other hands, branch lines might be built from the Northern Railway to the coast and tap the traffic which the FCAB then controlled. As the secretary, A.W. Bolden, had put it some years previously:

> The main object of the Directors is to prevent, if possible, branch lines to the Coast which might very well compete with our own line . . . there is always the possibility of these being built, but that the probability might be more remote if we secure the working of the Longitudinal and give a good service over it . . .[57]

It was precisely that kind of prescience and business acumen that marked the success of the FCAB as an enterprise, though, as events were to prove, in the long run the Northern Railway would become a headache for the company, not least because successive Chilean governments had a particular interest in it.

Thus, in the first decade of the resumption of working the lines by the FCAB, after the Huanchaca lease expired at the beginning of 1904, things looked promising. Competition had been blunted, and the generally buoyant situation – though with troughs – in mineral traffic from both Chile and Bolivia, coupled with growing up-traffic from Antofagasta which reflected that boom in increasing local demand for imported goods of many kinds, produced highly profitable results, as the following table indicates.

TABLE 2. FCAB results 1904–1913

Year	Gross Receipts £	Working Expenses £	Net Receipts £
1904	643,474	314,291	326,858
1905	805,821	439,765	366,055
1906	1,007,088	605,076	401,199
1907	1,022,698	666,178	356,519
1908	1,187,442	689,237	498,204
1909	1,189,099	573,243	609,655
1910	1,399,076	692,050	707,026
1911	1,588,258	836,819	751,439
1912	1,751,099	977,019	774,089
1913	1,916,643	1,074,924	841,719

Sources: Personal communication, G.W. Craig to the author, September, 1986; *FCAB Annual Reports, 1905–1914; The Times* (Company Reports), 1905–1914.

Such results enabled the board not only to provide good dividends and keep plant in good repair, but also to raise new capital when required. Its record to 1914 earned it the accolade of outside observers, such as *The Times* which commented that year:

> . . . the dividend-earning capacity of the Antofagasta line compares very favourably with that of the British-owned railways in Argentina and Brazil . . . it is, with the possible exception of the Peruvian Corporation, the premier industrial undertaking on the Pacific Coast . . . [58]

A week later, after the company's AGM had taken place, the paper pointed out that, in the first ten years' working of the lines by the FCAB itself, 'the gross receipts from the entire undertaking had multiplied three-fold, and their net profits were 2½ times as much'.[59] At the same time, however, the newspaper reminded readers of the company's dependence on the economies of Chile and Bolivia and of how much they relied on mineral extraction and export in world market conditions over which they had no control. Those circumstances were soon to be made crystal clear.

Meanwhile, the company could look back on a successful decade. Its network had expanded considerably in both Chile and Bolivia, so much so that in the summer of 1913 the board took the decision to separate completely the administration of its properties in the two countries, which took effect from February 1914. The general manager for Chile – then W.H. Robinson – would continue to be based in Antofagasta, and the general manager for Bolivia would be in La Paz. This was a logical decision, given the distance of Antofagasta from La Paz, the different nature of the two countries and, far from least, the increasing complexity of the company's operations in both of them. The first incumbent in Bolivia was H.T.A. Warren, recruited from the Uruguay Railway.

Water

If the primary preoccupation of the FCAB in its formative years was to safeguard its lines, management both in London and on the ground had another vital concern to protect and expand. And it was no less a life-line than the railway for the communities it served. 'Where nitrate is, water – by nature – is not,[60] and neither the mineral extracting industries nor the ports could have survived in the generally waterless Atacama desert without a reliable supply of fresh water. By the early concessions on which it was based, the FCAB had not only the right but also the obligation to provide that service, as well as meeting its own considerable needs. And demand for water for both industrial and domestic use grew almost insatiably as the desert economy developed, requiring fresh concessions and new plant.

By the original agreements – transferred from the Huanchaca Company – the FCAB was permitted to tap the Rivers Loa and San Pedro in return for providing Antofagasta and intermediate places with a free supply of 5 per cent of the water brought down to the town and up to 10 per cent for the settlements *en route*. This free supply was for public use, and half-price was to be charged for water delivered to state vessels and barracks. Beyond that, the price to the public was fixed at $1.40 (1 peso, 40 centavos) per cubic metre, that price to be held, irrespective of exchange rates. The pipeline, some 340 kilometres in length and 10-inch diameter, with a capacity of 2,000 cubic metres a day, was laid by June 1892, when the supply was turned on in Antofagasta's principal square, the Plaza Colón. Reservoirs were built at San Pedro de Atacama, with a capacity of some 30,000 tons, but within a few years the supply was quite inadequate to meet the need. In 1899, however, springs were found at Polapi, 25 kilometres north of San Pedro, and a concession obtained to tap them for twenty-five years. A pipeline 5 inches in diameter was then laid from Polapi to the reservoirs, and opened in 1901: that concession imposed the obligation to supply, free of charge, water for state railways, educational establishments, state vessels, barracks, and other public institutions. Later concessions, in 1904 and 1905, to tap other springs at Palpana and Colana in the same region carried similar obligations. With the nitrate boom, however, demand continued to outstrip supply, partly because of other factors such as interference with the exposed pipelines. The general manager reported in January 1905:

> We have had considerable trouble lately with the water supply on account of persons maliciously closing down valves up the country, and we have had to put on extra men and continually inspect the line. As the consumption now is equal to the supply, any stoppage . . . uses up the small reserve . . . The consumption of water by the Fisco and the Municipality is also out of

all proportion to the size of the town ... I intend to fix a maximum consumption ... and I shall have the support of the Nitrate Companies whose output will be reduced if the consumption in Antofagasta is not brought within reasonable limits.[61]

To meet the rising demand, particularly from the nitrate *oficinas*, the FCAB laid a second pipeline from the reservoirs in 1906: it reached Cerrillos, 205 kilometres from Antofagasta and about the same distance from San Pedro in October 1907, costing £365,000, and was extended to Antofagasta by October 1913. This had a daily capacity of 6,500 tons, much of which originated in another concessionary source, the Siloli springs, lying across the Chilean-Bolivian boundary, north-east of Calama. Permission to tap them was authorized by the Chilean government in June 1906, and by the Bolivian authorities in September 1908, the latter imposing an obligation to provide one-third of the water taken in Bolivian territory for public use. The Siloli main from the springs to the reservoirs at San Pedro was 56 kilometres in length, with a capacity of 6,500 cubic metres a day.

Even then, however, it was not always enough. Demand from the *oficinas* inevitably fluctuated, depending on the profitability of nitrate in world markets, always an unpredictable factor. In 1911, for example, a buoyant year for the fertilizer, it was reported that:

At the present moment we are in the uncomfortable position of not being able to supply the demands that are made upon us, and have been forced to limit our supply ... to keep up our reserves. The consumption has gone up to 2000 tons per day, as against 1400 during the same period last year. The average amount of water which arrives at Antofagasta ... is 1200 daily. The condensers produce 400 tons, giving us a total of 1600 ... We use for our own service locomotives some 200 tons, leaving a balance of 1400 tons, as against 2000 tons which is required by the town ...[62]

In consequence, after consultation with the local authorities, rationing was imposed. Moreover, as Antofagasta developed, amenities had to be improved, not least sanitation, and in that same report the general manager indicated that the supply of water would have to be increased 50 per cent in 1912.

In future years the water network, like the railways, was extended and condensers at the coast installed, as at Mejillones where the workshops were, though pipelines from the main inland sources of water progressively reduced dependence there on desalination plant. The water undertaking became an increasingly profitable business: whereas in 1904, out of total income of £643,474, water accounted for £19,001, in 1913, of gross receipts of £1,916,643, water earned £104,868.

On the whole, despite market fluctuations, and at least until the collapse of the natural nitrate industry in the early 1930s, the water business did well, the ratio of operating expenses to income being consistently lower than the running of the railway lines themselves. Much more crucial than its profitability to the company, however, was its strategic significance. When, for example, the threat that the Chilean Northern Railway Company might build branch lines to the coast and cut the FCAB's nitrate traffic was exercising both the board in London and the general manager in Antofagasta, the latter felt that the threat was, in fact, groundless apart from the rival company's problems in building branch lines to the *oficinas* and operating them at a profit in the face of a well-run and long-established network

> The stronger lever we have is the water question: if we did not supply the Oficinas with water, they would be unable to work, and on the whole I have no fear whatever that the Longitudinal will divert our traffic.[63]

A week later he was even more emphatic. Referring to a proposed deviation of the Longitudinal Railway which might compete for nitrate traffic, he said:

> The water difficulty is ever before them, and even if they were to make this deviation they would have to carry water in tanks for their own use. Supposing the Oficina were eventually built, it would have to rely upon us for its supply of water, and we could make terms with them, stipulating that all their traffic would be delivered to us at the Junction where the Longitudinal Railway would cross our Line.[64]

Control of the vital necesssity for life in the Atacama desert was, then, the key to the company's fortunes when the national economies flourished. And, since the major economic issue with traffic was the agreement of tariffs with both government and users, provision of water was a critical lever in such negotiations. But it never went unchallenged, and much of the time of managers on the west coast had necessarily to be spent on defending the company's investments and interests in water.

The challenge came from two sources, the users for industrial purposes and domestic consumers. And both could generally count on the support of government, national and local. It was in the interests of the national government to maximize revenue through mineral exports in economic terms, as well as to cater for regional needs in political ones. Both objectives implied that government could not be indifferent to the fact that the FCAB had a virtually monopolistic position on water supply in the Atacama. Industrial users looked naturally to minimize production costs and, despite the excellence of its service, resented the FCAB's quasi-monopoly. As a result, throughout its history, the company faced constant threats to its water business on several fronts. A particularly interesting example occurred in the years before the First World War.

In the latter years of the nineteenth century and the first decade of the twentieth, a number of comparatively small concerns, mostly British, had begun to work the huge copper deposits of Chuquicamata but, in 1910, Albert C. Burrage, an American entrepreneur from Boston, acquired their concessions with the agreement of the Chilean government. At the same time, a revolutionary new process for exploiting low-grade ores – the Jackling process – was being introduced into copper mining, particularly by the very rich mineral capitalists, the Guggenheims. In 1911, Burrage sold his Chilean interests to Guggenheims for some US $25 million. This was the origin of the Chile Exploration Company (Chilex), founded in 1912. Actual plant construction began a year later, and what was to become the world's largest copper mine started to produce in 1915. For the FCAB as owner of the branch line to Chuquicamata since 1902, these were highly significant developments. Chilex might well prove to be a very good customer, indeed, both for up-traffic of construction material through Antofagasta and for down-traffic on its production. But although it was obvious that an agreement would be advantageous to both companies, water supply bedevilled their relationship from the very beginning. In August 1912, the general manager of the FCAB reported:

> We see by the "Prensa" of the 24th August that the Chuquicamata Syndicate, represented by Messrs Duncan Fox and Company, have decided on the bold step of attempting to induce the Government to cancel our concession of 24th June, 1889 for the use of the Loa water, and are asking for it to be transferred to them . . .[65]

The company's lawyers were instructed to challenge this which they did successfully. But negotiations with Chilex on water supply proved to be a very protracted business and, for both the general manager and the board, a considerable nuisance at a time when demand for water everywhere was increasing, and they had other preoccupations. 'It is very evident', the general manager wrote in October, 1912,

> that further capital expenditure will be necessary to meet the ever increasing consumption. At the present time we have . . . two pipe lines, of a total capacity of 10,000 tons . . . The consumption in our pampa to the different nitrate oficinas has increased enormously . . . Our idea is to apply for a fresh concession, the intake being still at Calama, and lay a pipe line from that point to serve exclusively the nitrate districts . . . We suggest a pipe line of a capacity of 6,000 tons per day or perhaps greater, at a cost of some £150,000 to £200,000. If . . . we were unable to secure the desired concession, it would mean our having to lay a new pipe line from San Pedro, at an approximate total cost of some £250,000 . . .[66]

Meanwhile, negotiations with Chilex dragged on and on: a year after that report was written, the writer saw that company's representatives, Messrs. Yeatman and Hellman 'with regard to the application they had made for a freight, water and petroleum contract'. 'They were informed', he went on,

> that we were willing to enter into a separate contract for each of these items for a minimum period of five years. This information was not [to] their satisfaction . . . Mr. Hellman . . . stated that he considered his Company had not received every facility that we might have given, which I repudiated and impressed upon them that we had gone out of our way to assist them and that unfortunately they had shown hostility at every turn, going to extremes and doing their utmost to obtain our water rights at San Pedro . . .[67]

The meeting ended without agreement, and it is clear that it was the question of water which was central to the issue. Apart from his pique with Chilex, the manager was also peeved by the fact that that company's agents were a British firm.

There followed a long and complicated series of events involving both companies' local representatives and, eventually, their boards, their legal advisers in Chile and government ministers in direct negotiations. Early in 1914 Chilex successfully secured from the Chilean government a concession to take 15,000 tons of water a day from the San Pedro river: the basic question for the FCAB was whether the intake should be above or below its own outlet. The secretary and local management feared that, if Chilex secured the higher intake, it would give that company the power, when the flow was low, to affect supplies to the FCAB both for its own use and to meet its obligations under the original concessions for both domestic and industrial use under its contracts with customers. Here, both companies had powerful levers to employ, and skilled advocates to use them: the FCAB had its concessions and an efficient working railway from Chuquicamata to the coast; the American company, with its very ambitious plans for copper development, could argue with ministers the great value to Chile of that growth, and it could also threaten to seek concessions to build competing lines to the coast, by-passing Antofagasta. It could also relate its discussions on tariff rates with the FCAB to the question of water.

For the general manager of the FCAB, it was a very busy time, necessitating frequent trips to Santiago to see ministers and officials as well as his advisers, and keeping in constant touch with London. One complication was that there were a large number of other pending questions with the Chilean government relating to proposals to change the gauge of the lines, the supply of water to the Longitudinal Railway and to Antofagasta, tariffs on freights, and other matters, in which its customers – notably nitrate producers – had a lively interest. Robinson wrote:

> It is regrettable that amongst the difficulties we have had to contend against is the attitude the British firms who have any connexion with the Antofagasta (Nitrate) Company invariably take up and endeavour to block any concessions for which we are in treaty with the Government ... You cannot realise the trying and harrassing time one undergoes in surmounting all the difficulties to be met with in treating any subject of importance with the Government, which becomes accentuated as time goes on ...[68]

Obviously, those firms had their *own* interests to defend and advance, and it is hardly surprising that they took advantage of the company's difficulties.

The board grew increasingly concerned about relations with Chilex, and in 1914 assumed the key role in negotiating with Guggenheims. In July, what was called 'the London Agreement' was initialled: as Robinson in Antofagasta was informed:

> ... Generally speaking, the idea is that in exchange for the Chile Exploration Co. renouncing *for all time* their claim to have the Intake above ours, we have agreed to facilitate in every possible way the delivery to them of the full 15,000 tons of water per day granted to then under their concession, they to make use of our Intake so long as they give us their traffic ... The ... Co. will construct its own Pipe Lines from our intake to Chuquicamata and its own Reservoir near the intake ... They will have extended their Freight Contract to 10 years ...[69]

The agreement also included a clause stating that Chilex would not seek to build a competing line.

Unfortunately, that agreement, so painstakingly reached on a *quid pro quo* basis, fell through since Chilex raised further objections, having obtained from government a concession to make its intake above that of the FCAB. In the event, however, both companies realized that it was in their pragmatic interest to collaborate rather than to conflict. Subsequently, Chilex built its own water pipe line and, like all customers on freights, always drove a hard bargain; but FCAB did not suffer too much from either the tariff agreement or the challenge to its water monopoly. Moreover, though the threat re-appeared from time to time in the future, a competing line from Chuquicamata to the coast was never built. The FCAB continued to handle traffic to and from Chuquicamata through Antofagasta under whatever management the mine operated – Chilex, Anaconda (1923) and, finally, the Chilean government after the nationalization of the foreign-owned *gran minería* in the early 1970s. World supply and demand for copper were throughout more important than local circumstances for the company's profits, and given Chuquicamata's status as the world's largest body of copper ore, overall the results were positive.

What the Chilex water issue illustrates in the history of the FCAB is the importance of that commodity in the evolution of the company, and the preoccupation of management at the local level with the significance of the relationship of water supply to all other issues. But that management had also more mundane matters to think about, in the operation of an enterprise which, by 1914, had become, far and away, the most important foreign business operating in Chile's northern desert.

Notes

1. *The Times*, 4 January 1889.
2. *Ibid*, 19 December 1927.
3. *Ibid* 25 November 1921.
4. Joslin, *A Century of Banking*, p. 186.
5. *The Times*, 26 June 1918.
6. Board meeting, 10 April 1889. Minute Book No. 1. folio 21.
7. Ibid, 2 January 1889. Minute Book No. 1. ff. 6 and 7.
8. Cited by Césareo Aramaya Avila, *Ferrocarriles Bolivianos: Pasado, Presente, Futuro*, La Paz, 1959, p. 52. My translation.
9. *Ibid*. My translation.
10. Mitre, 'The Economic and Social Structure of Silver Mining', *loc. cit.* p. 248.
11. *The Times*, 30 June 1894.
12. *Ibid*.
13. Mitre, 'The Economic and Social Structure of Silver Mining', *loc. cit.* p. 150.
14. Board Meeting, 25 March 1897. Minute Book No. 1. ff.266–67
15. *Ibid*., 15 May 1897, Minute Book No. 1, ff. 273–74.
16. *Ibid*., 15 June 1897. Minute Book No. 1, f. 279.
17. *The Times*, 9 July 1897.
18. Board Meeting, 10 February 1898. Minute Book No. II, f.15
19. *Ibid*., 7 April 1898. Minute Book No. II, f.21.
20. *Ibid*., 23 February 1899. Minute Book No. II, f.47.
21. *The Times*, 25 March 1898
22. *Ibid*., 5 July 1902.
23. *Ibid*., 13 December 1900.
24. *Ibid*, 27 May 1904.
25. Bowman, *Desert Trails of Atacama, loc. cit*., p. 80.
26. General manager to secretary, Antofagasta, 8 March 1904. Letter No. 5.
27. *Idem* to *idem*, Antofagasta, 1 April 1904. Letter No. 10.
28. *Idem* to *idem*, Antofagasta, 24 June 1904. Letter No. 24.
29. *Idem* to *idem*, Antofagasta, 7 November 1904. Private.
30. C. Cowley, 'Memorandum on the Antofagasta Company and its subsidiaries, August, 1949', p. 12. Typescript in FCAB archive. cf. Oscar Bermúdez Miral, 'Las oficinas salitreras adyacentes a la linea del ferrocarril de Antofagasta a Bolivia', *Boletín de la Asociación de Geógrafos de Chile*, No. 3 (1967), *passim*.

31. General manager to secretary, Antofagasta, 8 March 1904. Letter No. 5.
32. *Ibid.*
33. *Idem.* to *idem.*, Antofagasta, 1 April 1904. Letter No. 10.
34. *Annual Report* for 1905, p. 8.
35. General manager to secretary, Antofagasta, 5 April 1904. Letter No. 12.
36. *Idem.* to *idem.*, Antofagasta, 22 October 1904. Private.
37. *Idem.* to *idem.*, Antofagasta, 9 May 1904. Private.
38. *Ibid.*
39. General manager to secretary, Antofagasta, 16 May 1904 Private.
40. *Idem.* to *idem.*, Antofagasta, 22 October 1904. Private.
41. General manager to secretary, Antofagasta, 16 October 1904. Private.
42. *El Industrial* of Antofagasta, 5 August 1919. Cited by Floreal Recabarren, Antonio Obilinovic and Juan Panadés, *Coloso: una aventura histórica*, Universidad de Antofagasta, 1983, p. 86. My translation.
43. General manager to secretary, Antofagasta, 2 August 1904. Letter No. 30.
44. Board minutes, 18 February 1908. Minute Book No. 3, f. 237.
45. Acting general manager to secretary, Antofagasta, 26 August 1908. Letter No. 198. cf. Recabarren *et. al., Coloso, op. cit.*, pp. 112–18 which quotes the contemporary press on the subject.
46. Board Minutes, 1 December 1908. Minute Book No. 4, f.35.
47. General manager to secretary, Antofagasta, 17 December 1908. Private.
48. AGM, *Report of Proceedings on 10th June, 1909*, p. 11.
49. *The Times*, 13 July 1907. Report of Meeting.
50. General manager to secretary, Antofagasta, 17 June 1904. Letter No. 23.
51. *Idem.* to *idem.*, Antofagasta, 7 November 1904. Special.
52. Extraordinary general meeting, *Report of Proceedings on 10th December, 1908*, p.5.
53. Fifer, *Bolivia, loc. cit.*, p. 191.
54. General manager to secretary, Antofagasta, 28 June 1906. Private.
55. *Idem.* to *idem., Antofagasta, 26 August 1907. Private.*
56. *Idem,* to *idem.,* General manager to secretary, Antofagasta, 30 May 1913. Private and Confidential.
57. Secretary to general manager, London, 13 February 1914. Private.
58. *The Times*, 3 June 1914.
59. *Ibid.*, 10 June 1914.
60. Fawcett, *Railways of the Andes*, p. 122.
61. General manager to secretary, Antofagasta, 23 January 1905. Private.
62. *Idem.* to *idem.,* Antofagasta, 5 January 1911. Letter No. 326.
63. *Idem.* to *idem.,* Antofagasta, 12 October 1910. Private.
64. *Idem* to *idem.*, Antofagasta, 19 October 1910. Private.
65. *Idem.* to *idem.,* Antofagasta, 30 August 1912. Letter No. 413.
66. *Idem.* to *idem.,* Antofagasta, 11 October 1912. Private.
67. *Idem.* to *idem.*, Antofagasta, 17 October 1913. Private.
68. *Idem.* to *idem.,* to secretary, Antofagasta, 29 December 1913. Private.
69. Acting secretary to general manager, London, 24 July 1914. Letter No. 228.

3
LIFE, LABOUR AND PUBLIC RELATIONS

Introduction

Running a large-scale business anywhere is, obviously, a complex affair, requiring a variety of skills. This is particularly true – and no less obvious – of foreign enterprises operating in alien environments where native talent is insufficient. For the FCAB, expanding rapidly in the decade before the First World War, neither Chile nor, much less, could Bolivia provide the managers, the engineers, the accountants or the clerks, let alone the men to drive the trains and maintain them. Hence, until fairly recent times and as, gradually, national education systems and economic change advanced, expatriate staff were a prominent feature. This was not true, however, of all spheres of activity. Operating as a foreign concern in both countries, the company had to rely upon the expertise of national legal advisers to comply with the laws of the countries, and sometimes, the influence of prominent public figures to safeguard its interests. And here, it is interesting to note that that same remarkable continuity of service seen in boards of directors and professional staff also obtained. For example, Alberto García de la Huerta was appointed the company's legal representative in Santiago in 1908, 'as an ex-secretary of President Riesco [and] in a position to attend to our ministerial work well, and to further our interests'.[1] He remained on the company's books until 1941 when ill-health forced him to retire, somewhat reluctantly. Similarly, at the local level, in Antofagasta itself for dealings with the provincial and municipal authorities, Francisco Carey was appointed in 1907, but not until July 1938, did the manager report that '... we have formally accepted the resignation of Señor Carey as from the 1st instant', adding that 'his Firm has been appointed as the Company's lawyers in Antofagasta'.[2] Carey, in fact, was succeeded by his son, and he by his son. In both cases, over thirty years' service suggests that it was not self-interest alone which motivated the two men.

Legal skills were one thing; managerial and operational expertise another and had to be recruited from abroad, especially, of course, the United Kingdom. Contract staff were engaged for the higher levels of posts, usually on an initial three-year basis, and renewable on satisfactory performance. The contracts spelled out in meticulous detail what was expected of the employee and the terms on which he or she was engaged (female employment being particularly concerned with medical matters), not only salaries and leave but also conduct. For example, the initial contract made between the FCAB and George Craig, appointed assistant engineer draughtsman in 1925, stated in clause 4:

> He shall pay due and becoming respect to the Civil and Religious Institutions and customs of the place he may be residing in, abstaining from all interference therewith, nor in any way interfere or take part in the political affairs of the Country.[3]

He was also, incidentally, enjoined not to marry within three years of his employment without the express consent of the board or its manager in Antofagasta. Such terms, today, would, of course, be unacceptable but in an earlier time were simply the norm.

For its part, the company's terms and conditions of service (see Appendix 2) spelt out its obligations as an employer in the provision of accommodation, furniture and amenities, and included helpful advice on climate, clothing, and other matters intended to orientate the expatriate before arrival. For work in regions ranging from barren desert to high mountains, such orientation was essential, particularly since most of the expatriate staff, at least on arrival, did not speak Spanish, though the company – as a paternalistic and, on the whole, benevolent employer – sought to remedy that defect:

> There is a tendency [wrote the Acting General Manager in 1910] among our contract clerks to shirk the learning of Spanish, and I would suggest that for the future their Contracts be endorsed with the condition that the annual rises provided for are conditional on their making satisfactory progress in this language. You may not be aware that we provide a teacher, and classes are held twice a week, lasting about one hour.[4]

Language-teaching was, however, a minor preoccupation: much more important for foreign workers were the overall conditions of life and work in new and strange surroundings.

The environment, particularly in the early years, was forbidding. Sanitation in both Chile and Bolivia was rudimentary, and the problem of health care was a major concern to individuals and management alike. Similarly, housing facilities, especially for men with wives and families and particularly outside towns, were far below the standards that even working-class expatriates had experienced in the home country. Again, and perhaps no less important for men working long days – and, often, nights – opportunities for recreation were very strictly limited. It is hardly surprising in such circumstances that a fair number of employees sought solace in drink, the result not only of the physical, but also of the human, environment. In both Chile and Bolivia, drunkeness was a major social evil, as most travellers tales testify:

> The chief end of the rotos' life seems to be to get drunk. He works only for this, and nine-tenths of his kind are in a state of intoxication at least once a week . . . For this reason Monday is called the 'rotos' holy day' for he is so drunk on Sunday that he has to take Monday to 'taper off'.[5]

And managers' reports frequently refer to the unofficial holiday of San Lunes, as well as to particular expatriate staff at the lower levels who paid respect to 'the customs of the place'.

On the death of an engine driver in 1908, for example, the manager stated:

> The Doctor reports that he was a very alcoholic subject and that so long ago as February of last year had been under treatment for this cause. He went to the Hospital on the 6th instant, suffering from a sprained ankle, which was attended to and he was given a bottle of lotion to rub on it. The same day, however, he had to be taken into the Hospital, having drunk the whole contents of the bottle of lotion.[6]

Nor were hospital staff themselves immune:

> I regret to report [wrote the manager on another case] that on several occasions we have had trouble with Nurse X owing to her being the worse for drink and I have had to ask her to send in her resignation.[7]

And, as a final example from the mid-1920s, when Arthur Heskett, then general manager of the Bolivian section, was travelling from Parotani to La Paz, two trains collided:

> The men lead by Don Arturo leapt from the coach and rushed up to the locomotive . . . I saw Don Arturo climb up on the footplate and the next thing to appear was a bottle flying through the air into the bushes alongside the track . . . The bottle was soon followed by the driver, very drunk, kicked off the engine . . . he had been quite drunk lying in the tender while his Bolivian stoker did his best to drive . . .[8]

From the beginning, the board of the FCAB in London and its local managers recognized the need to combat such vices and to provide their employees, both foreign and national, with reasonable working and living conditions. They were not, however, always in the position of being able to do as much as they might have wished, subject as the company's fortunes were to the vagaries of the economies of Chile and Bolivia, and to the dependence of those countries on world markets for minerals. Nevertheless, the records show that, despite inevitable labour troubles, the company consistently sought to keep the goodwill of its staff as a fair employer, and that it had a good measure of success is indicated by the length of service of so many of its employees. Naturally, this was in its own interests and, like every communications enterprise, it clearly recognized how much the whole depended on the parts. Disruption of whatever kind at any particular point on the main line, such as Baquedano or Calama, would affect all of it. Moreover, as the single largest foreign business in the province of Antofagasta, employing more expatriate staff than any other for decades, the FCAB had the responsibility of setting an example to other foreign companies in contributing to the social as well as to the economic evolution of the region and this responsibility was discharged.

Health and medical care

When, in 1904, the FCAB commenced the working of the lines, Antofagasta then a town of some 30,000 people – had one hospital, El Salvador, built in the 1870s. Ironically, it was situated next to the municipal graveyard, prompting President Germán Riesco on his visit in 1905 to remark: 'Really, it is no more than the cemetery's ante-room'.[9] Small and ill-equipped, El Salvador reflected the dismal state of public health provision in Chile in the first quarter of the century. And in Bolivia it was even worse. At the same time, the town was frequently afflicted by plagues – bubonic, typhoid and malaria, partly in consequence of a primitive drainage and sanitation system, as managers in that period observed too often.

From the outset, the company had provided its own medical service, with a British doctor and a nurse for the expatriate staff but the increase in the number of employees in the decade and the continuing prevalence of outbreaks of disease called for an expansion of the service. In the wake of a particularly virulent outbreak of bubonic plague, it was decided to replace the existing small hospital which, in any case, had no drainage, with something better. The general manager wrote early in 1906:

> I have arranged to construct a commodious hospital on the Company's land

> at the corner of the calles Centeno and Carretas . . . [usually Zenteno, after a hero of Independence: Carretas has long been known as Iquique] in the same piece of land lower down the calle Centeno a small isolation hospital will be erected . . . Rooms will be provided in the Hospital for the Doctor, nurses and dispenser and there will be private rooms and two classes of wards.[10]

The hospital services provided by the FCAB seem to have worked well for the next twenty years, during which, besides, municipal and national provision improved. By 1912, a modern drainage system had been installed in Antofagasta, and the incidence of epidemic disease fell markedly. Six years before, the *Junta de Beneficencia de Antofagasta*, a regional charity, started to raise funds and make plans for a modern municipal hospital, with a grant-in-aid from the central government. Though cash was hard to get – and the FCAB contributed annually to the *Junta* – in 1913 the first buildings were opened, though it was 1927 before the plan was complete. Another benefactor was Antonio Luksic, member of a well-known entrepreneurial family in the region whose surname will occur again in this story.

The development of municipal medical services had its effect on those provided by the company for its employees. In 1915, the general manager at Antofagasta queried whether there was any point in continuing them:

> I am very seriously considering the advisability of closing the hospital at the end of the present year, and making such arrangements with the Local Authorities for them to give us every facility in the new town hospital in connection with our staff . . .[11]

This was partly because the chief British contract doctor, Dr Young, wished to return to Britain 'for personal reasons' – actually to volunteer for service in the war – and the complications of replacing him at that time were obvious. The board in London, however, ever conscious of its obligations to its employees, took a different view. 'The Directors', wrote A.W. Bolden, 'do not want to appear to break faith with the staff in any way . . .'.[12] And, in a subsequent letter, he was more explicit:

> We think it would be a fatal mistake to allow our staff to feel that they have not the same medical advantages to look forward to as they have had hitherto. It may be, with the lapse of time . . . that the new Antofagasta Hospital will be found to be adequate to meet all the requirements . . . but that would seem to be a matter of time for overcoming the prejudice which today probably exists in the minds of the European employees. We feel both a legal and moral obligation to our staff whilst we deduct the 1% from their salaries (to contribute to the service) . . . very careful consideration should be given before we decide to decrease in any way the facilities now available.[13]

Both parties continued these arguments for the next two or more years, the general manager on the spot pointing out the improvements at the municipal hospital – to which the FCAB regularly contributed – the use made of it, and not only by native workers, and the expense of keeping up its own hospital with two contracted nurses. For its part, the board in London continued to show a marked reluctance to close it down unless and until it were absolutely convinced that the expatriate staff would willingly accept the closure.

Later records on this subject are somewhat sparse, but it would appear that a *modus vivendi* was reached. Though the hospital was cut back somewhat, it remained in existence until 1924, and a nurse was retained for routine treatment of minor ailments and accidents, as was the pharmacy. For many years, the company had employed, in addition to doctors contracted in Britain, a number of Chilean practitioners whose clinics the staff attended, and who were also retained, not only for work in Antofagasta but also to visit weekly other places such as Coloso and Prat. Similar arrangements existed in the company's other stations in Chile and Bolivia. But, with the departure of the two British doctors during the First World War, the company had to rely increasingly on local expertise, and in time it became obliged to. In 1924, the Chilean government decreed that doctors of foreign nationality might not practice in the country unless they possessed Chilean qualifications. But the writing had been on the wall long before then. As early as August 1919, the general manager, after discussing the matter with a visiting director, A.H.A. Knox-Little, reported that the future of the hospital depended on its getting British doctors:

> ... we are convinced that this could not be arranged unless the doctor first obtained his Chilian qualifications ... To do this he must of course have a good working knowledge of Spanish and it would appear impossible to get through under two years at least ... It would therefore seem practically impossible for us to employ an English doctor ...[14]

He recommended that the acting chief medical officer, Dr Figueroa, who had worked three and a half years for the company, and had given up his private practice to do so, be appointed chief of the medical department: the alternative would be to get an English doctor, working somewhat surreptitiously, though he did not think they would get away with that. His recommendation on Figueroa was accepted but the problems of getting an English doctor remained, and when the law of 1924 was passed, the idea was abandoned and the hospital closed. Good medical services, however, were maintained, partly through the construction, in 1924, of a nursing home for the large British community in the city, funded by the many companies active there, and with British nurses under contract to staff it. This survived until 1939, when the last two British nurses volunteered for war service, and the home was closed.

Housing and other amenities

In a highly eulogistic article on the FCAB in 1945, a Chilean newspaper remarked that it had been

> ... the most effective agent of progress in the [Antofagasta] region; for the worker, the best school to turn him into a craftsman; for the employee the safest and surest shelter for him to learn to appreciate the meaning of integrity, sobriety and family life ... [15]

Apart from pointing out that the company had started its medical service for employees long before the state itself had intervened in that sphere, the article set out in some detail what the FCAB was then providing for its Chilean workforce of some 2,500 and their dependents, a total of almost 8,000 people, in the way of housing, including water and light, and recreational facilities, as well as pensions for retired employees and donations to their families for funeral expenses when they died. In short, thought the writer, the FCAB was a model employer. Though, clearly, throughout its history, far from all its employees could think that, the company's early management did establish, however paternalistically to begin with, traditions of fair dealing with the staff.

It was obviously in its interests to do so, given the complex but integrated nature of its business, and the expansion of the Bolivian and Chilean mineral economies in the period before the First World War. Competition for native labour was often acute, and from the beginning both central and local management recognized that salaries and wages, however important they are, alone do not necessarily make for good industrial relations. Similarly, in order to attract and retain an increasing number of skilled and semi-skilled expatriate staff, the company had to provide a reasonable environment for work and living. Northern Chile and highland Bolivia, however scenically arresting, were underdeveloped regions, presenting sizeable problems of adaptation to the foreigner. And not all could easily adapt to quite unfamiliar geographical and climatological surroundings, ranging from arid desert to high mountains: the incidence of drunkeness is an indicator of that, perhaps no less the result of weakness of character than of sheer boredom, particularly outside working hours. While, through its provision of medical services, the FCAB tried to ensure healthy bodies, it also thought about healthy minds, at first primarily for expatriate staff but also, increasingly, for its Chilean and Bolivian employees. The improvement in their conditions over time was partly the result of, first, growing government intervention in labour and social issues, notably from the 1920s and, second, increasing unionization – this will be dealt with later. But, in many respects, the FCAB anticipated what governments were to enact and unions demand.

With contracted employees, the company undertook to provide accommodation and basic services, and local management spent a good deal of time improving amenities. An early letter illustrates what might be involved. The general manager wrote in 1906:

> I am arranging to remove the employés of the workmen class from the houses in the Calle Baquedano . . . putting them into houses which are being built on the West and South sides of the North Yard and use all these houses for the better class employés, a certain number for married men and the remainder as bachelors' quarters. There is no room up there to build a tennis court, the only site for this would be at the back of the Administration Avenue if we can secure the land there. The first house . . . is now used partly for quarters and partly for the bachelors' mess. The two small rooms are now insufficient as there are 30 members and the number is increasing. I am therefore putting on a second storey to the house and when this is done one side of the ground floor will be used as a large dining room and another for a billiard room – I am ordering two small billiard tables – and the upper part as a library and part as living quarters. I have also ordered . . . a gramophone . . . Later on . . . I shall put up a separate building for the mess and billiard rooms, library etc., and the tennis court will be adjacent to it . . .[16]

While life for expatriates in the larger communities, such as Antofagasta, Oruro and La Paz, was clearly more attractive – though in the early days only marginally – than living in places such as Mejillones, Calama and Coloso, the management was very conscious of the difference.

> I shall be glad [the Manager wrote from Antofagasta in 1907] to have the authorization of the Board for the purchase of a piano and pianola for use of staff in Mejillones . . . as there is of course even less distraction for the staff out of working hours in Mejillones than here.[17]

Five years later, when the staff, including the workmen, petitioned the manager for a better and bigger building, to be used as a school by day and for recreation at night, he had no hesitation in supporting it, 'knowing the feelings of the Directors in regard to the Company providing their staff with suitable quarters for recreation'.[18]

Broadly speaking, successive boards of directors were sympathetic to such requests – ranging from better accommodation to books and magazines for the libraries, ping-pong balls and billiard cues – and they allowed local management wide discretion in its evaluation of needs. Only when adverse economic circumstances hit the company was this attitude affected. Overall, it had a good reputation: at the AGM in 1924, for example, the chairman, Lord Lawrence of Kingsgate, referred with pleasure and pride to the fact that the President of Chile, Arturo Alessandri, had gone out of his way in his speech on the recent opening of Congress to draw attention 'in cordial terms to the Antofagasta Railway as a company which has distinguished itself by the interest which it has shown in the welfare of its employees and workmen'.[19]

That interest was not only expressed in providing recreational facilities. Pension funds were instituted for both expatriate and local staff, Chilean and Bolivian, and the company frequently contributed to other similar services. For example, as early as 1907, the employees on the Bolivian section formed a mutual benefit society: 'its main objects . . . to provide financial assistance in cases of sickness or death' and the manager recommended a monthly subvention 'so long as the Society is exclusively composed of Railway servants', a proposal the board accepted.[20] Individual cases of hardship were generally treated sympathetically where employees concerned were seen as hard-working and loyal: such a case was that of Mr W.H.F. in 1922 when his wife was ill and wished to return to England. In his ten years with the company he had not claimed his entitlement to home leave 'and for financial and other reasons does not find it convenient to take such leave at present . . . In all the circumstances we recommend that the Board authorize . . . a 2nd class passage for Mrs F. just as though she were accompanying her husband on home leave'.[21] The board agreed, as it did on numerous requests from the manager for financial assistance to families of deceased staff. Two cases in 1916 illustrate the point, when the general manager spelled out the general question before illustrating it:

> I should like to draw your attention to the frequency with which the Administration is called upon to assist the families of deceased employees, both British and Chilian . . . I consider that to employees who work loyally for the Company for a great number of years some stimulant should be given in the way of knowing that on becoming incapacitated for further duty or death their families will not be left destitute . . .[22]

The two cases he then cited were those of the long-serving housing inspector at Mejillones and the locomotive foreman at Calama, who had worked for the FCAB for almost thirty years. Both men had left widows with large families, so the management decided to pay the bereaved a lump sum equivalent to six months of their husbands' wages and, in addition, allowed them to stay in company houses in Mejillones 'until such time as they find . . . means sufficient for their sustenance.'[23]

The provision of accommodation for at least a period was probably as welcome to the widows as cash, since they and their families would be living in a fairly large community of their own kind, and Mejillones had the added attraction of beautiful and extensive beaches, as well as the amenities the company itself provided. The place had grown dramatically by the time the above letter was written, and it was not only the consequence of locating the workshops there for repair and maintenance of locomotives and rolling stock: the company also constructed holiday chalets which contract staff and their families stationed anywhere in Chile and Bolivia could use for annual seaside holidays. For the engineer, accountant and clerk, working for most of the year in, for example, stations in the Bolivian highlands such as Uyuni and Oruro, the change from the thin air and, not infrequently, cold and bleak winters, to the much warmer climate of the Pacific coast must have been something to look forward to.

Annual reports for the 'boom' decade down to the First World War indicate a rising curve of expenditure for works at Mejillones, including housing for both senior staff and employees and workmen; provision of water (from condensers), sanitary services, light and power for the workshops provided by two 110 kw generators, as well as such social services as a large club house for senior staff – British and Chilean – and another for workmen, as well as a cinema. In late 1912, for example, the general manager put in to London an estimate of almost £65,000 to cover the construction of 75 four-roomed houses for married staff, 36 three-roomed houses, 20 two-roomed houses and 82 individual rooms in blocks for single staff. Criteria for housing of contract staff were explained by the general manager in 1911:

> When a contract clerk arrives from England he is provided with a room containing the following furniture: Bedstead with mattress; Washstand; Table; Chest of Drawers or Wardrobe; Chairs. Bedding etc. can be purchased locally or through the Company for cash, but . . . it is preferable for the employee to bring these with him. Contract mechanics etc., are provided with an unfurnished room and all married contract employees with an unfurnished house. Both have the privilege of buying their furniture from the Co. and paying for them in easy monthly instalments, but this arrangement does not include bedding etc . . . [24]

Obviously, in the early years, housing conditions for contract staff were still fairly primitive in almost every place where the company operated, at least in comparison with what they could expect in the United Kingdom at their level. Water obtained from indoor taps and lighting from flicking a switch or turning on gas were not common amenities: indeed, as late as the early 1920s expatriate staff were advised to take out paraffin reading lamps. Over time, of course, the situation improved but in many places it was years before it did. And, for the native workforces it was decades. But, for the times, the FCAB did its best, and senior staff were certainly reasonably housed.

Robbery and violence

If local management had to care for its staff, it also had to safeguard its company's property. And given the wild nature of the country through which its lines ran, this was no easy task. Moreover, in both Chile and Bolivia, crime was very common and considered by most foreign observers as being, in part at least, linked to too much drink. Banditry was rife. One traveller wrote in 1899:

> One cannot pick up a newspaper without seeing several attacks by bandits, generally accompanied by brutality and murder . . . there have been shown to us the photographs of eleven brigands in prison here who are to be shot. One of them coolly confessed to twenty-eight murders . . .[25]

The writer was referring to incidents in the coal-mining region of south-central Chile, having earlier declared: 'Miners in no part of the world are noted for a high standard of life and morals'.[26] And the generalization applied no less to the nitrate, tin and copper miners of the north than it did to the coal-miners of the south. It was probably too sweeping, but the nature of life and work in Chilean nitrate *oficinas* and Bolivian tin mines certainly produced its crop of criminals. A typical outrage occurred in late 1906, when the general manager regretted to report that the pay train

> . . . was attacked by Bandits at dusk on the 10th inst. at the Hut of Gang No. 14, Km. 228, and the amount of $65,644 was stolen. The attack was so well organized and carried out with such rapidity that no defence was possible. The Bandits, seven in number, armed with carbines, held up the gang previous to the arrival of the train and locked them up in the hut. They then divided into parties, two for the engine, three for the Pay Coach, and two for the coach in which Mr. Minturn and the Travelling Auditor were travelling, and rushed the train as it stopped before the Sectional Engineer or Paymaster . . . could present their Winchesters or revolvers . . . The Paymaster had a narrow escape, a shot being fired through the pay window as he lifted it . . .[27]

The police at Calama, and a troop of mounted police, pursued the robbers, caught three and recovered part of the money and, as a result, the manager continued, he had arranged 'with the Officer in command of the Gendarmes that for the future a military guard shall accompany the pay train'.[28]

Two years later, he reported on an incident in Bolivia which, regrettably, involved his own employees: a large number of robberies of goods in transit from Antofagasta had occurred and, after investigation, he said:

> . . . we have detected an organized system of robbery among train crews and other employes (*sic*) in Bolivia, whereby trains were stopped at lonely spots between the frontier and Uyuni, goods taken from them and buried in the ground, to be afterwards removed by accomplices in carts. The ramifications . . . are very wide, no less than 35 persons in Uyuni having been imprisoned . . .[29]

Such incidents were not uncommon and called for close co-operation with local authorities. On another occasion, relating to robberies at Prat, the 'absolute want of public authority to maintain order' obliged the manager, through the Intendente, to get 'a ''piquet'', consisting of an officer and 8 men, to be stationed there', the company to provide accommodation and furniture for them.[30]

Expenditure on security and apprehension of criminals could be considerable. In 1918, for example, a massive robbery of half a million Chilean pesos occurred at Calama: most of it was eventually recovered, after forty robbers – including local staff – had been arrested. In fact, the entire local staff at Calama were arraigned and replacements had to be sent from Antofagasta to keep the line running. The manager had to employ not only police but also experienced trackers, providing free transport and food, and he also felt that the FCAB should pay all involved for what, in the event, proved a successful police operation:

> . . . such as the Prefect of Police, Officers of Carabineers etc: then our Chief Detective, Garces, certainly deserves a reward for the splendid work he has done; for two days and three nights he was at work on the Toco Pampa, in the saddle or on foot, and has certainly shown exceptional genius in tracing the . . . criminals . . .[31]

He arrested two in a burrow at the point of a revolver. Although the FCAB recovered a proportion of such costs through insurance, it did not recover all of it, and, as for the manager, it was an expensive consumption of time, the correspondence and local consultations going on for just short of a year.

In the Calama case justice was done for the crime committed, largely because some of the accused confessed and implicated colleagues. Sometimes however, the suspects, though arrested, went scot-free. In 1924, the international train from Bolivia was attacked at Sierra Gorda by four men with revolvers who robbed and shot dead a travel agent: several suspects were tracked down but there was insufficient evidence to convict them. Those who were convicted for similar crimes are recorded in a rogues' gallery of photographs, preserved in the company's archive in Antofagasta, along with cases of arms which were used to capture them.

If there was any advantage to the FCAB in the record of robbery and violence on its lines, it lay in the relationship between the company, the local forces of law and order and the political authorities who commanded them. The common interest to combat crime created co-operative relationships and reinforced the company's long-standing role as a contributor, in many ways, to local and regional well-being.

Public relations, regional and national

In the running of an increasingly complex transport network and ancillary services, the FCAB was fully aware of the importance of good relations at all levels. Its tariff policies depended on central government's approval according to the concessions granted to build both railway lines and water facilities; in Bolivia tariffs had to be approved every year, in Chile every three years. And when approved, they had to be negotiated with customers, often a tortuous business. Similarly, subject as the company was to both national and regional legal requirements, including taxation, good public relations were essential to smooth operations. Moreover, as the most significant employer of both foreign and native labour in the Antofagasta region of Chile – at least until the rise of the great copper complex of Chuquicamata – and an important one in Bolivia, the FCAB was expected by the sizeable expatriate community and by the local population to play its part in the overall life of the regions.

Its best advertisement, of course, was the services it provided. For passengers, when the international line from Antofagasta to La Paz was completed in 1917, the railway offered a twice-weekly service at a standard comparable to that of any railway in the world, and, for first-class travellers, a luxurious one. One such, travelling as a boy in 1921, recalls his impressions vividly:

> The passenger trains were ... painted a tasteful green with white roofs, their burnished brass work glinting in the sun ... the passenger coaches – day coaches, sleeping cars, diners and kitchen car were spotless ... The locomotives too were gleaming ... their brass work and steelwork highly polished, and usually the whole crowned by one or more highly polished brass domes ...[32]

Like him, another passenger recorded with pleasure the railway's cuisine and its dining car, 'the centre of social life on South American trains', and she continues:

> The meals served in these crowded, stuffy . . . *coches comedores* are marvellous examples not only of excellent food but of efficient service . . . a meal that starts with hors d'ouevres and moves with military precision through Scotch broth, fried congrio, chicken and rice, beefsteak with potatoes and vegetables . . . caramel custard and coffee . . . [33]

Clearly, few of the common people of Bolivia and Chile could take advantage of such luxuries, though they had reason to be grateful to the FCAB in other ways. One such was the provision of fire-fighting services.

In the arid regions of northern Chile, and not least on the nitrate *pampa*, fire was a frequent hazard. Moreover, since rain fell but rarely, most constructions were of wood, and fires, once started, spread rapidly. This was as true of towns such as Antofagasta as of the *oficinas* in the desert. But no national or provincial fire service existed: the tradition has always been that fire-fighting is a voluntary service, supported by private contributions for the supply of the men (*bomberos*), uniforms, equipment and so on. From the beginning, the FCAB played an active role in providing such services in the regions it served. In 1904, it founded the Sixth Company of Firemen, initially for the security of its own properties in Antofagasta but becoming one of seven units of the municipal fire brigade. It provided uniforms and equipment for the volunteers, many of whom were expatriates: Chileans in the corps had the privilege of being exempt from obligatory military service. The *bomberos*, rather like Masons, had a sense of corporate attachment and their own rituals, such as a torchlight funeral procession when one died. It was a proud thing to be a *bombero*, a member of a special club, and most members were highly enthusiastic:

> Often after business hours [wrote an observer in 1914] the bomberos may be seen racing along the streets dragging their light hand engines, smartly making the necessary connections with their hosepiping, and squirting a few gallons of water into the air to test the mains. [34]

And the enthusiasm was infectious. The success of the Sixth Company at Antofagasta prompted the staff at Mejillones in 1911 to petition the general manager to fund a brigade there, a request he passed to London with his full support:

> . . . considering the very good results obtained at Antofagasta and the keeness with which men participate in this work – or pleasure it appears to them, I feel that every encouragement should be given . . . [35]

The board agreed to his request for £1,000 for uniforms and helmets for fifty to sixty men and the necessary equipment and, as the years passed, the service was extended to other stations. Equipment was renewed as technology advanced and, throughout, the foreign community played an active part. One example is Arthur Heskett who served for many years and actually became overall chief of the Antofagasta fire-service. But there were many other employees who also played their part in providing municipal services with the backing of the FCAB.

That philanthropic role was quite extensive, though again examples are legion and selection inevitable. Some activities were not entirely altruistic. In the educational field, for example, in 1917 the general manager was approached by Dr Guzmán, the company's senior medical consultant in Antofagasta, on behalf of the Society for Chilean Students Abroad for a donation of $1,500. The society's object was

> ... to send intelligent young Chileans to the States and Europe to admit of their studying in a practical manner any branch connected with the profession they may be engaged in, to become accustomed to modern business methods, and for improvement generally ... For instance [he added to indicate that the sum could be an investment] – in the case of a member of the Chilian staff ... at Mejillones ... the Company ... would be assisting to pay his passage and expenses ... to serve his time in one of the large workshops at home whence he would return ... a far more valuable employee than when he left ...[36]

Three years later, the intendente of Antofagasta drew attention to the lack of educational facilities at Coloso, and asked the FCAB to cede part of its property for the building of a school for some 200 children: the manager supported the proposal since, as he put it, 'it is infinitely better for the children to be attending school than roaming about the yards, moles etc.', and the board gave its consent.[37]

Other activities were more selfless, such as donations to Chilean charities on a regular basis or, more particularly, extraordinary sums at times of regional and national crisis. The vulnerability of the nitrate industry in the world economy often meant sharp fluctuations between boom and slump for producers in Antofagasta and their workers, and in times of depression the latter could find themselves out of work at very short notice. Such circumstances obtained at the outset of the First World War, with the complete disruption of trade, and after recovery during the war itself, in its aftermath with a sharp fall in world demand for nitrate. In both 1914 and 1919, the region saw thousands of workers thrown suddenly out of work, and with no alternative employment. They and their families had to rely on charitable institutions to feed them, and those charities depended on voluntary contributions. In 1919, the FCAB donated £100 a month to the leading charity in Antofagasta, which it had supported similarly in the previous crisis, at a time when, because of the contraction of business, it had had to discharge some of its own staff. Again, in November 1922, when an earthquake and tidal wave wreaked havoc in the provinces south of Antofagasta, though causing little damage to that port itself, a relief fund was opened in London to which the company contributed substantially, as did, of course, other British interests in Chile such as banks and merchant houses. But there were also more light-hearted causes to support, as the following example illustrates:

> Up to the present we have been in the habit of granting rebates to Bands of Musicians and Theatrical Companies travelling over the line and, in order to put the matter upon a definite basis, I wrote to the Inspector Fiscal suggesting a rebate of 25% upon passages, baggage etc.[38]

This was in line with the company's belief in *mens sana in corpore sano* in those regions where public entertainment might rely entirely on itinerant performers, including operators of travelling cinemas. It gave donations, sometimes in cash, sometimes in kind – furniture, equipment, use of premises and so on – to a wide variety of sporting and social clubs, even including a lease of land to the German community in Antofagasta to establish a shooting range. When war broke out in 1914, the situation was slightly embarrassing, particularly since the manager thought the German Shooting Club was using its ground to signal to German warships, but he did not wish to create local ill-feeling. Fortunately, the lease expired later in 1914 and was simply not renewed.

All these activities showed how much the FCAB realized it had a reputation to live up to and, clearly, it was in its interests to be seen to be a co-operative and benevolent company, properly contributing to worthy causes. So far as the British community was concerned – one of the largest foreign element in the region – what the FCAB did, others followed, or where others, such as the large nitrate companies, took initiatives, the participation of the company was generally regarded as imperative to their success. Thus, in the establishment of a British church, with a clergyman, in the early days, it made not only financial contributions but also provided practical assistance. The manager stated in 1907:

> Pending the construction of a Church Building, I have given permission for Divine services to be held in the Cuartel of the Company's Bomberos. I have also provided Mr. Blake with one of the Cia's houses in the married quarters . . .[39]

Whether Mr. Blake's sermons, in those surroundings, were of the 'fire and brimstone' variety is not recorded.

As in matters spiritual, so in matters temporal affecting British interests, the FCAB played its part as, for example, in the establishment in 1918 of a branch of the British Chamber of Commerce in Chile at Antofagasta, at the suggestion of the parent body, then located in Valparaiso, though later in Santiago. It was set up under the aegis of the Antofagasta British League, the umbrella body for the expatriate community, and the then-manager, Robinson, was a member of the committee along with representatives of such long-standing British houses as Antony Gibbs, Duncan Fox, Buchanan Jones and the Anglo-South American Bank. As in Valparaiso, so in Antofagasta, the British presence and activities were important ingredients of regional development, and the FCAB was prominent in almost all of them. How prominent for the British community was illustrated in 1911 when George V was crowned:

> A Committee has been formed here to organize a fitting celebration of the Coronation, and they approached us ... They pointed out that as the Railway Co. has quite two-thirds of the total British population of Antofagasta in its employment, the contributions from the other British firms would be largely influenced by that given by the Railway, and suggested that we should subscribe £500. It is proposed to hold a combined athletic sport and gymkana, a smoking concert and a dance ... All classes of the British colony will thus have an opportunity of participating in the celebrations.[40]

And the money was forthcoming since *noblesse oblige*.

Friends in high places

The oligarchic nature of society in both Chile and Bolivia meant that until fairly recent times the political nation was small and the suffrage very restricted. But, within the oligarchies, politics were highly competitive, and personality generally more significant than ideology. For foreign companies, having to deal with both regional and national authorities on a wide variety of issues, it was important to have the right contacts and to cultivate relationships which would defend and advance their interests. Given the volatility of politics in both countries, however, this was not easy, and this was particularly true of Chile where, after the revolution of 1891 had destroyed strong presidential government and implanted a multi-party system, while the head of state remained in power for five years his ministries changed with bewildering frequency since they depended for Congressional support on fluctuating alliances and coalitions. A foreign company might establish good connections with a particular minister only to find his term of office very short. There was, however, greater continuity among subordinate bureaucrats, and it was also necessary to get on with them. Companies also had to avoid any charge of interference in national and regional political affairs, and standard instructions to staff in almost all businesses made that a categorical injunction. This did not mean, of course that, at the managerial level at least, they should not seek the support of influential figures. And, since most matters of controversy between government and private interests were of a legal kind, and a majority of politicians had been trained in the law and remained in practice while sitting in Congress or holding high office, lawyers figured prominently in the lists of important contacts companies sought to make. These observations were true for all companies, including the FCAB.

At the regional level, the intendente or governor of the province was a crucial figure as the direct representative of central government but in his own domain virtually the king. Of this the company was well aware, as the following example illustrates. In 1911, the Intendente of Antofagasta was a certain C. Astaburuaga, a lawyer by profession and, indeed, a partner of the company's chief lawyer there, Francisco Carey. When, later in the year, he resigned the intendancy to concentrate on his private practice, he was recruited by the general manager on a retainer of £500 a year, a step which had been planned long before. It was an astute move, as the manager spelled out:

> He will not only be of considerable value to us as a lawyer but also as a good friend to have at court with the government officials, and whoever is nominated to fill his post is bound to be a friend of his ...[41]

Later in the year he proved his worth. At the time, the FCAB still had pending in Santiago the important question of the extension of a second water pipeline from Prat to Antofagasta and the tariff to be charged on supplies. The matter had been going on a long time, partly because of ministerial changes in Santiago, when Astaburuaga drew his successor's attention to it, pointing out to him 'that the matter is of such importance as to warrant his drawing the special attention of the new Minister to it' he also arranged 'for the public to become aware of the delay by "inspired" notices in the local press'.[42] Though there were further delays, again because of changes of minister, the application went through, work commencing in June 1913, and the line was opened in October. And it was essential:

> Until the construction was finished we did not receive sufficient water from the Interior to supply the demand and our condensers were worked (*sic*). We also had to restrict ... any increase in the supply of private services, which were limited to 55 in 1913, making a total of 864 ... The condensers are now closed down and we are laying new mains in the town ... and increasing our private services rapidly ...[43]

The records show that it was the persistent advocacy of such as Astaburuaga that got that result.

Similar arrangements existed in Bolivia. When, for example, in 1905, a retained lawyer retired for reasons of health, he was replaced by a certain Sr. Salinas Vega, 'the Editor of "El Comercio", the most important paper of Bolivia and the Government organ'.[44]

A large number of people were retained in this way, and it was an expensive business. As the manager put it in 1905:

> It is difficult to describe Santiago affairs in a letter, but speaking in a general way I can assure you that influence there is an outrageously costly article for foreigners, and that schemes which ought, if the country interests were consulted, to go through without difficulty, have to be paid for dearly by their promoters ...[45]

And he cited specific cases of would-be concessionaires paying between £5,000 and £1,500 – depending on the value of the concession – to get lawyers to see the business through.

But, however efficient and well-connected the company's lawyers might be, personal intervention by management at the highest levels was often required. Visits to see ministers and also, occasionally, presidents in Santiago and – until the separation of administration of the Bolivian lines in 1914 – to La Paz were quite frequent. In Chile in particular, this was partly a consequence of the frequent ministerial changes and the need not only to get to know the new men but also to brief them on the company's significance in the regional and national economy. Similarly, in London the company maintained a close relationship with Chilean diplomats, particularly in the 1920s when Agustín Edwards was ambassador for many years. An ardent anglophile, who was also a prolific writer on Chilean history, much of it translated into English, he had a family connection with the FCAB in that it was his father, with the same name, who had been a founder of the Antofagasta Nitrate and Railway Co., forerunner of the FCAB itself. As a member of the richest family in Chile, which also owned the country's leading newspaper, *El Mercurio* – incidentally, also the longest-running newspaper in Spanish – Edwards was worth cultivating, and he was frequently consulted by the board in London.

Public relations at the upper levels of government and administration were helped enormously by the company's attention to official visitors to the north. On his visit to Antofagasta and Mejillones in 1905, for example, President Riesco, accompanied by a large retinue of ministers and high officials, was given royal treatment: the manager subsequently reported that:

> The President and his party were enthusiastic about Mejillones Bay and the

> necessity of the railway and pier being built as quickly as possible, so I think their visit will facilitate matters . . .[46]

Indeed it did: the documents accepting the company's proposals to acquire land for the new works were drawn up and signed on the President's flagship, the *O'Higgins* and a month later, despite yet another change of the minister responsible, a government decree gave the FCAB what it had asked for. The month before the manager had been in La Paz where he had 'several interviews with the President and the Ministers, who all expressed themselves as most anxious that cordial relations should exist between the Government and the company'.[47] In fact, reference was made in almost every annual report of the period to the good relations the company enjoyed with host governments, but they had to be kept in repair. Consequently, it became customary when new intendentes or new presidents came into office for the general manager to call on them, and close relations were often established. This was certainly the case with Arturo Alessandri, a dominant figure in modern Chilean history, though a controversial one, and president of Chile twice in the 1920s and 1930s. His first contacts with the FCAB were before he became president of Chile for the first time in 1920: as chairman of the Huanchaca Company, Bolivian-based but with sizeable Chilean investment, he was involved in negotiations with the railway company on tariffs for the carriage of tin ores from Bolivia to Antofagasta in 1919 and, despite strong differences of opinion on the business side, struck up a personal friendship with the-then Manager, Robinson. They got on well, and when, as President-elect, Alessandri paid a visit to the north in November 1920, he was fêted by the company which provided special trains as well as lavish hospitality. A month later, they met again in Santiago, as Robinson reported:

> I called on Señor Alessandri who only arrived back from the north the day before, and found him surrounded by numerous people . . . Immediately we were announced he excused himself from the rest, received us with great cordiality and took us into a private room where we settled down for a good long chat . . . He was full of praise for our railway and said quite emphatically that . . . it was the only properly managed railway in Chile . . .[48]

They discussed a number of projects in which the FCAB was interested, such as the proposed link with Argentina through Salta, the line from Arica to La Paz, and industrial relations, Alessandri commenting on the favourable record of the FCAB in that respect. And, Robinson went on:

> He mentioned that he was so pleased with what he saw on the Antofagasta Railway that he had requested Señor Briones Luco [a prominent member of

> Congress for the north] to send a cable to the Directors thanking them for their kindness ... on saying good-bye, he reminded me of our past friendship and said he would be offended if I ever went to Santiago without calling upon him even if there were no business to discuss ...[49]

Before that interview took place, he had informed London of Alessandri's visit to Antofagasta, and Bolden had stressed how important good relations were.

> I am quite sure [he wrote] that it will have occurred to you as it did to us that when you are in Santiago at any time interviewing the President, you will be able to impress him with the satisfactory service we give and the condition of our lines and rolling stock generally and argue that even if our tariffs are a little on the high side compared with the State Railways, it is much better that they should be and that the country should benefit by a good Railway service, as well as the moral claim that we have that in investing so much Capital in our business to the benefit of the commercial community in the districts we serve, we are entitled to a fair return on it ...[50]

Unlike some of his successors, Alessandri shared those views and, indeed, at one point in his first presidency even suggested that it might be better for Chile if the FCAB took over the management of the state railways, as it had taken over the running of the northern sector of the *red central*. Yet, the social legislation introduced by Alessandri as a reforming president had quite an impact on the operating costs of the company, as we shall see.

The importance of public relations, then, at all levels was fully appreciated by the FCAB and, from the beginning, it sought to foster them. But that was not always easy, and as the Bolivian and Chilean economies developed, new complexities appeared.

Industrial relations

Though, in both Bolivia and Chile, labour and trade union organizations had their antecedents in the nineteenth century, largely in the form of mutual aid associations, they only began to be an organized social force in the first twenty years of the twentieth century. A leading authority on the subject summarizes the factors which created them as follows:

> ... in general, labour movements developed when industrial development had created a substantial urban labour force, when immigrant workers from Europe brought with them ideologies and models of union development (mostly anarchist and anarcho-syndicalist), when political elites realized that

> they had to come to terms with such movements if only to tame them, and when . . . miners (in copper, nitrate and tin) provided a focus for working-class protest.[51]

The historical deep divide between rich and poor in both countries, coupled with highly oligarchical political systems, deepened as population and urbanization increased, and as the national economies became more enmeshed in the world trading and financial system, thus becoming increasingly subject to its fluctuations. Though labour unrest at particular times often derived from specific causes, the general situation of the workers was the backdrop, but it remains a moot point in working-class history whether labour relations were at their worst in times of depression or at periods of expansion. In the former, workers might be goaded into direct action by sheer economic pressure, but they were no less likely to press their demands when the economic cake was obviously growing and they wanted a larger slice of it. In Chile, in particular, the steady depreciation of the peso, with endemic inflation hitting the poorer classes hardest, was a constant factor. This was recognized by the FCAB in 1912, after a decade of intermittent strikes, when in that year, on the manager's report of the latest strike by lightermen that 'labour unrest generally [was] due partly to increased cost of living', the board approved his action in authorizing an increase in wages 'to employees paid on a currency basis to the whole difference between the rate of exchange and 1/-, such increase on the basis of the exchange rate for July representing about £1761 per month . . .'[52] Strikes became more frequent, however, and workers' demands for higher wages the fulcrum of industrial relations. And, at the same time, the labour movement became more organized under the influence of particular leaders, such as Luís Emilio Recabarren (1876–1924) in Chile and José L. Calderón (1861–1948) in Bolivia, both of them printers by profession and well aware of the significance of the communication of ideas.

Their ideas were, in the early years, anathema to government, the upper classes and foreign interests alike, and the normal reaction to agitation was repression. That was the temper of the times, and it obtained no less in the industrialized countries of western Europe and in the USA than it did on the west coast of South America. But fair-minded employers sought to strike a balance between a totally negative attitude to labour unrest and yielding completely to workers' demands, partly because of the increasingly integrated nature of their businesses.

The FCAB depended on a varied native workforce, divided into *obreros* and *empleados*, workmen and employees, the distinction between them underlined both by what they did and by what and how they were paid. Ordinary workers were paid weekly in cash; more skilled staff usually on a monthly basis. Among the former were gangers, lightermen and loaders at the ports, stokers, signalmen and general service staff from office boys to cooks in canteens. The *empleados* had a higher social status as men with a higher degree of responsibility – station-masters, supervisors of manual labour, inspectors and clerks. This class of worker had a more substantial stake in loyalty to the company than manual labourers who, in boom times at least, could always seek alternative employment in the nitrate *oficinas* or the tin mines. And in such times competition for labour was acute. Managers' reports for the first decade of the century indicate how heavily wage competition affected the company.

> ... labour is exceedingly difficult to obtain here now [the general manager reported in 1907] and the Permanent Way Gangs on the Chilean section between here and Calama have been 40% below their complement for some time, owing to the fact that the men find more lucrative employment in the Nitrate Oficinas ... in consequence I have sanctioned the proposal of the Resident Engineer to increase wages up to $4,000 a day if necessary, this being the minimum amount paid by the Oficinas ... [53]

And in the following April, he felt obliged to increase the wages of brakemen, and in May those in the workshops, for the same reasons.

When it came, however, to concerted action by the workers in demands for shorter hours or wage increases, a tougher stance was taken. A very serious situation arose in 1906, the middle of a turbulent decade in industrial relations. On 6 February both the dockworkers and the railwaymen in Antofagasta went on strike when management refused their request for an extended lunch hour. The following day, after a march through the town by the strikers, who had added a demand for a wage increase to their request for a longer mid-day break, the intendente, Carlos Merino Caballo, called out the marines and armed a number of civilians who, during a workers' meeting, fired on the crowd. Estimates of the dead ranged from 30, the official figure, to over 100, that of the strikers. The latter's reaction was to set fire to many properties in the central part of Antofagasta, though an attempt to blow up one of the company's trains in a siding failed 'owing to their not having the necessary detonators'.[54] Moreover, the drivers and stokers elsewhere on the line remained at work and most services were maintained. Nevertheless, for some days the situation was tense, and the general manager, Usher, sent a telegram to the Foreign Office in London:

> General strike in Antofagasta engineered by professional and political agitators. Local authorities exceedingly weak and declare have not sufficient force protect lives and property ... Have armed foreign employees and now sending women children aboard Kosmos 'Polynesia'. Request Foreign Minister to communicate at once with the Chilean Government.[55]

The British Minister in Santiago, Mr Kerr, saw the Minister of the Interior who told him that further ships and troops were being sent and that the ringleaders of the unrest would be arrested. The strike was suppressed, though Usher came in for fierce criticism from the Chilean press, having, it was alleged, threatened to call in British warships if the Chilean authorities would not act decisively, a charge he denied. He felt it necessary, however, to instruct two of the company's lawyers to see that 'truthful statements' appeared 'in one or two of the leading papers ... not [to] be supposed to emanate from the Railway'.[56]

A similar situation obtained a year later, exactly to the day, 6 February, and it met with the same response. Drivers and firemen at Antofagasta struck for higher wages, the work, according to the manager, of 'outside agitators' who intimidated those not wishing to strike, though 'none of the men from the workshops, traffic or mole have joined the movement'.[57] With the voluntary aid of such workers, stern action by the manager, and the support of the local authorities, the strike was defeated and services were little affected. The leaders were ejected from their houses on company property by court order, and a number of men were blacklisted for future employment, but there is little doubt that what effectively broke the strike was the support given to the company by the forces of law and order: 'throughout the strike', the manager reported:

> ... all trains on the main line were escorted to and from the outskirts of the town by mounted police and/or Cavalry, and in fact I may say that from the beginning every assistance was rendered by the Intendente and the Police and Military Officials ...[58]

In any strike action, a basic problem for its organizers was how to get colleagues upcountry to join in. In 1907, for instance, once trains left Antofagasta, manned by loyal staff, their running was taken over by staff at other stations who were not on strike. Those who did remain at work were subsequently given a bonus on their pay, and relations with the authorities were also cemented by the building, at the company's expense, of new barracks for the cavalry in Antofagasta. On this occasion, there was no violence, in stark contrast to the massive strike in Iquique and the nitrate fields of Tarapacá that same year, when a large force of troops massacred over 500 people, though some accounts put the figure as high as 2,000. An attempt to involve workers in Antofagasta in the strike in Tarapacá failed completely, partly because of the large number of troops sent up from the south.

It was the general view of management that labour troubles were largely the work of agitators, a view shared by the board in London. Referring to the events of 1906, the chairman, at the AGM on 16 July that year stated that:

> In that part of the world there were numerous agitators, who had left countries where more particular attention had been devoted to them ... Many had left Argentina, for instance, through the stringent measures put in force there against them ... he had no doubt that the Chilean government would soon see the necessity of adopting similar measures in connexion with Anarchist propaganda ... [59]

Local management, however, was very well aware that, agitators apart, workers had genuine economic grievances, not least a depreciating paper currency as well as rises in the cost of living. And it did its best to help workers on particular occasions. One such occurred in August 1906, when an earthquake practically destroyed the major port of Valparaiso, violently affecting shipping and not least foodstuffs from the Central Valley to the north. The manager reported:

> When the news of what had occurred in the South reached here, the Storekeepers and Butchers took immediate advantage ... to increase their prices to an exorbitant extent, which, if maintained, would inevitably have resulted in riots ... [60]

He, together with representatives of other foreign firms, took immediate action to hold down meat prices by arranging with an American shipchandler, who provisioned ships in the bay, to 'sell meat at a reasonable price', and getting the Huanchaca Company in Bolivia to send down cattle on the line to ensure supplies. This reduced the price of meat at the port from $1.00 to $0.60 a pound. But he did even more, partly in the light of a threatened wage demand from employees. As he explained:

> I do not see why we should be put to further expense and the risk of labour trouble by the actions of the local Storekeepers, and I have therefore arranged to increase our own Provisions Department, and sell the necessaries of life ... to all married employees ... In order to force down prices, I let it be known that I was intending to do this, and despatched the IVY to the South to purchase supplies ... this measure has undoubtedly checked the rise to a certain extent, and has been received with general satisfaction by Railway employees of all grades ... [61]

Whether his actions could best be described as self-interest or altruism, they were certainly imaginative, not to say unusual. But they were not unique. In 1912, the lightermen at Antofagasta went on strike and, ignoring procedure, by-passed the manager and approached the captain of the port, a government official; he was informed that if they went through the proper form 'we should be only too pleased to take into consideration and discuss any complaints or suggestions for improvement that they may wish to put forward'.[62] While Robinson thought 'they had been led away by a few of the socialistic type', the men returned to work, a meeting was arranged and matters settled amicably, 'the more so as the majority of the men's claims were most reasonable'.[63] At the same time, employees who were paid in Chilean paper received an increase of 20 per cent without recourse to strike action.

Thus, on the one hand, while management shared the prejudices of most employers of the place and period with regard to labour organizations, it also tried to be fair to its workers, and its record in that respect was certainly better than that of most of the nitrate producers. Relations with labour, however, were to become increasingly complex with the passage of time, as movements for unionization, against the background of 'the social question', became more political and as politicians seeking power became more conscious of their potential. But what more than anything else shaped those developments were the fluctuating fortunes of the Chilean and Bolivian economies to which the future of the FCAB was inextricably linked.

Notes

1. General manager to secretary, Antofagasta, 18 March 1908. Letter No. 170.
2. General manager to managing director (A.W. Bolden), Antofagasta, 8 July 1938. Private. Official.
3. I am indebted to Mr Craig for a copy of this contract.
4. Acting general manager to secretary, Antofagasta, 2 February 1910. Letter No. 278.
5. Frank G. Carpenter, *South America, Social, Industrial and Political*, p. 239.
6. General manager to secretary, Antofagasta, 12 February 1908. Letter No. 164.
7. *Idem.* to *idem.*, Antofagasta, 12 October 1907. Letter No. 14.
8. Personal communication. Lt-Col. A.D. Heskett to author, 9 February 1988.
9. Isaac Arce, *Narraciones Históricas de Antofagasta*, Antofagasta, 1930, p. 189. Cited in María T. Ahumada Manchot, Adolfo Contador Varas, Guadalupe Durán Díaz and Jorge Stavros Bracamonte, *Antofagasta: repertorio del patrimonio histórico más representativo de la ciudad, 1866–1930*, Universidad del Norte, Antofagasta, 1982, p. 171.
10. General manager to secretary, Antofagasta, 19 February 1906. Letter No. 93.
11. *Idem.* to *idem.*, Antofagasta, 19 November 1915. Private.
12. A.W. Bolden to general manager at Antofagasta, London, 3 December 1915. Letter Book 2.
13. *Idem* to *idem.*, London, 31 December 1915.
14. General manager to secretary, 1 August 1919. Private.
15. *La Hora*, Santiago, 26 July 1945. My translation. I am indebted for this reference to Professor Silvio Costillo of Santiago.
16. General manager to secretary, Antofagasta, 19 February 1906. Letter No. 93.
17. *Idem.* to *idem*, Antofagasta, 21 February 1907. Letter No. 118.
18. *Idem.* to *idem.*, Antofagasta, 24 May 1912. Letter No. 399.
19. *The Times*, company meetings, 18 June 1924.
20. General manager to secretary, Antofagasta, 12 October 1907. Letter No. 142.
21. General manager to managing director, Antofagasta, 18 August 1922. Letter No. 854 (Staff Memo. No. 372)

22. General manager to secretary, Antofagasta, 6 October 1916. Private/Official.
23. *Ibid.*
24. General manager to secretary, Antofagasta, 29 March 1911. Private.
25. W. Anderson Smith, *Temperate Chile: A Progressive Spain*, pp.317–18.
26. *Ibid.*, p. 317.
27. General manager to secretary, Antofagasta, 15 November 1906. Letter No. 110.
28. *Ibid.*
29. General manager to secretary, Antofagasta, 29 January 1908. Letter No. 161.
30. *Idem.* to *idem.*, General manager to secretary, Antofagasta, 26 February, 1908. Letter No. 166.
31. General manager to managing director, Antofagasta, 15 February 1918. Letter No. 635.
32. Personal communication. Lt-Col. A.D. Heskett to author, 9 February 1988.
33. Alicia O'Reardon Overbeck, *Living High or at Home in the High Andes*, London 1935, p.24.
34. Francis J.G. Maitland, *Chile: its land and people*, London, 1914, p. 273.
35. General manager to secretary, Antofagasta, 1 December 1911. Letter No. 374.
36. *Idem.* to *idem.*, Antofagasta, 20 April 1917. Private/Official.
37. *Idem. to idem.*, Antofagasta, 18 February 1921. Letter No. 776 and 27 May 1921. Letter No. 271.
38. *Idem.* to *idem.*, Antofagasta, 2 December 1908. Letter No. 213.
39. *Idem.* to *idem.*, General manager to secretary, Antofagasta, 17 August 1907. Letter No. 135.
40. Sub-general manager to secretary, Antofagasta, 2 June 1911. Private.
41. General manager to secretary, Antofagasta, 22 February 1911. Private.
42. *Idem.* to *idem.*, Antofagasta, 13 October 1911. Letter No. 367.
43. *Annual Report*, 1913, p.16.
44. General manager to secretary, Antofagasta, 3 February 1905. Private.
45. *Ibid.*
46. General manager to secretary, Antofagasta, 28 February 1905. Private.
47. *Idem.* to *idem.*, Antofagasta, 23 January 1905. Private.
48. General manager to managing director, Antofagasta, 3 December 1920. Private/Official.
49. *Ibid.*
50. Managing director and secretary to general manager, London, 25 November 1920, Correspondence Vol. 6, ff.231–32.
51. Alan Angell, in Simon Collier, Harold Blakemore and Thomas E. Skidmore (eds) *The Cambridge Encyclopedia of Latin America and the Caribbean*, Cambridge University Press, 1985, p. 324.
52. Board meeting, 10 September 1912. Minute Book 6, f.167.
53. General manager to secretary, Antofagasta, 10 January 1907. Letter No. 114

54. *Idem.* to *idem.*, Antofagasta, 19 February 1906. Letter No. 93.
55. General manager to Foreign Office, Antofagasta, 7 February 1906. Telegram (London: Public Record Office, Foreign Office Archives, Chile) F.O.371/17.
56. General manager to secretary, Antofagasta, 19 February 1906. Letter No. 93.
57. *Idem.* to *idem.*, Antofagasta, 8 February 1907. Letter No. 117.
58. *Idem.* to *idem.*, Antofagasta, 21 February 1907. Letter No. 118.
59. *The Times*, Company Reports, 17 July 1906.
60. General manager to secretary, Antofagasta, 31 August 1906. Letter No. 106.
61. *Ibid.*
62. General manager to secretary, Antofagasta, 19 July 1912. Letter No. 407.
63. *Ibid.*

4

TRIALS AND TRIUMPHS IN TURBULENT YEARS 1914–1930

Overview

Between the outbreak of the First World War and the Great Depression of the late 1920s and early 1930s, the FCAB, like virtually all foreign companies operating in Latin America, experienced quite large changes not only in its economic position but also in its operation and local relations. Its degree of integration in the mineral economies of Bolivia and Chile made it largely a passive victim of external shocks, such as occurred in 1914 and in the Wall Street crash over a decade later. Moreover, within those countries the period saw increasing unionization and a much more strident militancy among workers, trapped as they were, too, in situations over which they had little or no control. At the same time, in both countries, the political scenario became increasingly complex as politicians and governments were forced to take heed of growing popular pressures for change, and government was obliged to look more carefully at the role of the state in both economic development and social progress. The inexorable advance of technology also meant that for a business to survive and grow it had to adapt to new machinery and new methods of operation, both mechanical and managerial. These were quite new challenges to the FCAB, and it had to respond to them.

The First World War and its impact

The general outbreak of hostilities in Europe in August 1914 had an immediate and dramatic impact on the Latin American economies, and particularly those of Bolivia and Chile. The Bolivian economy had already had a bad year in 1913: 'the value of total exports declined 32 per cent between 1913 and 1914 reflecting a 31 per cent decline in tin production for this same period. Along with this decline . . . there was a severe decline in agricultural production ... due to adverse weather conditions'.[1] This situation was compounded in the first few months of the war by the abrupt disruption of international trade and finance. Yet, Chile, which had had a good year in 1913, largely due to buoyant nitrate revenue, was hit even harder when war broke out, and primarily because of its dependence for government revenue on export taxes on nitrate, amounting to 50 per cent of the total. At that time also Germany received about a third of all Chile's nitrate exports.

Immediately Great Britain declared war on Germany on 4 August 1914, her government embarked on a series of measures designed to drive German commerce from the seas, prohibiting first, on 5 August, all British trade with the enemy, and then extended on 11 March 1915 – and in contravention of international practice – to neutral shipping. Similarly, on the financial side, early in 1915 'United Kingdom residents were forbidden to carry out banking transactions with overseas branches of enemy firms and from doing business with enemy banks outside the country'.[2] Later, in 1915, the British government established a 'black list' of persons and firms in neutral countries with whom trading was forbidden, a powerful instrument in countries such as Chile where German shipping and trading interests were second only to those of the UK. Chilean interests linked to Germany would think twice about challenging the still most formidable financial and maritime power in the world. Though that power suffered setbacks, as in early November 1914, when an inferior British squadron was defeated by the Germans at the battle of Coronel, off the south-central coast of Chile, that failure was soon redeemed when, a month later, a powerful German fleet was virtually annihilated by the British navy in the battle of the Falklands. Thereafter:

> The British drew an invisible noose of distant blockade around Germany. German ships were arrested. Neutral ships were brought into British ports, and their cargoes checked. Later, British consuls in far-away countries issued neutrals with a clean bill, if they conformed to the rules.[3]

For Chile, these developments were extremely serious, compounding the immediate effects of the war in disruption of shipping and finance. That 'far-away' country remained neutral throughout the conflict, and thus subject to the British 'black-list'. More important was its critical dependence on foreign trade: in 1913, customs receipts provided 35 per cent of government revenue and, as noted, another 50 per cent came from export taxes on nitrate, and about four-fifths of that product in foreign markets was destined for use in agriculture. The sharp curtailment of that source of income in 1914 was a serious blow: no less important was the impact of the war on the regions in which the FCAB operated. And it was sudden. Within ten days of Britain's declaration of war, the general manager of the FCAB at Antofagasta was reporting that:

> ... all the European firms and those connected with the Nitrate Industry have reduced the wages of all their staff 20% and in some instances more, the consequence is that during the past week every train has come down loaded with workmen leaving the Nitrate District and they were given a free passage to the South by the Government on a transport ... sent up for this purpose. Some 4,000 have already left and an equal number are waiting to go ... I should mention that ... 17,000 men are employed in the ... Industry in the district served by this and the Aguas Blancas Railways and 47,000 souls including women and children ...[4]

Antofagasta's northern neighbour, the nitrate province of Tarapacá, was hit even harder: by late August, 10,000 workers had moved south and 'by mid-September 14,000 workers and their families had been shipped south. Within three months the total rose to 30,000'.[5] The Chilean nitrate industry was in its biggest crisis since the War of the Pacific: of the 143 *oficinas* working in the republic in July 1914, only 43 were still producing six months later. Even so, stocks accumulating at the ports far exceeded exports, rising to almost 2 million tons compared with under half a million tons at the earlier date. A financially embarrassed government sought to alleviate the situation, proposing a programme of public works to reduce unemployment: the programme submitted to Congress included building railway lines from the state-owned central line to the coast in both provinces, subsidies and loans to nitrate producers to keep *oficinas* open and a new drainage system for Arica. Soup kitchens were opened in various places. But the government did not have the money for the public works which, so far as railway lines were concerned, might have been a serious, future competitive threat to the FCAB, so much so that the local manager suggested to London that it might 'make a protest to the Chilian Minister in London' at a proposal 'far from friendly'.[6]

For local and central management alike it was a serious time in Chile, and matters were not helped by the Bolivian situation. In Bolivia, President Ismael Montes had embarked on a programme of monetary reform which antagonized the private bankers who, thereupon, restricted credit. Political tension resulted, 'which has necessitated the President placing the Republic in a state of siege, which ... will restrict business transactions and the output from the tin mines'.[7] As it happened, that crisis was short-lived, and, indeed, it was to prove so in Chile as well, though at the time it was worrying enough. And the crises in both countries, with the impact of world war, were closely intertwined. The decline of the Chilean nitrate industry had a 'knock-on' effect in Bolivia since it forced the repatriation of Bolivian workers – a sizeable number – from Chile itself. 'A report by the Prefect of Oruro, Eduardo Diez de Medina, mentions the repatriation in 1914 of 8,000 migrants from the north of Chile'.[8] And, as with the Chilean nitrate miners moved to the south in 1914–15, the Bolivian workers returning home were suspected of having socialist ideas. In fact, Chilean influence on Bolivian trade unionism was a factor in its growth.

All this lay in the future as the FCAB sought to grapple with an unprecedented situation and carry on business as usual as much as it could in the first months of the war. Recognizing the totally changed situation of the nitrate industry, the lack of shipping for both export and import trades, and the possibility that the situation would persist for some time, the local management took immediate measures to make economies. Wages were reduced, staff put on half or part-time, and the services provided were cut, Sunday traffic – passenger and freight – being eliminated completely. A basic problem was how to pay the men since the war created a financial crisis in Chile, with a run on the banks and the difficulty of obtaining local currency. Similarly, with customers no less affected, all transactions had to be put on a cash basis in order to try to meet at least wage bills. All construction work in progress was stopped, including the conversion of the narrower lines to the standard Chilean and Bolivian metre gauge and the placement of new water pipelines. The secretary in London, Bolden, reflecting the views of the board, fully appreciated the local problems and generally supported management's measures to tackle them. The following is a typical example:

> With regard to the Government's request [he wrote at the end of August, 1914] that we should continue our Capital works so as to employ as much labour as possible, the Board were quite in accord with your view strongly opposing this ... we confirmed ... the necessity for shutting down all superfluous works ... from the point of view of everything not actually required to run the traffic offering.[9]

He also took the trouble to inform local management of the war situation as seen from London.

One particular problem on which the board had to take a decision quickly was that of orders placed in England for materials required for new capital works in Chile, such as the change of gauge, as well as new rolling stock. Early in August the board decided to ask the manufacturers to suspend work on the orders for a period of six months rather than cancel them since that course would mean payment for work done as well as, possibly, some compensation. Moreover, the company had obtained favourable quotations originally, and the board feared increased cost if new orders were placed. Cancellation, thought the secretary, would cost between £60,000 and £70,000. In the event, however, due to the unexpected duration of the war, and continuing difficulties on cash flow in 1914–15, the scheme for changing the gauge on the Chilean lines was suspended indefinitely in 1915 and was not, in effect, taken up again until the mid-1920s. In Bolivia, nevertheless, the work went ahead and the change from 2′ 6″ gauge to one metre between Uyuni (612 kilometres) and Oruro (925 kilometres) was completed by early February, 1916. This meant that there was then 'an interchange of traffic, without transhipment, with the Bolivia Railway at the junctions of the lines of the company with those of the Antofagasta Company' whereas 'formerly transhipment was necessary at three of these'.[10]

Another problem the war created was related to the fact that the German house of Vorwerk and Co. were the financial agents of the FCAB in Valparaiso, and had been closely associated with the company from the beginning. But British wartime regulations insisted that:

> ... it is high treason to do any business through the King's enemies and the fact that Messrs. Vorwerk & Co. have a German partner in their Valparaiso house brings the law into operation at once. Certain German banks and financial interests in London have been allowed to re-open ... but only in connection with dealings before August 5th ... they are not to be allowed to enter into fresh business ... except such as may be absolutely necessary and arising out of previous transactions ...[11]

This put local management in an awkward situation, since Vorwerk handled all freight accounts, and the manager at Antofagasta, Robinson, was puzzled. He wrote:

> We do not quite understand what your intentions are regarding Messrs. Vorwerk and Co., we quite appreciate ... and realize we cannot utilize them in remitting our bills to you or in accepting any class of German Bills but outside that, seeing that they are a Chilian firm, both Messrs. Fischer and Grizar, the partners, are both Chilians by birth and we could not see where the legal side of the question came in ...[12]

Less than a month later he reported that all financial dealings with Vorwerk had been suspended but, on the same day, the secretary in London despatched a letter indicating that the British Treasury had decreed that branches of firms with headquarters in hostile territory but themselves on neutral ground might deal with British customers, provided that no transaction with the head office were involved. So Vorwerk in Chile were retained as agents of the FCAB, but only until January 1915.

A similar situation obtained with regard to company goods being shipped on German steamers when the war broke out. The British embargo on trade with the enemy applied to a consignment of rails being carried by the Kosmos line, and it forbade payment for discharge in Chile. The manager there was instructed to bargain with the Kosmos agent in Valparaiso and the German captains to take delivery of the cargo against a guarantee to pay for it when the war was over. The supply of essential materials was another problem since it was tightly controlled by the British government through the Ministry of Munitions which set up a Railway Committee to vet all applications for the manufacture and provision of such goods. The ministry had a list of priorities for manufacture, category A for essential production for the war effort, category B for work 'indirectly essential to carrying on the war' and so on.[13] As the war went on, the system was refined and, early in 1917, a sub-committee for South American railway requirements was set up. A.H.A. Knox Little as a director of the FCAB sat on it to represent interests on the West Coast. Forecasting its functions, the company secretary wrote:

> The procedure will probably be that the Ministry of Munitions will advise this Committee how many tons of steel, for example, can be spared. This Committee will then collate the requirements of each Company and authorise a supply to them in accordance with their requirements and the value to the Country of the traffic carried. We look to being treated as reasonably as any other South American Railway, and probably from the point of view of traffic carried, rather more so.[14]

And the FCAB was, because by that time its circumstances had changed completely.

The dramatic collapse of the nitrate industry in 1914 was very soon reversed since a natural product which had been used primarily as a fertilizer to make things grow was also, when mixed with charcoal and sulphur, an effective agent to kill. The demand for gunpowder as the war went on revitalized the nitrate industry of Chile within a few months of its eclipse at the outbreak, and the need for munitions also stimulated demand for the copper of Chuquicamata and the tin of Oruro. By March 1915 the general manager was reporting:

> We are pleased to be able to mention that the Nitrate Industry appears to have got over the worst. Oficina 'Eugenia', in Aguas Blancas, is starting work, and is advertising for seven hundred men while 'Aconcagua', 'Carlos Condell', 'Rosario' and 'Hijinio Astoreca' are asking for another four hundred between them. It is doubtful whether these men can be supplied locally.
>
> The price of Nitrate, which fell as low as 5/8d at the end of last year, is now up another 1/- which ... puts the industry on a more satisfactory footing.[15]

Workers returned from the south as the recovery continued, fuelled by the insatiable demands of the war:

> Notwithstanding the excessive sea freights, shipping is distinctly brisk, both for the United States and Europe, the former taking large quantities. As instance, Du Pont are using 20,000 tons of Nitrate per month for explosives.
>
> Antofagasta Nitrate Co. are still working their six Oficinas, and they are now asking for some one hundred cars a day, equivalent to some 2,000 tons of Nitrate.[16]

And, a week later, the general manager reckoned that the company's weekly returns would amount to £20,000.

As in Chile, so in Bolivia, the initial disruption of trade in late 1914 was followed by a rapid recovery of tin exports and prices, so much so that President Montes by 1917 'was able joyfully to announce to Congress that Bolivia in the previous year had for the first time passed the 100 million boliviano mark in her national exports'.[17] It was Montes who also inaugurated the recently-completed line from Oruro to Cochabamba on 26 July 1917, a ceremony 'carried through with much enthusiasm as were the other celebrations lasting for 2 or 3 days'.[18]

In the improved economic circumstances, the problem of cash flow which had preoccupied local management in late 1914 and early 1915, were soon overcome. However, and despite having sizeable stocks of commodities such as coal at the outbreak of war, obtaining supplies to keep the lines running was not easy, partly because of the lack of shipping. And there were particular problems at that time. The company, following the example of many nitrate *oficinas* in 1913 and 1914, had embarked on the conversion of its locomotives to oil instead of coal-burning. Indeed, that substitution in northern Chile had proceeded apace before the war, because of higher costs of coal: in 1913, petroleum traffic on the lines increased by more than 250 per cent over 1912. But the conversion of the locomotives during the war depended on the supply of steel boiler tubes, not least from the UK, and steel was, of course, a priority commodity for the war effort. Twenty-two engines were intended for conversion in the initial stage but, by mid-November 1915, only eight had been changed because of this bottleneck. To cut costs, the board was anxious to press on, and did its best to get the necessary permission for shipments. Fuel, both coal and oil, was another problem because of the war's demands. 'One never knows', wrote the secretary in February, 1916:

> . . . what the Government authorities may requisition and we hear only this week of a steamer loaded with a part cargo of coal being suddenly commandeered and the fuel put ashore again, so that it is quite impossible

> to arrange anything definite ahead, and we shall have therefore to snap up anything that is offering [sic] . . . [19]

Many Chilean and Bolivian customers still used coal-burning plant and, historically, the company had imported supplies from the UK, the USA and Australia, as well as taking quantities from the Chilean coalfields of the south-central region of Arauco, where the London-based Arauco Company was a major supplier. Given the increasing risks of German raiders affecting British shipping, the board sought to rely more on Chilean supplies for Antofagasta, leaving local management to make arrangements on the spot for delivery. At the same time, it continued to secure such British steamers and cargoes as it could, though it was a tortuous business. As the secretary explained early in 1916:

> You are aware the s.s. 'Crown' left with about 5,500 tons of Crown Patent Fuel over a fortnight ago and we have another steamer, the 'Elleric' to load early in March with Newport 'Abercarn' coal. I would mention that it has taken us a fortnight to get the Government license to ship this coal, and only after very strong representations repeated as on previous occasions that we were assisting very importantly the requirements of the British Government by carrying Nitrate, were we able to convince the Coal Export Committee . . . [20]

The government's need for gunpowder, and nitrate to make it, was the company's strongest lever in getting permission for supplies to keep the railway running and, as the war continued, its arguments grew ever more persuasive. In the first two years of the war, however, everything was in flux, and the correspondence between London and Antofagasta sometimes became acrimonious as both parties were frustrated by the situation created by the war.

The conversion the of locos to oil-burning proceeded, though not without great difficulty, not only because of the supply position but also because no one, either in London or in Latin America, really could estimate in advance what economies on fuel would be made until the new experiment had been thoroughly tried and tested. A local fuel crisis arose early in 1916 when there were strong differences of opinion between London and Antofagasta on the policy of supply, the local management criticizing the board for vacillation on the coal/oil equation and not ensuring supplies, the latter accusing the general manager of not giving sufficient information to allow it to make correct decisions. Tempers cooled, however, as the problems were ironed out and, with the entry of the USA into the war in April 1917, supply problems eased.

Some other problems were of a very different kind but still needed careful handling. In July 1915, the company had appointed as its agent in Valparaiso Mr A.F. Loveday who subsequently became the correspondent of *The Times* in Chile and in that capacity wrote a number of articles on German influence in Chile 'directed not only to keeping Chile neutral but also to obtaining control of the destinies of the country'.[21] He drew attention not only to the pro-German organizations in Chile and their possible political influence but also to the fact that German diplomats from other South American states which had severed relations with Berlin – including Bolivia, Peru and Uruguay – had found a congenial home in Chile. He also proposed to write a book on Chilean commercial affairs and asked the local manager to subscribe to it. For the board in London, however, his activities created some disquiet since, running a large company registered in a belligerent country but operating in a neutral one, it had to ensure that its employees conformed to its long-standing belief of not getting mixed up with local politics.

> The Board [wrote Bolden] would be sorry to put a curb on any usefulness of Mr. Loveday's work in connection with assisting the Allied cause but it would quite conceivably create a dangerous position for us if our appointed Representative was shewn to be taking sides ...[22]

Loveday was then reminded of standing orders, forbidding overt political activity, but the board did not object to him writing the book – to which, in fact, the local acting manager had already given his support – because

> ... it was to be propaganda which would not really be of a political nature but was rather stating the case commercially for Great Britain and her Allies as compared with what the Germans have done ... in Chili ... provided that no political controversies were engendered, you could subscribe and should keep any information regarding our Company to generalities, our idea being that the Capital of the Company, quantity of Nitrate transported, a statement regarding the lines in Bolivia and generally the growth of the Company's business could be set down ...[23]

The more 'loaded' questions in a list submitted by the putative author for information were to be ignored.

This traditional and cautious attitude taken by the FCAB was pragmatic in the circumstances of the Chilean position in the war. The British 'black-list' of German interests there was very effective and, in fact, Germany was virtually eliminated as a serious commercial competitor through its operation, even long-standing German nitrate interests in the north being forced to sell out, sometimes to American concerns. And while protests were made against the policy in both Congress and the press, it was applied fairly rigorously, with the support of US interests even before that country became an ally of the UK.

For the FCAB, the nitrate boom of the war years provided a bonanza in traffic, as production and exports expanded as indicated in the following table.

Table 3. Nitrate production and exports, 1914–1918 ('000 tonnes)

Year	Production	Exports
1914	2,463	1,846
1915	1,755	2,023
1916	2,912	2,980
1917	3,001	2,776
1918	2,859	2,919

Source: J.R. Couyoumdjian, *Chile y Gran Bretaña, loc.cit.*, pp.274–75.

Together with the recovery of Bolivian tin and other minerals such as borate and antimony, and with the increase of up-traffic in foodstuffs, fuels and passengers which economic reactivation stimulated, the short-lived drop in productivity and profits was reversed. And whereas total receipts in 1914 fell by over £370,000 on the results for the exceptional year before, offset by economies of over £200,000, in 1915 the net profit was only £51,000 less. Recovery accelerated in 1916, gross receipts being a record, and the results for 1917 were even better, allowing the board to recommend a dividend in 1918 of 10 per cent, less income tax, plus a bonus of 2 per cent on fully paid deferred stock to both the preferred ordinary and deferred stockholders, free of tax. While the nitrate trade was the major factor in this result, 'It was also partly due to the efficiency of the management, for the ratio of expenses to receipts was only 55.91 per cent., which is certainly a remarkably low percentage under existing conditions'.[24] The conditions included, for the duration of the war, a considerable degree of undermanning and, consequently, a heavier load of work for staff in employment.

For King and country

At the AGM of the company in June 1919, the chairman, the Hon. Charles N. Lawrence (as he then was) referred:

> ... to the really wonderful showing which has been made by not only our staff, but the staff of so many British undertakings in Latin America, who volunteered in their country's cause and, to our deep regret, in many cases, rendered the last sacrifice ... Regarding the staff who have been responsible for carrying on our business ... I am pleased to say that both Mr. Hunt [acting general manager in Chile] and Mr. Backus [general manager in

Bolivia] have continued to display the zeal and ability which were expected of them ...[25]

And he paid generous tribute to all the other staff in both Latin America and London who continued to work for the company during the war. Those who saw active service – no fewer than 160 – were listed in the *Annual Report* for 1918, a Roll of Honour which ranged from two directors, Major Greenwell of the Hampshire Carabineers, and Colonel H. Le Roy Lewis, who served as British Military Attaché in Paris, to those of humbler station in the company's service but no less significant in contribution to the war effort. Of the other officers and other ranks, 12 came from the London office, 100 from the Chilean section and 48 from the Bolivian, representing virtually all the specialized departments – administration, accounts, engineering, locomotives, stores, medical services, traffic and waterworks. Out of the total, 38 were killed in action, reported missing and presumed dead or invalided out, while 12 received decorations or were mentioned in despatches. Only one was taken prisoner. The most decorated was an engineer, R.J. Andrews, who rose to the rank of Acting Brigadier-General, was awarded the DSO and Bar, the MC, and the *Croix de Guerre avec Palmes*, as well as the Freedom of the City of London and a Sword of Honour. Early in 1919, Andrews requested re-engagement by the FCAB and was willing to be taken back at his previous salary of £240 per annum. The company was anxious to accommodate him but in a different job with higher pay. But he was still in uniform when the offer arrived, after he had left for duty at Archangel during the Russian revolution. There he was taken prisoner, and not repatriated until mid-1920. The company's offer was renewed in August of that year but, wrote the managing director to the general manager at Antofagasta, 'We have written him on several occasions since without receiving a reply ... [and] have therefore decided to withdraw our offer'.[26] In the event, Andrews joined the Royal Irish Constabulary but it was tragic that so adventurous a life should end early in 1923, 'as a result of an untimely accident while working in his garage'.[27]

The war service of Andrews and so many of his colleagues was a matter of justifiable pride to the FCAB but it is doubtful if that service could have been discharged so effectively without the company's cooperation from the outset. Almost immediately war was declared a number of contract and other employees in Chile and Bolivia applied to local management for the termination of their working agreements in order to return to the United Kingdom to volunteer for active service. By early November 1914 the ground rules for severance had been worked out between local management and the board in London: those who had completed less than one year's service were granted a free passage home;

those with from one to two years' service, a free passage, two weeks' salary and expenses according to contract, and those with from two to three years' service and over, free passage, a month's salary and the expenses to which they were entitled. Moreover, all such employees were notified that

> . . . after the War, and always provided there is a vacancy, they will be re-engaged, and in every case given preference over other applicants [though] it has been clearly defined that we cannot hold out a promise of immediate work as everything indicates that it would be some considerable time after the War before the Nitrate Industry recovers . . . [28]

The last cautionary clause was, of course, written when few could then anticipate either how quickly the industry would recover from the trauma of 1914 or how suddenly, in the aftermath of war, the industry would again collapse. During the war, when the nitrate industry's fortunes turned on the fertilizer's new importance in the manufacture of explosives, local management was short of experienced staff. But, with the end of the conflict, the sudden fall in demand for nitrate and its impact on the company's operations reversed that situation, and it found itself unable to re-engage many of its former staff. It also found itself faced with new complexities in the countries in which it operated, both with native labour and with national governments.

Economic crisis and labour unrest

The depression in the world economy which occurred in the years immediately following the Great War had a particular impact on Chile, primarily because of that country's dependence on nitrate. Whereas in 1918 a total of 2,919,717 tons had been exported, in the following year this fell to 803,961 tons. Between the Armistice in November 1918 and the beginning of 1919, some sixty *oficinas* in the nitrate region had ceased working and over 2,000 workers and their families had been transported south. Those *oficinas* which continued producing merely added to the stocks accumulating in Chile which rose from some 900,000 tons at the end of June 1918 to almost 1,500,000 tons by the same date a year later. At the same time, stocks held by the principal Allied powers – the United States, Great Britain and France – stood at nearly 1,500,000 tons at the end of 1918. Not surprisingly, with such a glut, the price of nitrate fell from the 13 shillings a quintal charged to the Allies just before the Armistice to less than 9 shillings a year later. Government ordinary revenue, which normally depended heavily on taxes on exports and imports, moved from a comfortable surplus in 1918 to a heavy deficit the following years, obliging the government to take extraordinary measures, including in 1921 and 1922 new loans, mostly from the United States, partly to cover the fiscal deficit, partly to finance necessary public works. Although the nitrate market recovered in 1919 and 1920, as more normal conditions were established and stocks were reduced, this was a temporary improvement, and not until the mid-1920s was some stability restored.

As the economic prosperity of the war years gave way to the slump and both unemployment and prices soared, Chile experienced a period of acute social unrest which often manifested itself in public demonstrations and strike action by workers. Thus, meetings to protest against the cost of living in Santiago attracted thousands in both 1918 and 1919, while the number of strikes rose from thirteen in the former year to seventy-three in the latter, ten of them in the nitrate zone. A prominent part in these activities was played by the Workers' Federation of Chile (FOCH), founded originally as a mutual aid society in 1911, but becoming increasingly militant as the years went by. Membership was open to all workers, and in 1919 the FOCH adopted as its basic unit of organization the union, grouping all workers in an area irrespective of calling or status. Increasingly, too, it adopted an anti-capitalist creed. Its political, but independent, counterpart was the Socialist Workers Party (POS), founded in 1912 to participate in electoral contests and press for improvements in working conditions. The tense social climate and economic crisis of the post-war years created favourable conditions for the growth of both organizations. Moreover, as it happened, the national state of uncertainty was compounded by a political crisis which turned on the presidential election of 1920, and on the personality of Arturo Alessandri, the best-known candidate.

Alessandri had spent a lifetime in Chilean politics but he really sprang to prominence as Liberal candidate for a senatorial seat in 1915 for the nitrate province of Tarapacá. There he conducted a demagogic campaign, attacking the Chilean oligarchy for its neglect of the lower classes, and receiving much working-class support. Congressional elections in March 1918 had given the opposition a majority in both chambers of Congress but that opposition, the Liberal Alliance, was deeply divided between those who sought – like the government parties – to preserve the status quo and those, like Alessandri, who recognized the need for basic reform. He was adopted as presidential candidate by those factions, but the Alliance split, some Liberals joining forces with the more conservative parties to support Luis Barros Borgoño. The election campaign, fought in the grim social and economic situation of the immediate post-war years, was marked by Alessandri's scathing denunciation of the traditional oligarchy and promises of a sweeping programme of reform, backed particularly by the Radical Party which in 1919 had declared itself of the same mind. This coincided with the rash of labour agitation, particularly in the nitrate regions, and government repression, ensuring Alessandri the support of the workers. But the result was very close and was challenged by both sides. Finally, Congress passed the issue to a Tribunal of Honour which on 30 September declared Alessandri the victor in the electoral college – elections were then indirect – by 177 votes to 176. Congress then ratified the decision and Alessandri assumed office as President on 23 December 1920. How far he would be able to keep his electoral promises, however, with Chile engulfed in economic depression and a heterogeneous Congress an unknown quantity remained to be seen.

Such were the turbulent circumstances in which the FCAB had to operate in Chile in the immediate post-war period. The nitrate crisis had an immediate effect: at the beginning of 1919, the general manager in Antofagasta reported pessimistically on the accumulation of stocks and the scarcity of shipping, concluding that 'The general opinion is that the slump will last over six months and that the recovery will be gradual'.[29] But even this was too sanguine. When the annual report for the year was presented to the shareholders for the general meeting held in London on 29 June 1920, it revealed that, compared with 1,076,947 tons of nitrate carried on the company's lines to the ports in 1918, only 230,217 tons were transported the following year, and at the meeting itself the chairman, the Hon. Charles N. Lawrence, elaborated on the significance of that fact. Nitrate was the key to the company's earnings from water, from up-traffic to supply the *oficinas*, from shipping and from passenger receipts in addition to the freight charges the commodity itself represented. Gross receipts had fallen by 43 per cent in consequence, and 'the year culminated in giving us the lowest net profits since 1907'.[30] This was despite the fact that working expenses had been reduced by over 40 per cent in the period as a drastic programme of economies was introduced to meet the dramatic fall in income.

Preoccupied as he was throughout 1919 by the general situation, the general manager in Chile, A.G. Hunt, had also specific problems to think about. One of these was the question of the railway's tariffs, a political as much as an economic matter since government approval was required by law for any increase and it was not a propitious time, economically or politically, to ask for tariffs to be raised. Nevertheless, given the soaring cost of materials that year, owing to post-war shortages, both the board in London and Hunt in Chile agreed that an application for an increase in tariffs to offset these costs should be made, and, further, that it should be of the order of 15 per cent. What followed illustrates the complexities faced by the FCAB as a foreign-owned company in Chile and the tortuous nature of the negotiations involved.

After close consultation with the company's representative in

Santiago, Señor García de la Huerta, Hunt formally lodged the petition on 7 April 1919. Ten days later, however, the State Inspector of Private Railways, Señor Mardones, who was favourably disposed towards the company himself, told Hunt in Santiago that the then-Minister of Finance, Luis Claro Solar, had advised the Minister of Railways that certain nitrate railways in the North 'were contemplating asking for an increase in tariffs and asking him not to grant any such application because of the prejudice which would be caused to the Nitrate industry'.[31] Hunt continued:

> The fact that señor Luis Claro Solar is the lawyer in Santiago for the Antofagasta Nitrate Company leads one to suppose that the note [from Claro to the Minister of Railways] was instigated by that Company. After receiving such a note it is improbable that the Minister of Railways would grant an increase in tariffs without first consulting his colleague the Minister of Finance who, it is obvious, is determined to squash any such idea ...[32]

However, since it was believed that 'the present Ministry was not expected to last much after the end of April' Hunt decided to let his own petition 'hang fire', and cabled London to that effect, after which he returned to Antofagasta.

By the time he returned to Santiago at the beginning of June, a new ministry had been formed and the company's application had been boosted by a favourable report from Mardones. But it was not yet plain sailing. The new Minister of Industry, Public Works and Railways, Señor Manuel O'Ryan, had only received his appointment as the result of a political deal between his Democratic Party and the majority Liberal Alliance whereby the Democrats were given a portfolio in the government in return for their continued support of the governing party. Hunt reported:

> Having once allowed O'Ryan to get the portfolio the policy seemed to be to censure and ridicule everything he did ... As a consequence he seemed afraid to put his signature to anything but the most insignificant decrees, and it appeared almost hopeless to expect that he would put his name to such an important concession as that we were asking for ...[33]

Only after 'various interviews' and at the cost of some concessions by Hunt did O'Ryan agree to sign the appropriate decree, granting the company a 15 per cent increase of tariffs except for second-class passengers who were to be charged only 5 per cent more since the Minister had to 'show his party that he was doing something for them'.[34] It was now the beginning of July and at that point the Minister resigned. Rather than starting all over again with a new minister, Hunt thought it best to get a decree from O'Ryan while he still could, and the decree was rushed through in the nick of time.

The negotiations had taken over a month and, as Hunt put it, 'To go into the full details of all the complications and intrigues would fill a long letter'.[35] He had been obliged to concede the point on passenger fares but on the other hand had secured two important concessions apart from the general 15 per cent increase. First, no time limit was attached to the new rates and, secondly, the decree itself stated that the increase was justified, 'an important statement which would strengthen our hand should there be any subsequent outcry, or political movement against the increase'.[36] The board in London approved Hunt's actions and the new tariffs came into effect in September 1919, with the exception of nitrate freights and second-class passengers where the increases became effective from the beginning of 1920. But, although satisfied at the time, neither the board nor Hunt could anticipate that within a few months the tariff question would have to be raised again in the light of developments which also mirrored the general situation in Chile, as the FCAB became embroiled in the most serious labour dispute in its history to date.

The trouble began at the beginning of November 1919 when certain workmen of the locomotive department protested against a company instruction to undertake some small additional duties, and ten firemen were suspended. Earlier in the year, as an economy measure, a number of men had been suspended and remained unemployed, and the local trade union suspected that it was to avoid taking them back that additional duties had been imposed on the firemen. The threat was made that unless the order suspending the firemen was withdrawn a general strike would be called. On 3 November, a Monday, the entire staff of the locomotive department at both Antofagasta and Mejillones did not turn up for work and, although most of the workmen in other departments did, a committee of the socialist federation ordered them out. As was customary in such situations, the general manager consulted the Intendent of Antofagasta who promised the necessary forces to protect lives and property, and troops were stationed at various places in the town and a force of police sent from Chuquicamata to Calama. The commander in Antofagasta thought it advisable to send a small detachment to Prat station on the line to the important junction of Baquedano, and requested a train for that purpose, but the train encountered a crowd of some 2,000 men, women and children before it left Antofagasta, and their clear intent was to prevent the train from leaving. Moreover, the railway line, which here had a fairly steep grade, had been greased, and the engine was forced to stop, to be attacked and stoned by the crowd.

> Women climbed on to the engine [Hunt graphically reported] and had to be thrown out by three soldiers who were in the cab. The troops in the train

> fired their carbines in the air and it is said some revolver shots were fired by the crowd. As the police were unable to disperse the crowd and protect the train and as the latter could not proceed owing to the greased condition of the rails it was decided to return to Antofagasta station . . .[37]

One man in the crowd received a bullet in the lung and died but it was uncertain who had fired the shot.

The intendent was then informed that, without a guarantee of safe conduct, no more trains would be run, and his advice to yield to the men's demand to withdraw the order on extra duties and re-instate those suspended was rejected, as management thought this would be interpreted as a sign of weakness, leading only to larger demands. It did, however, agree to meet a delegation of the men that afternoon. At that meeting, it was agreed that the men would return to work the following day and management would suspend the instruction on additional duties to study the matter further.

The same evening, however, the local Federation (part of the FOCH) held a meeting and, although the FCAB's own employees were prepared to return to work the next day, they were over-ruled by the leaders of the Federation. On the Tuesday 'not a single workman turned out to duty, although . . . the majority wished to do so'.[38] The management then informed the intendant that 'we considered that the strike was now a question of outside influence, with which we considered the authorities should deal' but he subsequently produced a list of demands put forward by the workmen, including a 50 per cent increase in wages, overtime at weekends, the establishment of a benevolent fund and, most ominous of all, recognition of the Federation by the company. At a meeting with delegates at the intendency later, management explained that such demands required detailed study and, after protracted discussion, it was agreed that the men would return to work immediately in return for an undertaking by the management that it would reply to general petitions before 1 January 1920. Meanwhile, the instruction on extra duties – the initial cause of the dispute – was withdrawn, the suspended firemen were re-instated, and the company promised no victimization of those who had acted as workers' spokesmen. And there, for the moment, the matter rested.

Hunt's observations on these events are worth quoting at some length:

> We have not yet received the petition referred to but we know that the men's demands will be exorbitant and indeed unreasonable, and we do not suggest that it will be possible to give them anything approaching what they are asking for. At the same time we are sure that unless we give something we shall have another strike about the end of the year, if not before. The men are earning practically the same wages, and in many cases less, than before the war, as owing to the crisis reductions of wages have been introduced.

> There is not the slightest doubt that the cost of living in Antofagasta has at least doubled during the last five years, and the men are finding it extremely difficult to obtain food and clothes for themselves and families. The working hours of the Engine and train men are very long, some of our Drivers frequently working eighteen hours without a rest. A very large proportion of our men have a number of years' service with the Company, and we are sure that they have no desire to leave the Company's service or to go on strike. This is a very important factor in a place like Antofagasta where with the exception of our men no other Railway workers are available. The recent strike was no doubt organized by a number of professional agitators who are at present in this district. We believe that if the matter is fairly studied and the men are given a small increase in wages and in certain other ways their conditions are bettered we shall have no further trouble with them, and on the other hand we shall disarm the Socialist Federation, because unless they are able to get the Railway Company's men to strike it will be very difficult for them to organize further strikes of any kind except perhaps at the nitrate Oficinas . . .[39]

Hunt's concluding optimism about the loyalty of the men and the power of the Federation was misplaced. When the petitions came in from all departments, they were all on Federation paper, and some were signed by members of the Federation who were not employed by the company. Moreover, most petitions asked for recognition of the Federation which was anathema to the management. At this time, the second week of November, Antofagasta was plagued by a rash of strikes fomented by the Federation, and involving a variety of trades. So serious did the situation become that the intendant called a meeting on 17 November of prominent public figures, such as the local judge, the chief of police, the colonel of the regiment at the port and the bishop. The press were also invited. They were informed that the intendant, who was shortly leaving for Santiago, had sent numerous telegrams to the capital, asking for reinforcements since he had insufficient forces to protect lives and property in the case of a general strike. It was finally resolved to send a delegation to Santiago consisting of the bishop, the chief alcalde and the general manager of Borax Consolidated, Mr Pridham, 'to place our position before the Government and get them to do something to meet the seriousness of the situation'.[40] By the time it left, the lightermen at Antofagasta and Mejillones had joined the labour protest and all shipping was paralysed. This was bad enough for the company but worse was to come: on 28 November, contravening their agreement to work until management replied to their petitions by 1 January, the entire workforce went on strike. It did so after the company had tried, on the advice of the intendent, to remove one Teodoro Dahl, regarded as one of the chief agitators: he was offered a better post some distance from Antofagasta but, after some vacillation, he declined and the men rallied to his support.

They demanded his reinstatement in his post at Antofagasta and declared that unless there was an immediate reply to their petitions they would stop work.

As it happened, the managing director and secretary of the FCAB – A.W. Bolden – had arrived in Antofagasta on 23 November, and he immediately assumed the leading role in the affair on the company's side. Meanwhile, sailors from the *Esmeralda* and the *Prat*, two Chilean cruisers berthed at Antofagasta, were landed to run the company's electric light plant and telephone exchange, a duty they performed for the nineteen days the strike lasted. Bolden and Hunt then had several days of fruitless negotiation with the men's representatives who, according to the latter 'refused to discuss anything else until the question of wages was settled' and on that question management was awaiting a reply to a cable to London. Finally, on 8 December a concrete offer was made of 15 per cent increase to the lower paid and 10 per cent to those earning over 300 pesos a month but this was rejected and the men refused to consider other points in their petitions. Throughout, Bolden and Hunt, in the neutral ground of the intendency, faced some thirty-five men, some of them Federation spokesmen not employed by the company. While all this was going on, essential trains were run by soldiers of the local regiment who had some experience of railways: such trains were the lifeline for food supplies to the nitrate *pampa*. But the impasse persisted.

Things began to move after the arrival, on 9 December, of the *S.S. Peru* with eighty lancers under the command of Lt-Col. Adolfo Miranda, and a complement of drivers and firemen from the Military Railway Battalion. Miranda, sent from Santiago on a special mission to settle the strike, proposed arbitration of the issue, a proposal not favoured by management since it felt it had offered as much as it could in wage increases and arbitration would not help. Miranda suggested some small percentage increases, to which the management finally agreed, and a further meeting was held at the intendency, under the chairmanship of Intendent Cabero, but with Miranda present, and he it was who insisted on the withdrawal of the leading Federation representative. But the men refused the enhanced offer. In the further, rather futile discussions, reported Hunt:

> It became apparent that although Col. Miranda was a strong man and had arrived with the intention of taking a firm attitude with the men, he found that they were too obstinate for any result to be obtained in that way and had arrived at the conclusion that discussion in the present form would give no results . . . [41]

Thereupon, on 11 December, Miranda insisted that arbitration was the only way forward under a decree of 1917, and Bolden and Hunt, after consulting their local legal representative, Señor Carey, finally agreed. After much prevarication, extending over several days, the men accepted arbitration, but only after trying to set conditions which would commit the company to far more than it felt it could afford financially, and force it to accept a Tribunal of Arbitration in which they would have the larger say. This, Miranda declined and, the intendent having left Antofagasta and Miranda being appointed interim intendent, it fell to him to appoint the arbitrator. He chose Admiral Salustio Valdés, commander of the *Prat*, a nomination which pleased the management since 'being a Naval man and a disciplinarian, it was almost certain that he would not support the Federation or any petition contrary to discipline'.[42]

The Arbitration Tribunal with Valdés presiding first met on 16 December but it took seven full days of detailed discussion, which were exhaustively reported in the local press, before both sides defined and agreed which matters were to be left to the arbitrator. The men, however, agreed to return to work on 18 December, and Valdés issued his award on 31 December.

On the key issue of wage increases, he awarded higher percentages to the different categories of workmen than the company had offered but somewhat less than the 35 per cent across the board he himself had earlier suggested. These ranged from 25 per cent to the lower paid to 15 per cent to the higher, and when the management 'impressed upon him the seriousness of the effect upon the Company's finances' he acknowledged this but 'explained that he did not feel that he could reduce his award because of the very serious labour situation . . . some sacrifice would have to be made . . . to quieten things down'.[43] He undertook, however, when next in Santiago to explain things to the President and suggest that the company be given an increase in tariffs. As it was, the company was not dissatisfied: arbitration was a binding agreement and resort to it had blunted the Federation's influence; while the men were not entirely happy, they accepted the award and had returned to work, and a strike which had threatened very serious consequences had been brought to an end. Moreover, in his statement accompanying the award, Valdés, while recognizing that the strike had its origins in low living standards and in the lack of adequate laws to regulate relations between employers and workers, went out of his way to castigate

> . . . the incessant propaganda of agitators . . . exploiting the worker's good faith and disturbing his judgement, inciting him to rise up against that capital which maintains work.[44]

For its part, the leading daily in Antofagasta praised both the award and Valdés for

> . . . building a bridge between the enterprise and the strikers, to make it easier

for owners and workers to shake hands, establishing in the company whose activity is so necessary to regional progress a truly lasting harmony.[45]

That harmony was impaired in April when the Federation in Antofagasta succeeded in mounting a two-day stoppage by all workers, including those of the railway, but this was a political strike to protest at the arrest of Luis Recabarren, leader of the POS, whom the government charged with incitement to plot against the authorities. The incident passed off quietly, and when the Federation sought to stir up further unrest, the majority of the company's employee's refused to take part. When, subsequently, the Federation presented an ultimatum to the authorities, threatening a further strike unless its demands for the dismissal of certain officials were met, again it failed to persuade the workers to participate. 'Our information', wrote Hunt,

leads us to believe that the proposal was frustrated by the refusal of the drivers . . . to join in, as with these men we would have been able to run a train service and the attempt would have been a fiasco, the Federation being greatly dependent on the complete stoppage of the Railway to make their action felt by the Commercial Houses etc.[46]

A more serious threat arose three months later when the maritime workers from Iquique to Antofagasta mounted a series of strikes relating to work practices and the government had to appoint a commission to investigate their grievances. Some railway workers petitioned on several issues in the general state of labour unrest, seeking, in effect, to upset the arbitration award of Valdés, but this the company resisted and Valdés himself advised the workers 'that the Railway Company was complying with the spirit as well as with the letter of the Judgement' and this they accepted. While the maritime strikes affected the company's traffic and a number of drivers and firemen were without work, they were not suspended and continued to receive full pay though this was, for the company, a very expensive business. The maritime workers' return to work in July saved management from a harsh decision as to whether it was too expensive to go on paying men without work or risk an all-out strike by suspending them. But there was little doubt, as Hunt reported:

. . . that the drivers, firemen and shed hands appreciated the action of the Company and brought all their influence to bear against joining the strike, just at that particular time that everybody was convinced that a general stoppage of work would take place, and, had the Railway men gone out, no doubt this [a general strike] would have happened and we were fortunate in keeping the men content and thus avoiding what might have been serious trouble.[47]

The company's handling of the serious dispute of 1919–20 not only revealed the philosophy of its management from the top down: it also set the tone for the future conduct of industrial relations. While sharing the prejudices of most managers of the time against organized labour, it was far from indifferent to the conditions of life and work of its employees, and sought to meet their grievances as far as it thought it reasonably could, consistent with running the business efficiently and profitably. Bolden frequently expressed his views on the subject in the turbulent 1920s, inveighing heavily against 'agitators' but, at the same time, recognizing that their effectiveness often derived from just causes. After his return to London and the 'political' strike of 1920, he declared:

> The writer felt from all he saw that unless the Chilian Government seriously dealt with the many agitators or took some measures to redress the conditions of living in the Province in the matter of prices, that there was bound to be trouble from time to time.[48]

Over a year later, referring to a lock-out of maritime workers which proved successful, he wrote:

> You know well the Board's policy of treating the staff and employees with reasonable consideration but when agitators are at work and the men allow themselves to become tools in their hands resulting in impossible demands, then it behoves us to take a firm stand . . . If the men could only see it, we act in their very best interests in doing so.[49]

That policy of firm fairness was pursued by the company to the best of its ability in a difficult decade. And, on the whole, it had more success in retaining the loyalty of its workforce than other foreign enterprises in the region. Alessandri himself paid tribute to the company after a visit to the north which he made as president-elect in November, 1920, travelling on the company's trains: in a subsequent interview with Hunt, the latter reported:

> He seemed to be impressed with the difficult character of the workmen in the North . . . but he made an exception in regard to . . . the Antofagasta Railway: he had spoken to a number of them and asked about conditions and was pleasantly surprised to find that all replied that they were well placed . . .[50]

The compliment was paid at the end of a very good year for the FCAB, largely the result of the dramatic, though short-lived, improvement in nitrate traffic, the company handling four and a half times the amount of nitrate it carried in 1919. Moreover, to compensate for the higher wage costs from the arbitration award – amounting to some 2 million pesos – the company applied for an increase in tariffs of 15 per cent and, in the teeth of fierce opposition from the nitrate companies, was finally granted an increase of 12 per cent, though the negotiations, as in 1919, were difficult and protracted and the increases did not take effect until 1921. The negotiations were assisted by the company's offer to establish a retirement fund for native staff, a *quid pro quo* for the tariff increase urged by the Chief of the Chilean Naval Commission in London, fortuitously the same Rear Admiral Valdés who had chaired the arbitration proceedings. 'Tranquillity in labour circles', Bolden commented, 'is absolutely necessary for Chili as for all other countries and ... the introduction of the fund will undoubtedly have some effect in that direction with our work people'.[51] It was in the same spirit, though on a more minor matter, that the board, at Bolden's prompting, agreed to the request of the general manager in Chile for 'a decent biograph' in Coloso where it was 'exceptionally difficult to keep the men ... without some attraction ... at present there is absolutely nothing to keep them there during their leisure hours'.[52]

The maintenance of good relations with the workforce was, however, always threatened by the erratic behaviour of the market, notably nitrate, and the boom of 1920 was followed by a severe slump in 1921. This was, in fact, worse than the crisis of 1919, the company carrying less nitrate than in any year since 1906 and, with the knock-on effect on the water business, up-traffic and passenger income, gross receipts for the lines and the waterworks fell by over 56 per cent compared with 1920. Economy was the order of the day from the middle of January, as the general manager reported:

> The Traffic Department is suppressing a number of goods trains and the crews are being discharged. The Locomotive Department is reducing running staff and some of those remaining will be reduced in rank and rate of pay. From the workshops we are discharging about 100 men ... All overtime in the workshops has been stopped. The Permanent Way Department will reduce gangs and the other Departments will make such reductions as are possible ... We are in all cases selecting for dismissal the shorter service men and will also take the opportunity of including certain undesirables ...[53]

These were hard times, indeed, but despite the fact that by August 1921, the total workforce had been reduced from some 4,150 to 2,600, that hours had been reduced to what was, in effect, a four-day week, with a consequent fall in wages, and that the labour situation elsewhere in Antofagasta was marked by frequent disturbances, the FCAB weathered the storm. It retained the loyalty of its long-serving staff and ameliorated the lot of those it could not keep. It agreed, for example, with a direct request from President Alessandri to pay seven days' wages to all staff dismissed at a time when the law did not require any employer to give

Senior staff at FCAB in 1923: A. W. Bolden, with walking stick, is seated in middle of front row

Metre gauge train in Ascotan

Converted metre gauge locomotive in Ascotan

Permanent way gang at work, *c.* 1928

The first metre gauge train arriving in Antofagasta North Yard from Mejillones in 1928

Train in La Paz station, Bolivia

Rolling stock, *c.* 1914: sleeping car

Rolling stock, *c.* 1914: second class carriage interior

FCAB Antofagasta offices and rolling stock, *c.* 1914

FCAB Antofagasta offices and rolling stock, *c.* 1914

Rolling stock: 4-6-2 passenger locomotive, Uyuni, Bolivia, 1925

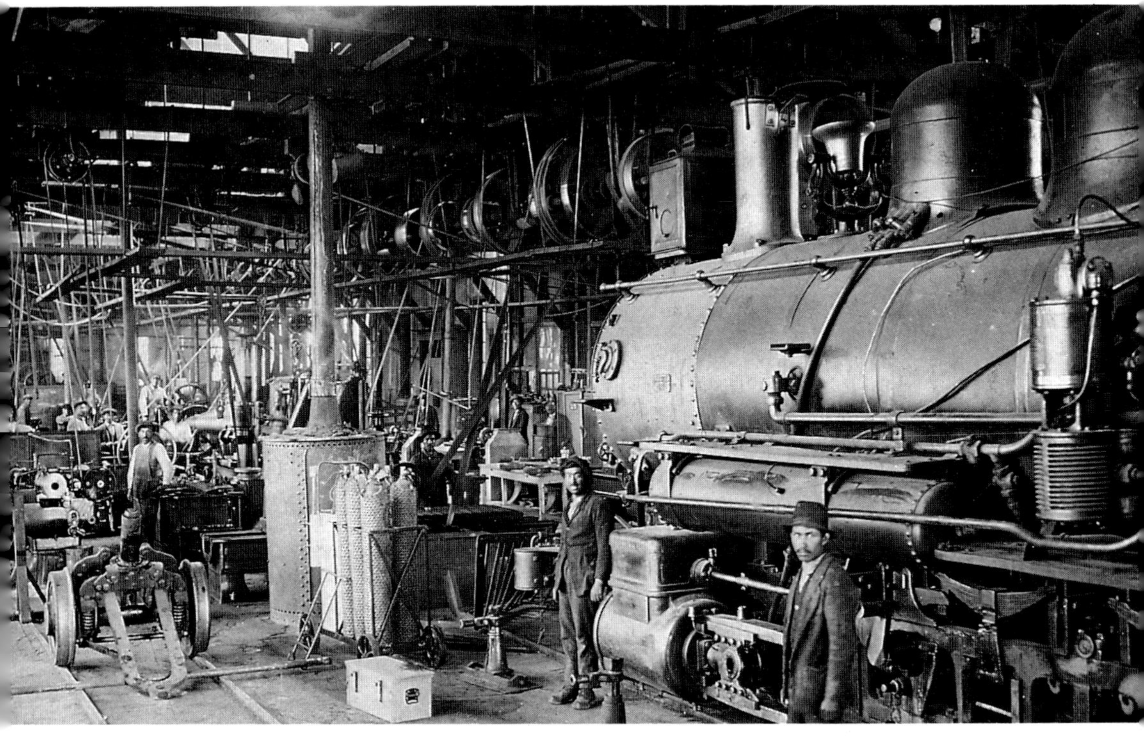

Main railway workshops, Uyuni, Bolivia, 1925

The snow plough at Montt station, Collahuasi branch, *c.* 1930: l-r G. W. Craig, District Engineer, M. Hardy, Traffic Inspector, Sr. Leguizamon, Roadmaster

Punto Alto on the Collahuasi branch: l-r G. W. Craig, Chief Engineer, J. Hill, Waterworks Engineer, R. H. Dobson, Managing Director. This was the highest railway line in the world at 4,826.35 metres (15,834.48 feet). The line was lifted in 1958.

Conchi Viaduct No. 2, 1913. This spectacular feat of civil engineering was closed to traffic in 1914

George Craig in 1930. He retired as Chief Civil Engineer

Arthur Heskett ('Don Arturo') at work in his office, 1925

Blessing of diesel electric locomotives at their inauguration, 24 May 1961

any notice at all to workmen on daily pay and, despite the austerity of the times, it awarded wage increases to permanent staff in both 1921 and 1923. When, in 1921, Federation leaders attempted to promote a strike, the majority of the men refused, and not until 1924 did the company face a labour problem similar to that of 1919–20. There was, in fact, a genuine appreciation by the workforce which the company was able to retain that, despite its problems, it attended to their interests as far as it could, and the opinion expressed by one of the senators for Antofagasta, elected in March, 1921, reflected that belief: he 'said he had talked with a number of the railwaymen ... and that of all the workmen he had spoken to, ours seemed to be the most contented and best treated'.[54] As the nitrate market improved gradually in the next few years, the company was able again to expand its business and increase its labour force. By the mid-1920s, however, certain events on the national stage had been set in train which were to have a profound effect on Chile itself and also on the foreign companies which operated there. Meanwhile, in neighbouring Bolivia, the company had been faced with analogous problems to those it confronted in Chile in the management of its railway network and industrial relations, in the years which saw the rise of trade unionism and the consequences of the First World War.

Bolivia

Trade unionism in Bolivia was both a later development and had a more sporadic growth than in Chile, partly owing to the less unified nature of the country, its more fragmented social structure and the slower pace of industrial development. One of its earliest manifestations, however, was the attempt made by railway workers to establish mutual aid associations. These inevitably involved the FCAB, owning as it did the main line from Antofagasta to La Paz and operating several other lines leased by the Bolivia Railway Company. As noted earlier, to all intents and purposes, the FCAB owned the Bolivia Railway Company, and its general manager in Bolivia, from the separation of the administration of the main line and branches in 1914, was also the general manager of the Bolivia Railway Company, though he reported separately on the operations of the respective lines to two different boards. The workers on the lines, however, were, in effect, under the same employer.

Among the most significant early working-class organizations was the League of Workers and Employees of the Railway which had its origins in a dispute involving office workers of the Bolivian Railway Company and management in 1919. It came into existence early in August that year when some seventy of the company's employees drew up a document committing them to set up an associations for the furtherance of workers' rights, and invited workers of other companies and trades to join them. Many did so, and the League became a nationwide organization, reformist rather than revolutionary in character and working within the existing legal framework while seeking to change it. In March 1920, owing to differences over tactics among the leadership, the League split but by that time other organizations of workers had emerged. Prominent among these was the Oruro Railway Federation, composed exclusively of workers on the Antofagasta-Bolivia line, more of a trade union than a mutualist organization, and with more avowedly socialist views. It looked to government to enact labour legislation on such issues as working hours, compensation for accidents at work and pensions.

The company's first real experience of the new mood of many Bolivian workers – a number of whom had also worked in Chile and had been influenced by developments there – began in December 1919, when the workers of the Antofagasta-Bolivia Railway and of the Bolivia Railway Company presented the general manager, J. Backus, with a detailed petition for an improvement of working conditions, ranging from wage increases and paid holidays to provision for accident and pension benefits. The matter was still under consideration when A.W. Bolden arrived in La Paz in January during his return to England from Chile, and so was able to discuss the petition on the spot with Backus and also consult board members in London by cable. As a result, agreement was reached with the men on several issues, leading to an amicable settlement on 9 February 1920. The workers obtained wage increases of from 10 per cent to 15 per cent, the right to fifteen days' paid holiday a year, travel concessions on the lines, stipulated working hours for all grades, as well as certain administrative changes, though other issues, such as a life pension scheme, were referred to London for further consideration. But what might have been a serious strike was avoided and, although the railway workers did go on strike briefly in 1921 and 1922, these were part of national political protests and not the result of working grievances.

As in Chile, so in Bolivia local or regional industrial disturbances were, more often than not, the reflection of national circumstances, and Bolivia, a mineral-exporting economy, shared with Chile the vicissitudes of the post-war era. What nitrate was to Chile – and to the FCAB – tin was to Bolivia, and fluctuations in world demand were almost immediately reflected in the country's economic position, and in the equation between supply and demand for the mining work-force as well as in the traffic of its communications system. Although, in 1919 and 1920 the tonnage of tin carried by the company's lines kept abreast of wartime demand, in 1921 it fell by nearly 41 per cent, as the market price of tin fell from £215 early in the year to £150 in August on the London market. For the FCAB and the Bolivia Railway Company a fall in mineral traffic also entailed a decline in import traffic of mining materials and passengers, many of whom were closely connected with mining. The company's receipts from the Bolivian section of the Antofagasta-La Paz railway fell, in 1921, by over 36 per cent, and, while the fall on the lines run by the Bolivia Railway Company was not quite so dramatic, it was bad enough.

Again, as in Chile, so in Bolivia the response of management to adverse circumstances took two main forms: maximum economy in operation, and application to government for an increase in tariffs. As the general manager reported in his annual review for the FCAB for 1921:

> In view of the poor traffics and general trade depression, economies have been enforced wherever possible, and all work which was not absolutely essential was stopped . . .[55]

Certain work was, in Bolivia, always essential owing to a climatic regime which was much less predictable than that of Chile: moreover, the lines there ran over far more difficult terrain and maintenance costs were proportionately higher. Fortunately for the FCAB the early 1920s were comparatively free from climatic disasters, and economies in operation could be effected.

On tariffs, however, there was a major problem in difficult times, namely the rate of exchange of the Bolivian currency, the boliviano. Under the Speyer Contract which gave birth to the Bolivia Railway Company, the FCAB had the right to surcharge tariffs to compensate for any fall in exchange below the par value of 19¹/₅*d* to the boliviano. Tariffs were collected in Bolivian currency but if the sterling equivalent of the boliviano fell below that parity the company had to seek redress through a tariff surcharge or carry the cost of a falling exchange, something it could not do for a long period, given its obligations to shareholders under the Speyer contract. In 1921, because of the impact of the world recession on Bolivia, the boliviano declined to a low point of 13½*d* by November, and the company was obliged to ask government for a surcharge on tariffs in compensation for the loss on exchange. After long and difficult negotiations, the Bolivian government finally agreed to a 20 per cent surcharge on tariffs, not the true rate under the concession but one to which the FCAB agreed 'in view of the conditions for business generally'.[56] The fall in exchange in 1921 meant a loss in earnings to the FCAB of some 27 per cent and the agreed tariff compensated the company by only 15 per cent, so it was, in effect, subsidizing the Bolivian government. As usual it took the longer view:

> . . . we felt it was better [reported the Chairman, the Hon. C.N. Lawrence, to the AGM of the FCAB on 20 June 1922] to have an amicable

> understanding with the Bolivian Government rather than insist on the full surcharge for the time being, because of the really depressed state of business generally in Bolivia.[57]

At the same time, the company had entered into negotiations for a revised tariff structure for the lines of the Bolivia Railway Company, as well as parity of treatment for tariffs on the Bolivian section of the Antofagasta line.

After the traumas of 1921, the years to the middle of the decade marked an improvement in the company's fortunes in Bolivia as they did in Chile. Despite marked fluctuations in the price of tin on the London exchange in the early 1920s, the tonnage for export shipped by the FCAB through Antofagasta rose by 71 per cent in 1922 over 1921, by 5 per cent in 1923 and by 3½ per cent in 1924. Moreover the gross receipts of the Bolivia Railway Company rose from the level in 1921 in each of the following years to 1925. As for the parent company, the FCAB, despite the years of depression, 1919 and 1921, growing industrial militancy and the complex problems of running a difficult network in a foreign environment, the results were satisfactory overall. By the mid-1920s the level of profitability had recovered to that of the boom during the war, as the following table indicates.

Table 4. FCAB results, 1914–1925

Year	Gross Receipts £	Working Expenses £	Net Receipts £
1914	1,541,995	843,485	698,510
1915	1,322,056	674,673	647,383
1916	1,852,655	1,004,884	847,771
1917	2,239,384	1,252,060	987,324
1918	2,370,200	1,482,287	887,913
1919	1,346,592	881,715	464,877
1920	2,370,079	1,614,959	755,120
1921	1,031,489	738,121	293,368
1922	1,287,847	671,661	616,186
1923	1,927,995	1,016,967	911,028
1924	2,062,940	1,150,751	912,189
1925	2,183,109	1,335,311	847,798

Source: FCAB Annual Reports, 1915–1926

Such results, together with other income, for example, from investments, and allowing for expenditure, including taxation, enabled the company to meet every year its obligations to holders of the 5 per cent cumulative preference stock and to pay a reasonable dividend every year to holders of ordinary stock, ranging from 3 per cent in the worst year,

1921, to 7 per cent in 1923, 1924 and 1925. These results were not spectacular on a total capital investment of over £13½ million but they were steady and the board's dividend policy was always consistently cautious, reflecting the directors' recognition of the fact that mineral traffic in both Chile and Bolivia was the mainstay of the company's viability, and that traffic was unpredictable from year to year. At the same time, a careful financial policy of building up reserves was pursued: by the end of 1925, the Reserve Account stood at £1 million and the Renewals Account at just over £1½ million. As events were to prove in later years, such prudence would be more than justified.

Political crisis and state intervention

If the volume of traffic was always an unpredictable factor in the running of the company's lines and ensuring profitability, so was the political environment in which the company operated. The growth of union organization in both Chile and Bolivia in the post-war period was one indication of mounting social pressure in difficult national economic circumstances, and that pressure became an increasingly important factor for politicians in both countries. Government found itself obliged to pay more attention to popular unrest and while many executives clung to outmoded ideas on working-class discontent, seeing the hand of the agitator in every disturbance, others recognized that times were changing and that if social pressures were not alleviated through appropriate legislation more dangerous disorders would result. At the same time, new emphasis was given to the role of the state in the national economy as successive governments grappled with the dislocations of a world economic system on which they had practically no influence.

In Bolivia, Bautista Saavedra, president from 1921 to 1926, exemplified the new type of leadership. Unlike his prominent rivals in the comparatively new Republican Party, he was not a *hacendado* but an intellectual and an astute organizer who sought his political base in the growing commercial and middle class of La Paz as well as in the burgeoning working-class organizations of miners and railwaymen. As early as September 1920, before becoming president but as one of a ruling junta of three, he proclaimed the right to strike and set up a government labour arbitration system. As president, in 1921 he presented to Congress a wide-ranging programme of social reform, including proposals for accident compensation, amplification of the right to strike and legislation to improve arbitration. Though his proposals were watered down in Congress 'these laws were ... the first (such) ever passed in Bolivia ... a major victory for the working classes and a primary step in ... a long and hard process of social advancement through legislation'.[58] In 1923, he introduced a major tax reform aimed primarily at the tin magnates, increasing their contribution to the national treasury almost fourfold between 1923 and 1924 and causing the powerful Simón I Patiño to remove his heaquarters from Bolivia to the United States. Subsequently, Patiño, in return, loaned the government £600,000 for railway construction against a guarantee by Saavedra not to raise taxes on tin again for five years. This transaction was of direct interest to the FCAB since the loan was to be used to complete the line from Potosí to Sucre, begun under the aegis of the government, but not completed hitherto for lack of funds. Now, with cash available, the FCAB contracted with the government to continue construction without taking part in the financing, and expecting the line, when completed, to benefit the line from Rio Mulato to Potosí which the FCAB operated under the lease from the Bolivia Railway Company.

If the Saavedra regime brought benefits to the company in Bolivia, the same could not be said of events in Chile, where a complex series of political developments in the mid-1920s foreshadowed substantial changes for the company's operations and quite new problems for management both in Antofagasta and in London.

The election of the reformist President Alessandri in 1920 proved a false dawn for Chile. For the next four years his programme of social reform and economic measures to alleviate the worst effects of the post-war depression was stultified by the opposition in Congress, particularly in the Senate where it had a majority, while the Alessandrista parties controlled the deputies. In those four years, no fewer than sixteen cabinets were formed, the value of the peso fell by a half and by 1924 the treasury was so exhausted that pay for civil servants and the armed forces was six months in arrears. Public demonstrations increased and a large number of organizations protesting at the obstructionism of the Senate sprang up. Congressional elections were due in March 1924, and in the feverish state of the country, Alessandri and the opposition agreed in January that in return for his willingness to abstain from interference in the elections, the opposition would accept procedural changes in congressional business to speed things up, including the passage of an income tax law originating in late 1922 but not yet on the statute book. They also agreed – foolishly as it turned out – to support a proposal for a bill authorizing salaries for congressmen, contrary to previous practice.

Alessandri, however, so mistrusted the opposition that he reneged on his electoral promise, and the whole weight of the government machine, including the army, was thrown behind his supporters in the elections of March 1924. This gave the Alessandristas control of the Senate as well as the deputies but, to the country's astonishment, the new Congress proved no more responsible than its predecessor, wasting months in sterile debate on insignificant issues, though the lower house debated the congressional salaries bill and passed it to the Senate in June. This issue for the army was the last straw. High-ranking officers, including General Luis Altamirano, inspector-general of the army, began plotting to overthrow Alessandri, while middle-ranking officers met frequently to discuss service conditions and the state of the nation. Prominent among them was Major Carlos Ibáñez del Campo.

The crisis came to a head in September 1924: as the Senate debated the salaries bill, some fifty junior officers in the public gallery vociferously applauded those who opposed it. This was on 2 September, and the action was repeated the following day: then, in response to a request from Alessandri, the protesters, led by Ibáñez, presented a list of projects they thought essential. Drawn up by Ibáñez, the list ranged widely from the withdrawal of the congressional salaries bill; new laws on promotion, salaries and pensions for the forces; stabilization of the peso; immediate payment of back salaries to public servants, to what was to concern foreign businesses in Chile more than such matters, a package of measures later known as the social laws, designed to improve the conditions and status of workmen. An alliance of convenience was formed between the high command of the services and the junior officers, whose junta accepted Alessandri's designation of Altamirano as Minister of the Interior – Prime Minister – General Juan Pablo Bennet as Minister of War and Admiral Francisco Neff as Minister of Finance. Alessandri vetoed the bill on congressional salaries, and when a very subdued Congress met on 8 September, it passed in one afternoon all the legislation proposed in Ibáñez's list, including the social laws, many of which, in essence, Alessandri had put forward in his first four years as president.

He, himself, offered to resign but instead the forces suggested six months leave of absence abroad, which he accepted. Thereafter, Altamirano acted as President until 23 January 1925, when the middle-ranking officers, suspicious of his contacts with diehard conservative politicians, sprang a successful coup, deposed the government and installed a respected civilian one in its place. They also called for Alessandri's return which took place in March, and the new cabinet included Ibáñez as Minister of War. But differences between them forced Alessandri to resign, whereupon all the political parties and finally Ibáñez also, who made no secret of his presidential ambitions, agreed on a single candidate for new elections. Emiliano Figueroa Larrain, an amiable, elderly but not particularly astute public figure, thus became President of the republic for a year and a half while Ibáñez, from his position as Minister of War, quietly and efficiently built up his own following, and in February 1927, became Minister of the Interior. Two months later Figueroa resigned after Ibáñez initiated a clean-up of the public services which included the dismissal of Figueroa's brother as head of the Supreme Court. In May 1927, new presidential elections in Chile saw Ibáñez triumphant, and he embarked on a four-year term of autocratic but efficient, honest and prosperous government.

This summary digression into the complexities of Chilean politics in the 1920s is the essential backdrop to the operations of the FCAB in those turbulent years, to the new challenges it had to face in rapidly changing circumstances, and to its response to them. At the AGM of the FCAB on 16 June 1925, in his review of the previous year's results, the chairman – now Lord Lawrence of Kingsgate – made reference to both the Chilean Income Tax Law and to the recent legislation on social affairs in both Bolivia and Chile, all of which seemed likely to affect the company's working expenses. Since most of the new legislation – amounting in Chile to six new laws covering workmen's contracts, a labour code, health insurance, workmen's compensation, arbitration and conciliation, and the position of *empleados* as opposed to workmen – was on the statute book but not yet governed by legally-approved *reglamentos* for their implementation, it was impossible to say categorically what all that meant for the company. While recognizing that governments in Chile and Bolivia had every right to raise revenue for essential purposes, he pointed out the implications for an undertaking such as the railway:

> . . . like the manufacturer of boots or any other commodity, extra charges on us can only be recouped by extra tariffs . . . we are most anxious not to increase our tariffs if it can possibly be avoided and therefore we have not taken any steps yet with regard to income tax but we are afraid that the other legislation . . . will eventually bring about increased charges which may force us to ask both Governments to reconsider with us the tariff question.[59]

He also referred to the growth of the Chilean bureaucracy the new laws entailed, and to the heavy burden of extra work laid on senior management 'in an endeavour to comply with the various laws and at the same time safeguard the interests of this company'.[60]

Even without the new laws, safeguarding the company's interests in 1924 was arduous enough. In the heady political atmosphere, labour problems multiplied throughout the country and the general manager in Antofagasta had his hands full both at the beginning and the end of the year. In fact, the dispute between management and labour which began in January and lasted for three weeks was, far and away, the most serious and threatening for the FCAB since the troubles of 1919. It began with the presentation of petitions by all the different branches of the labour force not only in Antofagasta but also Baquedano and Calama. There were fifteen in all, and they were fairly wide-ranging though the key request was for a permanent increase in wages. While General Manager Hunt was broadly opposed to this, he had some sympathy with the men, partly because of the fall in the value of the peso but also because the new income tax law had just come into force and that appeared at first sight to impose a 2 per cent tax on all wages. Moreover, as he pointed out,

> ... it is obvious that the amount they suffer on account of the law is by no means limited to the two percent which is deducted from their wages, as all tradesmen will of course raise their prices (and landlords are already raising the rent of houses) to compensate them for having to pay the tax on their profits, all of which will have the effect of increasing the living costs for the consumer ...[61]

Thus, although the Minister of Finance decreed at the end of January that the 2 per cent impost did not apply to workmen on a daily wage, the cost of living factor remained, and Hunt felt that some increase in wages was justified. Consequently, he sought and obtained from the board in London permission to apply

> ... a general increase in salaries and wages ranging from 10% to 15% on all currency salaries or wages, or else an arrangement to apply a surcharge on same whilst the Chilian "peso" is quoted above 35 to the £, leaving us to decide which of the two alternatives we should adopt ...[62]

In the event, he adopted the latter course and the men were so informed in Circular No. 22A.

Throughout the early negotiations, involving many meetings, Hunt's life had been complicated by the Intendent of Antofagasta who throughout sided with the men and even discussed with them their petitions before they were presented. He also frequently called Hunt to his office to warn him that, according to his secret police, a strike would shortly be called, while Hunt, at the same time, was holding quite amicable meetings with the workers' delegates. He himself declared:

> One very notable fact in connection with the recent trouble is that all petitions were respectfully worded and were signed only by actual employees of the Company, most of whom have several years' service, and that in none of these petitions is there any mention of Federations or other matters of this nature ...[63]

This attitude, which was maintained throughout the dispute, was undoubtedly due to the conciliatory, but firm, attitude adopted by local management, backed by the board in London, and to the men's recognition of the company as a fair employer, as its dealings with them over the years had shown. In his first considered comments on the dispute at the end of January, the managing director, A.W. Bolden, referred to that history:

> The first impression of the Board was to refuse entirely to accede to any request or demand for an increase in wages, whether temporary or permanent. As a result of the strike at the end of 1919 the wages of the Clerks and Workmen were certainly put on an improved scale and what at that time was considered as an eminently fair basis and in May, 1921 ... when commercial houses and others were reducing staffs owing to business depression, we voluntarily gave our workpeople 10% to 15% increase in wages so that today we consider that ... they are being quite fairly paid and there is no justification for any permanent increase in remuneration ...[64]

He went on, however, to say that, in view of the fall in the value of the peso and its effect on the cost of living,

> ... the Board felt that there was some reason for trying to meet the situation temporarily until the value of the dollar (ie. peso) should improve and we therefore gave you authority ... to increase currency salaries and wages by such a percentage as the number of dollars to the £ sterling exceed 35; when exchange reached 35 to the £1. or below that figure then any such concession would be automatically withdrawn ... you have been authorised to shew the practical sympathy of the Company with its employees by making some temporary concession over the rate of exchange in order to tide them over temporary difficulties ... [but] ... Any question of a permanent increase in wages and salaries ... is quite unacceptable.[65]

For the board, and, indeed, for the general manager, that was the sticking point.

Consequently, when the men virtually unanimously rejected Circular No. 22A, and stuck to their claim for a permanent increase, Hunt stood firm, despite pressure from the intendant who, in the run-up to the March congressional elections, clearly had a political axe to grind. In the event, and only after many more tortuous meetings between management and men at the intendancy, with the intendant in the chair, the workers' delegates accepted the company's proposal, with some mathematical amendments on the exchange rate itself, to which the board had agreed.

Throughout the negotiations a lively interest in the dispute was taken by the regional press, and notably by the leading daily of Antofagasta, *El Mercurio*, which justified its extensive coverage by pointing out that not only did a third of the population of Antofagasta itself depend on the railway for its livelihood but also that some 50,000 workers and their families in the copper-mining complex of Chuquicamata and the nitrate *oficinas* were in a similar situation, reliant on the company for their basic necessities. It consistently paid tribute to the good sense on both sides, and to the determination of both management and workers to avoid a damaging strike. When accord was reached at the end of February, the paper offered its readers the following eulogy to Hunt:

> From the beginning . . . Mr. Hunt, setting a splendid example which might well be considered by all business directors in the country, immediately got into direct touch with the petitioners, giving them all the necessary facilities to negotiate man to man, respecting their right to make petitions while at the same time defending the vital interests in his charge . . . As a result of this wise and rational way of doing things (unfortunately rather rare) a solution has been found . . . a bilateral victory in which both sides have gained and no one has lost . . . [66]

Hunt himself, despite three weeks of arduous and often frustrating discussion, felt that the outcome would be satisfactory to the company.

> At no time during our recent discussions [he wrote] was there any sign of the extreme attitude shown by the men in 1919, nor was there any attempt to bring persons outside the staff into the discussions, except, of course, the Intendente . . . It is unfortunate that the trouble occurred but we think that we have got out of it at a minimum cost, taking into consideration the political situation . . . [67]

With those views the board agreed: 'we congratulate you', Bolden wrote, 'that they [the points in dispute] eventually resulted in the abandonment by the employees of all the claims which you have not been able to meet'.[68]

Nevertheless, the additional cost of the settlement to the company amounted, according to Hunt, to £5,838 in February 1924 and to £6,180 in March, apparently trifling sums, but a portent of what was to come as the political and economic situation in Chile got worse and as the costs of the new social laws and other state-directed imposts began to bite.

The loyalty and reasonable attitude of the labour force in the early part of the year was, however, eroded in the course of it, owing partly to the unstable national political situation and partly to the popular expectations aroused by the new social laws. Piqued at their exclusion from the negotiations of the company directly with its employees, local and regional unions became more militant and this development coincided with a rise in exchange, which meant, of course, that the company's formula of a sliding scale for wages and salaries based on the international value of the peso came into operation, apparently reducing incomes. In Antofagasta, militants formed the *Unión Ferroviaria*, claiming 1,500 members, with branches in Mejillones of 600 men and in Calama with about 100. The new social laws, passed by Congress in September 1924, and published then, but not yet in force, were grist to the union's mill, as the *reglamentos* governing their operation wound their tortuous way through Congress. In these circumstances, the *Unión* affiliated itself to the *Federación de Empleados de Antofagasta*, a somewhat somnolent organization which the *Unión* sought, and came, to dominate. Unfortunately, a certain Ramón Alzamora, secretary of the *Unión*, became secretary of the *Federación* late in 1924 and he happened to be an employee of the FCAB, and a leading organizer in what ensued. (He was also, in fact, an anarchist and later a founder-member of the Socialist Party.)

Both organizations, with other societies and unions, mounted a series of demonstrations in the autumn of 1924 to protest against a government decision to postpone the introduction of Law No. 4059 relating to *Empleados Particulares*, originally intended to come into effect on 27 December. As drafted, that law and, indeed, the other social laws envisaged by the military government, seemed particularly favourable to white-collar employees (*empleados*), though it did not embrace workmen. But it stipulated a 48-hour week, with overtime at pay and a half to 56 hours, one month's notice or its equivalent in cash to any employee discharged, together with one month's salary for each completed year's service for anyone discharged. It also laid on employers the obligation to divide annually amongst its employees 20 per cent of its net profits up to 25 per cent of annual salary. Among its other provisions was a retirement fund to which employees earning up to $12,000 had to pay 5 per cent of salary, the employer to contribute a similar sum. Not surprisingly, employers' federations and managements in general protested, and the government postponed the introduction of the law until April 1925. For the FCAB, Hunt had a preliminary estimate made of the law's likely cost to the company as the law then stood: it amounted to £46,000 per annum, and he informed the Minister of Railways in October 1924 that such an increase in working expenses would oblige the railway to solicit a higher tariff for what it carried. He also associated the company with the protests being made by other employers in Antofagasta – notably the Chile Exploration Company and the nitrate firms. And he put his finger on the real problem:

> The fact of the matter is that the new Military Government are trying to please everybody, but principally the masses. The laws have now been passed and published, and, although there is talk amongst the commercial people of the possibility of their being modified, we cannot believe that now that every employee and workman in the country knows of the benefits which are given to him by the new laws any modification will be possible which will deprive the workers of these benefits . . . [68]

The workers' demonstrations, urged on by such as Alzamora, culminated in the threat of a general stoppage of work throughout Antofagasta on 1 December. All employees in the province were notified by the societies, which also informed the government of their intentions. Though the strike was aimed at government, the employers could not stand idly by, and they thrashed out a common response, namely to inform the intendant, the government's local representative, that they did not recognize the *Federación*'s right to call workers out, and that any workers so doing would be deemed to have resigned, with the loss of all benefits, but could be re-engaged as new employees from 2 December. For his part, the intendant declared publicly that the forces of law and order would defend the right of any employee to work if he so wished. All of a sudden, on 1 December, the FCAB found itself in a cleft stick: while its own employees went on strike and stopped trains running, employees of the other companies remained at work. The sanction of the Employers' Federation on sacking strikers, therefore, left the company in the isolated position of being the only one which might have to do that after 1 December. Hunt, with good reason, feared that a general workers' protest against the government might be turned to a particular attack against the company alone, and, therefore, limited action to stopping a day's pay for the workforce on strike on 1 December. As it happened, however, his fears of a further stoppage did not materialize in 1924, largely because the government declared 9 December a public holiday on the centenary of the battle of Ayacucho, Spain's last stand in the Wars of Independence. Since 8 December was a normal public holiday (*Puríssima Concepción*) and workmen, unlike *empleados*, were not paid on such occasions, their overall loss of earnings in early December was enough to deter them. But the situation remained delicate: while, as Hunt, wrote:

> Legally we have a right to advise all employees who absent themselves from work without permission, or without a medical certificate, that their services are terminated by the abandonment of their work . . . At the same time we did not feel that we could recommend this . . . action because serious trouble would doubtless result . . . The authorities might support us very enthusiastically at the beginning . . . but as matters become more and more serious they might wish to pass the responsibility on to the Railway Company . . . to give way in the stand we might take up.[69]

Although 1924 was bad enough for the company's industrial relations, 1925 was worse. On 17 January, the stevedores at Antofagasta declared a strike against the allocation of work by employers, alleging that 'activists' were penalized. It lasted a week during which the company's workers were persuaded to come out in sympathy on 22 January, when the *Unión Ferroviaria* told management of that intention and asked for its opinion. This was brief and to the point: 'the Company did not recognise that the "Unión Ferroviaria" have the right to declare a stoppage of work on the Railway'.[70] As a result, while some staff at Mejillones continued working, the Chilean employees and workmen at Antofagasta stopped for two days, thus halting the train service completely. On 23

January, the acting intendant, Manuel Vargas, issued a decree, accepting the stevedores' demands and ordering a resumption of work. So the railway went back to normal. Only later was it known that the intendant had acted on secret instructions from the government in Santiago to settle the dispute on the very day that, in Santiago, the military junta was overthrown by the coup inspired by Ibáñez. Interestingly enough, Hunt reported that the *Unión*'s spokesman had 'volunteered the information that the Railway staff had absolutely no claim whatever to put forward and that the stoppage had been arranged simply and solely as a sign of sympathy with the bay workers who were on strike'.[71] In other words, times had changed and changed completely. Whereas previously, as the troubles of 1919 and early 1924 had clearly shown, the FCAB, through pragmatic treatment of labour disputes directly with its workforce, retained their loyalty as a fair employer, national and regional issues now impinged on that relationship, and the company's freedom of action was seriously impaired. Hunt, in Antofagasta, was well aware of the implications of the new role of the state in social and economic affairs, and how it might affect the company. Writing at the beginning of 1925 on the impact of the social laws and growing state intervention in what had hitherto been largely a matter for management and men, he put forward a plan of action to meet the new contingencies. Whereas hitherto,

> . . . the General Manager personally has exercised a very close control over all staff matters, not only in regard to salaries, but also in regard to such matters as the distribution of . . . accommodation, medical attention, messing facilities, clubs, sports etc. In addition, whenever there have been questions with the men, the General Manager personally has always interviewed the men's representatives . . . there is a risk of other important duties such as dealings with our clients, the Government and the local authorities, and the general organization of the Railway, being neglected . . .[72]

His solution, reached after consultation with other provincial companies – the Chilex, and the Antofagasta, Loa and Lautaro Nitrate Companies, all large concerns – was to establish a welfare department under a senior manager to relieve him of staff matters and the distractions to which they often gave rise. 'We are convinced', he wrote, 'that one of the principal reasons why the four large firms mentioned were able to hold their own during the recent stoppage was the existence of their Welfare Departments . . .'.[73] The new laws, he pointed out in a subsequent letter, would require additional staff and more accommodation: the existing offices were already overcrowded and, being constructed of timber, were a fire hazard, particularly since 'in the Administration alone we have an archive containing papers which have accumulated for the last twenty years'.[74] That archive was on the top storey and the weight of paper there had already made necessary the installation of props below. He proposed a new building made of reinforced concrete and reckoned it would cost about £29,000.

To these suggestions, the board agreed, Bolden himself taking a lively personal interest in everything to do with the new legislation and the general welfare of the workforce. It was clear to all that the old paternal relationship between the FCAB and its staff had been overtaken by events, and was no longer enough in the rapidly changing circumstances. The increase in capital and running costs was seen as a justifiable and necessary expenditure if the FCAB was to retain its reputation as a good employer and, indeed, keep pace with other foreign concerns, and notably the Chilex at Chuquicamata, in the provision of social services for the staff.

Despite such improvements, however, labour unrest continued during 1925 against the backdrop of the unsettled political situation and the implementation of the new laws. On 13 February, a general strike struck Valparaíso, the result of workers' demands on poor housing, which led to a Decree-Law reducing rents on accommodation deemed by sanitary inspectors to be unhygenic, 'legislation which the Government are evidently framing and promulgating as a result of pressure brought upon them by the working classes'.[75] In March, management refused to accept a demand by the *Unión Ferroviaria* to dismiss a worker in Mejillones, who did not belong to it, after his involvement in a fight with a member of the *Unión*, and later in the month workers of the Nitrate Railways Company put in demands for wage increases of up to 60 per cent, threatening to involve employees in other concerns, including the FCAB. At the same time, bay workers in Mejillones were on strike from 10 to 24 March for an increase in piecework wages: though an interim solution was found, the men struck again in May and only returned to work on 8 June, with increases of from 30 per cent to 35 per cent. In April, there was serious trouble in the nitrate *oficinas* as strikes took place both in protest at the companies' dismissal of 'agitators' and in furtherance of wage claims, while Chuquicamata had a strike from 29 April to 3 May, on the insistence of management to dismiss workers regarded as 'revolutionary and a bad element in the camp'.[76]

The successive governments in power after Alessandri resigned in 1925 until Ibáñez assumed control in 1927 were somewhat ambivalent in their attitude to labour questions. While supporting the new laws to benefit the workers, they were unequivocally opposed to "agitators", and the firmness of employers in the north on that issue reflected that fact. Hunt commented in the middle of 1925:

> The military are taking advantage of the state of siege [martial law, declared that month as a precaution in Antofagasta] to clear the nitrate oficinas of all

> persons of a revolutionary character. They are being arrested and transported to the South and some of the worst characters have been taken on board a warship in the bay. Although some hundreds of people have been dealt with in this way during the last few days there have been no disturbances of a serious nature.[77]

He, however, took no severe action with regard to the workers of the FCAB until its most acute labour problem of 1925 erupted at the end of September.

On the 26th of that month, management received a general petition from all employees and workmen asking for the additional surcharge on wages (the sliding scale related to the value of the peso) to be replaced by a fixed addition of 40 per cent for those with salaries up to $400 a month and 30 per cent for those above that rate. On advice sent from London by cable this was refused on 1 October and a strike was called that evening. On that very day, President Alessandri resigned and the Intendent of Antofagasta, Lt-Col. Jiménez, urged the company to concede the men's demands in view of the national situation but, fully supported by London, Hunt refused on the ground that to yield under duress would simply lead to more exorbitant claims being made. Nor, despite considerable pressure from the intendant and the prefect of police, was he prepared to accept arbitration which, as it happened, the men also rejected. However, in order to break the deadlock in discussions, and with London's approval, he put to the intendent on 3 October a compromise proposal, guaranteeing to maintain the sliding scale on the peso previously agreed until 1 April 1926, and that if by then Chile's recently established Central Bank were working with exchange fixed at anywhere between $39 and $42 to the pound, the company would annul the sliding scale mechanism and grant a 20 per cent fixed increase to salaries and wages. This, 'the men indignantly refused and stated that their representatives were not empowered to discuss any other proposal than the 40 per cent and 30 per cent fixed increase'.[78] The strike continued but a skeleton train service to run provisions to the *oficinas* was run by the English personnel, assisted by troops provided by Jiménez. On 5 October, the Acting Intendant of Iquique, Colonel Enrique Bravo, arrived at Antofagasta and, as Jiménez's superior officer, took over the intendency and assumed command of the regional forces.

What exacerbated the local situation was the coincidence of the railway strike with a national crisis after Alessandri resigned, handing power to the Minister of the Interior, who sought to get all the parties in Santiago to agree on a single candidate, Figueroa, as president. But the Minister of War, Carlos Ibáñez, initially disagreed, even going so far as to issue a proclamation, calling for elections to be postponed until the parties had been cleansed of corruption. The high commands of the army and navy split on the issue, the navy supporting Figueroa and opposing

Ibáñez, and 'the general public opinion was that it was only a few hours before the commencement of an armed conflict with the Army on one side and the Navy on the other'.[79] It was in this heady atmosphere that Bravo urged Hunt to accept arbitration in the company's dispute with its men, fearing that the national political crisis would be reflected in worse regional disturbances. A flurry of cables passed between Hunt and London from 5 to 13 October, as he recognized the gravity of the situation and looked for a reasonable solution. On the latter date, he sought and secured the board's approval for an improved offer to the men, namely 30 per cent and 20 per cent increase for the different grades, pointing out subsequently that under the sliding scale arrangement with the recent improvement in exchange lower paid men were taking home less pay:

> There is no doubt [he wrote] that this reduction of salary in the case of all the lower grade men had a good deal to do in creating the atmosphere suitable for a strike, and, although looking at it from a gold point of view, the reduction is perfectly explicable, it is very difficult to defend against public opinion based on a currency outlook . . .[80]

There followed an extraordinarily long and fruitless round of negotiations, involving the intendant, in which the men adamantly stuck to their claim for more than the company had been prepared to pay, namely increases of 35 per cent and 25 per cent but less than their original demand for fixed increases of 40 per cent and 30 per cent. During this period, and after consultation with the managers of the larger nitrate works, Hunt refused to accept arbitration as proposed by Colonel Bravo and was backed by the managers, much to the latter's annoyance. Finally, the exasperated Colonel informed Hunt that he had no further recourse than to involve central government. This was on 17 October, by which time the political crisis in Santiago had blown over and the threat of civil war had faded with Ibáñez agreeing to the compromise candidature of Figueroa.

But when the Minister of the Interior replied to Bravo's cable, it was to request the company to accept the men's latest claim, and, if it would, a recompensing proportionate increase in traffic tariffs would be proposed. Since 'it would be a very serious thing indeed for us to refuse such a request from the Government' and since the latter had implicitly accepted the company's financial arguments by itself suggesting a *quid pro quo* on tariffs, there seemed to Hunt 'to be no other course but to accept'.[81] At the same time, he insisted that the men return to work at once, that they should receive no pay for the three weeks the strike had lasted, and should make no other claim of any kind on the company. These terms were accepted, and most of the men returned to work, but feelings against non-strikers ran high for some time though when management 'discharged three of the ring-leaders', including Ramón Alzamora, 'as a protest against the lack of discipline and the disorder in the work', a threatened strike for their reinstatement did not materialize.

Although labour problems in the next few years were not as severe as in 1925, that year was, in effect, a watershed in the company's relations with government. While the social laws of 1924 were subsequently frequently amended, their implementation involved a sizeable growth in the bureaucracy, and – together with other legislation – gave to ministers and officials, no matter what government was in power, a much greater say than hitherto in the running of companies like the FCAB. The cost implications had to be kept under review by private concerns, but much more time-consuming for management was the intervention of new officials and statutory bodies in their affairs, thus adding considerably to their other preoccupations. Running the railway as a profitable business was often difficult enough, given the terrain over which the lines ran and the climatic regions they crossed, making problems of maintenance a permanent concern. So were good relations with customers, actual or potential, in the periodic fixing of appropriate tariffs for their freight, and providing passengers on an important international line with a high standard of service. Moreover, as we have seen, as a large employer of both native and expatriate staff with varied skills and functions, the company faced an increasingly complex problem of personnel management, now often involving the authorities at both regional and national level. Finally, in all these tasks, effective public relations, and, therefore, the company's public image to a wide variety of interests, was also a basic ingredient. And although, as mineral-exporting economies, reliant to a high degree on foreign capital, both Chile and Bolivia did not have complete freedom of manoeuvre in relations with overseas interests, successive governments in both countries had considerable scope in seeking to expand the role of the state in the national economy, often at the expense of those interests.

Throughout the 1920s nitrate exports remained of crucial importance in Chilean finances, the export tax on the fertilizer being the largest item on the income side of the budget. But since the First World War, when Germany's reliance on Chile for supplies was cut off by the Allied blockade, that country had pioneered the development of synthetic nitrate and set an example many other countries were to follow. The growth of the synthetic market posed the greatest threat to the natural product, and hence to Chilean national income, though international supply and demand in the nitrate business had always fluctuated markedly since its primary value as a fertilizer turned on the vagaries of international agriculture. With synthetic nitrate being increasingly produced, that imponderable factor was compounded by cost considerations, as buyers naturally sought the cheapest source. As a result, the Chilean government adopted a more interventionist stance in national nitrate affairs, affecting both producers and carriers of the fertilizer, though in the long run the growth of synthetic competition proved inexorable.

As a major carrier of nitrate to the coast, and principal supplier of the industry's needs, not least water, in the province of Antofagasta, the FCAB took a keen interest in the subject. By the late 1920s, however, though still very important in its operations and profits, nitrate was losing its former critical importance for the company, as other mineral traffic, notably from Bolivia and Chuquicamata, continued to increase. In 1924, for example, its lines carried 42 per cent less nitrate than in 1925, amounting to a fall in gross receipts of over £320,000: nevertheless, dividends were kept at their previous level, owing not only to the rise in other mineral traffic but also due to a reduction in running costs as local management strove to effect economies by laying off redundant staff and stopping all but essential operations. With reserves still in a healthy state, it was not thought necessary to add to them despite the difficulties of that year. The nitrate industry recovered somewhat in 1927 and with good traffics in the tin of Bolivia and the copper of Chuquicamata, coupled with further reductions in running costs, again a satisfactory dividend was paid to stockholders. But while the company thus gained on the roundabouts of other minerals what it lost on the swings of nitrate, the Chilean government was not in a similar position. Neither were the producers whose nitrate the railway carried. Together they were a powerful combination.

In 1925, after the serious strike in October, the company had not thought it opportune to take up the government offer of an increase in tariffs to compensate for its acceptance of the wage claim. In 1926, however, with results by the middle of the year not looking good, it prepared a request for an increase of 10 per cent on existing rates, but this was fiercely opposed by the nitrate interest through the Association of Nitrate Producers. This not only opposed any increase at all in railway tariffs but itself petitioned the government to arrange for a reduction of 20 per cent in existing freight charges, having previously urged the government to reduce the export tax on nitrate, its chief source of revenue. As the President of the Association, Mr Jones, pointed out to Hunt, who was then on a visit to Santiago, they could hardly expect government to cut export taxes for producers if the latter then had to add to their costs through higher charges on freights. In the light of this, and the then deteriorating nitrate situation, Hunt recommended that the tariff request be withdrawn as a gesture of goodwill towards the government, and the board in London agreed. At the time, the Chile Exploration Company was contemplating seeking a concession from government to build its own line from Chuquicamata to the port of Tocopilla, thus posing a serious threat to the FCAB's traffic to Antofagasta and while the company had, under its original concessions, strong legal arguments against that course, both Hunt and the board felt their hand would be strengthened by the withdrawal of the claim on a tariff increase.

Though this was done, and was suitably appreciated, the Chilean government had its own ideas for helping the beleaguered nitrate industry without cutting export taxes as the Association urged. In addition, in August 1926, the latter applied to the Chief Inspector of Railways for a reduction of 20 per cent in the tariffs of the Nitrate Railways Company in Tarapacá, the Taltal Railway, another important carrier, and of the FCAB, and published the matter in the Chilean press, much to Hunt's disgust. While the application remained in abeyance, national politics again intervened. In February 1927, Carlos Ibáñez engineered the resignation of the cabinet and his own appointment as Minister of the Interior, formed a new ministry composed of able and trusted supporters, and began a programme of sweeping administrative and economic reform. As Minister of Finance, he chose Pablo Ramírez, one of whose first acts was to meet representatives of the Association

> to discuss immediate steps to be taken in order to re-open the nitrate oficinas which have suspended work. He opened the meeting by saying that so long as he was Minister of Finance it was quite useless for them to expect any reduction in the export duty, but that he would be glad to assist them in other ways, such as by reducing the import duties on . . . commodities which they require for elaborating nitrate. He also promised that he would obtain for them a rebate in the tariffs of those railways serving the nitrate districts . . . [82]

When, a few months later, the unhappy president, Figueroa, resigned, and Ibáñez took his place after a special presidential election in May with 98 per cent of the votes cast, Ramírez was confirmed in his post. By then, however, he had already acted.

On 11 April, at a meeting with representatives of the nitrate-carrying railways, Ramírez requested 'for reasons of national convenience a general reduction of 10 per cent in the railway freights' to and from the *oficinas* for the period to 31 December 1928.[83] While Hunt carefully marshalled the arguments against the reduction for the benefit of the board, he pointed out the dangers of opposing the request too strenuously, and a flat refusal might lead the government to

> . . . annul all the decrees authorising increases in tariffs since the year 1916, and then fix for each Railway the tariffs which in the opinion of the Government are equitable. We can hardly believe that the Government would adopt such

extreme measures . . . but we must not lose sight of the fact that the present Government is virtually a dictatorship . . . Should we eventually agree to concede something, we think it would be only just and reasonable to ask the Government to give us, during the time the rebate is in force, an assurance that there shall be no increase in our expenses by new taxation, either direct or indirect . . . [84]

Though the railway companies had been given six weeks' to reply, the period was none too long, since their respective boards and local managements agreed that a common strategy was essential, and there followed a series of consultations both in Chile and in London. Finally, each company prepared its own memorandum, arguing against the reduction in the light of its particular circumstances but taking care to say nothing indicating either a refusal or an acceptance. Assuming that the minister would stick to his guns, at interviews to be arranged with him in Santiago, the companies agreed on common conditions of acceptance, such as the temporary nature of the reduction and no increase in taxation. When the interviews took place at the end of May and the beginning of June, the minister did, indeed, maintain his position on freight rates, though he did accept a period of one year rather than eighteen months from 1 July, 1927, for the lower rate to apply, and promised due consideration of all the other points made. The cordial nature of the proceedings was recorded by Hunt when he wrote:

> It is, of course, most unfortunate that we have had to sacrifice a portion of our profits, but we think . . . that we have got out of a very difficult situation at a minimum cost, and that we have created a very favourable atmosphere with the present Government . . . [85]

These sentiments were echoed by the chairman at the AGM in the same month but, as matters turned out, their confidence in the government was quite misplaced.

During the course of the long discussions on the nitrate tariff question, the minister's hand had been strengthened by the deliberations in Congress concerning a new law creating the Superintendency of Nitrate and Iodine, a proposed government agency giving very wide powers to the new body and underlining the intention of the Ibáñez government to have a large say in anything to do with the industry in future. As originally drafted, the proposals included an article giving the force of law to the suggested temporary tariff reductions but, as part of his deal with the carriers, the minister undertook to delete that article and, in fact, did so. Had this not happened, all the railway companies would have been exposed to the threat that in future government could claim the right to fix its own tariffs for carriage, ignoring the fact that the basis of the companies' freight charges was the original concessions under which the railways had been built, and around which a large body of procedure had emerged over time. Obviously, the raising or lowering of tariffs was a matter for discussion with government at any particular juncture and, broadly speaking, compromise had generally ruled and justice was done in the eyes of both parties. That understanding had now been threatened by recent events, and was to be so again. Hunt wrote in July 1927:

> . . . the Chilean Government are now very much alive to the fact that they are virtually partners in the Nitrate Industry, and we can be quite sure that the new Government Nitrate Committee which is being created by law will not miss any opportunity of exercising its rights . . . of close inspection and control over the rates charged by carriers . . . our tariffs generally will be very closely watched . . . and any reduction we propose for other commodities will be used as an argument in favour of a reduction in the nitrate tariff . . .[86]

While, so far as was practicable, the FCAB had sought throughout to have uniform tariffs on its lines for the commodities, it made its own contracts with customers, the more important of whom, such as the Huanchaca Company in the early days and the Chilex in the 1920s, might for particular reasons seek, and be given, specific agreements. Hitherto, government had not intervened in such business matters, apart from exercising its legal right under Chilean railway legislation to approve any modifications to the agreed tariff structure, and Ramírez had acted correctly in *requesting* the FCAB and the other carriers to accept a *temporary* reduction in freights for nitrate which took the form not of actually changing the tariff book but by the granting of *rebates* to the nitrate producers of 10 per cent on nitrate itself, a similar amount on coal, and 15 per cent on oil fuel. Both the fixed period for these concessions, and the fact that they were rebates on tariffs underline the *voluntary* nature of the companies' co-operation with government whose agent, the Minister of Finance, had recognized that situation by not pressing for a mandatory law. But, as Hunt and, indeed, the board in London feared what had been done once could be done again.

Long before the end of June 1928, the expiry date of the nitrate rebate system, there were clear signs that the government intended to squeeze the railways by making a temporary arrangement more permanent. In October 1927, it set up a committee of three engineers, 'one from the Railway Inspection Department, one from the Superintendence of Nitrate . . . and one from the Inland Revenue Department . . . to study the tariffs which should definitely be established on the nitrate-carrying railways for the transport of nitrate, coal and petroleum'.[87] Six months later, after an interview with the Superintendent of Nitrate, Señor Delcourt, Hunt reported on the possibility of pressure on the railways to continue the rebates beyond the stipulated date, at a time when the Nitrate Producers' Association was working on another petition to government for a further reduction in freight tariffs in addition to the temporary rebates, a proposal which he thought 'would have the tacit, if not the active support of the Chilian Government'.[88]

That government had by then committed itself wholeheartedly to supporting nitrate producers in Chile in any price war with synthetics, through cost-cutting and subsidies, and part of the programme involved the carriers. In May, they received a request from the Superintendent of Nitrate, speaking for the Minister of Finance, to continue the rebate system for a further year on the argument that government efforts to assist the industry had resulted in increased output and exports, thus giving the carriers an increased tonnage to offset the cost of the rebate system. After discussion with the representatives of other carriers, Hunt found it difficult to refute this argument entirely, pointing out that:

> The tonnage of nitrate transported on the Antofagasta Railway for the ten months from the 1st July, 1927, until the 30th April, 1928, was 622,904 tons, which is the biggest tonnage . . . transported in the corresponding ten months during the last nine years, . . . it is difficult to deny that the Railway has benefitted by the measures which have been adopted by the Government to reorganize the Nitrate Industry . . .[87]

How far the rebates had contributed to that result he was not sure.

On that issue, however, the board was quite emphatic. Having agreed the rebates on quite definite terms, and in deference to the government, it was not disposed to extend the concession beyond 30 June, and Hunt was instructed to make that plain. This was also the attitude of the other chief carrier, the Nitrate Railways Company, which was in constant touch with the FCAB in London. Hunt framed his reply to government accordingly but with mixed feelings

> . . . as we felt that there was no doubt that it would be very badly received . . . and would probably create a very difficult situation as between the Government and ourselves . . . we are of opinion that it would be bad policy to start a serious question . . . at the present time . . . in view of the very strong public sympathy which the Government would have . . .[88]

At about the same time, the Nitrate Railways Company received an official reply to its refusal to continue the rebates, coupled with the threat that if it did not change its mind a law would be passed by Congress to fix the rebates which might then be increased. In the light of this information, Hunt held back his reply while consulting London again, and in his very full report on the matter pointed out that the publication in the Chilean papers of reports of the profits made in 1927 by both the Nitrate Railways and the FCAB

> very much increase the diffculty we have in convincing the Government that the financial position of the Railways does not allow the continuance of the rebates ... The present Minister of Finance is kept very well informed on such matters ...[89]

The board, however, remained adamant, and Hunt rehearsed its arguments with Delcourt at a meeting in Santiago on 15 June though, while the atmosphere was cordial enough, the Superintendent gave no ground, insisting that the rebates be continued and that the railway companies agree by 20 June: otherwise, a law enforcing government policy would be sent to Congress on 21 June and there was little doubt it would be passed. He did undertake, however, to put to the minister a suggestion from the board that if, perforce, rebates had to be continued, the FCAB might receive some compensation in the form of lower tariffs on certain imports such as rolling stock.

That also proved to be a protracted business, but on the rebate issue, no matter how affable conversations of company representatives and government officials might be, the latter held the whip hand. In 1928, the FCAB, along with the others, caved in, agreeing to continue rebates until the end of that year and, in the event, after further similar negotiations and pressures, to the end of 1929. The agreements were made under protest and there was some comfort to the company in the wording of the decree for the first extension of the system, which made explicit that it resulted from an accord between government and the railways, 'thus maintaining the principle that modification of our tariffs can only be made after obtaining our agreement'.[90] But these were idle words: a determined government, such as that of Ibáñez in the late 1920s, could always threaten foreign companies like the FCAB as hostages to fortune, no matter what legal or constitutional means were available for defence. In that respect, the debates on rebates for the nitrate industry in the late 1920s were a portent: future governments, under growing social and economic pressure, would be no less reluctant to use their power.

The fight by the FCAB on rebates was much more a matter of principle than of price. At the AGM on 11 June 1929, the chairman, now A.W. Bolden, who had taken over in March 1928, after Lord Lawrence had died in December 1927, estimated that the cost of the rebate scheme to the company would amount to over £150,000 by the end of 1929:

> ... large amounts to us in the aggregate ... not only lost gross receipts, but all lost profit; calculated over the tonnage of nitrate produced and transported

> over our lines, it means about 1s 9d per ton, which could scarcely in itself affect the sale of nitrate in one way or other ...[91]

He emphasized, however, that the company's tradition of service to the countries in which it operated was a guiding principle in its business there, based on the mutual interests of both parties.

The rebate issue of the 1920s offers a classical illustration of the new complexities faced by the company in its dealings with government but the example it provides of the time-consuming and tortuous negotiations involved could be duplicated in other matters. The Ibáñez government had set its sights on nothing less than the regeneration of Chile, creating in the process a whole new range of policies and new instruments to put them into effect, many of which survived the regime itself. And, while economic policies were based on the encouragement of foreign capital, its entry and operation in the country were to be regulated and governed by more clearly defined terms in accordance with what government saw as the national interest. Moreover, Ibáñez had come to power with a promise of administrative reform, and his team was imbued with unprecedented zeal not only in implementing new legislation but also in investigating the existing state of affairs. Consequently, and not least for foreign companies operating on long-standing concessions, management was often faced with vexatious questions in defending their interests, involving much more discussion with government officials and hence a far heavier work-load than before.

So far as the FCAB was concerned, it would be tedious to catalogue the numerous contentious issues raised by government representatives in the period, and one example must suffice. A particularly complicated issue arose over that part of the Longitudinal Railway operated by the FCAB on account of the Chilean Northern Railway Co. At the end of 1927, the Comptroller General of the Republic set up a commission of three to look into the accounts of the line as well as those of the Antofagasta Railway. Unfortunately, it was headed by a certain Señor Armando Fabregas, a former employee of the FCAB, who early in 1926 had accused the company of falsifying its books and charging the state-owned Longitudinal Railway with expenses properly chargeable to the Antofagasta Railway. At that time, and after an inspection by appropriate officials, the accusation was refuted and Fabregas was subsequently dismissed for incompetence. Now, armed with his new credentials, he sought to re-open the whole issue, but acted so arrogantly that the company protested to the Comptroller who replaced him by the more conciliatory Enrique Pérez de Arce. Even so, the affair dragged on for a full two years, as the various reports of the commission were considered by different government departments and as the company's general manager argued its case, often in meetings with ministers in

Santiago. Changes in official personnel over the period did not help, and the volume of correspondence between Hunt in Chile and Bolden in London on the various issues raised testifies to the complexity of the affair and the difficulty in reaching an accord. The essence of the dispute was the system of book-keeping used by the FCAB for the accounts of the Northern Railway, providing inquisitive, not to say inquisitorial, officials with ample scope to raise all kinds of matters related to its running. These all needed the painstaking attention of management, its accountants and legal advisers. On the question of the Northern Railway, discrepancies in accounting practices were finally ironed out and a compromise formula adopted for the future, but the whole business had taken an inordinate amount of time, paperwork and money. It had, however, been necessary in the company's interests, in defence of which no less attention had to be given in the period to a large number of other differences with government, ranging from taxation to the company's ownership of land-grants made under earlier decrees but now subject to revision. On one matter, however, concerning both the national interest and the company's business, they reached complete accord: this was the conversion of the gauge of the main line and branches of the Chilean section of the Antofagasta railway from 2 feet 6 inches to one metre, a major undertaking of railway engineering and one of which all those associated with it were justifiably proud.

All change on the line

The question of widening the main line had been discussed by the board of the FCAB for some years before a definite decision was taken. This was in 1913, at the height of the nitrate boom in the years before the First World War when the company's business in Chile was expanding rapidly, and the reasons for changing the gauge from 2 feet 6 inches to one metre were cogent enough: as the then-chairman, the Hon. C.N. Lawrence, told the AGM on 10 June that year:

> That the wider gauge must be adopted at some time is a certainty and the longer it is put off the more expensive it would become, because in any case we would be compelled to provide new Rolling Stock to cope with our growing traffic and renew our tracks, which, in some parts, are old and of a light weight of rail. With the wider gauge we shall secure greater capacity, effect economy in working and be able to improve the speed of the passenger service ...[92]

He also pointed out that this would avoid the break of gauge at Uyuni in Bolivia where the original line from Antofagasta met the Bolivian railway system of one metre gauge, passengers had to change trains, and traffic had to be transhipped. Other reasons for the change of gauge in both Bolivia and Chile were that the governments of both countries wished to have the one metre system in operation in the national network.

The Chilean government authorized the change on its side of the frontier on 13 December 1913, by a decree of the Minister of Railways, and the FCAB began the work at once, ordering new rolling stock and beginning the conversion of its modern 2 feet 6 inches stock to make it suitable for the wider gauge. At that time, it was anticipated that the main line from the Bolivian frontier to Antofagasta and Mejillones, as well as the branch lines running from it, would all be converted by the middle of 1916. But the outbreak of the First World War in August 1914 put an immediate stop to the work on the Chilean side, though not on the Bolivian, 'so as to have only one break on the system and avoid the changes at the various points where our own lines join those of the Bolivia Railway Company'.[93] In fact, the metre gauge line of just over 300 kilometres between Uyuni and Oruro came into operation in February 1916. The Chilean section, however, posed far greater problems of coversion, the main line was longer and had more branches, and, in the uncertain business and financial climate of the early years of the war, the board thought it best to postpone that part of the operation. Consequently, it first put back and then, in 1915, cancelled the contracts it had made with British suppliers of material for the conversion operation in Chile. Not until 1926 was the work resumed and there were several reasons for this, some related to the high prices of materials and rolling stock in the immediate post-war years, others to the recurrent crises in the nitrate industry, particularly in 1919 and 1921. In the meantime, however to alleviate the problem of transhipment of freight at Uyuni, 'a bogie-changing apparatus was installed (there), by means of which the bodies of the wagons were lifted by jacks and the bogies changed according to the gauge of the track on which the vehicles were to run to their destination'.[94]

Yet, in the post-war period, while the question of conversion to metre gauge was always on the board's agenda, the company was in no great hurry to undertake it, and there were several valid reasons for this. First, the existing gauge – narrow though it was compared to both the metre gauge and the British standard of 4 feet 8½ inches – proved remarkably satisfactory for the traffic it carried, both passengers and freight. The width of the sleeping and dining coaches on the international service to and from Antofagasta was three times the gauge; nevertheless, 'the standard of comfort in the passenger stock was as high if not higher than anywhere else in the Andes'.[95] As for goods, some twenty-two tons of nitrate, for example, could be carried safely on a wagon of just over seven tons tare, that is three times the paying load to the tare of the wagon. The existing rolling stock, kept in good repair by the company's workshops in Chile and Bolivia, still had in the early 1920s several more years of work in it while the costs of converting it did not seem worth the candle. Moreover, it was recognized that the capital cost of conversion would be quite considerable and, at the time, it seemed doubtful that it would be fully justified by the economic advantages it might bring, unless a large amount of new rolling stock were ordered in addition to the new rails, switches and so on that metre gauge would entail. Indeed, as late as the middle of 1925, the general manager at Antofagasta, Hunt, was somewhat doubtful whether the outlay involved would be worth all that much: commenting on reports from his senior technical staff, he said of the chief mechanical engineer (Mr Hilary R. Hood) that

> . . . the principal economy which he expects in his department's expenses would be that resulting from the acquisition of more powerful and up-to-date locomotives.
>
> The Resident Engineer does not anticipate that the conversion will cause any marked economy in the expenses of his department, while the Traffic Manager does not prophesy any particular economy . . . until the present . . . rolling stock is replaced by metre gauge rolling stock of greater carrying capacity . . . [96]

He did add, however, an interesting comment on the relationship of conversion to the impact on costs of the 'social laws':

> A point which has not been touched upon by the Traffic Manager is that of increased speed which will be made possible by the change to metre gauge. With the new laws which shorten the hours of labour, increased speed becomes of some financial importance, in that it might make it possible to decrease the expenditure in overtime . . . [97]

Despite that point, his conclusion was 'that the expenditure cannot be justified economically', and he was quite right. With its existing gauge and with a highly professional staff of engineers and, on the whole, a loyal workforce, the system had coped remarkably well with the increased traffic of the war-time boom and the better years of the post-war decade. The bottleneck of transhipment at Uyuni was a nuisance but nothing more since it took only three or four minutes to change the bogies for each wagon, fully loaded, for the appropriate gauge of its destination. In the light of all these circumstances, the board agreed with the recommendation of its local general manager 'to wait and see', supported, in fact, by a decree of the Chilean government of 16 October 1923, agreeing to postpone the date for completion of conversion on the section from Antofagasta to Mejillones until 22 December 1926, and on the line from Baquedano to the Bolivian frontier at Ollagüe, including branches, until 22 December 1928. At that time, the government of the day fully accepted the company's explanations for the delay, namely 'difficulties resulting from war conditions and post-war conditions', but, as the critical dates got nearer, the pressure on the company from the government increased. Moreover, the arguments of the latter for conversion to metre gauge had already been bolstered by the company's earlier agreement, in taking over the Chilean Northern Railway Company in 1919, to lay a third rail of metre gauge between Antofagasta and Baquedano where the state-owned Chilean Longitudinal intersected the Antofagasta railway: this had been completed in June 1921, giving through connection south to Santiago, Valparaiso and beyond, and north to Iquique.

Another factor in delaying the conversion north of Baquedano was the fear that this would lead to pressure from the government for permission to run its metre gauge trains on the company's lines and thus raise the spectre of competition for its traffic. Hunt was much exercised by this question in 1924 when the Minister of Railways sent a note via the FCAB's representative in Santiago, Señor García de la Huerta,

> ... expressing the Government's interest in an early completion of the metre gauge conversion, particularly on the section from Baquedano to Calama, and asking us to report upon the progress of the work ... this might be the "thin end of the wedge" and their next request might be that we should allow their trains to run to Antofagasta and possibly up our central nitrate zone ...[98]

And he referred to conversations he had had previously with officials about the company's lease of that part of the Longitudinal Railway which it operated under the Chilean Northern Railway Company: they had hinted that 'it might be convenient to them to take over the ... Railway before the termination of the time stipulated in the contract'. 'All this' [he continued]

> seems to indicate that they may be building the foundation for a future policy of penetration into our system with State Railway metre gauge trains, either for commercial reasons or possibly military reasons ... So long as we do not convert the line North of Baquedano ... the Chilian State Railways cannot possibly insist on an interchange arrangement, as they could not, of course, run their metre gauge trains over our 2′ 6″ line ...[99]

Summing up his reasons for recommending a cautious posture, he added:

> There is no question that the party which is at present in power is strongly in favour of "Chili for the Chilians" ... and while from the point of view

> of the Chilian Government such a policy may appear attractive, it is necessary for us to do everything possible to protect our interests and not allow our business to be prejudiced by any competition on the part of the Chilian State Railway trains which might penetrate into our system.[100]

In his long and considered reply, the managing director, A.W. Bolden, accepted the force of the argument while presenting his own. He pointed out that a large amount had already been spent on the conversion in the yards at Antofagasta, on a certain length of two-gauge track between that port and Mejillones, and the completion of the work from Antofagasta to Baquedano. More importantly, the concession for the change of gauge stipulated that the interchange of traffic with the Longitudinal over the whole of the FCAB's system should be based on Argentine practice, namely that the company owning the lines passed over did the entire haulage, took the whole of the tariff and paid to the company owning the wagons an agreed figure for their use based on a rate per wagon axle. The real danger here would probably be agitation to lower tariffs from such interest groups as agriculturalists and government officials. That was a risk but, should the FCAB not complete the conversion, that would be

> ... a sufficient excuse for the Chilian Government if they thought well to do so to construct a metre gauge line from Baquedano northwards through our Nitrate district ... There could be, we think, some very plausible arguments brought forward of the necessity for the Government constructing such a line ... It could be said that we had contemplated giving what the Government required, that is, metre gauge facilities, that we had made an agreement with the Government ... and that we had now broken our word and therefore the Government must do the work themselves by having their own line. The argument would be somewhat unanswerable and it is obvious what intense competition would result ...[101]

This seemed to the board a greater evil than completing the change of gauge on the company's own lines, if possible 'in our own time'.

In the event, that is precisely what happened, and the dates for completion stipulated in the decree of 1923 were kept. From the middle of 1926 it was 'all systems go' as the FCAB embarked on the biggest and most complex engineering operation it had ever undertaken. On the European side, orders were placed for new locomotives, wagons and rails, though the board's intention of ordering all the new material from British workshops was partly thwarted by the dislocations arising from the General Strike of 1926, and some rails came from Belgium. In Chile and Bolivia, meticulous planning was essential if undue interference to traffic were to be avoided during the work, and it was also necessary to convert existing rolling stock to metre gauge, a mammoth task which fell on the workshops at Mejillones which had to cope with 61 locos, 103 coaches and 2,140 wagons, as well as the assembly of the imported material. 'The problem to be solved was to adapt the programme so that sufficient rolling stock for both gauges would be available for traffic requirements at all stages of the work'.[102] Thus, the plans allowed for certain sections of the main line to remain with the third rail laid to metre gauge to enable traffic to be handled on both gauges until the work was finished, and for other sections – some 173 kilometres of track on the Bolivian side, and 113 kilometres on the Chilean – for the track to be spread. A mere six days was allowed for the latter task and permission was obtained from the Chilean and Bolivian governments to close the main line to international traffic from 5 to 10 July 1928, for that final operation to take place. Suffice to say that, thanks partly to good weather in a region between 10,000 and 13,000 feet above sea-level where storms are frequent, and to the enthusiasm and hard work of the thirty-five gangs which had been formed to carry out the work, the schedule was kept, and the first through metre gauge international train left Antofagasta for La Paz on the evening of 10 July. Reporting on that event, Hunt graphically described the festivities:

> The station had been decorated with the flags of the British, Chilian and Bolivian nationalities and special lighting was arranged so that the public could get a good view of the locomotive and coaching stock . . . we arranged a commemorative ceremony at the station prior to the train's departure. The "Intendente" of the Province, the "Alcalde", other authorities, and the more prominent business people of the town were invited . . .[103]

After appropriate speeches had been given,

> . . . the train left for its destination to the accompaniment of enthusiastic cheering and music by the Band of the "Esmeralda" Regiment, which the "Comandante" kindly lent for the occasion . . .[104]

Complete metre-gauge working was instituted on 6 December 1928, actually two months before the schedule laid down, and it was rightly said

> . . . that the formidable task was accomplished without accident or inconvenience to the Company's numerous clients is a tribute to the officers and staff responsible for the successful termination of a work the most difficult perhaps in the Company's annals . . .[105]

This, the board recognized in paying a bonus to over 100 of its staff who, in Hunt's words, 'have by their special efforts contributed to the successful carrying out of this important and complicated work, and have by ingenuity and attention to detail saved the Company many thousands of pounds'.[106] As it was, Bolden reported to the AGM on 11 June 1929:

> ... altogether to December 31st last the total expenditure was some £1,170,000, of which we calculate some £800,000 represented the capital proportion of the work governed by the increased weight of rails, the new switches and crossings, the enlarging of banks and cuttings, and new rolling stock, as apart from renewal, and the cost of conversion of 2ft. 6in. rolling stock to metre gauge etc. About £150,000 remains to be spent and of this we calculate some two-thirds will be the capital proportion ...[107]

For that outlay, the company had carried out its promise to the Chilean government and avoided the danger of a competing line being built. It had also improved its service, cutting the journey time from Antofagasta to La Paz from 42 to 31 hours and eliminating the need for passengers to change at Uyuni. Despite earlier reservations on the economies conversion might bring, the new metre gauge rolling stock was an improvement. The 300 wagons of 10 tons tare could carry 30 tons of freight, and the 23 new tank engines could haul on heavy grades loads which had previously required 2 of the old gauge engines. Moreover, because of the deliberately prudent financial policy of successive Boards in building up both reserves and renewal funds, the money was there to finance the massive operation without either the need to raise fresh capital or reduce dividends.

The 1920s were, indeed, a decade of trials and triumphs for the FCAB. It had weathered the economic and political storms in a turbulent period for the countries in which it operated. And it seemed in 1929 that it could only go from strength to strength, for few could then foresee what lay in store for the world economic system in the years that lay ahead.

Notes

1. Herbert S. Klein, *Parties and Political Change in Bolivia, 1880–1952*, Cambridge University Press 1969, p. 45.
2. J.R. Couyoumdjian, 'Anglo-Chilean Commercial Relations during the First World War and its Aftermath', 1914–1920', Ph.D. thesis, University of London, 1975, p.102. Subsequently published as *Chile y Gran Bretaña durante la guerra mundial y la postguerra, 1914–1921*, Santiago 1986.
3. A.J.P. Taylor, *English History, 1914–1945*, Oxford University Press, 1969, p. 14.
4. General manager to secretary, Antofagasta, 14 August 1914. Private. Confidential.
5. Bill Albert, *South America and the First World War. The impact of the war on Brazil, Argentina, Peru and Chile*, Cambridge University Press, 1988, p.50. Citing other sources.
6. General manager to secretary, 14 August 1914. *loc.cit.* (n.4).
7. *Ibid.*
8. Guillermo Lora, *A History of the Bolivian Labour Movement*, ed. and abridged by Laurence Whitehead and trans. by Christine Whitehead, Cambridge University Press 1977, p. 71.
9. Secretary to general manager, London, 28 August 1914. Private. Letter Book Vol.1. f.27.
10. *Annual Report for 1915*, (1916), p.8.
11. Secretary to general manager, London, 14 August 1914. Letter Book Vol.1., f.257.
12. General manager to secretary, Antofagasta, 28 August, 1914. Private. Official.
13. Secretary to general manager, London, 29 June 1916.
14. *Idem.* to *idem*, London, 8 February 1917. Letter Book Vol. 3. f.264.
15. General manager to secretary, Antofagasta, 26 March, 1915. Letter No. 537.
16. *Idem.* to *idem.*, Antofagasta, 29 May 1915. Private. Official.
17. Klein, *Parties and Political Change, loc. cit.*, p.52.
18. *Report of the Bolivia Railway Company to December 31 1917*, n.p.
19. Secretary to general manager at Antofagasta, London, 11 February 1916. Letter Book Vol. 2, ff.332–3.

20. Secretary to general manager at Antofagasta, London, 25 February 1916. Letter Book Vol.2, f.352.
21. *The Times*, 2 February 1918.
22. London manager and secretary to acting general manager at Antofagasta, London, 21 February 1918. Letter Book Vol.4, ff.196–7.
23. *Idem.* to *idem.*, London, 4 April 1918. Letter Book Vol. 4, ff.241–2.
24. *The Times*, 18 June 1918.
25. *The Times, Company Reports*, 25 June 1919.
26. Managing director to general manager at Antofagasta, London, 14 April 1921. Letter Book, Vol.6., f.453.
27. Acting secretary to general manager at Antofagasta, London, 1 February 1923. Letter Book, Vol.7., f.680, No.248. See also *The Times, Obituaries*, 19 January 1923.
28. Acting general manager to secretary, Antofagasta, 6 November 1914. Letter No. 523 (Staff Memorandum No.179).
29. General manager to secretary, Antofagasta, 3 January 1919. Private, Official.
30. *The Times*, Company Reports, 30 June 1920.
31. General manager to secretary, Antofagasta, 16 April 1919. Private, Official.
32. *Ibid.*
33. General manager to secretary, Antofagasta, 25 July 1919. Private, Official.
34. *Ibid.*
35. *Ibid.*
36. *Ibid.*
37. General manager to secretary, Antofagasta, 7 November 1919. Private, Official.
38. *Ibid.*
39. *Ibid.*
40. General manager to secretary, Antofagasta, 21 November 1919. Private, Official.
41. *Idem.* to *idem*, Antofagasta, 13 January 1920. Private, Official.
42. *Ibid.*
43. *Ibid.*
44. *El Mercurio* of Antofagasta, 2 January 1920.
45. *Ibid.* 3 January 1920.
46. General manager to secretary, Antofagasta, 30 April 1920. Private, Official.
47. *Idem.* to *idem*, Antofagasta, 6 August 1920. Private, Official.
48. Managing director and secretary to general manager at Antofagasta, London, 29 April 1920. Letter Book No.6.
49. *Idem.* to *idem.*, 27 October 1921. Letter Book No.7. Private, Official.
50. General manager to secretary, Antofagasta, 3 December 1920. Private, Official.
51. Managing director and secretary to general manager at Antofagasta, London, 28 October 1920. Letter Book No.6.

52. General manager to secretary, Antofagasta, 9 April 1920. Letter No. 737.
53. *Idem.* to *idem.*, Antofagasta, 21 January 1921. Private, Official.
54. *Idem.* to *idem.*, Antofagasta, 18 March 1921. Private, Official.
55. Extracts from Bolivian manager's report dated La Paz, 7 April 1922. *Annual Report for 1921*, p.22.
56. *Bolivia Railway Company, Annual Report for 1921*, p.5.
57. *The Times, Company Reports*, 21 June 1922.
58. Klein, *Parties and Political Change in Bolivia*, p.71.
59. *The Times, Company Reports,* 17 June 1925.
60. *Ibid.*
61. General manager to managing director, Antofagasta, 8 February 1924. Private. Official.
62. *Ibid.*
63. General manager to managing director, Antofagasta, 22 February 1924. Private. Official.
64. Managing director and secretary to general manager at Antofagasta, London 31 January 1924. Letters to Chilean manager. Private. Official (*Note*: In the Company Archive, numbered letter books end with No.6. in May 1921 until Jan. 1948 when a new enumeration was instituted).
65. *Ibid.*
66. *El Mercurio* of Antofagasta, 28 February 1924 p.3. My translation.
67. General manager to managing director, Antofagasta, 22 February 1924. Private. Official.
68. Managing director to general manager at Antofagasta, London 27 March 1924. Private, Official.
68. General manager to managing director, Antofagasta 24 October 1924. Private. Official.
69. *Idem.* to *idem.*, 5 December 1924. Private, Official.
70. General manager to managing director, Antofagasta, 30 January 1925. Private. Official.
71. *Ibid.*
72. General manager to managing director, Antofagasta, 1 January 1925. Private. Official.
73. *Ibid.*
74. General manager to managing director, Antofagasta, 16 January 1925. Private. Official.
75. *Idem.* to *idem.*, Antofagasta, 27 February 1925. Private. Official.
76. *Idem.* to *idem.*, Antofagasta, 8 May 1925. Private, Official.
77. *Idem.* to *idem.*, Antofagasta, 19 June 1925. Private, Official.
78. *Idem.* to *idem.*, Antofagasta, 25 October 1925. Private. Official.
79. *Ibid.*
80. *Ibid.*
81. *Ibid.*
82. General manager to managing director, Antofagasta, 4 March 1927. Private. Official.
83. *Idem.* to *idem.*, 22 April 1927. Private. Official.
84. *Ibid.*

85. General manager to managing director, Antofagasta, 24 June 1927. Private. Official.
86. *Idem.* to *idem.*, Antofagasta, 8 July 1927. Private. Official.
87. *Idem.* to *idem.*, Antofagasta, 4 November 1927. Private. Official.
88. *Idem.* to *idem.*, 20 April 1928.
87. General manager to managing director, Antofagasta, 25 May 1928. Private, Official.
88. *Idem* to *idem.*, 8 June 1928. Private. Official.
89. *Ibid.*
90. General manager to managing director, Antofagasta, 6 July 1928. Private. Official.
91. *The Times, Company Reports*, 12 June 1929.
92. *FCAB Annual Report for 1912,* p.10.
93. *FCAB Annual Report for 1915*, p.11.
94. *Facts and Views concerning the change of Gauge from 2ft 6ins. to one metre*: the Antofagasta (Chili) and Bolivia Railway Company Limited, June, London 1929, p.5. This 19-page pamphlet was produced to accompany the *Annual Report for 1928*.
95. Fawcett, *Railways of the Andes*, p.118.
96. General manager to managing director, Antofagasta, 22 May 1925. Private. Official.
97. *Ibid.*
98. General manager to managing director, Antofagasta, 13 June 1924. Private. Official.
99. *Ibid.*
100. *Ibid.*
101. Managing director to general manager at Antofagasta, London, 17 July 1924. Private. Official.
102. *Facts and views* . . . p.9.
103. General manager to managing director, Antofagasta, 13 July 1928. Private. Official.
104. *Ibid.*
105. *Facts and views* . . . p.17.
106. General manager to managing director, Antofagasta, 7 December 1928. Private. Official.
107. *The Times, Company Reports*, 12 June 1929.

5
A CRITICAL JUNCTURE 1930–1935

The impact of the world economic crisis, 1930–32: Chile and Bolivia

If the outbreak of the First World War and, likewise, the post-war years of depression were times of crisis for the mineral exporting economies of Chile and Bolivia, in retrospect they appear as mere rehearsals for the traumas which began with the Wall Street crash of late 1929. For both countries, the collapse of foreign markets for their products which ensued was compounded by the drying up of foreign capital and by the heavy indebtedness which they had incurred in the boom years of the later 1920s. By that time, the United States had replaced Europe as the main source of loans and investment, and both President Hernando Siles in Bolivia (1926–30) and President Carlos Ibáñez in Chile (1927–31) relied heavily on that source not least for programmes of public works. But they were also heavily dependent on mineral exports, in Bolivia, tin, and in Chile, nitrate and copper. As a major carrier of all three commodities, so was the FCAB.

Although it was 1930 before the impact of the world economic recession really made itself felt, the writing was on the wall by late 1929, despite the generally good results that year for the company itself. In his annual review of the previous year's working at the AGM in June, 1930, the chairman, A.W. Bolden, could point to the facts of increased traffic over 1928 in all three major commodities, and, in fact, a greater tonnage of tin carried from Bolivia than in any year in the company's history. In consequence, up traffic of materials required for the mining districts of Bolivia and of Chuquicamata had also increased. But he also drew attention to a 'lesser movement of nitrate in the second half of the year and a tendency towards decreasing production', to 'a decreasing tonnage' of copper carried at the same time, and, not least, to the effect of the falling price of tin on output. That decline, caused by world overproduction of tin, began as early as 1927, when its price on the market was US $917 a ton, falling to $794 a ton in 1929 as the depression took hold and reaching $385 a ton in the bottom year of 1932. Even Bolden, an 'old hand' and a remarkably prescient businessman, could not have foreseen how deep the depression would go, how long it would last, and how far it would affect the company he had served so well since 1907 and would continue to do so to the day of his death in 1941. As it was, as chairman and managing director, he bore a heavy responsibility in the company's hardest years, as did all senior managers.

Chile was particularly affected by the impact of the world crisis:

> Not only did Chile's foreign trade suffer severely – it suffered more than that of any other country in the world. In a table prepared by the League of Nations, covering 39 countries "representing about 90 per cent of the total value of world trade", Chile heads the list with respect to percentage decline in the value of both exports and imports between 1929 and 1932 ...[1]

On exports, nitrates and copper were the key elements, as the collapse of prices and demand in the world market for these commodities created a rapid fall in domestic production. Copper production fell from 320,630 tons in 1929 to 103,173 tons in 1932, while in the same period the exported production of nitrate fell precipitously from 2,898,000 tons to a mere 250,000. The export value of these two commodities combined – representing in the late 1920s about 75 per cent of total exports by value – fell from an average of 1,674 million pesos in 1927–29 to 183 million pesos in 1932, that is by no less than 89 per cent.

But if the trade position deteriorated badly, so did the financial situation, an equally eloquent indicator of Chile's economic dependence on the outside world. Here, however, compared with the mining sector, there was a time-lag in the impact of the world economic crisis. Heavy borrowing by the Ibáñez government was the basis of its large public works programme and the key to the country's undoubted well-being to the late 1920s. How far Chile was living beyond its means was exposed in what followed. In 1929, foreign borrowings reached 443 million pesos, and rose further to 682 million in 1930, but in 1931 they fell sharply to 54 million, in 1932 to 22.4 million, and in 1933 to nothing at all. Coupled with a rapid fall in export earnings, this drying up of foreign capital created an acute balance of payments problem, made more severe by charges on the debt. The drain on the Central Bank's reserves to cover the deficit simply could not be sustained: on 15 June 1931, Chile defaulted on her foreign obligations, and on 30 July introduced exchange control to protect the remaining reserves, keep up the external value of the peso, and maintain the inflow of essential imports. Such, in basic outline, was the economic impact of the international crisis on the world's most exposed economy, and the social and political consequences were no less profound.

The mining industry bore the initial brunt of the collapse. Whereas at the end of 1929 some 91,000 men had been employed, mostly in the north, by the end of 1931 the figure had fallen to 31,000, and a common social feature of the period was the desertion of the northern mining camps as the unemployed and their families moved south. While national unemployment statistics for the period are notoriously unreliable, those for the Santiago Labour Exchange show over 68,000 registered as seeking work in January 1932, and almost 129,000 towards the end of the year. There are no statistics for underemployment, of course, though during the depression most employers of labour cut working hours and wages and 'according to one estimate, real statistics fell some 40% from 1929 to 1932, while the price of staples nearly doubled'.[2]

These economic and social characteristics of the period had their inevitable political counterpart in the most confused years in Chilean history since the wars of independence. Its major prop of economic prosperity cut from beneath it, the Ibáñez regime embarked on a widespread programme of retrenchment which served only to fuel discontent further, leading to a hardening of the government's attitude towards its critics. This, again, inflamed popular passions, promoting mass demonstrations and mounting tension which reached its climax on 25 July 1931, with large-scale violence on the streets of Santiago, demands by professional associations for full public liberties, and the death of two protesters. On the 26th, in the face of impending chaos, Ibáñez resigned and went into exile in Argentina, amid wild scenes of public rejoicing. After further disorders, including a mutiny in the fleet, the former vice-president, Juan Estéban Montero, was elected president in October, but his programme of severe economy at a time of deepening economic distress and rising unemployment proved unpopular, and in June, 1932, he was forced out by a coup organized by the head of the air-force, Colonel Marmaduke Grove, Carlos Dávila and Eugenio Matte, an avowed socialist. More confusion followed as, a few days later, Dávila, formerly Chilean ambassador to the United States, was ejected by his co-conspirators only to secure sufficient military backing to turn the tables a week later and exile Grove and Matte to the Pacific island of Más Afuera. A few weeks later, he became provisional president of 'the Socialist republic of Chile', ruling by decree. The republic lasted 100 days but, despite much feverish activity, he had no answer to the country's problems and was, in his turn, ousted by another military coup. The

Socialist republic, however, did put on the statute book a large number of decrees which went unrepealed, and were to be resuscitated in the early 1970s. The organizer of the latest coup, General Bartolomé Blanche, urged on by fellow officers, then handed over power to the President of the Supreme Court, Abraham Oyanedel, who restored constitutional government and organized free congressional and presidential elections on 30 October 1932. The overwhelming victor was that same Arturo Alessandri who, as president in the early 1920s, had sponsored the social laws of 1924 and the constitution of 1925. He now was to preside over six years of stable government and the resuscitation of the Chilean economy after the traumas of the world depression.

Bolivia, too, faced a deepening economic crisis, compounded by a serious and growing international dispute with Paraguay over possession of the Chaco Boreal, a vast, sparsely populated lowland plain, where the frontier between eastern Bolivia and western Paraguay had been ill-defined since the colonial era. The history of the dispute was long and complex: suffice to say that by the 1920s both countries had built forts along the Pilcomayo river to contain penetration by each other's nationals, and these forts became the focal points of increasingly serious border clashes between the forces of both states, and the fuel of nationalist fervour. An arms race ensued, and a serious incident towards the end of 1928, when Paraguayan troops attacked the Bolivian fort of Vanguardia, seemed to threaten outright war. Though this was averted, through the mediation of the United States, and both countries backed down in 1929, each continued war preparations, Bolivia earmarking 20 per cent of its 1929 budget for military purposes. Moreover, in addition to that drain, no less than 37 per cent of the budget was allocated to the service of Bolivia's huge foreign debt.

In these circumstances, the collapse of tin was a catastrophe, and the attempt by President Siles to extend his rule beyond his mandate while coping, ineffectually, with the economic situation, failed completely. The political opposition plotted his removal but it was student rioting in La Paz on 22 June 1930, which sparked off a series of successful provincial revolts, leading to Siles's overthrow five days later. An interim military junta took over but relied on a civilian cabinet, made up of prominent politicians from the traditional, oligarchical parties, until elections in January 1931, placed Daniel Salamanca in the presidency. But, although both the junta and Salamanca took various measures to improve the economic situation, these were mere palliatives, given the gravity of the crisis. The plain fact was that no Bolivian government, whatever its complexion, had sufficient power to alleviate the situation: that power rested more in the hands of the international bankers to whom Bolivia was so heavily indebted and, more immediately, in the hands of world producers of tin, including the Bolivian barons, of whom Simón Patiño was the most significant.

It was Patiño who played the leading role in the first serious attempt to institute an international system of control over production and prices, in a world in which four producers – British Malaya, Bolivia, the Netherlands East Indies and Nigeria – accounted for 80 per cent of the world supply, and in which Bolivia was the highest-cost producer. In June and July 1929, the Tin Producers' Association was formed in London, its objective to restrict production on a voluntary basis in order to raise prices by reducing both stocks and current output. But it failed when the low-cost producers, with their competitive edge, declined to come in. Prices continued to fall, and late in 1930 more drastic measures were adopted. Since the colonial powers, Britain and the Netherlands, together with Bolivia, had the lion's share of world production, the tin companies turned to their governments to agree 'to enforce production restrictions and determine quotas'.[3] They agreed, and on 1 March 1931, the International Control Scheme, assigning quotas, came into effect.

For the Bolivian government, this arrangement gave it 'a control over its chief industry which it had never before exercised',[4] and, while the initial effect was negative on the country's overall economic position by further restricting production in the short term, that result was reversed in the long run as prices were stabilised and began to rise from the mid-1930s. Before then, however, rock-bottom was reached in mid-1932 when the price of tin was at its lowest, and the Control Scheme adopted a drastic proposal to stop all production of tin for July and August, and to cut quotas thereafter so that world production would be no more than one-third of the level of 1929. These decisions were taken precisely at the time that President Salamanca, who had pursued a forward policy in the Chaco Boreal, reacted violently to the latest Paraguayan incursions there, rejected the advice of his senior army officers, and ordered immediate reprisals. Thus began the Chaco war with Paraguay, with Bolivia in a chaotic economic situation which the world crisis of the early 1930s had exacerbated, if not created, and which, as in neighbouring, normally less volatile Chile, had suddenly presented all foreign interests in both countries with quite unprecedented problems.

The crisis and the FCAB: the men in charge

In confronting the most critical years of its history to date, the railway had, at least, an intangible asset in the quality of its senior management on the ground. Its general manager in Antofagasta from 1918 to 1929, A.G. Hunt, had retired from Chile in April of the latter year with the highest grade in the Chilean Order of Merit, conferred by special recommendation of President Ibáñez himself in recognition of Hunt's twenty-five years' residence in the country and of his contribution to its progress. He remained closely associated with the FCAB, however, first as a member of the board and a director from June 1929, and later as its chairman and managing director on the death of A.W. Bolden in 1941. And, like the latter, he died in harness, in October 1946.

To succeed Hunt in Chile in 1929, the board chose another 'old hand', A.E. Heskett, who had first gone to Antofagasta in 1906 and had risen rapidly in the company's service, being appointed general manager in Bolivia in 1921 at the age of forty, a post he held until his transfer to the similar position in Chile. The latter post he held until his retirement in September 1947. Like his predecessor, Heskett was a first-rate administrator who was also decorated by the Chilean government. And, by all accounts, he was a remarkable man who integrated himself into the life of the environment in which he worked. 'There is no institution in the province', said an obituary in the leading daily of Antofagasta,

> nor any national service which does not owe something, and at times something valuable and very important, to his good will, and to his willingness to serve this country which, without ceasing to be British, it pleased him to regard as his own. He had acquired our manner of speaking and in almost half a century of living in Chile, he had become familiar with the mysteries of our tongue, with our nods and winks and with our silences to a degree never perhaps attained by any other "gringo". It was simply that he had got inside the workings of the national spirit as few other foreigners could.[5]

Such qualities of 'Don Arturo', as he was popularly called, would stand him in good stead in the trying times that lay ahead in 1929, and from 1930 he was ably assisted by another long-standing servant of the FCAB, W. Wells. Two years younger than Heskett, Wells had begun his career as a water engineer in Antofagasta in 1907 but, like so many who began with a technical background, moved into administration, being appointed deputy manager in Chile at the beginning of 1930, and acting general manager whenever Heskett went on leave. On the latter's retirement, Wells succeeded him as general manager until his own retirement early in 1951. To succeed Heskett as general manager in Bolivia in 1928, the board chose W.A. Pickwoad, another with a long-service record in both Chile and Bolivia. He was to remain in La Paz until October 1944, when he became general manager of the Central Argentine Railway.

The long experience of such staff in senior management – and it was shared by their colleagues on the technical side such as engineers and traffic managers, inspectors and accountants – was paralleled in London by a knowledgeable board of directors, led by Bolden. And there can be little doubt that his was the guiding hand in the framing of overall policy and in the careful management of both the company's finances and the stock holders' interests. Throughout the critical years, he was in constant touch with his local management, and, as the company records show, he had a meticulous eye for the detail of its operations as well as for its overall performance. Over the years, as chief executive, he had developed the practice of paying long personal visits to Chile and Bolivia, and his correspondence reveals not only a shrewd understanding of events in both countries but also an appreciation of what it was like for his staff actually to run the business there. Moreover, he had a high degree of financial acumen, and it was due largely to his prudence and foresight that the FCAB entered a most difficult decade far better prepared for adverse circumstances than many other British companies operating in Latin America. Thus, in 1929, for example, he announced to the AGM the setting up of the Andes Trust, by segregating certain assets hitherto shown in the books as 'General Investments': £2 million was the sum involved, and he explained the purpose of the new subsidiary company as follows:

> . . . our future balance-sheets would, under the heading of "Investments", include the capital stock of the Trust and Finance Company. Unless it were necessary to do so for dividend equalization purposes or some other financial requirement, we would not bring into our Antofagasta Railway revenue account the income on those assets, and it would remain with the Trust Company; but what we should do would be to show in our own revenue account the true financial operating results of the railway and waterworks undertaking, and that is what I think we should do, as otherwise the results are not a true index of what we receive for our services to our clients.[6]

The investments held by the Andes Trust, owned and controlled by the FCAB and with the same directors were, in effect, 'a reserve for the lean years' but not until 1932 – the depth of the depression – was the dividend of £100,000 from the Trust brought into the railway revenue account. Summing up the results for that year, Bolden also summarized where the business stood as well as his own financial philosophy:

> The one bright spot in the picture is that the financial position generally of the Company is still sound . . . by the wisdom of the past, both by the board not having distributed profits up to the hilt and by the Shareholders having agreed to our policy, we have put ourselves into a position to meet, at any rate with some success, just such times of great falling off in business as we have experienced during the last three years . . .[7]

Even so, it was a long haul from depression to recovery and none knew that better than those who had to make it.

The crisis and the FCAB: Chile

Although it was the sudden collapse of world commodity markets in 1930, including nitrate, both natural and synthetic, which undercut the Chilean economy and the railway's traffic, the latter had already been threatened by developments in the nitrate industry in the late 1920s. These revolved around Chilean government policy towards one of its major sources of income and the impact on Chile of American capital and technology. While Chilean governments, from Ibáñez onwards, sought to combat the rising competition from synthetics in association with the Nitrate Producers' Association, American capital, and largely that of the Guggenheim empire which had owned and developed the copper of Chuquicamata since 1912, had moved decisively into Chilean nitrates. In 1924 the Guggenheims had bought from the Chilean government the Coya Norte nitrate field for over US $3 million and, early in 1925, they had taken over the Anglo-Chilean Nitrate and Railway Co. Ltd., a British company which owned nitrate grounds in the same region and also the railway linking the grounds to the port of Tocopilla north of Antofagasta. At about the same time, the Guggenheims' brilliant consultant metallurgist and later a senior employee, E.A. Cappelen Smith, who had already introduced more cost-effective technology at Chuquicamata, invented what became known as 'the Guggenheim process' for reducing the raw material or *caliche* to pure nitrate: this, compared with the traditional 'Shanks process', which produced from 55 per cent to 75 per cent nitrate from *caliche*, recovered 90 per cent and was, therefore, much more cost-effective. In the mid-1920s, Guggenheims had built a new plant using the new process at María Elena near Coya Norte, with an annual production capacity of 600,000 tons, and with the Tocopilla Railway as its lifeline to the coast. More than that: not far south-west of María Elena lay the richer nitrate fields of Pedro de Valdivia, for which the British Lautaro Nitrate Co. Ltd. had made an offer to its assumed owners, the Chilean firm of Barburizza y Cía, but, after a court case over an alleged flaw in the latter's ownership, the government of the day imposed:

> ... a heavy fine on this ground and an obligation to build two plants with a capacity of 500,000 tons per annum. There was difficulty in finding all the money to meet these obligations. Messrs. Guggenheim came forward, undertook to raise the money and to build one Guggenheim plant at a cost of £4,500,000... [8]

This, they eventually did, but not before taking over the Lautaro Nitrate Co. in 1929, when its capital was £8 million, raised by Guggenheims to £14½ million.

The further, no less complex, details of these transactions do not concern this narrative, but the relevance of this digression to the fortunes of the Antofagasta Railway may be stated simply. At the time the Guggenheims acquired the Lautaro interests, that company owned 26 *oficinas*, all using the Shanks process, and 418 square miles of nitrate *pampa*, much of it in the hinterland of Antofagasta which the FCAB served. The new Guggenheim plant at Pedro de Valdiria on the Tocopilla *pampa*, with a productive capacity of 750,000 tons of nitrate a year, and using the Tocopilla Railway for carriage, was intended, with María Elena, to be the basis for the Chilean nitrate industry of the future; and to be cost-competitive with synthetics in world markets and a continuing source of revenue to the Chilean exchequer. In that respect, the interests of the Guggenheims coincided with those of the Chilean government but for the nitrate interests of Antofagasta and those elsewhere in the north, these new developments posed a serious threat.

Heskett, in Antofagasta, was well aware of this. Writing some months before the nitrate crisis of 1930 really bit hard, and contemplating the outlook for that year, he sent a gloomy message to London:

> I am afraid that all that has been written and calculated with regard to the prospects for 1930 ... has been completely altered by the recent radical change in the nitrate situation as far as the Antofagasta Pampa is concerned ... the object in view of Messers. Guggenheim's [*sic*] seems to be a monopoly of the Industry as the fusion of the Lautaro and Anglo-Chilean interests practically means that Messers. Guggenheim dominate the Tocopilla, Taltal and Antofagasta Pampas. It would appear that the great object is concentration of elaboration in certain oficinas which can work fairly cheaply, in order to reduce the unit cost...[9]

Consequently, *oficinas* in Taltal and Antofagasta, using the Shanks process, were being closed down and, with Chuquicamata – bought from the Guggenheims by the massive American Anaconda corporation in 1929 – cutting production of copper bars from 14,000 to 8,000 tons a month, and 'the wretchedly low prices for tin and other minerals', Heskett had already begun to cut costs. Workshop hours were reduced by one-sixth and a gradual reduction of up to 10 per cent of the men there was initiated; re-painting of buildings was cancelled, and other economies were effected on the maintenance of the permanent way as the track settled down after the change of gauge. Timetables and speeds were appraised 'in order that we can arrive at what may be termed the most economical load'.[10] And certain works involving capital expenditure, such as workers' houses at Calama, were postponed until better times.

But this was only the beginning. In May, Heskett was reporting that nitrate traffic on the Aguas Blancas railway – the only line worked by the FCAB which had not been converted to metre gauge – had virtually ceased, and he had been discussing with the traffic manager the possible closure of the port of Coloso. Throughout the year, indeed, stations on that line and on the main line from Antofagasta were being shut down as traffic dried up, and resultant economies were made. Frequent meetings with heads of departments to discuss further economies became a feature of the general manager's duties as staff continued to be dismissed or had their hours and wages cut. This was not a straightforward affair, however, as was explained in one report by Wells, acting general manager:

> The true effect of the economies carried out will not be clear for some time, for the reason that when men are dispensed with, we are faced with the consequent liabilities under the social laws, and although these amounts are spread over some months, they tend to depreciate the economies effected.[11]

Nevertheless, dismissals, particularly of *obreros*, were inevitable in the circumstances and no business was immune. In August, for example, Mr Baseden of the Chilex at Chuquicamata:

> ... informed us that, owing to the condition of the copper market, they have decided to suspend all new construction ... He therefore asked us not to incur any further expense in connection with the concession for the siding at Kilometre 211 ... he did not know for how long this policy would continue, but ... it might be anything from two to five years ... He also remarked that they were effecting economies and had dispensed with the services of some 50 employees and 160 men ... [12]

For the FCAB, every service suffered, despite the social laws: thus, its obligations under the law for compulsory provision of health and invalidity facilities were trimmed by the following measures:

> 1) The salaries of the Medical Officers in Mejillones and Calama have been reduced.
> 2) The elements in the first-aid boxes supplied to the permanent way gangs and out stations have been reduced to the smallest quantities compatible with the needs for purely first-aid requirements.
> 3) One of the Doctors in Antofagasta has been dispensed with. His principal duty was to attend the Hospital on certain days, but we have arranged for this to be now done by the Doctor who visits Baquedano, paying the later $400 per month more for the extra work. The salary of the discharged Doctor was $1,400 per month ... [13]

Saving 1,000 pesos a month by such measures may seem like cheese-paring, but economy was the order of the day. By September, however, after yet another officers' conference in Antofagasta, where the dismal traffic prospects were surveyed, it was clear that 'economies must now be made on a more permanent and comprehensive basis' entailing a thorough revision of all departments. Such measures included consideration of the removal of the greater part of the stores department from Mejillones to Antofagasta, further reductions of *empleados*, and, above all, the withdrawal 'from main line service [of] the whole of the converted engines; 500 wagons and several coaches', at an estimated saving of £1,500 to £2,000 a month in maintenance.[14] A short time later, Wells reported:

> As a further measure of economy, we have asked for the authority of the Railway Department to discontinue the daily service of trains to and from Mejillones as from the 1st October next, and run trains only on Monday, Wednesday and Saturday. The number of passengers travelling on this branch does not warrant a daily service . . . three trains either way per week . . . will amply meet requirements.[15]

And so it went on. A further 37 men lost their jobs at Mejillones: 'This now brings', Wells wrote, 'the total number dismissed since the 1st March last to 109 employees and 729 workmen'.[16] He did, however, suggest the establishment of a fund to be charged to monthly expenses 'in order to provide the necessary indemnity and payment in lieu of notice payable under the social laws' which, since March, had cost the company some £7,700.[17] And not only Chilean employees were affected: the closure of further *oficinas* led in November to the forced retirement of several contract staff then on home leave, and the imposition of greater duties without additional pay on several others, should they wish to return under those conditions. By the middle of December, Heskett, who had recently returned from home leave, felt that 'with regard to expenses, we have brought these down to the lowest point that we feel is consistent with the proper upkeep of the Company's property.'[18] Even so, though 1930 had been difficult enough, worse was to come.

Meanwhile, in that very year which saw the rapid development of the nitrate crisis, the Ibáñez government, in association with Guggenheims, embarked upon an ambitious and complex plan to concentrate all national nitrate resources into the hands of one company, called originally COSANA (The National Nitrate Company) but later COSACH (The Chilean Nitrate Company). This was created by a law of July 1930, and almost all the nitrate producing companies in Chile accepted the arrangements for merging their businesses in the COSACH. Its objectives were admirably spelt out by A.W. Bolden to the AGM of the railway company in June, 1931:

> COSACH will permit of the concentration under one control of production, shipping, selling, finance and, in fact, all the ramifications connected

> with the production and marketing of nitrate, and iodine, and it is claimed that a considerable saving will be effected thereby and consequently an improved situation for Chilean nitrate of soda created in the world's markets.[19]

The share capital was to be £75 million, one half of which was to go to the Chilean government, and the bond capital was to be some £40 million. Bolden continued:

> The Chilean Government will own 50 per cent of the Ordinary Shares in consideration for ceding to Cosach, Fiscal nitrate grounds containing some 150,000,000 tons of nitrate, and the abolition of the present Export Duties on nitrate and iodine. The Government were also guaranteed certain sums for the first four years, which I understand may be called anticipated income on its shares and in lieu of the Export Duties ...[20]

The other half of the shares were to be divided among producers, with the Guggenheims acquiring the lion's share and assuming formal direction of the COSACH, and the long-term aim was to eliminate the Shanks *oficinas* and concentrate production through the Guggenheim process in large plants, such as María Elena and Pedro de Valdivia, with two more such plants to be built eventually, one in Tarapacá and one on the Antofagasta *pampa*. Such, in outline was the plan. But, in the words of one authority:

> The corporation was a disaster ... It began operation on March 20, 1931, with thirty-eight *oficinas* and 48,478 labourers, and by June 30, 1931, only six *oficinas*, employing 17,000 workers were in operation. Production fell from 205,000 tons to 85,000 tons a month ... By June, 1932, COSACH had lost thirteen million dollars, defaulted on its bonds and reduced the nitrate labour force to 10,000 men.[21]

No venture of such magnitude could have been worse timed, with the nitrate market continuing to shrink and stocks remaining far too high. And, apart from its economic failure and it social consequences, the COSACH became a positive political liability to Ibáñez, as his opponents seized on that issue as proof that he was losing his grip and had sold out to American capital.

The immediate effect of the COSACH on the nitrate interests was to accelerate their decline everywhere except on the Tocopilla *pampa*, and for the FCAB a further diminution not only of nitrate freights carried down but also of traffic carried up to service the *oficinas*. Already by the end of 1930, of the thirty *oficinas* hitherto served by its lines, only one, Chacabuco, was still working, and throughout 1931 the general manager and his staff continued to look for economies in working additional to those they had made, perforce, in the previous year. Dismantling of buildings and the closure of stations continued on the now profitless Aguas Blancas Railway; administrative savings were effected by the fusion of departments, and Mejillones was again subjected to close scrutiny. Services were further reduced, as the following example illustrates. '... we have recently forwarded to the Government for approval', the general manager wrote in April 1931,

> proposals for the modification of our existing train service to meet the need for curtailing the trains to a minimum, in view of the reduced number of people travelling ... The principal modifications are that the International train from Antofagasta to La Paz will run on Tuesdays and Fridays instead of Wednesdays and Sundays ... The daily train from Antofagasta to Calama will be suppressed on Tuesdays, Thursdays and Fridays, being replaced on Tuesdays and Fridays by the International train ... The daily train from Calama to Antofagasta will be suppressed on Wednesdays and Saturdays, and replaced by the Down International ...[22]

Little was overlooked: earlier Heskett had queried whether the company should still pay passages 'for the wives of employees who marry young ladies living on the Coast immediately prior to their becoming due for home leave privilege'

> We may mention [he continued] that since the Board agreed to pay the wife's passage on leave, some five or six employees have married ladies whose home must be considered as Chile ... as undoubtedly your attention would be drawn to passages being paid for wives when only a few years ago you contracted a single man. We must add to get married on sailing day and go on home leave seems to us to be outside the spirit of the Board's ruling ... we ... would suggest that a period of one year after marriage must elapse before the wife's passage can be paid by the Company.[23]

There were, of course, still some occasions when no expense *could* be spared, such as the visit to Chile of the Prince of Wales and Prince George in February 1931. The royal party was met at Ollagüe by Heskett; the Acting British Consul at Antofagasta; Admiral Von Schroeders, the Chilean Minister of Marine; the colonel in charge of police in the zone, 'one or two detectives and a suitable guard' who had travelled overnight by special train from Antofagasta.

> The royal train arrived ... punctually at 4.00 pm. [Heskett wrote] and was hauled from Ollagüe by engine No.183 suitable decorated with flags, and a cast of the Prince of Wales's feathers which had been made in the Mejillones Workshops was placed in front of the smoke box ... His Royal Highness's suite consisted of the party detailed in your private official letter ... and fortunately none of them seemed to be unduly affected by the altitude, but

> when His Royal Highness knew that we had to continue rising a little as far as Ascotán, he asked that the speed might be increased to get out of the altitude as soon as possible. This wish was echoed by his suite, but did not stop His Highness and Prince George from leaving the train at Cebollar and again at Ascotán to photograph some llamas, and what he was pleased to term "wild men", who happened to be a few permanent way labourers at Ascotán . . .[24]

The train ran on schedule to San Salvador, Calama and Portezuelo, the Prince meeting British expatriates and Chilean authorities at each stop, and finally boarding an aircraft at Portezuelo for Santiago. Before leaving, he presented both Heskett and Pickwoad, who had accompanied the party from Bolivia, with a silver cigarette case as a souvenir, and 'expressed his great satisfaction at the arrangements which had been made for his comfort'. This occasion was, no doubt, a welcome break for Heskett from his other preoccupations, especially economies. He subsequently reported that, along with other British subscribers, he had put the FCAB down for £100 as a contribution for a fund to stage a horse race for the Prince of Wales's Cup at the Club Hípico in Santiago, but added:

> I provisionally paid the subscription in the name of the Company. If, however, you feel that the Company should not subscribe in view of the present economical (sic) situation, I could easily have the name changed.[25]

In fact, the board approved though Heskett doubted that the sum of £2,500 required would be raised 'as many firms who had promised to give fairly large sums had to reduce their subscription on account of the very bad state of business'.[26]

Soon it was back to the old routine of sending bad tidings to London of late remittances, poor traffics, and the need to meet tax bills, amounting to £30,000 in May and to a similar sum in November. Nevertheless, the response to the crisis was not entirely negative, and, in any event, despite the difficulties, the company's long-term interests had to be defended. Thus, although Heskett frequently referred to the danger of the development of the Tocopilla nitrate *pampa*, especially with the construction of the Guggenheim plant at Pedro de Valdivia, he did pursue, with the backing of London, a consistent policy from early 1931 of seeking to persuade the Chilean government to allow at least part of the *oficina's* output of nitrate to be shipped via the Longitudinal Railway through Antofagasta. That port and the surrounding region had been badly hit by the nitrate crisis and by the recent changes in the industry, so he could count on the support of the local business community and of local officials such as the intendant. Unfortunately, however, he could not count on the COSACH whose 'leading men' he described as

'Guggenheim nominees' and, given the 'big monetary interest' of the Guggenheims in the Tocopilla Railway, it would not be easy to persuade the government to influence a decision to divert traffic from that line to the Antofagasta railway. Heskett worked hard at this issue throughout 1931: he had long discussions in May with both the Director of Railways and the Minister of Development, both of whom seemed sympathetic, and he reported optimistically in June that:

> All efforts are being made in Santiago to interest the Government in the proposal. The Minister of Fomento had spoken to the President of the Republic, who was quite interested, and we were assured of other strong support in other influential quarters . . . [27]

Despite this, however, little progress was made, largely due to the opposition of the officials of COSACH, and by the end of October Heskett's optimism had quite evaporated:

> I can assure you that we are maintaining the most friendly relations with the "Cosach", but at the same time it might easily strain those relations if we persist too much in attempting to obtain part of the "Pedro de Valdiva" output, more especially as it is very evident that the "Cosach" authorities are dead against the idea . . . [28]

In the event, nothing came of this very time-consuming business: by the end of the year, it was clear that the COSACH was a failure, as Chile slid even deeper into depression. Nevertheless, the episode illustrates how the management of the FCAB in both London and in Chile sought to salvage something from that situation, though the circumstances were very much against them.

It was a similar story on Chilean government tariffs, another issue which much exercised both of them during 1931. Consistent with its general policy of favouring domestic industries and foreign-owned enterprises considered vital for the Chilean economy as a whole, in April, 1931, the Ibáñez government issued two decrees affecting import tariffs on fuel oil. By this time, the FCAB had long pursued the policy of converting its engines from coal to oil-burning, as had, indeed, many nitrate *oficinas* for elaboration since imported petroleum was now a cheaper fuel than either Chilean or imported coal. The import duty on the company's oil had been fixed at $12.00 per ton for 1931, rising to $15.00 per ton for 1932, $18.00 per ton for 1933 and $21.00 per ton for 1934. This progressive tax on imported oil fuel also applied to the copper producers, but by the decrees of April the COSACH was declared exempt from it and its duty fixed at $3.00. This rate was levied on the oil for the Chilex power plant at Tocopilla and for the Andes Copper Mining Co. at Chañaral to the end of 1934. The rate for Chilex on oil intended for other uses was $12.00 for the same period. 'The decree lays down', it was reported:

> ... that these rates will be continued ... after ... 1934, provided it is found that electric power can be produced cheaper by the use of imported fuel than by national fuels. On the contrary, should the national fuels prove equally or more economical, then, as from 1st January, 1935, the maximum duty will be applied on imported petroleum used by the Copper Companies i.e. $21.00 per ton ...[29]

Meanwhile, of course, the FCAB was subject to heavy discrimination on fuel import duties, and representations to government officials were duly prepared since, as the general manager put it, 'we consider that we should also receive the same treatment as ... the nitrate and copper industries, seeing that we are affected just as much as they are by present industrial conditions'.[30]

Thus began another long-drawn out saga for senior management in Chile, strongly supported by Bolden in London who even obtained assistance from the four prominent British banks involved in the affairs of the COSACH, 'to bring some pressure to bear on the Chilian Government to assist the British-owned nitrate-carrying railways ...'.[31] After consultations with the local representatives of the other railways affected, who had also been ordered to protest, Heskett prepared a petition for the Minister of Hacienda. His report on subsequent events is worth quoting at some length to illustrate the tortuous nature of what was involved and the capacity for prevarication of the Chilean officials with whom he had to deal.

> We decided [he reported] to present this [the petition] personally to the Minister of Hacienda and explain the motives and it was only through the good offices of Mr. Vatcky of the Anglo-South American Bank, that we were finally able to secure an interview. We found the Minister in such a state of nerves that he could hardly attend to any business ... He said that he had no time to discuss anything and asked us to take the matter before the Superintendent of Salitre ... I said that this matter had received favourable attention by the four big bankers who were responsible for the "Cosach" loan in London, and that they had only been able to put out the loan on the undertaking of the Chilian Government that protection would be given to the British-owned nitrate-carrying railways ... he begged us to go to the Superintendent of Salitre who in due course would have to report on this petition. We therefore proceeded to interview Señor Ayala, when it became evident that, as far as he was concerned the fate of the railways was immaterial to him and that all he was interested in was the future of nitrate ... he was quite indifferent and told us that the petition would have to be reported on by the Superintendent of Mines and Petroleum. As this official [Heskett continued, wryly] is also president of the Commission for

> fomenting the coal industry, it appeared somewhat improbable that we would obtain a favourable report from this quarter ... In truth, the sole hope of obtaining any relief ... is through the present Minister of Hacienda, but as he has been so severely criticised for granting relief to the copper industry, it is doubtful if he would go to the extent of issuing another decree giving us relief ...
>
> ... my colleagues [he concluded] came to the conclusion that the best we could hope for was to get the duty fixed at $12.00 per ton until ... 1934 but ... several weeks will elapse before any decision is taken ... [32]

'Several weeks' was far too sanguine. A month later, encouraging noises came from the Minister of Fomento but, in July, he and his sub-secretary resigned, and his successor had to go over the question again. In fact, the papers had been sent to so many 'interested parties' that nothing had been achieved by the end of the year when yet a new Minister of Hacienda looked at all the reports again, but only after another burst of activity from Heskett in Santiago. Given the political and economic situation in Chile throughout 1931, it is, perhaps, hardly surprising that delays in decision-making occurred but Heskett put his finger on the real problem:

> The present economical (sic) situation in Chili is so bad [he wrote in December] and the Government are so pressed for funds, that settlement of any question which would entail relief from duties or anything financial is particularly difficult. [33]

As with other questions pending between the FCAB and government, the issue of the progressive import tax on petroleum remained on ice for the whole of 1932, and it was not until the advent of settled government towards the end of that year and the introduction of policies for the economic recuperation of Chile that overall settlement on a number of issues was agreed in the following years. Meanwhile, the company was not yet out of the wood as the economic depression reached its nadir, and ever-more drastic measures to cut costs had to be introduced.

The most dramatic of these for all employees and workmen came in the middle of 1931. By that time, actual traffic income and prospects for the near future were both so dismal that the board in London reluctantly decided that there was no alternative to a real cut in salaries and wages, amounting to 10 per cent for all personnel – management, *empleados, obreros*, doctors, lawyers, all, in fact, who had somehow survived the already draconian measures introduced as the crisis grew. This was to come into force from 1 July 1931, and it proved a Pandora's box. In Antofagasta, Heskett convened a meeting with chiefs of departments and Mr Fairweather, the inappropriately-named deputy manager of the Bolivian Section, ' with the object of finding the best way to meet the Board's wishes'. Against Heskett's own inclination, his staff felt that the

10 per cent cut should not be applied to the first $600 for Chileans and to 200 bolivianos for Bolivians, 'being considered as a fair living cost in the North of Chile and in Bolivia'. Moreover,

> The principal difficulty with which we are faced in considering a reduction in salaries is that the contracts which the employees have under the Law cannot be varied without their consent ... if the employees refuse to accept a reduction, it will be necessary for us to cancel their services; indemnify them in accordance with the Law, and re-engage others under fresh contracts if possible at reduced rates. If it became necessary to take this step ... it would cost us on the Chilian Section anything between £12,000 to £15,000 and this ... would offset any saving which would be effected by the reduction in salaries and wages for two or three years ...[34]

The board, while insisting on the cut of 10 per cent, compromised on the proposal, and agreed to an exemption up to $400 for Chileans and a proportionate sum for Bolivians.

Implementation of the reduction in salaries was a painful process. A number of the British contract staff felt unable to accept and left the company's service, while some key personnel on the technical side, who had already assumed additional responsibilities as a result of the previous economies and had not had increases in pay, requested exemption from the new terms. While clerical and administrative staff could generally be replaced by locally-recruited men at lower salary levels, highly-trained technical staff, such as shop foremen, mechanical inspectors and water engineers, were a different case, and senior management in Chile had no alternative but to present the arguments to the board. Moreover, as was frequently pointed out, redundancy was itself an expensive business, both with regard to expatriate staff whose contracts had been materially altered, and for whom, in addition, passages home had to be paid, and with regard to Chilean *empleados* under national legislation. Fortunately for the FCAB, the great majority of the latter accepted the reductions, probably as much from the fear of permanent unemployment in crisis-ridden Antofagasta province as from the sense of loyalty to the company itself. And as for expatriate staff, many of whom had had only that employer throughout their working lives, they were well aware that the employment situation at home was itself highly unpredictable. Nevertheless, for all from the board down, it was a matter of cruel necessity: only as and when the economic situation improved – and that was a very slow process – could the situation be reversed. In fact, even for senior personnel such as Heskett and Wells, it was mid-1935 before one half of the 10 per cent reduction was restored, and not until the beginning of 1937 that the balance was made up. Nothing could illustrate more graphically the depth of the depression in the early 1930s and the duration of its effects, though the following table makes the same points in cold figures.

Table 5. FCAB results (Chilean section only), 1926–1935

Year	Gross Receipts	Working Expenses	Net Receipts
	£	£	£
1926	1,450,874	978,591	472,283
1927	1,274,840	770,289	504,551
1928	1,388,104	808,437	579,667
1929	1,501,604	936,278	565,326
1930	1,006,077	739,929	266,148
1931	618,820	446,569	172,251
1932	357,702	334,212	23,490
1933	398,240	307,675	90,565
1934	567,950	375,404	192,546
1935	516,561	293,444	223,117

Source: FCAB Annual Reports, 1927–36

As may clearly be seen from these statistics, falling revenues from 1931 were countered by drastic reductions in working expenses: even so, the results in net receipts, particularly in 1932–33 – the real trough of the depression – indicate how tough it was to keep the section in the black and why economy was the *leitmotiv* of so much correspondence in those years.

The crisis and the FCAB: Bolivia

Some years before the onset of the world economic crisis, the FCAB had already faced a major problem in Bolivia relating to the arrangements it had made in 1908 with the Bolivia Railway Company (BRC) and the Bolivian government (see above pp. 53–54). The 5 per cent first mortgage bonds of the BRC, representing £5,750,000 and bearing the government's guaranteed interest for a period of twenty years, were due to mature on 1 January 1927, and, as the chairman of the FCAB, Lord Lawrence of Kingsgate, informed its AGM on 14 June 1927:

> The Bolivian Government faithfully fulfilled its guarantee obligations, and during the 20 years contributed over £2,000,000 towards the payment of interest on those bonds, this being the amount required over and above the income of the railways, that income being . . . the rentals paid by us as lessees [of the lines], which rentals were percentages of the gross receipts . . .[35]

He also pointed out that, throughout that period, his own company had not been called upon to assume those obligations, as it had undertaken to do if ever the government reneged on its promise. Unfortunately, however, the rentals had never been sufficient to provide the full amount of interest on the bonds 'and consequently there was no basis for financing the redemption of those Bonds when they matured on 1st January, 1927'.[36] Thus arose the question of the future of the bonds and, the FCAB then holding £4,042,400 of the total with the remaining £1,707,600 held by representatives of other nationalities, it was almost inevitable that the FCAB should take the leading role in the subsequent negotiations with the Bolivian government on the financial reorganization of the BRC. The government had a further interest in the matter in addition to the guaranteed interest it had paid on the first mortgage bonds: at the beginning it had agreed to purchase at par £2,500,000 of second mortgage bonds 'for the provision of part of the capital required for construction of the railways', also at 5 per cent but on which it had received no interest. Those bonds were due to mature on 1 January 1932. The other relevant factor in the complex financial equation of the BRC as it stood in 1927 was that, in addition to its position as majority bondholder, the FCAB held the entire capital stock of the company, US $10,000,000.

To cut a rather long and exceedingly complicated story short, in November 1927 negotiations began between, on the one hand, representatives of the Bolivian government of President Siles – namely the Ministers of Finance and of Public Works and Communications and three other nominees – and, on the other, a commission for the bondholders. This consisted of Bolden, by now chairman of the FCAB, representing the majority holders; Huntington Adams of New York for the minority holders, and Heskett, still then general manager of the Bolivia Railway Company and of the Bolivian section of the FCAB. The discussions in La Paz were detailed and protracted but, finally, an agreement *ad referendum* was reached on 21 January 1928. The text is wordy and involved, and only its major proposals are relevant here.[37]

The £5,750,000 of 5 per cent first mortgage bonds were to be replaced by new 40-year 5 per cent (Income) Bonds maturing on 1 January 1967, of which £1,707,600 held by holders other than the FCAB were to be called 'Series A', and the balance of £4,042,400 'Series B'. To get the assent of the 'Series A' holders – the minority interest – the FCAB agreed, so long as it operated the lines of the Bolivia Railway Company, to guarantee a minimum of 3 per cent interest a year to them. The Bolivian government was to receive US $2,700,000 of the capital stock of the BRC in exchange for £419,332 to the FCAB, of the original second mortgage bonds held by the Bolivian government. A further £373,068 of the same bonds were cancelled in consideration of the FCAB cancelling an equal amount due to it by the BRC for unrecovered expenditure on the construction of lines. The FCAB should increase its rentals – to 40 per cent of the gross receipts for all lines – and sums would be set aside each year from those rentals both to amortize the minority holding in new bonds and to create a fund to amortize the advances made by the Bolivian government during the first twenty years of the concession in respect of its guarantee on the old first mortgage bonds.

Summing up the implications for the stockholders of the FCAB, Bolden felt that

> Generally speaking, the arrangement seems a reasonable one for all parties. The Bolivian Government had invested in the railways in purchase of bonds and by guarantees some £4,648,000 and had received no interest thereon during the 20 years. The First Mortgage Bondholders other than the Antofagasta Company had received their full 5 per cent interest for that period but with the expiry of the guarantee period it was clear that the full 5 per cent would not be forthcoming. Therefore, what was done was to give the First Mortgage bondholders all there was to be had . . . I do not see what more could reasonably have been expected: the Antofagasta Company was neither morally nor legally liable for another farthing; it had added its guarantee to that of the Bolivian Government until maturity, and its bonds rank equally with those of the other bondholders. It is true that the lines of the Bolivia Railway Company converge towards the Antofagasta Company's main line, but that is one reason why we went into the business . . . the bondholders generally benefit from the fact that having our own organization in Bolivia enables us to work the lines cheaper . . .[38]

The actual implementation of the agreement, which was, in fact, amended in 1929, and which required the consent of the vast majority of holders of the original bonds, turned out to be a very long process. Although by the end of the 1920s, over 97 per cent of the total issue of the original first mortgage bonds had been deposited in token of acceptance of the new scheme, it was as late as 1955 that the last of them to be surrendered were exchanged for the so-called 'new Series A', leaving £12,460 undeposited out of the £1,707,600 ascribed to the minority holders when the agreement was made. By then, of course, circumstances had changed quite dramatically both for Bolivia in general and for the FCAB in particular, and those circumstances were shaped in the early 1930s. Meanwhile, by the agreement of 1928, Bolden for the FCAB had blunted the possibility of the actual expropriation of the Bolivia Railway Company which had been threatened, few can say how seriously, by President Siles in 1927. Bolden had retained the leases on the lines nominally in that company's charge – important feeders to the FCAB's main network to and from Antofagasta – and, while the

Bolivian railways were destined to be an unpredictable asset and would henceforth cost more in rentals, the risk was justified by the potential, as he saw it. Despite that optimism, the uncertainty remained, and in the early 1930s Bolivia had to face not only an economic crisis but also a disastrous war.

The doleful litany which characterized so much of Heskett's correspondence from Chile in the early 1930s had its counterpoint in Pickwoad's reports from La Paz. And whereas in Chile the collapse of nitrate had led to the formation of the COSACH, falling tin prices in the late 1920s had, as already noted, involved Bolivia in the operations of the International Control Scheme from early 1931. The assignment of production quotas to the major tin countries proved an essential element in both reducing stocks and raising prices but it was a slow process and it entailed the closure in Bolivia of many small mines, considerable unemployment in the industry, as well as a reduction of exports and a fall in income for carriers such as the FCAB. In 1931, Bolivia had been given a quota of 34,620 tons when the Control Scheme began in March, but in June that was cut to 28,818 tons. In 1932 the original quota was 24,756 tons, reduced to 18,318 tons in June, and cut yet again in July to 14,687 tons. The latter figure was the quota also given for 1933: it represented a cut of no less than two-thirds of the Bolivian tonnage exported in 1929. Prices of tin on the London Exchange ranged from a high of £145 a ton at the beginning of 1931 to £102 a ton at year's end, while the corresponding figures for the following year were £159 and £105. Not until 1933 did recovery begin, as prices moved between a range of £228 a ton and £142 a ton, and that recovery was maintained in 1934 (£241 and £222) and 1935 (£245 and £209). The overall improvement in prices and the ironing out of wide fluctuations on a yearly basis showed how effective the surgery had been but the operation had been painful.

As in Chile, so in Bolivia, the FCAB was not only affected by the fall in 'down' traffic of minerals, especially tin, but also by a sharp decline in 'up' traffic, consisting to a large extent of materials required by the mining industry, such as machinery and fuel oil, while passenger receipts also fell off in both directions. Reporting on the results for 1930 of the Bolivian section of the Antofagasta Railway at the end of March 1931, Pickwoad stated that 'as a result of the crisis, our receipts are the lowest recorded since 1922',[39] but, two years later, in his report on 1932, he said that 'we have experienced the worst year from the point of view of receipts since the separation of the Sections',[40] that is, since 1914. Consequently, beginning in 1930, economies had to be introduced, and the story had the same familiar ring as in Chile:

> The question of reducing our Working Expenses to the lowest possible limit has received careful consideration, and no expenditure, except that which is

absolutely necessary, is incurred by any Department, consistent with the proper upkeep of the Company's property. Considerable reductions have been made in the staff, but the full benefit of this will not become apparent for a few months yet, owing to gratifications, etc. which have to be paid to employees who have been dismissed, in accordance with the Laws of the Country ...[41]

In mid-1931,

> ... reductions were made on salaries and wages, the workshops were put on short time and arrangements were made to reduce the working time of the gangs to five days per week during the dry season, in addition to which we have continued to dispense with the services of workmen and employees as opportunity has offered.
>
> The International trains, which previously had been run on different days, were combined between La Paz and Uyuni, and owing to the small amount of cargo received, arrangements were made for carrying this on passenger trains, and only on very rare occasions has it been essential to run cargo trains.[42]

Much more drastic an economy measure was implemented in 1931: whereas in previous years, including 1930, the Section's accounts included on the debit side sums of £30,000 each for debenture amortization and renewals, no charges in those respects were made from 1931 onwards, and, indeed, that situation did not change until 1936 when an allocation of £10,000 for renewals appears in the accounts.

It was, inevitably, the same old story that Pickwoad had to tell when wearing his other hat in the company's interests in Bolivia, namely as general manager of the Bolivia Railway Company. The leased lines which the FCAB ran and had to maintain – Oruro to Viacha, Rio Mulato to Potosí, Uyuni to Atocha and Oruro to Cochabamba, more than 400 miles of track – were no less affected by the general crisis afflicting all parts of the Bolivian economy. Decreased traffic in goods and passenger services on these lines, taken in conjunction with the rentals payable to the Bolivian government added up to deficits in the years 1930 to 1932 inclusive, and to meagre net profits in the following years, with nothing set aside for renewals between 1931 and 1935. Revenue fell by almost a third in 1931 over 1930, and by a fifth in 1932 over 1931, though from 1932, despite the general depressed state of the economy, and especially mineral traffic, some improvement occurred 'attributable largely to the transport of troops, munitions and materials for the Bolivian government' arising from the Chaco War with Paraguay, which began in earnest in July that year. Hence,

> The number of passengers carried was 202,367 in 1933 against 129,295 in 1932, but receipts did not benefit to the same extent as the increased

> movement was mainly concerned with the transport of troops, for which half the ordinary public tariff is charged . . . Of Public goods, 124,231 tons were transported, an increase of 23.54% compared with the 100,559 tons in 1932 . . . mainly in items of Up traffic such as General Merchandise, Articles for the Mining Industry, Explosives, Bolivian Flour, Coal and Sugar . . . [43]

Further increases in both passengers and goods traffic were recorded for both 1934 and 1935, as the Chaco War continued its bloody, and, for Bolivia, its eventually disastrous progress. The Paraguayan army of some 70,000 men under the astute command of Colonel José Félix Estigarribia, drove the unacclimatized and poorly-led Bolivian forces west, captured their forts in the Chaco Boreal and decimated their best units. When a truce was declared in June 1935, Bolivia had lost some 50,000 men, Paraguay some 35,000, and the definitive peace treaty in 1938 saw the transfer of the Chaco from the one to the other. But, as time was to reveal, the loss of territory by Bolivia and the experience of the war itself was to have a profound effect in the long run on Bolivian society and politics, culminating in the revolution of 1952, a genuine watershed in Bolivian history.

All this lay in the future. Meanwhile, for the Bolivian Section of the Antofagasta Railway, as well as for the BRC, the war, while adding to management's problems, also provided opportunities for improving results somewhat and, not least, for playing a role in Bolivia's war effort. As Pickwoad reported in 1933:

> With the outbreak of hostilities, and in order to assist the Country as far as possible, gifts were made to the Government by individuals and firms. This Company, at that time, offered to prepare a Red Cross train and transport wounded soldiers free of charge, but after consultation with the Government it was agreed that the Company should give two 'Fordson' tractors for the purpose of making roads, as it was at that time thought that the wounded could be better attended at the various base hospitals owing to the lower altitude of the Chaco compared with La Paz and the consequent quicker healing of wounds . . . [44]

Having secured the board's approval for this humanitarian gesture, Pickwoad proceeded ' and the tractors were duly handed over to the Government in September 1932'. However, he continued:

> The number of wounded transported over our lines increased considerably, as the Base Hospitals were not organized for such a large number of cases. As the men received no treatment of any description from the time they left Villazon until the time of arrival at destination, after travelling, in many cases, for approximately two days, the Company's Doctors and employees suggested to me that the Company convert two Second-class coaches into Red-Cross coaches, all expenditure for such conversion and subsequent

> upkeep, including meals provided for the troops, medicines, wages of Red-Cross nurses etc., to be met out of a voluntary contribution of 1% from their salaries and wages. This I agreed to, and I would wish to place on record that all our staff, both National and foreign, with the exception of some three or four Bolivians, willingly lent their support to this most humanitarian suggestion. Two American Second-class coaches were converted . . . each having . . . 33 beds, and they were put into service in January last and have done exceptionally good work . . .[45]

He subsequently informed London that the coaches had been 'of very real service to the Country and very much appreciated by the wounded. We have carried some 2,750 cases during the year, and I am pleased to . . . record . . . only one death on the train during . . . this period'.[46]

There was, of course, another side to the war effort. 'During the year under report' (1933), Pickwoad went on in the same communication:

> considerable help was given the Government in our Uyuni Shops. In all, some 545 lorries of different makes were erected and tested, and last month a further 100 Ford lorries were erected and handed over in running condition to the Army . . . Two batteries of 105mm Howitzers and Mountain guns, with their respective gun limbers and battery wagons, were also erected and reformed in our Shops, and the Howitzers of the Pisagua Regiment repaired . . .
>
> During the year, we have transported 82,918 Officers and troops; 11,704 tons of war material and some 118 tons of troops' baggage etc.
>
> This heavy extra transport naturally disorganized . . . our general traffic movement, but . . . the work was carried out in an efficient manner, without complaints from the Government, and, in fact, we received various letters of congratulation from the Chiefs of Staff and Minister of War . . .[47]

Such services continued to be offered for the duration of the war, and during the demobilization, as Pickwoad reported in 1936:

> . . . prisoners should start returning within the next few weeks. Due to the lack of second class coaches for the transport of such a large number of men – I understand there should be some 24,000 prisoners in Paraguay – we are constructing benches round the sides and down the middle of our covered stock, which should enable the men to travel in a reasonably comfortable manner . . .
>
> As it was found that Kitchen Car No. 501 was not sufficient to meet all requirements, Covered Cars Nos. 8003 and 8017 were subsequently converted into Kitchen Cars and were most useful, not only to the Military Authorities, but to ourselves, as, in this manner, we were able to avoid long delays at stations and the supply of 'chicha', etc. to the troops . . .[48]

He, himself, was, in fact, appointed Director General of Transports during this period, to coordinate the necessary traffic movements throughout the country.

At first blush, it might seem that these activities contravened the company's long-standing injunction on political involvement by contract staff. But, as with other foreign businesses in Latin America, which enforced the same prohibition, a distinction was drawn between involvement in the internal politics of the host country, and providing service to that country in time of need. Had the FCAB operated in Paraguay, there is little doubt that its expatriate employees would have acted, with the board's approval, in a similar fashion, if requested to do so by the government and always provided that the service required did not compromise either the individual or his employer. It is, perhaps, interesting to note that Sir Robert Harvey, a director of the FCAB from 1908 until 1926, and a key figure in the Anglo-South American Bank, served Peru as Inspector-General of Nitrate from 1876 to 1879, and, when the Chilean army occupied the nitrate-fields of Tarapacá in the War of the Pacific, was offered a similar post by the Chilean government, a post he accepted in 1880. Having been taken prisoner by the Chileans first, he 'justified his pro-Peruvian conduct on the grounds of natural duty towards the government which employed him'.[49] Though Pickwoad was not employed by the Bolivian government until he acted as Director General of Transports during the demobilization, the analogy is near enough, and many similar examples could be cited.

Nevertheless, co-operation between the company's representatives and government on certain issues such as arose during the Chaco War did not automatically mean that they saw eye-to-eye on everything. Before the war, but after the depression had already hit Bolivia hard, the FCAB had leaned over backwards to assist the shattered economy by granting, as in Chile, rebates on freights on the lines it owned or leased, at a time when its own prospects were distinctly gloomy. Thus, as early as 1930, when a new freight contract was signed with the Patiño Mines and Enterprises (Inc.), far and away the most important tin producer and exporter, the tariff for carriage of tin was cut by 5 per cent in all contracts for shipments of 500 tons and over so long as the price of tin was below £180 a ton, and in addition, a general agreement was reached with government to give rebates on the transport of petroleum, mining materials, explosives, and what were called 'articles of first necessity', including foodstuffs. Interestingly enough, the general rebate of 5 per cent was 'not to be applicable to Coca in view of the low freight which this traffic already enjoys'.[50] At that very time, the Bolivian government was asserting that the company was liable to a tax of 8 per cent of 45 per cent of the gross receipts of the line from Ollagüe to Oruro, instead of the 3 per cent paid hitherto, and demanding payment of over 140,000 bolivianos in alleged unpaid taxes. Though the Supreme Court in Sucre ruled in favour of the company on the basis of the 3 per cent having been agreed in 1914, and enshrined in the law of the republic, the government raised the matter again a year later, sent the issue to Congress, and then, having been rebuffed once more by the Financial Commission of the Chamber of Deputies late in 1931, had a third go through the Chamber of Deputies in February 1932, and raised its claim to 9 per cent. This time the deputies supported the government – by one vote – but the Senate overturned that decision, and that was that.

Another vexatious issue between the government and the company in the years of economic crisis and international war concerned the completion of the railway between Potosí and Sucre. In 1924 the FCAB had taken over from the Bolivia Railway Company responsibility for the construction of the line on behalf of the government, the latter being responsible for finance. This was an important undertaking since it would link the legal capital, Sucre (also known as Chuquisaca and less commonly as Charcas or La Plata) with La Paz, the chief city and seat of government, via the line which ran from Potosí to the main line which had been opened in 1911. The work, however, had been subject to frequent delays owing partly to interruptions and damage caused by bad weather, which pushed up costs, but principally due to the government's inability to secure enough cash to complete it. In November 1929, for example, it secure a loan of 1,500,000 bolivianos from the Banco Nacional de Bolivia to complete the line but heavy rains caused such damage to the track already laid that the sum proved insufficient. A further loan of 2,700,000 bolivianos from the Banco Nacional, painfully negotiated by the government in 1930, was thought to be enough but again the weather intervened and exceptionally heavy rains not only interrupted the work some 15 kilometres from Sucre but also soaked up the funds in repair bills. Meanwhile, the FCAB had been doing what it could in construction, advancing the necessary finance which it expected to recover from the government. The loan from the Banco Nacional kept things going until March 1931, but then the board of the FCAB decided that the company could no longer provide advances, and the government was so advised. It was also requested to enter into negotiations to agree terms with the FCAB for the liquidation of the latter's responsibility in the matter and the repayment of the sums owing to it. The line was actually handed over to the government in March 1931, which then prevaricated over a settlement throughout that year and, indeed, throughout 1932.

> These same difficulties [Pickwoad wrote in April 1933] have unfortunately not disappeared, and the fact that the Government did finally nominate a Commission to take over the line did not help to any great extent, as the Government Engineer-in-Charge placed every possible difficulty in our way and made the most extraordinary and absurd objections to cubications, etc,. many of which had already been approved by the previous Government Fiscal Engineer and the amounts paid to the Sub-contractors responsible for the work. Though such objections will naturally not be accepted by the

Company, it has caused a considerable amount of extra work and constant bickering . . .[51]

Negotiations went on intermittently during 1933, and by the beginning of 1934 it seemed that agreement had been reached whereby, in essence, the government's indebtedness to the FCAB would be liquidated. Under previous agreements, the company had secured the right of importing goods into Bolivia free of customs duties, but those agreements were due to expire in November 1936. By the new settlement, it was proposed that these rights should be continued and that what would have been payable in duties should be deducted from Bolivia's debt to the company: meanwhile, the government would pay an annual interest of 5 per cent on the debt until its liquidation. It was estimated that this would take from fifteen to twenty years.

These proposals were approved by the Bolivian Congress in January 1934, but at that point, President Salamanca declared his unwillingness to accept them and stalemate ensued until, in November, shortly after a disastrous battle in the Chaco War, he was deposed by a military coup, to die, disheartened and disgraced, seven months later. Under the new government, led by José Luis Tejada Sorzano, negotiations with the FCAB on the Potosí-Sucre railway were resumed, and early in 1935 the agreement adumbrated the previous year was ratified. As for the railway line itself, now under direct government control, construction to Sucre was finally completed in 1936. Few lines of such modest length in railway history could have taken so long to be laid, despite the climatic factor, and, certainly, few could have been so surrounded by such long-winded controversy. For Pickwoad in La Paz and, indeed, for Bolden and the board in London, the settlement was a satisfactory solution to what the former called 'this long drawn out question'. Besides, both of them had had enough to think about concerning the company's interests in Bolivia, as the following tables indicate.

Table 6. FCAB results (Bolivian section only) 1926–1935

Year	Gross Receipts £	Working Expenses £	Net Receipts £
1926	411,551	267,071	144,480
1927	415,129	285,053	130,076
1928	453,738	301,388	152,350
1929	495,724	312,889	182,835
1930	369,622	290,551	79,071
1931	250,926	166,986	83,940
1932	178,635	119,007	59,628
1933	193,205	98,585	94,620
1934	234,813	107,454	127,359
1935	330,059	142,655	187,404

Source: FCAB Annual Reports, 1927–1936

Table 7. Bolivia Railway Company results (leased lines), 1926–1935

Year	Gross Receipts £	Working Expenses £	Surplus £	Rentals £	Net Profit £
1926	450,057	250,774	199,283	153,207	46,075*
1927	446,055	270,577	175,478	178,041	−2,966*
1928	426,817	253,380	173,437	170,727	2,656
1929	463,655	276,371	187,284	185,462	1,822*
1930	375,798	254,959	120,839	150,319	−29,539*
1931	254,854	179,334	75,520	101,942	−26,422
1932	203,845	135,355	68,490	81,538	−13,048
1933	230,726	113,380	117,346	92,290	25,056
1934	285,803	130,118	155,685	114,321	41,364
1935	432,496	173,288	259,208	172,998	86,209**

* Net Profit/Loss after £30,000 set aside for renewals.
** Net Profit after £3,714 set aside for renewals.
Source: Bolivia Railway Company, Annual Reports, 1927–1936.

Comparison with Table 5 (p. 173) indicates how far in Bolivia, as well as in Chile, the FCAB was affected by the world economic depression of the early 1930s. As Bolden frequently pointed out to successive annual general meetings in those years, whereas previously the company might have a bad year in one country as the market for its primary products and exports fell, it had hitherto found compensation in the other country whose basic commodities were not similarly affected. 'Over many years past', he said in 1931, 'there have been occasional crises,

> but when Nitrate has been bad, Tin and Copper seemed to have saved the situation and when Copper or Tin were under a cloud then Nitrate seemed to be the saving grace, but for 1930 we found no such partially satisfactory traffic position . . . Under the circumstances therefore only one thing had to be done, and that was to introduce every economy we possibly could, and means were taken to that end just at the earliest opportunity . . . [52]

Thus, while the implementation of policy in quite unprecedented circumstances fell to management on the ground, the framing of policy and justifying it to stockholders, as well as keeping the loyalty of the staff, were responsibilities which fell squarely on the chairman and the board.

The crisis and the FCAB: London

The confidence of stockholders in those who ran the FCAB had been a consistent characteristic of the company from its beginnings. Clearly, this was based primarily on its track record of success expressed in the dividends they received on their investments, but it also reflected their faith in the prudent financial management of the concern and in the quality of its leadership. Moreover, a Lawrence of Kingsgate or a Bolden created faith through the simple fact of longevity of service and, hence, of experience in the company's affairs. The records of annual general meetings and of extraordinary meetings called for particular purposes, such as changes in capitalization or the reorganization of the Bolivia Railway Company, are eloquent testimony of that confidence from the late 1880s to the early 1930s. They show practically no dissent from the floor with what was said from the platform. That reaction was now to be tested against the impact of the world economic crisis on the company's fortunes.

Although in 1930, when running costs were already being reduced in Chile and Bolivia in the light of future prospects, prior charges for interest on debentures, 5 per cent on cumulative preference stock and 4 per cent on consolidated ordinary stock were all paid, by the following year it was a different picture. As Bolden reported to the AGM in June 1932:

> The gross receipts of our undertaking for the 12 months ended 31st December last were the lowest for any year since 1905, and when we remember the great expansion which has taken place in the intervening years in the Nitrate, Copper and Tin Mining Establishments and their potentialities of production, we realise through what a severe time of depression we have been passing . . .[53]

He also referred to the recent death of the Hon. C.A. Campbell, who had been a director of the FCAB since early 1914, and added:

> In view of the times . . . the Board have decided not to fill the vacancy for the present, and so save for the Company the fees involved. We feel we would rather do the extra work that falls upon us, and follow up our policy of economy in every direction . . .[54]

He did not mention, however – it would have been inappropriate – that Campbell, a well-known City figure, had committed suicide by shooting, and that, at the inquest, the coroner reported that he 'had been worrying lately about world affairs and he had not been sleeping well'.[55]

In the light of the overall situation, no dividend on ordinary stock was paid for 1931, and none was paid for 1932. And, worse than that:

> We have been unable to pay anything – again for the first time in our history – on our £2,000,000 of 5 per cent Cumulative Preference Stock . . . and it was only by the aid of the dividend received from the Andes Trust . . .

> and from the income from our other Investments and Bolivia Railway Bonds, that we were able to pay our Debenture Interest . . .[56]

Despite all this, when the report and accounts for 1932 were received and adopted, as proposed by Bolden in the chair, the seconder, Sir Bernard Greenwell, himself a member of the board from 1905 to 1949, commented:

> The report was bad but I say this that it might have been very much worse if it had not been for your Chairman. He has an absolute mastery of the details and has made himself master of them for over 25 years. More than that he has the goodwill of the staff on the other side . . .[57]

No one demurred. As for 'the staff on the other side', Bolden went out of his way to encourage them in those hard times. When the overall cut of 10 per cent in salaries and wages – including directors' fees – was introduced in mid-1931, he sent a personal letter to Heskett in Antofagasta:

> I want to tell you that any sacrifice which must be imposed is very distasteful to us in the case of yourself and Mr. Pickwoad, and staunch friends, apart from being Employees of the Company, like Wells, to name only one among many, as it seems a poor reward after so many years of sacrifice; but the Directors felt that, including themselves, some gesture had to be made by the higher officials as well as the British Staff generally in order to convince the Chilian and Bolivian members of the staff of the absolute necessity to do something . . . Times and conditions are very trying; equally I know they are for you, and I wish we could see some relief, but I do not see much for the moment. We can only hope for the silver lining to the clouds to come along sooner than appears at present. One can only try and be as cheerful as possible under the circumstances . . .[58]

For him, however, as chairman and managing director, and for all his staff, the 'silver lining' took a long time to appear.

The moratorium on dividends was, *force majeure*, extended. Though a halting improvement in traffics and profits began in 1933, for that year, Bolden remarked:

> . . . the Directors decided they were unable to recommend the payment of anything on account of the arrears of Dividend on our 5 per cent Cumulative Preference Stock, which obviously, also involves no payment in respect of the past year on the Consolidated Ordinary Stock. It is three years now since the Consolidated Ordinary Stockholders received anything in the way of Dividends, and at the end of the current month [June, 1934] we will be two-and-a-half years in arrears on our Cumulative Preference Stock . . .[59]

Similarly, though the position improved further in 1934, 'our deliberations' Bolden declared, 'convinced us that

> it would be unwise to attempt at this stage to pay anything on account of the arrears of the Cumulative Preference dividend . . . it would have meant borrowing or selling securities with which to pay . . . and we do not think that is a course which we should follow . . . having met the Debenture Interest as we have done these last two or three years by recourse to our reserves, it is much better to leave it at that until we see more clearly what is forthcoming in the two countries in which we operate . . . [60]

Thus, despite improving traffics as the world economy recovered and Chile and Bolivia emerged slowly from the depths of the depression, the lights remained at amber for stockholders in the FCAB as, indeed, they did for most of its employees. Bolden and the board stuck closely to a policy of financial caution and they generally carried the stockholders with them: it seemed preferable to maintain a sound financial basis for the FCAB, with high reserves and good renewal accounts together with a profitable investment portfolio, rather than dissipate resources through a dividend policy of immediate distribution. Not until 1936 were dividend payments resumed on the 5 per cent cumulative preference stock, and these represented the arrears for 1932. Indeed, throughout the decade and beyond arrears in dividend payments were not overtaken, largely due to quite new complexities arising from the great crash of the early 1930s. Prominent among these was the bugbear of exchange.

The introduction of exchange control by the Chilean government at the end of July 1931, had its parallel in Bolivia not long after. When Great Britain went off the gold standard in September, Bolivia, firmly linked with the sterling bloc, was affected at once. Gold payments were suspended and a month's moratorium on all payments decreed. In May 1932, all dealing in gold was placed exclusively with the Central Bank, the government tightened its control over exchange rates and forced the tin mining concerns to deliver 65 per cent of their letters of exchange on foreign and specie currencies to the Central Bank. Despite government intervention, however, the currency of both countries – in Chile, the peso; in Bolivia, the boliviano – depreciated sharply on foreign exchanges. By early 1932, the peso had fallen to 60/65 to the £, compared with around 30 at the end of 1931, while the boliviano was fixed at 17 to the £, instead of the par value of 13.33. The tariffs of the FCAB were based on the gold peso in Chile at 40 to the £, ie. 6*d*., and in Bolivia on the rate of 13.33 bolivianos, ie. 18*d*, and the company had the right under its concessions to petition for surcharges on its tariffs when exchange fell below these rates. Negotiation, however could be a very protracted business, and, given the economic situation in both countries, it was decided not to press for the full surcharge to which the FCAB was entitled. This was despite the fact that the company in Chile was still allowing rebates for tariffs on nitrate, coal and petroleum, first instituted in 1927 but continued thereafter on a yearly basis at the request of the Chilean government, though by 1932, the rebate on petroleum had been reduced to 10 per cent compared with 15 per cent on both nitrate and coal. Bolden spelled out the situation to the annual general meeting in 1933 as follows:

> With regard to our receipts from the Chilian Section, a certain amount of traffic is based on sterling tariffs, and this applies to some of the traffic . . . carried to and from Bolivia; but all the same . . . the fall in exchange must adversely affect our business, and as I told you last year, our Manager discussed with the Chilian Government the putting into force of a surcharge to compensate us for that fall in exchange . . . to compensate fully for the fall in exchange would have meant a very considerable surcharge . . . Now the Board realise that when the business of a country is suffering . . . it is no use trying to secure the last ounce of one's rights . . . the Board felt that for foodstuffs and passenger traffic as well as certain Chilian national products, it was wise not to surcharge these . . . What we have done now is to put in force a surcharge on nitrate . . . which is sold in markets abroad on a sterling or a gold basis, and on certain other classes of traffic including 1st class passengers, and that surcharge is based on sterling. With the Government quoted rate of say 56 pesos to the £ sterling, we are putting on a 40 per cent surcharge and this £ sterling basis for the surcharge has been accepted all round as a fair and equitable arrangement . . . [61]

In fact, that arrangement did not come into effect until February 1933, though Heskett in Chile had first raised the matter about a year before. Throughout 1932, therefore, 'no benefit whatever was received in Chili from any surcharge to compensate for the fall in exchange'. [62] The delay was due primarily to the opposition of the Superintendent of Railways, Señor Mujica, who persistently raised objections on a variety of pretexts. The enabling decree for a surcharge on tariffs was, indeed, signed by the Minister of Fomento in somewhat fortuitous circumstances, as Heskett explained:

> Monday morning found Señor Lira [an adviser] and myself again at the Ministry of Fomento but Señor Mujica was absent with an attack of fever as a result of sun-bathing. This was unfortunate for Señor Mujica but fortunate for us, as we were thus able to deal direct with the Sub-Secretary who had agreed through a mutual friend, to get us the decree signed . . . [63]

Though, in the event, two draft decrees – one previously drawn up by Mujica, and one by Heskett in the latter's absence – had to be put to the minister, the outcome was satisfactory in that Mujica's more objectionable clauses were taken out, with his reluctant agreement after he returned to work, and with the addition of a clause to save his sunburned face 'stating that the Government reserved the right to cancel the authorisation if times improved'.[64]

Though Pickwoad in La Paz does not appear to have had a Mujica with whom to deal, his time was also increasingly taken up with the surcharge question. In March 1932, with the board's approval, he did secure a scale of surcharges ranging from 10 per cent to 20 per cent for traffic on the leased lines, to operate from 23 May, and a further increase from March 1933, as the boliviano fell to 20 to the £. Moreover, though successive Bolivian governments had hitherto maintained that the FCAB had no right to surcharge tariffs to compensate for exchange losses on its own lines, in January 1933, the government of the day ceded that point and allowed surcharges to be made on the same scale as on the leased lines with the exception of government traffic which was specifically exempted.

For the board in London, as for local management, the appearance of the exchange question in the years of crisis introduced a new and complicated element in the running of the railway, and it was to prove a permanent feature in its business thereafter. Applications to surcharge tariffs to counteract a fall in exchange became the norm, but negotiations were usually protracted and delays inevitable. Moreover, the company always feared the adverse effect of passing on the full cost to its customers, as Bolden frequently pointed out. In 1934, for example, he spelled out the new complexities to stockholders, in referring to the agreements reached in Chile and Bolivia on surcharges in 1933:

> Obviously it may not be practicable to increase tariffs as expressed in the currency of the Country to the full extent of the fall of that currency, vis-a-vis another currency, which . . . we always think of as the £ sterling, and whereas, for example, in Chili we are entitled to collect pesos of the value of 6*d*, which means 40 to the £, we now find the Chilian exchange fallen away on what is termed the 'export rate' to about 125 pesos to the £. Where a consignment formerly paid we will say for the sake of argument 20 pesos it would really not be practicable suddenly to charge it with 60 pesos. Not only could industry not bear the burden, but we should find ourselves losing traffic . . . Dealing still with the Chilian Exchange . . . it has fluctuated between about 60 pesos to the £ down to 49, the closing rate last year for the purposes of our accounts having been 54.53. The surcharge based on the latter rate would be 14.53 pesos on 40, or, say, about 36 per cent, but when we come to try to remit those pesos we would have to provide, say, 125 to obtain £1 sterling, and you will at once realise the very adverse effect on our affairs produced by such a situation . . .[65]

Within the year, however, the situation had deteriorated as exchange fell, and the surcharge in Chile in the latter part of 1934 amounted to about 20 per cent, giving the company about 8*s*. for every £1 to which it was entitled. This was insupportable, as Bolden subsequently pointed out:

> . . . despite the difficult position in Chile and Bolivia the Board felt it was not fair to the Company to continue to make this great sacrifice bearing in mind that exports of Nitrate, Copper and Tin and other minerals and metals were sold abroad for sterling or other foreign currency . . . [66]

Meanwhile, he himself had visited Chile to take personal charge of discussion on the surcharge question, and he succeeded in negotiating new rates of 66 2/3 per cent for nitrate and 50 per cent for coal and petroleum, instead of the 20 per cent then ruling.

> My negotiations [he reported] were very protracted and whilst I was in Chile the Government fixed the official gold value of the Chilean peso at 1½*d*. gold which in terms of sterling gave a figure of, say, 96 pesos to the £1 . . . Now, as our Chilean tariffs are expressed in pesos of *6d*. the new valuation meant that we should have been entitled to make a surcharge of 140 per cent but this the Nitrate Makers and the Government argued could not be permitted in the present state of the Industry . . .
>
> I found in Chile that the Government realised the seriousness of our position and were sympathetic, but at the same time they maintained that it was a question of everyone sharing the burden, the burden being the loss of markets for the Chilean Nitrate Industry, the results of world conditions, including the quotas for Chilean nitrate especially in those countries where the synthetic article is produced . . . [67]

Thus, while the new surcharges were something, the company was, in effect, still subsidizing the Chilean economy, though to a lesser extent. Moreover, exchange control was maintained in both Chile and Bolivia for some years, making the remittance of profits in local currency at a reasonable rate of exchange difficult: this, in turn, led to changes in accounting practices from 1933 onwards, and the appearance in the balance sheet of an exchange reserve account. Bolden summed up the situation in 1937, as follows:

> Although the total volume of traffic handled during 1936 was greater than that for the previous year, the sterling equivalent of the gross receipts was less . . . at last year's meeting . . . I made the remark "You cannot get away from this Exchange difficulty" and it is one of the main sources of our troubles. We have only to reflect that at one time we used to work in Chile with an exchange which was stable at 40 pesos to the £ . . . now the ordinary commercial rate is about 130 to the £ . . . In Bolivia we had a steady exchange of Bs.13.33 to the £ or say a Boliviano of 18*d* . . . the effective rate is now about Bs. 120 to the £ or say 2*d*. while the official rate is Bs.80 to the

> £ or say 3*d* . . . you will see how difficult it is to get back to anything like the former sterling receipts which, e.g. would mean increasing our Bolivian tariffs at least six times . . .[68]

And that, of course, despite permitted surcharges in Bolivia as well as in Chile – a constant feature of the decade – was quite out of the question.

In this respect, times had changed, and changed forever. While the depreciation of the exchange provided some compensation in lower local currency costs, such as wages in the earlier part of the period, that advantage was soon to be eroded by social and economic events in both Chile and Bolivia as successive governments increased the volume and scope of legislation designed to benefit the working classes. For foreign companies, as well as for domestic business, which had kept afloat during the years of depression, these developments were to pose yet another challenge to their economic viability.

Notes

1. P.T. Ellsworth, *Chile: an economy in transition,* The Macmillan Company, New York, 1945, pp. 7–8.
2. Paul W. Drake, *Socialism and Populism in Chile, 1932–1952*, University of Illinois Press, 1978, p.61.
3. Klein, *Parties and Political Change in Bolivia, op.cit.*, p.119.
4. *Ibid.*, p.119.
5. *El Mercurio* of Antofagasta, n.d. My translation. I am indebted to Lt-Col. A.D. Heskett for this press extract.
6. *The Times, Company Reports*, 12 June, 1929.
7. *Ibid.*, 9th June, 1933.
8. *Chile and the Nitrate Industry*, London, 1933, p.30. This is a 40-page pamphlet, marked 'Private and Confidential', containing 'information acquired for the Bank of London & South America Limited during a short visit of Directors to South America in February/April 1933'. In the author's possession.
9. General manager to managing director, Antofagasta, 21 February 1930. Private, Official.
10. *Idem.* to secretary (C. Cowley), Antofagasta, 4 April 1930. Letter No, 259.
11. Acting general manager to managing director, Antofagasta, 25 July 1930. Private. Official.
12. *Idem.* to *idem.*, Antofagasta. 29 August 1930. Private. Official.
13. *Idem.* to *idem.*, Antofagasta, 5 September 1930. Private. Official.
14. *Idem.* to *idem.*
15. *Idem.* to secretary, Antofagasta, 19 September 1930. Letter No. 282.
16. *Idem.* to *idem.*, Antofagasta, 31 October 1930. Letter No. 288.
17. *Ibid.*
18. General manager to managing director, Antofagasta, 12 December 1930. Private. Official.
19. *FCAB, Annual Report for 1930*, 9 June 1931.
20. *Ibid.*
21. Monteón, *Chile in the Nitrate Era*, p.172.
22. General manager to secretary, Antofagasta, 2 April 1931. Letter No. 312.
23. *Idem.* to *idem.*, Antofagasta, 20 February 1931. Letter No. 305. Staff Memorandum No.601.

24. General manager to managing director, Antofagasta, 6 March 1931. Private. Official.
25. *Idem.* to *idem.*, Antofagasta, 6 March 1931. Private. Confidential.
26. *Idem.* to *idem.*, Antofagasta, 29 May 1931. Private. Confidential.
27. *Idem.* to *idem.*, Antofagasta, 26 June 1931. Private. Official.
28. *Idem.* to *idem.*, Antofagasta, 30 October, 1931. Private. Official.
29. *Idem.* to *idem.*, Antofagasta, 15 May 1931. Private. Official.
30. *Ibid.*
31. General manager to managing director, Antofagasta, 22 May 1931. Private. Official.
32. *Ibid.*
33. General manager to managing director, Antofagasta, 24 December 1931. Private. Official.
34. *Idem.* to *idem.*, Antofagasta, 26 June 1931. Private. Official.
35. *The Times, Company Reports*, 15 June 1927.
36. Cowley, 'Memorandum on the Antofagasta Railway Company', *loc.cit.*, p.46.
37. For a full English translation, see G.S. Brady and W.R. Long, *Railways of South America* (3 parts, Washington D.C., Bureau of Foreign and Domestic Commerce, 1926, 1927, 1930). *Part III – Chile* (1930), pp.129–37. For a detailed discussion in Spanish of the agreement, its antecedents and consequences, see Césareo Aramayo Avila, *Ferrocarriles Bolivianos, loc.cit* pp.81 *et seq*.
38. *The Times, Company Reports*, 12 June 1929.
39. General manager, Bolivian Section, to chairman, La Paz, 30 March 1931.
40. *Idem.* to *idem.*, La Paz, 5 April 1933.
41. Letter of 30 March 1931. Cited in f.39.
42. General manager, Bolivian Section, to chairman, La Paz, 25 March 1932.
43. Bolivia Railway Company, *Annual Report for 1933* (1934) n.p.
44. General manager, Bolivian Section, to chairman, La Paz, 5 April 1933.
45. *Ibid.*
46. General manager, Bolivian Section, to chairman, La Paz, 24 March 1934.
47. *Ibid.*
48. General manager, Bolivian Section, to chairman, La Paz, 8 April 1936.
49. Blakemore, *British Nitrates and Chilean Politics*, p.27.
50. General manager, Bolivian Section, to chairman, La Paz, 30 March 1931.
51. *Idem.* to *idem.*, La Paz, 5 April 1933.
52. *FCAB, Report of General Meeting*, 9 June 1931, pp.2–3.
53. *FCAB, Report of General Meeting,* 7 June 1932, p.1.
54. *Ibid.*
55. *The Times*, 9 April 1932. In a personal letter to Heskett, Bolden wrote: 'A week before he committed suicide, we had a Board Meeting and after the Meeting he and Mr. Hunt and I were talking over the general situation and Mr. Campbell said ... he was not sorry for people like Kreuger who committed suicide but only for those who were left behind and that many of us had seen our best days ...'. Bolden to Heskett, London, 29 April 1932.

56. *FCAB, Report of General Meeting*, 8 June 1933.
57. *Ibid.*, p.13.
58. Bolden to Heskett, London, 4 June 1931.
59. *FCAB, Report of General Meeting*, 5 June 1934, p.4.
60. *Ibid.*, 4 June 1935, p.5.
61. *FCAB, Report of Meeting*, 8 June 1933, p.6.
62. *Ibid.*, p.7.
63. General manager to Chairman, Santiago, 10 February 1933. Private. Official.
64. *Ibid.*
65. *FCAB, Report of Meeting*, 5 June 1934, p.7.
66. *FCAB, Report of Meeting,* 4 June 1935, p.11.
67. *Ibid.*, pp.11–12.
68. *FCAB, Report of Meeting*, 15 June 1937, pp.3–4.

6
THE NEW COMPLEXITIES 1935–1973: Part 1

Overview: the political panorama

Though the world crisis of the early 1930s had similar repercussions on the economies of Chile and Bolivia, contrast is more revealing than comparison in considering, however briefly, the subsequent history of both countries. Unlike Bolivia, Chile had avoided serious foreign entanglements. What might have complicated matters here, namely the protracted territorial dispute with Peru over final possession of Tacna and Arica, had been resolved peacefully in 1929, not least through the statesmanship of Carlos Ibáñez. That issue thus had no place in the preoccupations of his successors who could concentrate on the revival of the Chilean economy and attendant social and political problems. But, for Bolivia, the disaster of defeat in the Chaco War, its enormous cost in men and money, and the deep divisions in society and politics which it had emphasized were to cast long shadows across the country's future development.

In Chile, the election in 1932 of Arturo Alessandri as President for the second time restored the historic tradition of governments taking power through the ballot box, a tradition which continued until the overthrow of Salvador Allende in 1973. Constitutional rule remained unimpaired even when, during this period, two incumbents died in office – Pedro Aguirre Cerda only half-way through his six-year term in November, 1941, and Juan Antonio Ríos in June, 1946. The suffrage was extended by stages to all citizens over eighteen (with the few exceptions which are common to most democracies, such as inmates of lunatic asylums), and elections came to be conducted in a free and fair fashion through the secret vote. Chastened by its experiences in the early 1930s, the military held aloof from politics and, despite continuing and often acute stresses in the social and economic fabric, Chile was a functioning democracy with a competitive and largely peaceful party political system. It was not, of course, perfect: for example, a complex system of proportional representation in elections of senators and deputies reinforced the fissiparous tendencies of Chilean politics in which personality has generally taken precedence over party programmes and discipline, and in which alliances and coalitions have been the norm rather than the exception. This often meant that, though his constitutional prerogatives were considerable, the chief executive lacked support in the legislature and, indeed, no president in the entire period could count automatically on the co-operation of Congress. Even Eduardo Frei (1964–70), whose massive victory in the presidential election was followed by the triumph of his party, the Christian Democrats, which secured an overall majority in the Chamber of Deputies in 1965, found his 'revolution in liberty' somewhat frustrated by the opposition in the Senate of the other parties which, in combination, outnumbered his own following. Most presidents of the period, at some time or another, on one issue or the next, had to compromise their programmes to get full congressional cooperation. Yet, despite such defects, Chile had a working system of government and administration which followed an evolutionary, not a revolutionary, path with eight presidents in succession attaining office through elections in the forty years between 1932 and 1972.

In marked contrast to Chile, in the twenty years alone before the revolution of 1952 Bolivia had no fewer than eleven occupants of the presidential palace, most of them men in uniform who came to power by seizing it, sometimes with the collusion of the political parties. Again in contrast, not one chief executive in Bolivia in that time, whether attaining the office by *coup d'état* and, much more rarely, through election lasted a full four-year term as the constitution laid down. In any event the electorate in Bolivia was far smaller than in Chile where racial and cultural differences were far less pronounced. Thus, in the early 1940s when voters in Chile numbered over 500,000 in a population of about 5 million, in Bolivia they were as few as 70,000 in a population of some 2 million. And the majority, the peasant Indian population, was effectively excluded from national political life. In the year of the Bolivian revolution itself, 200,000 citizens had the right to vote, some 7 per cent of the population compared with over 1 million in Chile or 18 per cent. In short, compared with Chile, Bolivia before 1952 had neither a working constitutional system nor an increasing democratic polity, and it took a fundamental revolution to change that state of affairs. But although, as will be seen in due course, that revolution was a watershed in Bolivian history in its sweeping effects on the structure of landholding, the ownership of the tin mines, the emergence of the Indian part of the population, and a whole range of social and economic improvements, as well as producing at least for the rest of the 1950s a more ordered system of government, it did not eradicate the role of the military in politics nor did it resuscitate the Bolivian economy.

For foreign business operating in one or the other country or, indeed like the FCAB in both, the period between 1935 and 1970 was one of great complexity. However different the political evolution of Chile and Bolivia – and that difference had a major impact on the FCAB itself – each country had to overcome the economic legacies of the world crisis at a time when social problems had been thrown into sharp relief, when the working-class were becoming better organized, their demands more insistent and their search for political expression more imperative. Though the nature of the national economies internally, and especially that of Chile, changed markedly in the period, their basic relationship with the international world of trade and finance remained much the same as before because of their undiversified export pattern. What nitrates had once been to Chile, copper would become; and while, in Bolivia, oil extraction and export and the development of other minerals besides tin assumed increasing importance, that natural resource kept its critical place in the country's economy. In addition, two other developments from the 1930s should be noted: as elsewhere in Latin America, economic nationalism found more strident expression in Chile and Bolivia than before, and governments of most political stripes put more and more emphasis on the role of the state in both the national economy and in social welfare. Foreign capital and enterprise was, inevitably, deeply involved in these developments, and boards of companies, as well as their central and local managements, had now to face new problems arising from novel perspectives.

Peace and war 1935–1945: Chile

The main achievement of the second Alessandri administration in Chile (1932–38) was the revival of the economy. While improving world conditions for exports such as nitrate and copper played their part, government policies, largely the work of the Minister of Finance, Gustavo Ross Santa María – 'a financial wizard' – were equally significant. Backed by a congressional majority of the right-wing parties (Conservative and Liberal) and the leading middle-class party (Radical), the government introduced legislation to promote construction activity, stimulate industry (party by increasing tariffs on imports of manufactured goods), ease credit and encourage savings. The results were summarized by one observer as follows:

> The value of Chilean exports which had dropped to 290 million pesos in 1932 had risen to 948 million by 1937 [Alessandri's last full year in office], while imports showed a corresponding increase from 214 to 429. Nitrate production was approximately five times what it had been in 1932. The industrial index (taking the fairly prosperous years of 1927–29 as 100) had soared to 148, and unemployment had virtually disappeared. From 1934 on, the treasury never failed to finish the year with a surplus.[1]

Among its more immediate measures, the government killed off the COSACH, that elephantine, bureaucratic and expensive attempt to rationalize Chile's nitrate industry. In 1934 it was replaced by the COVENSA (The Chilean Nitrate and Iodine Sales Corporation): by its terms of reference, major producers such as the Lautaro and Anglo-Chilean Nitrate Companies regained their autonomy as private concerns, while a new company, the Cía. Salitera de Tarapacá y Antofagasta, was formed to embrace all the other *oficinas* which were formerly part of the COSACH. All producers were obliged to turn over their nitrate to the COVENSA which had complete control of export and sale, and its directorate – made up of five representatives of private firms, five of the Chilean Treasury and a chairman who had to be Chilean – allocated annual production quotas. Profits were to be apportioned with 25 per cent to the state and 75 per cent to producers, the latter, however, being subject to an annual preferential charge for interest of 4 per cent plus 2 per cent for amortization on the £11 million bonds originally issued by the COSACH. Gustavo Ross, in fact, earmarked the government's 25 per cent share of the profits to service the foreign debt.

The COVENSA was successful in July 1934 in reaching agreement with synthetic producers on sales quotas to cover the chief consuming countries outside the United States, but this three-year agreement, while stabilizing the world market and ensuring Chile a share, was, in effect, the final recognition that the days of Chile's dominance were over for good. Improved cost-effective techniques and a greater concentration of production enabled Chile to hold about 10 per cent of the market in the 1930s, falling to about 4 per cent by the 1960s. This compared with about 65 per cent before the First World War.

The persistent decline of the Chilean nitrate industry from the years of the world economic crisis was naturally of great concern to the railway company as successive annual reports and chairman's speeches in the 1930s indicate. Whereas in the previous decade, and particularly in 'boom' years, the Antofagasta Railway had carried about 1 million tons of nitrate to the coast, representing, on average, over 40 per cent of the freight moved, in the 1930s this had fallen to less than 20 per cent, the actual tonnage ranging from a low of 103,000 in 1933 to a high of 198,000 in 1937. In fact, for the seven years, 1933 to 1939 inclusive, the average tonnage of nitrate carried works out at just over 155,000 a year. It is very difficult, however, to calculate the precise financial implications for the company of the decline of the nitrate industry in this period, the whole question being complicated by the rebates on tariffs granted by the company at the persistent request of the government which were themselves offset by amounts which varied from year to year representing the compensatory surcharges on freights allowed by government in the face of overall rising costs. Varying exchange rates make confusion worse confounded. But, if chairman's speeches are any guide, the fall in income from nitrate traffic, to which he referred from year to year, and the plain fact that that traffic had fallen by some four-fifths in ten years, both suggest that the revenue loss from that source must have been considerable.

Fortunately, however, what the FCAB and, indeed, the Chilean government, lost from the mid-1930s on the swings of nitrate they regained to some extent on the roundabouts of copper, but not before passing through a similar depressing experience as that commodity, too, was hit by the economic crisis beginning in late 1929.

In that year, to that date a record year for Chilean copper, the three huge American-owned mines of Potrerillos, El Teniente and Chuquicamata – known collectively as the *Gran Minería*, accounting for 90 per cent of total Chilean output – produced 317,000 tons valued at US $111 million when the price of copper on the world market was 17.47 cents a pound. And, again in 1929, the lines of the FCAB carried no less than 137,000 tons of copper bars for the Chilex subsidiary of the Anaconda Company from Chuquicamata to Antofagasta. Then the slump struck as the bottom dropped out of the world copper market, and prices and production plummeted over the next three years. By the end of 1931, owing to the drop in demand and the existence of high stocks accumulated in the boom years of the late 1920s, the world market price had fallen to 7.03 cents a pound, and *Gran Minería* production to about 200,000 tons. The position worsened in 1932, the result not least of a penal 4 cents a pound import duty on copper bars imposed by the United States. Sales of *Gran Minería* output fell to US $11 million that year, and the fall of copper in the depression is also sharply reflected in the smaller tonnage carried by the FCAB for the Chilex, from the record figure of 137,000 tons in 1929 to 77,000 in 1930, and to a low of about 35,000 tons in 1932. For the railway, it was not, of course, a matter merely of copper freights which were an important item in its income: no less important was 'up traffic' to supply Chuquicamata with machinery, fuel, and other necessities for both the plant and the workforce. Heskett put the matter succinctly in August 1934, when the copper mining industry had already begun its recovery:

> ... we have the excellent news to report that as the Anaconda establishment at Bute, Montana, has been closed down, the Chuquicamata establishment will push up their production during this month to 10,000 tons, and there is every probability that from September to the end of the year they will be producing 12,000 tons per month ... While the news as to the increased production, which means a larger down tonnage, is extremely welcome, a further fact is that with the pushing up of the production to 12,000 tons monthly, stores materials and replacements are bound to be required, and ... before long, we shall be receiving an increased Up tonnage, which is what swells our receipts.[2]

Although, as with nitrate, it would be tedious to disaggregate in the company's accounts the items on the income side directly attributable to the fluctuating fortunes of copper production at Chuquicamata, there is little doubt that by the mid-1930s copper had replaced nitrate as the most important Chilean commodity in down traffic on the FCAB's lines. As world stocks of the metal were reduced, demand recovered and the world price of bars rose in consequence – though hesitantly in 1933 and 1934 – the tonnage carried by the company increased from the low of 35,000 in 1932 to over 57,000 the following year, almost 100,000 in 1934, and to over 114,000 in both 1935 and 1936. It was not until 1937, however, that the record tonnage of 1929 was surpassed with a figure of over 170,600, to fall again to an average annual tonnage of over 140,000 in the last three years of the decade, still higher than in the late 1920s. But the really big boom in copper production in Chile and a sizeable increase in freight from and to Chuquicamata would come later with the growing demands of the allied powers in the Second World War which would prove that, unlike nitrates, copper at that time had nothing to fear from synthetics.

For successive Chilean governments, the rise of copper coincident with the decline of nitrate provided a welcome source of income. Already in 1925 a special income tax of 6 per cent on the mining industry's profits was instituted, to be raised to 12 per cent that same year, while the application of the social laws passed in 1924 significantly increased labour's share. As part of the economic recovery programme in 1932 and after, the policy of Gustavo Ross was both to impose an artificially high rate of exchange on the copper companies and include them in a law of 1934 imposing a tax of 6 per cent on profits of all Chilean industry: this meant that direct taxation of the *Gran Minería* had risen to 18 per cent, and, coupled with the indirect taxation created by exchange controls, by 1937 the tax share of Chilean receipts from the industry had risen to 38 per cent. By that time also, unionization of copper workers in the *Gran Minería* had proceeded apace, and they had become the 'aristocracy of labour' in the Chilean economy, earning wages well above the average. Other businesses were less favourably placed to meet increasing labour costs which were a marked feature of the 1930s.

This was partly in response to increasing inflation which in the decade 1930–1940 averaged 7 per cent a year, and in 1940–1950, 18 per cent, and government reaction to it. To counteract labour demands, government increasingly intervened by raising salaries and wages by law, forcing compliance on employers. For example, the Alessandri government had a reputation for being tough with workers, particularly unionized blue-collar ones, and it certainly put down strikes with severity, particularly in its early years: this did not prevent it, however, from passing a law in 1937 to give *empleados* a minimum wage of 300 pesos a month, as well as other legislation to their benefit on family allowances, unemployment relief and lump sum payments on retirement. Later governments were to go much further on both statutory wage provision and social security, adding to employers' running costs which, the law apart, were continually increased by their own response to workers' demands.

The FCAB had always prided itself on the good relations in general which its management had with its employees, relations which were kept in repair by the sympathetic attitude towards workers' difficulties shown from the board down, and also by the understanding of workers' problems which local management displayed. In 1933, for example, in requesting approval to pay a cost of living allowance, Heskett went into considerable detail on the workers' plight in Mejillones:

> Mr Hood [Chief Mechanical Engineer] has made a particular study of the conditions reigning at present in Mejillones, and I can only say that I agree with him that the patience and resignation shown by the people in that port must be admired and, I believe, are due to the confidence that they have in the Company, as they feel sure that directly the Company are in a position they will do their best to better the present conditions.
>
> Mr Hood paints a very distressful picture . . . as apparently during the hot weather the men have been obliged to pawn even their blankets, whilst their clothes are practically all worn out or sold. With the cold weather coming on, and the present epidemic of influenza, the conditions are really very serious, and it was for that reason that I felt it was my duty to put the matter very seriously before you . . . [3]

His proposals for a cost of living bonus were accepted and, in fact, the bonus was increased by 15 per cent for all *empleados* and *obreros* from 1 January 1935, without any representations from the men themselves. From that date also, all employees on short time had a six-day week restored. Before the second increase was announced, in 1934 Heskett had agreed to make a loan of one month's salary to all requesting it, repayment to the company to be made in instalments but when, in mid-1935, the employees petitioned for the cancellation of the debt, he refused since it was 'a debt of honour', while agreeing to extend the time for re-payment. His own reasonableness, however, was undermined at the same time by the Chilean government giving a 25 per cent increase in salaries and wages to all members of the armed forces and of the civil service, all of whom received an additional increase in the special allowance given for working in the desert regions – the so-called *gratificación de zona*. Not surprisingly in these circumstances, the FCAB's own workforce petitioned for yet a further increase in their own salaries or wages, and Heskett proposed to London that the cost of living bonus be increased by a further 10 per cent. His reasons were not, of course, entirely altruistic and he was quite candid on this:

> Our workmen in Mejillones and generally [he wrote in June 1935] are working with a very good will and seem absolutely contented, and the employees [i.e. white-collar workers] also seem fairly contented, but there are cases where it is absolutely impossible for them to make ends meet, and while we all feel that the moment is not one particularly propitious for embarking on further expenditure, I do really feel that we should do everything possible to avoid these requests from the employees being converted into demands, and the matter going to the Authorities for solution according to the Social Laws . . . [4]

Like his predecessor Hunt, he had had practical experience of dealing with the Chilean bureaucracy and regional officials, and that experience had shown that, to avoid trouble, they tended to support the men, however just or not the latter's case. The board in London accepted the proposal and, in thanking the board, Heskett remarked:

> We may say that we have had no trouble with the staff, whose petitions have been presented in a very reasonable manner, and we feel sure that the generosity of the Board in granting this further increase will have the effect of keeping our employees and workmen contented, which is a great thing in these days of unrest. [5]

As for the board's view itself, it was admirably spelled out by Bolden at the AGM in June 1936, in surveying the results for the previous year:

> Increased costs of living in both countries (Chile and Bolivia) as in all other parts of the world always lead to demands for increases in salaries and wages, and these have been met in a manner which the Board consider just and reasonable. The workmen in those countries can plainly see that there is increased traffic, that business appears to be improving and that the Railway Company is having increased receipts. They see also their own cost of living rising as a result of the depreciated exchanges and they are faced with their work bringing them a return which is not so good for them and their families as it had been. It is only natural that they look for some improvement in their terms of service. They do not understand, I am sure . . . that this Company being a sterling Company the increased currency receipts do not recoup us in the way they should. Our materials which we have to import for the operation of the Railway cost us very many more pesos and bolivianos compared with what they did when depreciated exchanges were not existing and we are not able to increase our currency tariffs sufficiently to compensate; they have been increased but not to the same extent that exchanges have depreciated: nor do I think that freighters could have afforded to pay in currency what would have been necessary to give us the same sterling results . . . [6]

In the context of Bolden's remarks on that occasion, it is worth noting that in both the annual reports of the FCAB and in the accounts of proceedings at annual general meetings from the beginnings in 1888, reference to salaries and wages as an important part of running costs had hitherto been rather rare: now, from the mid-1930s, they become almost a refrain, and phrases such as 'increases in currency salaries and wages' and 'additional contributions payable under the Social Laws' (as the *Annual Report* for 1937 put it) commonplace.

A significant year in the modern industrial and political history of Chile was 1936. Ross's recovery programme, which benefited the upper and middle classes, brought little solace to the workers who saw inflation eroding their already weak position. At the beginning of February, after futile petitions for wage increases, virtually the entire workforce of the state railway system went on strike, only to meet adamantine resistance from the government. Alessandri declared a state of siege, suspended the sittings of Congress, and ordered the army to run the railroad, while other sections of the working-class struck in sympathy with the railwaymen. He also closed down the opposition press and sent a number of left-wing leaders into exile, imprisoned others for incitement to disturb public order or placed them under house arrest. This naturally spawned a bitter reaction from the left-wing parties – the Socialist Party, founded in April 1933 and the Communist Party, founded in January 1922 – but thereafter bitterly persecuted by the Ibáñez government, and now in line with Moscow's international policy from 1935 of urging local parties to seek coalitions with middle-class and other left-wing democratic parties in a common front against fascism. Meanwhile, Chile's major centre party, the Radical, which had hitherto supported Alessandri's programme in Congress, had split into left and right wings, largely on the question of that programme and its implementation. The left wing gained ground not least because of Ross's intense personal antipathy to the party as a whole which he was never reluctant to express. At the height of the labour unrest in early 1936, the Socialist Party called on the radicals and communists to join them in opposition to what was increasingly coming to seem like a dictatorial government and, towards the end of February, the Radical Assembly of Santiago enthusiastically endorsed the call for a popular front. The party's Central Committee subsequently adopted this as its political programme, and the Chilean Popular Front was born. Though it took many more months of involved debate and manoeuvring among the opposition parties to make the Front effective, and despite the reluctance of right-wing Radicals to support it, it became a feasible political force when early in 1938 the parties composing it agreed on a common candidate for the presidential election of that year, the radical landowner and excellent campaigner, Pedro Aguirre Cerda. His opponent for the conservative forces in society was Gustavo Ross.

Aguirre travelled extensively through the country, meeting as many people as possible, and speaking on the Popular Front programme of sweeping change to benefit the masses, while Ross, confident of conservative support and his vote-buying capacity, stayed in Santiago. But what finally determined the narrow victory of Aguirre towards the end of 1938 was a totally unexpected event. The third candidate in the election was Carlos Ibáñez, returning from exile to contest it, and his following in alliance with the small, but disciplined, Chilean Nazi Party, led by Gónzalez von Marees, could count on some 15,000 to 20,000 votes, not enough to win but sufficient to deny Aguirre victory. But, following a peaceful march in Santiago on 4 September of some 12,000 of their followers, youthful nazis, probably at González von Marees' instigation, seized the main building of the University of Chile and the Social Security Building in the same vicinity at the heart of the city in what seems to have been an attempted coup. On 5 September the loyal paramilitary police, armed with tear-gas and machine guns, re-took the university and then used their captives as a shield to storm the Social Security Building. Though the rebels inside surrendered, the order then came from someone in government that none were to be spared, and sixty-two young nazis were killed in cold blood.

This event shocked the nation. It also led Ibáñez and von Marees, both then in jail, to urge their followers to vote for Aguirre and the Popular Front, as Ibáñez withdrew from the presidential race. Aguirre beat Ross by 222,700 votes to 218,609, and there is no doubt why he did. The expectations aroused by the Popular Front in the turbulent years, 1936–38, however, simply could not be met. In the first place, since the elections of 1937, the right-wing opposition parties had a clear majority in the Senate and formed the biggest bloc in the Chamber of Deputies, holding two more seats than the Radicals and left-wing parties combined. Four minor centre parties held the balance of fifteen seats between them, and their allegiance could not be taken for granted either by the government or by the opposition. But the latter could generally count on enough support to thwart government policies. Second, the Front itself was an unstable coalition. Though the Radicals were its major component, they could not stand alone, and their partners, notably the Socialists and Communists were, at bottom, antagonistic to one another, not least because they were in competition for the labour vote and the support of unionized workers. And, third, the rivalry between Radicals and Socialists in particular, while expressed in the altruistic language of differences on policy, was no less a matter of who should get the best jobs in government and administration. Frequent ministerial changes in Aguirre's first full year in office reflected both the obstructionist attitude of the right and the growing divisions on the left. The outbreak of the Second World War created deeper divisions, within the Radical Party between fierce anti-communists such as Juan Antonio Ríos and the left-wing which sought to keep the Communists in the Front, and growing bitterness between the latter and the Socialists who, by late 1941, wanted the Communists out. In short, by then the Front was clearly disintegrating: it only required the Central Committee of the Radical Party to decide on 16 January 1941, that that party's best interests would be served through 'independent political action' to sound its death knell.

Politically, the chief beneficiaries of the Popular Front government were the Radical and Communist parties, the former consolidating its hold on government and administration, the latter, while declining to accept ministerial portfolios and thus avoiding complicity in policies which went wrong, strengthening its support in the working and lower middle classes. Economically and socially, the Aguirre Cerda government disappointed its devotees, and its election platform of change to benefit the lower orders was only very partially carried out. Here, the chief beneficiaries were the Radical Party's most consistent supporters, the professional and middle classes, many of whom got jobs in the rapidly expanding civil service. Under Aguirre and, more particularly, under the Radical successor presidencies of Ríos (1941–46) and Gabriel González Videla (1946–52), social security provisions for various groups of white-collar workers, and certain key industrial workers, such as coalminers and railwaymen, were introduced, though the masses, and particularly the rural workers, benefitted little, and labour unrest continued to grow as inflation persisted. Still, such measures as were enacted did have an effect on employers' costs. Thus, in 1942, health insurance for white-collar workers was followed by the introduction of the *sueldo vital*, a legally-declared basic salary for the same groups. González put through in 1952 no fewer than six laws, reorganizing the social insurance system for blue-collar workers, instituting family allowances for civil servants, and integrating the various insurance arrangements for health provision. These were all piecemeal measures but they had to be paid for. And such legislation carried forward the earlier social security provision of the 1920s and early 1930s, expanding the role of the bureaucracy in internal affairs, and emphasizing the state's role in such arrangements. Future governments would amplify such legislation and underline these developments.

On the industrial front, the Popular Front government had one major achievement to its credit, the establishment in 1939 of the Chilean Development Corporation (CORFO) as a government agency to promote industry, improve the balance of trade and generally raise workers' living standards. It was to be a major stockholder in the enterprises it subsidized or created, affirming again the role of the state in economic affairs. Interestingly enough, the law creating it was part of a law for reconstruction of the devastated regions after the massive earthquake of 1939 which hit chiefly south central Chile, the only way the government could get Congressional approval for this major expansion of state intervention. No less interestingly, while its funds were to come from government capital and foreign (chiefly US) credits, the former was secured basically by a further tax on the profits of copper mining amounting to 15 per cent, almost doubling the effective rate of direct taxation on copper to a total of 33 per cent.

The advent of the Second World War was a mixed blessing for the Chilean economy. On the one hand, first it increased dramatically the growth of import-substituting industry, as supplies from former traders such as Germany and the UK were cut off. Second, the demand for Chile's minerals by the allies increased Chile's export earnings, and created a large foreign reserve. Third, it enabled US interests to replace those of European powers as Chile's major trading partner, and that was a permanent shift. On the other hand, however, the initial shortage of goods fuelled inflation further, and growing indebtedness to the US offset many of the other economic gains, especially as regards the CORFO which came increasingly to rely on US credits. Moreover, though at its creation, the CORFO might have seemed an instrument of economic nationalism, that sentiment was blunted by Chile's dependence on the United States. Thus, in January 1942, Washington and Santiago came to an agreement to impose a wartime ceiling price of 12 cents a pound on Chilean copper, in exchange for the US repeal of its excise tax of 4 cents a pound, in operation since 1932: in fact, it was not repealed until 1947, but it is calculated that the fixing of the copper price at 12 cents a pound cost the Chilean government over US $500 million in lost earnings to the end of 1945. The complicated diplomatic history of US–Chilean relations in the early 1940s cannot be considered here: suffice to say that, whatever their economic relationship, Chile did not break off diplomatic relations with the Axis powers until January 1943, and did not formally join the Allies in declaring war until over two years later.

For boards and managements of foreign businesses in Chile, the turbulent decade 1935–1945 required considerable adjustments to changing situations, not least in the matter of the wage component in running costs which rose inexorably throughout the period. And while a long-established company such as the FCAB was able for a while to maintain its paternal, but on the whole responsible, attitude towards the workers, that tradition began to break down as unionization increased and, often backed by the law, labour's demands assumed a keener edge. More and more of local management's time was taken up with such matters, and however crude an indicator it might be, the following table reflects, at least in part, the changes in profitability of which the wage factor was one.

Table 8. FCAB lines. Ratio of expenditure to gross receipts

YEAR	RATIO(%)
1935	56.52
1936	62.64
1937	64.55
1938	74.42
1939	81.72
1940	85.73
1941	86.40
1942	86.38
1943	78.71
1944	87.50
1945	84.36

Source: FCAB, Annual Reports, 1936–1946

Obviously, the changing ratio from year to year also reflected variable running costs, such as fluctuating fuel bills, maintenance of rolling stock and lines, repair costs for damaged track – usually the result of adverse weather conditions – and amounts set aside for amortization and renewals. Nevertheless, references to labour costs figure prominently in chairmen's speeches and in managers' reports. Thus, in his annual report to the board for 1936, Heskett wrote from Antofagasta:

> The cost of living has shown a continued tendency to increase ... Arising from a petition received from the employees for an increase in salary, the Board authorised that, as from the 1st May, 1936, the 25 per cent cost-of-living bonus granted to the currency paid employees and workmen, which had been in force since the 1st July, 1935, be added to the basic salaries and wages, and certain increases were granted as from the same date to assist the lower paid employees, more particularly the married men, and also the Permanent-Way gangs.
>
> ... in the early part of 1937 a law was promulgated, which, among other things, obliges employers to increase the wages of their employees by from 10 per cent to 60 per cent, according to salary earned and years of service, and this, together with other dispositions of the law, will have the effect of considerably increasing the Company's expenses ...[7]

A year later, he estimated that that Law (6020) meant an increased monthly expenditure of approximately 150,000 pesos, and he also reported that in August, 1937 further wage demands had resulted in a settlement reached

> ... on the basis of increases varying from 20 per cent, to 40 per cent ... It is estimated that the cost of these increases to workmen has involved the Company in an additional monthly expenditure of about 170,000 pesos ...[8]

So it went on. In his survey of 1938, at the AGM on 13 June 1939, referring to the new Pensions Law of that year, Bolden drew attention to 'the increased currency salaries and wages, as well as the increased contributions which we had to provide under the Social Laws of the country',[9] while in his report for 1940 Heskett reported at considerable length on the same subject in a year when working expenses of the railway, moles and waterworks had increased by almost £119,000 over 1939.

> This large increase is mainly attributable to the following: The improved official value of the Chilian peso . . . is estimated to have increased working expenses by nearly £50,000 and there were the extraordinary payments amounting to £32,412 which we had to make for Employees' Indemnities for years of service under the provisions of Law No. 6527. There was a 10 per cent increase in the rates of pay to the Antofagasta Bay Workers as from the 24th August, 1940, and a general increase of wages was granted to all workmen as from the 1st November, 1940 . . .[10]

The Law for Employees' Indemnities provided that workmen on the private railways were to be paid fifteen days' wages for each complete year of service, 'the period of service to be computed from the 13th November, 1940, and the indemnities calculated on the wage earned at the time of leaving the service'.[11] 'The law moreover stipulates that workmen

> . . . of more than 10 years' continuous service to their credit with the Company at the 13th November, 1940, are to be paid 15 days' wages for each of those ten years, the indemnity to be calculated on the average wage earned during the two years immediately prior to the 13th November, 1940 . . .[12]

He also referred to another recent law granting twenty-five working days' holiday a year with full pay to employees in the provinces of Antofagasta and Tarapacá.

Many of these laws were, in fact, long in gestation and the result of the Chilean equivalent of private members' bills introduced in the Chamber of Deputies by interested individuals. Law No. 6527, for example, on indemnities for workmen on private railways, had its origins in a proposal by two deputies as early as 1936, in order to bring the men into line with those on the State Railways. It aroused much opposition from the private railways, including the FCAB, and Bolden did not mince his words on the matter. He wrote:

> It would be manifestly unjust to impose obligations with respect to indemnities on private railways and exclude all other employers in Chile, to say nothing of making the indemnities retroactive with regard to past

> services. It is beside the point that such indemnities are already paid by the State Railways which can provide the funds required either by an increase in tariffs or from the general revenue of the country . . . if there is any likelihood of the projected bill being passed strong representations should be made to the government . . . [13]

Acting for the board, he repeated these arguments to the Chilean Ambassador in London, Agustín Edwards, who undertook to convey them to Santiago. In the event, the proposal floundered through several Chilean departments and committees, and did not become law for another four years. But it re-surfaced from time to time, requiring Heskett to make a number of visits to Santiago to make representations before different bodies. Once the proposal, amended, became law, however, there was nothing to do but accept it.

To such obligations imposed by law, the usual counter-attack was to seek an increase in tariffs on traffic carried by the FCAB, again usually a tortuous business involving long visits to Santiago, frequent meetings with men in authority from ministers down, close consultation with the company's advisers, and not a little frustration. It is true that such tariff increases were generally finally awarded, though rarely at the level requested by the company and certainly insufficient to meet rising wage and other costs. But it was always a long process, and the capacity of particular members of the bureaucracy to procrastinate was quite remarkable. Prominent among them was Heskett's old adversary, Señor Mujica, whose talent for Fabian tactics was only matched by his ability to hold on to his post as Superintendent of Railways for several years, despite frequent ministerial changes in the late 1930s and early 1940s. One example must suffice from a long catalogue.

On the promulgation of Law No. 6020, in 1937, conferring additional benefits on *empleados*, Heskett estimated that the annual cost to the company would amount to over 1,866,000 pesos (about £20,000 at the then relevant exchange rate), and he suggested to London that a request for an increase in tariffs might properly be submitted to offset that new cost. The board agreed and Heskett prepared his submission, taking care, as the company always did, to consult the local managers of other foreign-owned railways beforehand. A good deal of time was taken up in consultation with them, and the conclusion was finally reached that for the FCAB:

> . . . the least we could ask for would be that the existing surcharges on the tariffs for nitrate, coal and petroleum etc. for the nitrate industry should be increased to 100%, and that all articles exempt from surcharge . . . and all passengers and luggage should be surcharged 50% . . . [14]

Before the petition was submitted, however, the Minister of Finance himself, Gustavo Ross, and one of his aides, Osvaldo de Castro – no friend of the railway – visited Antofagasta, and Heskett conferred with them.

> We gave a full explanation [Heskett said] ... of the actual economic situation of the Railways as brought about by the introduction of Law No. 6020; the general all-round increase in the price of fuels and all commodities and the necessity that existed for improving the conditions of the workmen. Señor de Castro, as I fully expected, opposed our proposals ... but Señor Ross was exceptionally sympathetic ... He suggested that we should furnish him with a memorandum setting out the increased cost to the Company by reason of increased salaries and wages and the increased cost of essential materials ...[15]

As it was, Heskett concluded, even if the company succeeded in its requests, 'it will be seen that ... they would only compensate us for a little more than half the estimated increased expenditure ...'[16]

This was in April, and Mujica had not yet appeared upon the scene. Pursuing the matter some weeks later, Heskett went south but was himself then delayed as he explained in June:

> I came down here (to Santiago) without a Secretary as we have none to spare in Antofagasta with so many men on leave ... the weather broke, and we had rain, wind and cold with the result that I felt pains and found that the mozo had not packed my special medicine ... the rheumatism dug itself into my right knee and kept me to a certain degree out of action ...[17]

But this was only the beginning of the general manager's problems: Ross was too busy to attend to the FCAB, and left the matter to De Castro and Mujica. The former quibbled about the surcharge on nitrate, coal and petroleum but, eventually, a compromise was reached, and it then fell to Mujica to discuss a general surcharge on everything else. Heskett reported:

> He was as usual quite suave etc., but it is very difficult to tie him down. He first of all confirmed a telephonic conversation with me that he must know how we had been serving our bond interest, our income in gold, a comparative statement of wages and salaries over the last five years and a host of other information that was being asked for with the only idea of delay ...[18]

Mujica also said that he would have to go north to investigate before reporting to the minister, then 'finally promised faithfully to go deeply into the matter ....'[19] Although he abandoned the idea of going north, Mujica still had other cards to play: having been charged with drafting the decree on the nitrate surcharge, he then had published the FCAB's petition in the *Chilean Gazette* (*Diario Oficial*) as well as in the papers of

Santiago and Antofagasta, inviting all and sundry to make their comments. Heskett reported wearily:

> 'The result was somebody called Mustaki objected, he owning a tin pot oficina in the Tal Tal district . . .'[20]

This was too much for Heskett, who had been negotiating patiently for six weeks, and, through an intermediary, he contacted Ross who got the decree signed on 1 July. That left the general surcharge still to be arranged, thus giving Mujica ample scope for further mischief.

What it was, in detail, the archives do not record, but in the middle of August the exasperated Heskett wrote:

> . . . owing to the obstructive attitude taken up by Señor Mujica, I have been unable to come to any definite arrangement with the Government in regard to the general surcharge question, and under the circumstances felt it was a waste of time and money to remain longer in Santiago. I left Santiago on the 10th instant, but the previous day I had an interview with the Minister of Fomento and fully explained the situation to him. He was good enough to promise to go personally into the matter and see if something could be definitely settled. I therefore left instructions with Señor García de la Huerta to follow up the matter closely . . .[21]

García de la Huerta clearly did his best but he had to report to Wells in October that the Minister (who, himself, had promised so much) had averred that

> . . . according to the study made by Señor Mujica it appeared that the Company was not in such a difficult position as we had tried to make out; that we were not working at a loss, and that we could afford to be bear the increased expenditure which had arisen. He added that to authorise an increase in surcharge at the present time might create considerable discontent in the North . . .[22]

The minister promised to pass on a copy of Mujica's report – then still in draft – but when the final version arrived, Wells said it was 'entirely unfavourable to us, and at the moment we are preparing our observations thereon which we will forward to the Minister . . .'[23] These were sent in November, but it seems that they were made more persuasive by what occurred in the next few weeks. On 5 December, under the auspices of the central government, the far-flung province and city of Antofagasta began a week's festivities to broadcast to the country its distinctive contribution to national well-being. The city's guests of honour were the Minister of Fomento, Ricardo Bascuñan, and the Minister of Finance, Francisco Garcés Gana, but, as Wells, deputizing for Heskett who was on leave, reported:

> The Intendente and the Alcalde of Antofagasta were somewhat perturbed over the question of finding suitable accommodation for these gentlemen and their party, and I was asked if I could help out. I immediately offered to accommodate the Minister and his two daughters in the Guest House of Mr Heskett, and also to place my house at the disposition of the Minister of Fomento and his wife ... The Intendente formally made the offer to the Minister and they accepted ...[24]

This was, obviously, an opportunity not to be missed, and Wells seized it. He raised with the Minister of Fomento the outstanding question of the general surcharge, supplied him with a copy of the company's reply to Mujica's report – which the minister said he had not had time to study – and rehearsed the company's long-standing arguments.

> The Minister appeared [Wells wrote to London] to fully appreciate our position ... He assured me that he would attend to our petition as soon as possible ...
>
> Both Ministers expressed to me their best thanks and appreciation for the kind hospitality which had been extended to them by the Company ...[25]

Whatever influence these encounters had must be a matter of conjecture. It may be sufficient to note that Wells was able to tell Bolden in mid-December that the minister, 'without reference to Señor Mujica ... had instructed the Sub-Secretary to extend a decree authorising the surcharges for the Antofagasta, Aguas Blancas and Chilian Northern Railways ...'[26] For Mujica not to be consulted to the bitter end must have been, for him, 'the most unkindest cut of all'. Still, it should be noted that, first, the surcharges did not come into effect until 1938, so protracted had been the business of getting them approved and, secondly, the rates finally accepted were lower than what the company had requested, for example 30 per cent, not 50 per cent on 2nd and 3rd class passenger fares. In the meantime, moreover, after lengthy negotiations with the workmen's representatives over an increase in wages, Wells had been obliged, in September 1937, to concede rises in basic pay ranging from 40 per cent to 20 per cent, depending on existing levels, a measure which would cost the company an additional 160,000 pesos a month. That was the limit the board would allow, particularly since, at that time, the surcharge question had not been settled.

In effect, from that time forward it was company policy to link wage-settlements – whether imposed by law or freely negotiated – explicitly to increases in tariffs, though, in the earlier years at least, official approval for the latter was neither automatic nor prompt. Gradually, however, successive Chilean governments, while haggling over details, seem to have accepted the company's view as spelled out by its secretary after the latest wage settlement in 1945:

> The Board are very glad [Cowley wrote to Heskett] that you have maintained the *principle* that wages and tariffs are interdependent and that any increase in the former must be fully compensated for by a concurrent increase in tariffs . . .[27]

In addition to this time-consuming business for management, its lawyers and advisers, another feature of that period in Chile demanding increasing attention was the considerable growth of trade unionism and, to some extent, of working-class militancy. Whereas previously local management had, on the whole, been able to deal with industrial relations on a company basis – and did enjoy a just reputation as a fair and reasonable employer – it had to take more and more account of national political, social and economic developments. The leading British authority on trade unionism in Chile notes that 'The acceleration in the pace of industrial development with the coming of the Popular Front government produced a rise in the numbers in unions', citing figures to show that whereas in 1932, when the Ministry of Labour first began to collect statistics, the membership of legally constituted unions was 54,800, rising to 193,000 by 1942 and to 284,300 by 1952.[28] It is also noteworthy that 1936, the year that saw the birth of the Popular Front, also witnessed the foundation of the Chilean Confederation of Labour (CTCh), a national umbrella organization for unionized workers. Such general developments were bound to have a regional impact and in the province of Antofagasta there was a growing consciousness by workers of a particular employer, as to how their colleagues with other bosses were faring. Thus, as Heskett frequently pointed out, a favourable wage or salary settlement for *obreros* or *empleados* granted by the more important employers, such as the Chilex at Chuquicamata or the British-owned nitrate and railway companies such as the Lautaro, almost inevitably led his own workers to submit fresh petitions for similar treatment. Indeed, on several occasions he felt bound to protest to his fellow-managers at such actions where their repercussions did not seem to him to have been thought out. Naturally, he recognized that each company was different and that managers had to run their business to satisfy their superiors but there were occasions where common understanding had been breached unilaterally, as, for example, in 1936. Early that year the various syndicates of bay workers at Antofagasta petitioned their employers for a substantial increase in wages but this was rejected by the Association of Employers, which had long been recognized by all of them, and by the workers, as their negotiating body in all matters to do with labour in the bay. That association and the syndicates then agreed to submit the case to a government commission specially appointed to weigh the evidence. The next move, in the absence of an agreement, would have been for both parties to approach the local conciliation tribunal, under the Labour

Laws, and, if that failed, to go to arbitration. If *impasse* still prevailed, the men might then declare a legal strike. This procedure had been used many times before and seems to have worked effectively. On this occasion, however, as Wells reported:

> It was with some surprise that, in a recent edition of the local newspaper, we saw an announcement that the Anglo-Chilean and Lautaro Nitrate Companies had decided to increase the wages of their workmen by 10%. I immediately enquired from the Lautaro Company as to whether this included the bay workers, and found that it did, so that all the work which the Lautaro Company's representative had done for the Association – and he has been very prominent in finding means to refuse the petition of the bay workers – was lost . . .[29]

Subsequent attempts by the Lautaro manager, Mr Kruger, to justify his action did not convince Wells, who pointed out that this was not the first time that company had cut the ground from under the association's feet, and that all the employers had long accepted the latter's rulings, 'and that such rulings need in no way conflict with anything the Anglo-Chilean and Lautaro Companies might decide to do as regards the men in their Oficinas . . .'[30] Kruger saw the point but the damage had been done. Shortly afterwards, Wells underlined the problem in reporting that the Chilex had also recently conceded a wage increase of 10 per cent but only after securing from government a more favourable exchange rate to buy pesos for dollars, and on the clear understanding that the increase was 'not applicable to the bay workers, whose case they have left to be dealt with by the Association in Antofagasta'.[31]

Heskett, who had recently returned from a business trip to Santiago, was justifiably piqued by the nitrate companies' breaking ranks, and not least because the FCAB had at that juncture a petition from its own workers under consideration, which he felt unjustified in the light of a substantial increase in wages awarded only a few months previously. Now, additional pressure from the syndicates at Mejillones, Antofagasta, Calama, not to mention the bay, seemed inevitable. He also put his finger on a significant factor influencing the situation:

> . . . with regard to the political situation in Chile . . . it is considered, by those who ought to know, to be delicate in the extreme and what is more unfortunate for us is, that it is having a very adverse effect on the labour situation, due to the undoubted nervousness of the [Alessandri] Government, and apparently their desire at all costs to induce, if not even to go so far as to oblige foreign companies to improve the financial position of their employees and workmen, in order to avoid the revolutionary party [i.e. the Popular Front] making capital out of the undoubted hardships which the labouring classes are suffering owing to the high cost of living . . .[32]

Further evidence of the relationship between national politics and the regional picture emerged in the discussions on the petitions of the railway's workers. They submitted a fresh petition immediately on Heskett's return from Santiago where he had already come under pressure from the Labour Department in the light of the increases awarded by the nitrate companies and by the Chilex: now it was the intendant's turn. He sent for Heskett

> ... and pointed out that he had instructions from the Government that at all costs he had to keep the men quiet in the North, and now that the Lautaro Company and the Chile Exploration Company had satisfied the demands of their employees, he requested the Railway Company to do the same; and he further informed me that his idea would be to have a meeting between the representatives of all the federations etc. in the Railway, and the management, with himself as president and to draw up an "acta" agreeing to the new wage list ...[33]

All this was clean contrary to established procedure in labour disputes and Heskett so informed the intendant who was not only new in the job but also 'an extremely voluble gentleman'. As the good and experienced manager he was, Heskett had prepared his ground:

> The most careful enquiries [he reported] have been made of our employees and workmen, and I really can find no active discontent or under-current of dissatisfaction which might result in the presentation of demands, the result of which might lead to the formalities laid down in the "Codigo de Trabajo".
>
> Personally I feel that if the nitrate and copper companies had not come along with these increases we would not have been placed in the somewhat unenviable position which we now find ourselves, but while I think we have looked after both our employees and workmen exceptionally well ... I still have a feeling ... that we might improve the condition of the lower-paid men, as these are the men who have the hardest time to make both ends meet ...[34]

Having routed the intendant he therefore, proposed not an all-round increase in wages and salaries but, in consultation with his departmental chiefs, and in direct negotiations with the men's representatives, to identify the poorest paid and those in real hardship and raise their wages accordingly. In addition, the very worst paid – the permanent way men – were to be given a new base rate, and incorporated into the cost-of-living bonus scheme, from which they had hitherto been excluded. With the board's approval, these measures were taken, and proved acceptable to the men, not least because Heskett was able to show that the effect of the increases given by the nitrate companies and the Chilex did no more than bring them into line with what the FCAB had been doing for its workers for almost a year!

San Pedro and San Pablo volcanoes

Railway from San Pedro to Ascotan

Leaving Loa

Open cast copper mine, Chuquicamata, 1978

Antofagasta: the old wharf from Hotel Antofagasta

Antofagasta marshalling yards

Rolling stock, *c*. 1914: first class interior

Papal visit to Antofagasta railway

Early Venturi water meters and recorders (Antofagasta Museum)

Captured carbines and photographs of their late owners (Antofagasta Museum)

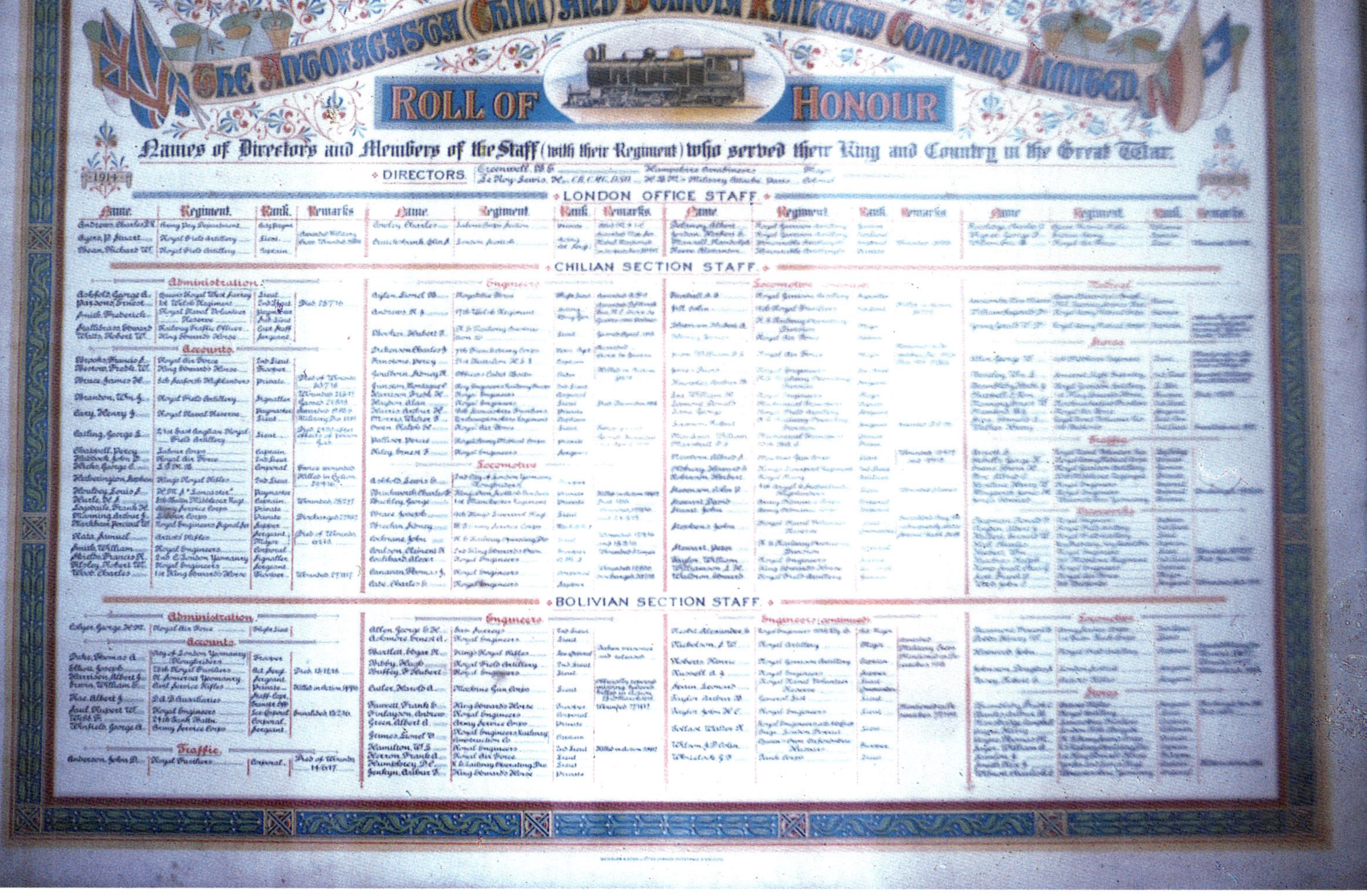

Roll of Honour: First World War

Freight train passing San Martin salt lake, *c.* 1985

This particular case – time-consuming though it was – well illustrates how misunderstandings could easily arise among the workers of the railway through wage settlements obtained by their fellows in other concerns, and how easily the government and local officials could completely misread the real situation. On this occasion, thanks to the firmness of Heskett and Wells, the FCAB emerged with credit from what, at first sight, seemed a tricky situation.

But the factors which influenced developments in the labour field in 1936 grew ever stronger as the years went by. In 1938, for example, the bay-workers petitioned for a 60 per cent increase in wages, the association offered 10 per cent and, after the various procedures under the law had been gone through and failed, the workers gave notice of strike action. The intendant then called on the Minister of Labour, Señor Bernardo Leighton, to intervene; and the minister made a special trip to Antofagasta to act as conciliator. After several meetings with the men and backed up by a telegram from President Aguirre Cerda himself, he succeeded in getting arbitration accepted and both sides agreed on General Julio Carvallo, commander of the Antofagasta garrison, for that role. His award favoured the men rather than the employers, having pointed out that:

> The prices of foodstuffs and articles of clothing have risen since 1932 by 145% and 80% respectively, whilst in the same period the men's wages have been increased by 40%.
>
> The award [Heskett wrote] gives a general increase in wages of 27% to the men, plus a house allowance of $80 a month to the married men, and provides for the wages to be either increased or decreased each six months according as to whether the index figure of the cost of living, as fixed by the Government Statistical Office, rises or falls . . . [35]

Here was another portent of things to come through government intervention: the linking of pay settlements with the cost of living index in a country which, since the late 1870s, had suffered endemic inflation, increasingly gained ground in future years, raising wage costs for employers who then recouped themselves in higher prices to consumers, thus perpetuating the inflationary spiral.

To return to 1938, in the wake of Carvallo's arbitration, all other major employers in Antofagasta received petitions for increases in wages, ranging in the FCAB's case between 25 per cent and 100 per cent. Heskett refused this absolutely in view of the 1936 and 1937 settlements in the light of living costs but, with the board's approval, he did accept the new principle of a six-monthly review of wages linked to the cost of living for the future. This meant, of course, that the policy of seeking increases in traffic tariffs to offset increases in wage costs became embedded in company practice.

A year later, he noted another extraneous influence apart from government, as employers received the customary petitions from workers.

> There can be little doubt [he opined] that all these petitions were engineered from Santiago by the . . . CTCh . . . to be discussed in May, which is always the time that these people choose, as then they are able to work on the feelings of the men by Labour Day demonstrations and such like means . . . That the 'CTCh' is at the back of this movement we have practically been able to completely confirm, and we were fortunate enough to be able to intercept a communication from the Anglo-Chilean Nitrate Railway Syndicate to our Antofagasta Syndicate asking for the latter's assistance and giving advice on to how to proceed . . . [36]

By a different letter of the same date, he expressed his exasperation at his own workforce's behaviour: referring to the benefits they had had he thought that:

> . . . there would seem to be very little for them to complain about. As we have repeatedly informed them, the Company are not slave drivers, and if they feel they are not being treated properly, or there are better Companies to work for, then we make no objection to their leaving and taking up other employment. The whole trouble is caused by about half a dozen elements of ultra-socialistic tendency, and it is always found that these men are probably the best office workers and never give the slightest cause for any complaint to be found with their work. If, therefore, they have to be got rid of, it is almost practically certain that they are being dispensed with because of their Socialistic tendencies.
>
> You will naturally ask how it is that all the rest of the employees, who have been with us for a large number of years, allow themselves to be led by a group of discontents (*sic*), and it is really a question of wanting peace, and they found it much more convenient not to oppose those people, as if they do so they are immediately singled out for reprisals, and unpleasantness occurs . . . our attitude will have to be more or less determined on what the majority of the old hands decide and to see if their influence, if they care to exert it, is sufficient to keep the rest in order. [37]

But the 'old hands' were getting older, and the times were changing, and, as in 1936, one could no longer count on the solidarity of managerial colleagues: in this instance, the Anglo-Chilean Company let the side down, 'the Company's Board in Santiago settling the matter there (i.e. their similar problem) with the intervention of the Minister of Labour and a Commission of workmen from Oficina María Elena'.[38] In the FCAB's case, as it happened, a satisfactory agreement was reached for the *obreros* but the *empleados*, 'assisted by two representatives from Santiago of the CTCh, who had been named by the Minister of Labour to settle the matter', proved recalcitrant.[39] The dispute went on for several more weeks, and Heskett's account is worth quoting at some length to illustrate quite graphically both how far regional problems could no longer be settled entirely at regional levels, and how much more complicated that circumstance had made them.

Early in August he informed London that

> ... owing to the interference of the CTCh, the Minister of Labour informed me that he had decided that the dispute should be settled in Santiago ... I was able to talk to the Minister on the telephone, and we had a long and quite straight talk on the matter, during which I informed him that the Administration of the Antofagasta Railway is in Antofagasta, together with the whole of our books and records, and that as the laws of the country, by which we carefully abide, indicated that the conflict should be settled in Antofagasta, I failed utterly to see why he should give way to the employees, who simply and solely wanted the matter transferred to Santiago in order that they might be able to persuade the Minister, or the President, or the CTCh, to bring influence to bear to make the Company give way ... I considered it a scandal that the employees were still being listened to when the north of Chili was probably in the middle of a crisis equal to that of 1932, and that rather than being in a position to give increases in salaries there was more likelihood of our having to get rid of about 20% of the staff. The upshot, however, was that he agreed to send his Visiting Labour Inspector ... He proposed arbitration, and I presume he would suggest himself as arbitrator, the result of which would, of course, be a foregone conclusion ...[40]

The inspector timed his visit to coincide with the outbreak of the war in Europe, and first tried to persuade Heskett that that development would undoubtedly benefit the province, a hope, he said, which justified the company yielding to the *empleados*. A concurrent strike in Iquique had recently been concluded by the Nitrate Railways Company yielding to the *empleados*'s demands: as Heskett said,

> This has considerably prejudiced our position here ... the ... Inspector informed me that his reports from the statistics of the Railway Department proved that the fall in traffics on the Nitrate Railways in Iquique was very much greater than that on the Antofagasta Railway, and that if the Nitrate Railway could better the condition of their workmen, he could see no reason why we could not do the same for our employees ...[41]

Who, precisely, in the railway department supplied the statistics is not recorded, but it is far from impossible that it was Heskett's old adversary, Señor Mujica, who was still superintendent there. That may be conjecture, but there is no doubting the difficult situation Heskett found himself in in 1939. 'The whole situation here is so uncertain, and the attitude of the Government so unsympathetic to any kind of reduction in staff, that our position is extremely delicate'.[42] Indeed, the inspector tried to get from him a categorical guarantee in the company's name that when agreement with the *empleados* was finally reached they should all be kept on indefinitely, no matter what, a suggestion that was just as categorically rejected. This was precisely at the time that management in both Chile and London were equally preoccupied in making drastic economies in the light of a very bad year for traffic, and when, as Heskett had pointed out to the Minister of Labour, 1939 looked like being comparable to 1932 in those respects.

The arguments went back and forth for more than another month, but this was one battle that Heskett simply could not win in the light of all the circumstances – the intractability of the employees, the support given to them by the inspector and, indeed, by government, the invidious comparisons being drawn between the FCAB and the Nitrate Railways and, most important to Heskett, that if the company did not reach some kind of compromise agreement acceptable to both sides, 'the Government were perfectly capable of stepping in and arbitrarily settling the matter'.[43] Consequently, compromise ruled in the final settlement of October: the men secured an increase of $80 a month (instead of the 16 per cent increase and the $100 a month they were pressing for to the last moment) and a sum of $220 for the five months the dispute had run (instead of the $500 back-pay they had sought) and the agreement was to run for eighteen months from 1 October 1939. In short, despite the difficulties, Heskett had done quite well, and it was he who fired the parting shot: 'I agreed', he said,

> to the insertion of a clause that the Railway Company would take no revenge, and pointed out that this was something we never did do, as we were a little above that method of administration . . .[44]

But the fact that he had to spell this out to those who did not appreciate it was itself a sign of changing times.

These new complexities, surfacing in the later 1930s but becoming more insistent as time went on, naturally occupied a good deal of management time and effort. But managers still had a railway to run, and directors the stockholders to think about. New circumstances would arise but some problems were perennial such as the unpredictability of weather, the water-supply side of the business, the renewal of tariff contracts with customers such as the Chilex and nitrate producers, and always, the assumptions outsiders made about a foreign business which played a major part not only in the national and regional economy, but also in the support of other services. The company's reputation had to be sustained though sometimes the assumptions outran the possibilities, and often they provided some light relief from day-to-day preoccupations. An example of what might be expected comes from 1938 when Heskett received an urgent message from the Minister of Lands and Colonisation, inviting him to commit the FCAB to put up $1 million or a minimum of $800,000 as an investment in a project to build 'a tourist hotel in Antofagasta at an estimated cost of some $5,000,000'. 'I was somewhat astonished', Heskett wrote:

> when he told me that the Anglo-Chilian Nitrate Corporation and the Lautaro Nitrate Company between them had subscribed $2,200,000, and that his object ... was to know what amount of shares the Railway Company would be prepared to subscribe, taking into account that the Railway Company would be ... most directly benefited by the proposed tourist hotel ...[45]

Heskett demurred, pointing, politely, to the company's current financial constraints – arrears of dividends to stockholders, overdrafts at the bank, and so on – and he did not feel that the minister's promise of 3 per cent a year profit was a 'lucrative investment'. He had, in addition, a more cogent argument for Bolden, though not for the minister:

> ... unless the weather in winter is a great deal more balmy than it has been for the last month or so here in Antofagasta, no tourist will want to come here unless they [*sic*] are attempting to get rheumatic fever; and I cannot see tourists coming here in summer with all the attractions there are in the South of Chile ...[46]

The minister's persistence lasted for several months, however, and Heskett – always deferential – diplomatically put him off, in consultation with Bolden agreeing finally to put in $400,000, provided evidence would be forthcoming that the hotel was actually being built, and that payment in instalments would be allowed. Fortunately, for political reasons the minister resigned in September, and Heskett informed London three months later that 'we are hoping ... the scheme will not be followed up'.[47] Nor was it, at least at that time.

Support for other causes was both more modest and more traditional. At about the same time that Heskett was requested to help put up a tourist hotel in Antofagasta, he was also being asked to support the Anglican faith in the same city. Up to 1931, like the other British firms, the FCAB had made an annual donation to church funds but they, too, were hit by the economic crisis and things spiritual were left to one chaplain whose parish embraced not only the two Chilean provinces of Tarapacá and Antofagasta but also, indeed, Bolivia. Following the example of the other British concerns, the FCAB also reduced its contribution between 1932 and 1935 but somewhat reluctantly as Heskett explained:

> We felt rather disappointed at the action of the British Firms here ... as it appeared they thought the Railway Company, who also subscribed handsomely to the British School and the Nursing Home, should bear the brunt of the maintenance of the Chaplain ... therefore, we reduced our subscription ... but in 1936, on the arrival of the Rev. Thompson, we agreed to increase it to £50 payable in Chilian currency at the official rate of exchange ...[48]

In pointing out that 'the Railway Company already pay approximately 50% of the total amount contributed in Antofagasta', he, nevertheless, sought leave to raise the subscription to £100, as it had been up to 1931, and to this the board agreed. Similarly, as times improved, the company reverted to its traditional benevolence towards its employees and others for their recreation, as the following illustrates:

> Antofagasta Golf Club. With reference to the consignment of golf clubs which you recently sent out for account of this Club; notwithstanding the fact that before the order ... was sent home we received permission to import them and pay for them with our own funds, the Exchange Control Commission have since insisted ... that payment for these articles cannot be permitted out of our own funds, and that an export credit must be obtained at what is known as the "Oro de lavaderos" rate of exchange ... $178.28 per £ ... what we propose to do to liquidate matters with the Golf Club is to charge them the difference between the freemarket rate (then about $95 to the £) and the rate of $178.28 per £.[49]

Nothing, it seems, was too much trouble: when the BBC's Latin American Service was inaugurated in 1938, Heskett wrote as follows:

> We will arrange for the weekly bulletin which the Corporation offered to send out regularly to be supplied to the Chilian Employees' Club in Antofagasta, and if you could arrange for an additional two copies to be sent out, we could hand these to the Chilean Employees' Clubs at Mejillones and Baquedano.[50]

In passing, but in the same context, his comments on the BBC World Service in English may also merit citation:

> It can [he wrote] be stated with certainty that the BBC news bulletins in English are very keenly listened to and greatly appreciated by the British residents in South America ...
>
> If there is any criticism from the British residents here it is perhaps that there is too much classical music included at times in the BBC programmes.[51]

Though the FCAB rarely blew its own trumpet – at least to the outside world – changing times called for imaginative tactics, and certainly in public relations, as Heskett pointed out in another letter:

> You will no doubt observe [he wrote to Cowley in 1938] in "El Mercurio" of Antofagasta of the 6th instant an article is published which outlines the benefits provided by this Company for its employees and workmen. We arranged with "El Mercurio" to have this published in Antofagasta, also in Santiago and Valparaiso, and we think you will agree that, *in these times when undertakings like ours are attacked on the slightest pretext whatsoever*, it is as well that the public in general should be made acquainted with the true facts of what the Company does for the benefit of its employees and workmen, both on its own initiative and in compliance with the social laws, and the very heavy expense to which it is put in this connection.[52]

The modest – though spasmodic – recovery of the company's fortunes from the depths of the depression which the years from 1935 to 1940 witnessed was continued in the following quinquennium, embracing the Second World War. It reflected the great expansion in Chilean copper mining and refining as wartime requirements of the Allied Powers increased, particularly after the United States became a belligerent towards the end of 1941. The following table illustrates both the growth of national output of refined copper and the significant proportion of the total shipped from the massive mine of Chuquicamata:

Table 9. Chilean refined copper production, 1940–1945 (thousands of metric tons)

Year	Total Chilean Production	Chuquicamata Production
1940	333,247	150,995
1941	442,857	216,848
1942	463,389	225,742
1943	473,763	238,021
1944	474,613	241,227
1945	450,999	237,619

Source: Tables VII and VIII in A. Sutulov (ed.), *El cobre chileno*, Santiago, 1975, pp.490–491

These figures indicate that, over the period, roughly 50 per cent of Chile's production of refined copper came from the single mine of Chuquicamata, but particularly significant for the FCAB was the fact that virtually the entire shipped tonnage from that source was carried on its lines, as the following table shows:

Table 10. Transport of copper bars by the Chilean section of the FCAB, 1940–1945 (thousands of metric tons). And receipts on traffic

Year	Tonnage Moved	Receipts (£ sterling)
1940	145,948	100,453
1941	225,389	155,119
1942	226,534	155,384
1943	231,099	186,430
1944	239,112	187,654
1945	247,066	193,924

Source: FCAB Annual Reports (1941–1946). *General Managers' Annual Reports, Chilean Section.*

Over the five-year period, about 18 per cent of the FCAB's gross receipts from all sources on the Chilean section came from copper shipments, but it must be remembered that this takes no account of 'up traffic' to Chuquicamata – machinery, fuel and so on – nor of passenger movement related to the growth of copper mining. It is impossible to disaggregate relevant figures for these items from the company's accounts, but they must have been considerable. And it is noteworthy that the number of employees of all kinds at Chuquicamata increased from 7,406 in 1940 to 9,670 by the end of 1944.

Yet despite the buoyancy of copper traffic, the company's net receipts over the decade 1936–1945 from the Chilean Section could hardly be called spectacular, and it is significant that payments of dividends in arrears on the 5 per cent cumulative preference stock were still ten years behind at the latter date, while, of course, nothing at all was paid on the consolidated ordinary stock in these years. Indeed, it was not until December 1956 that the FCAB was able to pay a dividend of 4 per cent on that stock, the first such dividend since 1930. Announcing that result, the then-Chairman, H.C. Drayton, pointed out that:

> Averaged out over the twenty-five years during which those Stockholders received nothing at all, it will represent only 0.16 per cent per annum, gross, which cannot be considered an adequate return . . . [53]

This is to anticipate. Returning to the years of peace and war, 1936–1945, the overall results for the Chilean Section were as follows (cf. Table 5, p. 173):

Table 11. FCAB results (Chilean section only), 1936–1945

Year	Gross Receipts	Working Expenses	Net Receipts
	£	£	£
1936	564,358	310,363	253,995
1937	722,555	406,516	316,039
1938	607,044	409,988	197,056
1939	576,849	407,629	169,220
1940	669,310	536,439	132,871
1941	788,141	629,922	158,219
1942	847,372	759,908	87,464
1943	1,049,921	889,362	160,559
1944	1,057,834	970,818	87,016
1945	1,112,710	985,195	127,515

Source: FCAB Annual Reports, 1937–1946

Both the increase in gross receipts and in working expenses reflect growing traffic but the important point to note (cf. Table 8, p. 206) is the rising ratio of expenditure to gross receipts. Managers' reports for the period, as well as chairmen's speeches, are eloquent commentary on this fact, as inflationary pressures forced up costs.

A typical year was 1941, when gross receipts on the Chilean lines rose by £18,831 over 1940 but, at the same time working expenses (including amounts set aside for renewals and debenture amortization, exchange losses and various obligatory reserves, such as employees' indemnities) increased by £93,483 for the same period. In his annual report for 1941 Heskett went into some detail to explain this situation:

> The salaries and wages bill showed an increase of nearly £20,000, mainly brought about by Law 7064, passed in September, 1941, which introduced a scale of obligatory increases in the salaries of all employees [i.e. white-collar workers] and became retroactive as from the 1st January, 1941. Expenses were further augmented by Law 6939, which obliges the Company to pay annual bonuses to its employees and workmen whether it earns profits or not, such bonuses operating from the year 1940. Therefore in 1941 we had not only to provide some £24,800 for the bonuses for 1940 but also to reserve an amount of approximately £28,750 for the bonus corresponding to 1941 and payable in the following year.
>
> A further additional charge in the 1941 accounts was some £16,000, being a contribution to the Reserve for workmen's indemnities payable under Law 6686 which was promulgated in 1940.
>
> Our Oil Fuel bill was higher by some £29,000 and the Materials bill by about £14,000. Chilean Income Tax charges were also up by £14,000,

> mainly because of the increase in the rate of tax imposed under Law No. 7145 . . .[54]

In consequence, an application was made in October 1941 for a 20 per cent increase in FCAB tariffs, not a realistic claim in the light of the additional expenses but only in the light of practical expecations. A few weeks' later – while that claim was still pending – the Minister of Fomento issued a decree authorizing the State Railways to increase their basic passenger, luggage and goods rates by up to 50 per cent on both the north and south sections. Heskett wrote:

> Seeing that we are in exactly the same boat . . . one would imagine that our modest petition for a 20% increase would be granted without much trouble or delay, but Señor Mujica in his usual over-zealous way thinks otherwise, as he has found it necessary to ask us to furnish a mass of statistical data, etc., to enable him, as he says, to study our petition. His idea no doubt is to make matters as difficult as possible for us . . .[55]

Unfortunately for the FCAB, and particularly for Heskett, history, or at least that part of it relating to 1937, was about to be repeated. As in that year, he had to repair to Santiago to press the matter, but once again, got caught up in a tortuous round of negotiations for which Mujica was largely, though not entirely, to blame.

Early December found Heskett in the office of the Minister of Fomento, Oscar Schnake, a leading member of the Socialist Party. 'This gentleman', he wrote, 'was exceptionally sympathetically inclined' but Schnake, while saying that he did not think the FCAB would have any trouble with its petition, insisted that all the formalities had to be carried out. This was nothing new, and it seemed that the enabling decree would soon have Schnake's signature. Then politics intervened. President Aguirre Cerda having died on 25 November, the Radical Party held a meeting on 14 December to choose its next presidential candidate with two antagonistic rivals, Juan Antonio Ríos and Gabriel González Videla in contention. Heskett had expected his decree signed, sealed and delivered on the 12th, but Schnake first of all absented himself from his office for some days, 'rushing around on political business', mainly in support of Ríos. On the 15th Schnake himself was proclaimed the Socialist candidate for the presidency, and thereupon resigned his ministry, not yet having signed the decree. His successor as Acting Minister of Fomento, Rolando Merino, then informed a company representative, Señor Armas, on 18 December, 'that he did not wish to concede any increase in tariffs to any railway . . .' and his private secretary – who had also worked for Schnake – added the next day that Merino 'did not wish either to hear or discuss the matter, and, further, he had decided not to concede audiences to any representatives of any railway who came to talk about an increase in tariffs'.[56]

Heskett, now back in Antofagasta, was justifiably peeved at this turn of events, but, as he wrote to Hunt, he had taken appropriate steps to put the matter right:

> As Señor Mujica was solely responsible for the delay in bringing the decree for the signature of the Minister, and had delayed until the moment when Señor Schnake decided to present his candidature for the presidency, Señor Armas informed Señor Mujica that we expected him to arrange the matter and see that the decree was duly signed. This official promised to do everything he could to help us, as he himself was convinced that the increase was justified . . .[57]

As it turned out, this was a downright lie. When management finally received, on 26 January 1942, Mujica's report to Schnake of 11 December 1941, far from supporting the increase, not only opposed it strongly but also went out of its way to raise a number of questions about the FCAB's finances in Chile which were to complicate matters even further. To Heskett, who returned to Santiago in February, it seemed that Mujica was:

> . . . trying to get his revenge for the set-back he received when I was able to settle the outstanding questions of the administration of the Longitudinal Railway with Señor Matías Silva when he was Minister of Fomento . . .
>
> Apparently Señor Mujica was very angry at the decision taken by Señor Schnake on the question of an increase in tariffs, and his report . . . while being absolutely incorrect, was written in really bad faith. It was quite evident that his intention was to put the Minister in such a position that if he had signed the decree he would have been liable to attacks and criticisms for agreeing to an increase in tariffs . . .[58]

In his report, Mujica first had estimated that the FCAB's extra income from a 20 per cent tariff increase would be about 10,000,000 pesos and all profit, blithely ignoring the rapidly rising costs of all kinds which were, of course, the reason for the petition in the first place. Second, he had assumed that, to meet its debenture and preference share obligations, the company could acquire sterling at the official rate of exchange in Chile when, as management knew from hard experience, it would be impossible to get drafts at that rate through the Exchange Control Commission. And, third, he had suggested that half the estimated yield from a 20 per cent increase should be retained in Chile: Wells observed:

> . . . this is absolutely out of the question as our profits are controlled by the terms of Art. 76 of the Railway Law and not in any arbitrary way which may occur to the Director of the Railway Department . . .[59]

Moreover, shortly afterwards, Wells reported that the *sueldo vital* for Antofagasta had just been raised, and that the salary bill for FCAB *empleados* from 1 January 1942, would, as a result, increase by some 3,000,000 pesos a year. 'This very heavy expenditure', he added, 'coupled with the ever increasing price of fuel oil and all materials, certainly calls for more compensation than a modest 20 per cent increase in tariffs'.[60]

Five months had now gone by since the request for that 'modest' increase had been submitted, and Heskett was not to know that the matter would take another seven. His first task was to deal with Mujica, whom he put into touch with the Head of the Exchange Department of the Bank of London and South America, suggesting at the same time that he also consult the Exchange Control Commission to find out precisely how the FCAB 'could purchase the necessary foreign exchange to cover our obligations'. 'We had to go very warily on this point', Heskett reported:

> . . . because Señor Mujica was asking some very awkward questions as to how we had been able to get foreign exchange without buying through the Exchange Control Commission. It was quite evident that what he was trying to do was to force us to disclose our sterling income, and if we had disclosed this he would most certainly have reported the matter to the Inland Revenue Department, and then the same question would have arisen as to our paying part of our Income Tax in sterling. We were able more or less to shelve the matter by simply insisting that the question of foreign exchange was not a matter for the Railway Department, and all that Señor Mujica had to say was whether or not the Railway Company was in a position to pay its obligations and meet increased costs . . .[61]

Ministerial changes delayed the matter throughout April then, suddenly in June, the whole issue was complicated by labour disputes. Towards the end of May, the Workmen's Syndicates at Antofagasta, Mejillones and Calama petitioned for a 60 per cent increase in wages, payment to everyone for a full month's work of 30 days, and monthly family allowances of 60 pesos for wives and 40 pesos for each child under 16, 'whether they are legitimate, illegitimate or adopted'. If accepted, this would cost the FCAB an additional 8 to 9 million pesos a year. Since management's comparisons with what other employers paid favoured the FCAB, lower sums were offered but rejected and, direct negotiations having failed, the matter went to the local tribunal of conciliation and arbitration, where it also resulted in stalemate. Strike action was voted from 20th June – in defiance of both the intendant's advice to the men and of the Law of Internal Security, prohibiting strikes in public utilities – but three days later Heskett received a call from the intendant, informing him that:

> ... the Minister of Interior had just given his instructions to indicate to me that the Government not only requested but exacted that the Company should accept arbitration. ... There was nothing to be done ... as the Minister ... was adamant, and a refusal to accept the Government's imposition would have placed the Company in a very unenviable position. The Minister of Fomento also rang up [Heskett reported] and asked the Intendente to inform me that the Arbitrator would work in close co-operation with him, and apparently the Minister ... had received a very strong indication from the Minister of Interior and probably the President that *as soon as the arbitrator made his award the question of tariffs must be settled* ...[62]

By the irony of fate, the Minister of Fomento was Oscar Schnake who had previously promised so much, and who had been put back into his old office by President Ríos on the latter's election earlier that very year!

The government-appointed arbitrator made his award in the middle of July: he gave an increase of salary of 6.50 pesos a day (instead of the 7.20 demanded), 25 pesos a month family allowance for wives, and children under 16, and allowed the guaranteed month, but flatly refused to make payments as retroactive as the men wished, thus saving the company some 900,000 pesos in a full year. Heskett thought it a satisfactory settlement in the circumstances, despite the additional cost, but he was under no illusions that the 20 per cent increase in tariffs for which he had asked was the maximum that he now confidently expected to get, although that claim had been based only on the increased costs of 1941. Yet, when he reiterated the company's petition in August, it was again referred to Mujica who immediately demanded the information that had been given to the arbitrator! This tactic was assisted by the loss of the file, but countermanded by the arbitrator who expressed satisfaction with the financial information given to him to arrive at his award. It was now the beginning of September, by which time Mujica – for reasons known only to himself or, at least, not recorded – had dropped all his objections and issued a favourable report. The matter then went to the Minister, and it looked like plain sailing.

Unfortunately, there were still rough waters ahead. After haggling over the tariff for sulphur (a growing traffic for the FCAB) second-class passages and Articles of First Necessity, the Minister gave way on the first and Heskett agreed to raise tariffs by only 10 per cent on the second and third items: the decree was then drawn up for the Minister's signature.

> At the last moment, however, [Heskett wrote] the Minister decided he would have to send the whole matter to the Economic Committee of Ministers, although he considered this a mere formality. The whole difficulty, however, is caused by the recent Emergency Law which has been passed to enable the President to meet the economic situation ... it is

> apparently the intention of the Government to try to avoid any companies, more especially foreign companies, exporting their profits, and the method they propose . . . is to instruct the Exchange Control Commission not to sell foreign exchange for this purpose. This, of course, places this Company in a very difficult situation, as we do not buy foreign exchange, but are able to send home what profits we make through our Bolivian clients paying us in sterling and also the Chile Exploration Company paying us in dollars. The whole question, therefore, revolves on the point that our profits must be disclosed as we have to present a statement of our results of working to the Inland Revenue Authorities for the purpose of Income Tax, and if the Government wish, they can easily find out that we have made a profit, and then they will probably enquire where the money is and what we have done with it.
>
> Their object in trying to stop companies exporting their profits is that also arising from this Emergency Law they are empowered to borrow money from the companies and invest this money in public works . . . I have just received a minute from the Sub-Secretary [of Public Works and Communications] asking the Company to provide $15,000,000 in quotas of $5,000,000 per annum, repayable in five years, with 6% interest, for the purpose of road building in the north . . . [63]

Both issues were rather awkward. On the first, while the company had never acted illegally and the practice of Bolivian clients paying in sterling and the Chilex in dollars went back decades, and had hitherto been fully accepted, Heskett feared that, under the new dispensation, giving

> . . . the Government almost unlimited powers over financial problems . . . they would insist on our Bolivian clients paying their Chilean freights in Chilian currency, and also that the Chile Exploration Company would be prohibited from paying us in dollars . . . [64]

As for the loan question, he regarded it as ‘a monstrous proposal’, savouring of ‘blackmail or highway robbery’, and, though he did not say so, he probably thought that the idea of the forced loan being used for road construction in the north, which would undoubtedly create more competition for the FCAB, was simply adding insult to injury. ‘It is quite clear to me’, he stated

> . . . that they are all convinced that the increase in tariffs is justified, but they appear to be trying to put the screw on by withholding the decree, in order, if possible, to force us to make this loan . . . [65]

How right he was events soon revealed. Having deliberately decided not to go to Santiago, where he might be pressed for an immediate answer, he left Armas to ‘mark time’ on the loan issue, only to be informed by him that:

> . . . it was evident from the behaviour of the Minister of Public Works and Communications, Señor Schnake, that he would not sign the decree authorising the increase in tariffs unless the Board announced their willingness to take up the $15,000,000 loan . . .[66]

In the event – and the records do not say why – on the same day that Heskett so informed London, Armas met Schnake for one and a half hours, the latter performed a complete *volte-face*, and agreed to issue the decree, which was signed by him on 2 October and by President Ríos, to take effect from 12 October 1942, that is, just a little over a year from when the matter was first raised. The questions of profit remittances and the loan were quietly put on one side but it had been an arduous business from start to finish, and no one knew that better than the general manager of the FCAB in Chile. But Heskett also knew that he owed much to others, and in March 1943, wrote as follows:

> I beg to thank you for your approval of my recommendation that Señor Armas should be given a bonus of $25,000, and that gentleman has asked me to convey to you personally his warm appreciation of your very generous act . . .[67]

It would be repetitious to recount for subsequent years the story of both tariff negotiations and labour relations affecting the FCAB in Chile, and the examples from the late 1930s and from 1941–42 may suffice to illustrate two of the basic issues facing the company which became regular features of its history. By the social laws of the period – to which additions and amendments were made in the following years – the *empleados* secured automatic increases in salaries linked to the cost of living and these were obligatory for employers. And, while *obreros* did not enjoy *legal* entitlement to the *sueldo vital* and had to bargain direct for higher wages, these tended to follow the same criteria, though it was not until the late 1950s that government sought to regulate pay increases by law for both categories of worker in line with rises in the cost of living. The pattern was completed, as already noted, by employers seeking compensatory increases in charges for the goods and services they provided.

To the complications of working out that equation, the Second World War added others, somewhat similar to those the company had faced in 1914. One of these was the problem of supplies, particularly of fuel, not only for the company's own needs for its rolling stock in both Chile and Bolivia but also for the mining establishments in both countries. During the 1920s, the FCAB and those concerns for which it carried fuel had deliberately turned to oil rather than coal for energy since at that time imported petroleum was cheaper than coal either produced from the Chilean mines at Lota and Coronel, south of the Central Valley, or shipped from abroad. Oil was also, obviously, cleaner and, coupled with advances in technology, a more efficient fuel. One consequence, however, of the economic crisis of the early 1930s was a marked increase in government intervention to assist the national coal industry, and successive administrations pursued a consistent policy of fostering it through such measures as raising import duties on oil. In consequence, the policy of conversion to oil was partially reversed and, indeed, government insisted, for example, that nitrate *oficinas* use national coal rather than oil in their operations. In his annual report for 1934, Heskett indicated how the FCAB in Chile was affected by these developments:

> The price of Chilean coal was such that it was evident a saving would be effected by using it wherever suitable. A trial made with one of the 33-class engines gave satisfactory results, and it was then decided to convert to coal-burning some 17 locomotives in all. These coal-burning engines are used exclusively for cargo traffic, and the passenger trains continue to be hauled by oil-burning locomotives.
>
> The stationary boilers of the Waterworks plant, the Main Shops in Mejillones, and the North Yard and Old Shops in Antofagasta, were converted to burn coal, and Chilean coal is now used for the Company's tugs. This change in the locomotive fuel made it necessary to provide storage and coaling facilities at Antofagasta, Mejillones, Baquedano and Calama . . . [68]

Unfortunately, however, this change of policy put the railway at the mercy of the Chilean coal industry in the matter of deliveries at Antofagasta, and Heskett's correspondence with London in the later 1930s is peppered with complaints on the subject. Whenever, for example, the miners in the south struck for higher wages – a not uncommon event – production and deliveries became erratic, and the only precaution management could take was to hold sufficient reserves to blunt that effect. This was precisely the situation at the beginning of the European war when shipping, and hence supplies from other sources, was severely disrupted. Late in 1939 Heskett had made arrangements to take 2,000 tons of Chilean coal a month during 1940, and had estimated oil requirements for that year at 12,000 tons. But, towards the end of November, he was reporting that

> . . . the difficulty of obtaining supplies of coal from the Chilean mines has become more acute as time went on, and although . . . we had accumulated 10,000 tons and felt that our position was secure, this stock has rapidly been dwindling owing to the coal companies falling down on their deliveries. The position was so acute that the Gas Company of Santiago at one time had coal for 24 hours, and the Antofagasta Gas Company had coal for three days; whilst the Melon Cement Company of Calera cut down their works to one oven . . .
>
> The shortage is entirely due to the numerous increases in wages which have been forced on the mine owners by the present Government in order

> to settle the innumerable strikes which have been taking place during the course of this year at Lota and Coronel. As a result of these increases, the miners now find that by working three or four days per week they earn sufficient money to provide for their families over the whole week, and three or four days' amusement for themselves ...[69]

In view of the coal crisis, the government set up a Coal Rationing Commission, headed by the Sub-Secretary of Fomento, Señor Arturo Zúñiga, with whom Heskett had several meetings in Santiago. Among the arguments he put forward for the FCAB to receive an adequate quota, was the dependence of Mejillones on assured supplies and, at the same time, he instructed Wells in Antofagasta to make the same point to the intendente, emphasizing that without coal neither the water-condensers nor the workshops could operate, 'and the town of Mejillones would have to be evacuated'. He also asked for the discriminatory duties on imported coal to be lifted so that he could rebuild stocks with supplies from England and, while Zúñiga himself was sympathetic, both the Chilean Coal Development Agency and the national coal companies 'moved heaven and earth to avoid this being done.' Finally, with the assistance of one of his senior advisers and a very prominent politician, Ernesto Barros Jarpa – a close friend of Zúñiga's – he secured a promise from the Lota Company to supply 2,000 tons of coal a month and the permission of the Rationing Commission for this to be done.

All went well for about six months. Then, in July 1940, Lota's supply dropped to less than 1,000 tons of coal, and to nought for August and September. At the same time, the Rationing Commission felt itself unable to stipulate a regular monthly quota for the FCAB. With stocks amounting to about a month's requirements by October, the position was serious. It was only slightly alleviated by the commission allotting 2,000 tons of imported coal due to arrive in October to the company, but at a price of $230 a ton and, while import duties were waived, all discharge expenses fell to the FCAB. 'This price', Heskett reported, 'is getting near to the point when it shows little economy over oil fuel based on the present contract price ... Furthermore, we have the constant worry of not being able to rely on regular supplies ...'[70] The coal arrived and the price was paid but the problem still remained.

Meanwhile, London had not been indifferent to the local supply situation, recognizing its critical influence in keeping the railway running and anticipating greater traffic in minerals through the demands of the war. Bolden and Cowley were in touch with the Exchange Control Department of the Bank of England on the question of payments for supplies, confirming that management in Chile and Bolivia were free to convert local currency into US dollars, and considering appointing a purchasing agent in the USA for fuel and other supplies which might not be available from the UK because of supply and shipping problems. Bolden explained:

> Our idea is that any U.S. dollars you and the Bolivian Section can obtain should be placed on current account with the J. Henry Schroder Banking Corporation of New York . . . As regards general stores and spare parts, our intention is to continue to obtain same from this side where possible not only on account of price but also because we could have the material inspected and would know that it conformed with the required specifications . . . Nevertheless with the war continuing and as time goes on we may be obliged to obtain an increasing percentage of our requirements from the United States and hence the need would arise for more dollars to be provided in New York . . . [71]

And this is precisely what happened, particularly with fuel supplies. By May, 1941, Heskett was reporting that:

> The production of coal in Chili has lately decreased in an alarming way, and the supply is totally inadequate to meet demands; in fact, the production of the Lota Mines has declined from 90,000 tons per month to 30,000 . . . some indication of the seriousness of the effects can be gathered from the fact that the State Railways have had to very considerably reduce both their passenger and goods train services . . . [72]

A shipment of 5,800 tons of American coal relieved the immediate situation but there was also an alternative, namely to go back to oil: by the same letter Heskett said that three more of the 33-class engines had been converted back to oil-burning, making fifteen in all, and 'this will enable us to very nearly consume our maximum contract quantity of fuel oil and to reduce our coal consumption considerably'. The oil contract was with the International Petroleum Company, and supplies came from the US. Perhaps surprisingly, those supplies were not affected by the entry of the United States into the war, though coal supplies continued to be a headache, and conversion to oil, where possible, was continued. Thus, late in 1942, it was reported that:

> The difficulties of obtaining Chilean coal are greater than ever, and it is extremely doubtful whether we shall be able to obtain an average of 1,000 tons per month during 1943 . . . Four of the 33-class locomotives are fitted for coal-burning, but in view of our decreasing stocks of this combustible, our inability to obtain adequate supplies, and the fact that we have a surplus of oil fuel at our disposal, we have given instructions for these locomotives to be converted to burn oil fuel, so that we shall now have the whole of the 33 class, the 181 class, and all the locomotives working on the Longitudinal Railway using oil fuel . . . [73]

Australian coal was tried in 1943 but found wanting, and throughout

1944 management was plagued with the supply problem affecting both American and Chilean coal and, in effect, survived on a month-to-month basis. But survive it did to the end of the European War in 1945 when supply problems eased and both freight rates and coal prices began to fall.

The fuel problem of the war years exemplified the difficulties of an enterprise operating thousands of miles from its home base, and heavily dependent on imported supplies to keep it running, or on local sources which were underdeveloped or erratic. And what has been said about fuel could be repeated for other raw materials and manufactured goods, such as machinery. In war-time conditions, all kinds of permissions had to be obtained, transport arranged, and payments made when the priorities of governments took precedence over everything else. Cowley spelled it out in a long letter to Heskett on supplies from the USA early in 1943:

> Long before America came into the War we gave Messrs. Caldwell and Co. [the American purchasing agents for the FCAB] full details of the nature of our traffics and our requirements and they took up the matter with the appropriate Authorities at Washington. The latter . . . have also received confirmatory information through the American Embassies at La Paz and Santiago. Messrs Caldwell & Co. have shown considerable energy . . . and their efforts have been rewarded with . . . success . . . shown by the fact that they have secured a general export licence which is renewable every three months and which is intended to cover all material we need to ship from the U.S.A. *This export licence, however, does not deal with priorities; there is . . . no question of obtaining anything in the nature of blanket priorities* and it is necessary for application to be made in each and every case and the matter then is adjudicated by the Authorities at Washington in the light of the circumstances then ruling . . .[74]

Heskett and his staff learned this the hard way, not least on fuel, and the supply problem throughout the war took up a good deal of time, indeed overtime, in keeping the railway running.

But now, with the war, there were fewer experienced staff to do it. As in 1914, expatriates left the company to offer their services to their country, and Bolden was quick to reassure them:

> With regard to members of the British Staff who might wish to volunteer for service, the Board have not yet made any regulations thereon but I have no doubt they would be at least as favourable as those detailed in your Staff Memorandum No. 179 of the 6th November, 1914, which were put into force following the outbreak of the war . . .[75]

Throughout the war, London kept in touch with the volunteers, and also informed Antofagasta and La Paz regularly of their progress, as the following extracts indicate:

> Mr. Guthrie obtained a Commission as a Second Lieutenant in the Royal Engineers early in October. Later on he expects to be sent on an Officers' Emergency Course. He asks us to send his kind regards to his many friends on the Railway. Mr. Gillitt has joined the Royal Air Force as a Pilot and Mr. Mitchell is a Writer in the Navy. The latter, who tells us that as soon as he has completed his training he intends to volunteer for draft abroad, seems to be very pleased and proud to be in the Navy . . . [76]
>
> We were very sorry to see from "The Times" of the 3rd instant that Flight Lt. Frank Gillitt was killed in action in October and shall be obliged if you will, on behalf of the Board, convey to Mr. Gillitt [resident in Chile] their sympathy with him and Mrs. Gillitt and family in their loss. [77]

Staff shortages and losses through the war inevitably threw greater stress on those who remained to run the railway, though the numbers involved seem to have been far less than in 1914. One loss, however, in the early years of the war, was far more difficult to replace than most.

On 19 June 1941, Cowley wrote to Heskett as follows:

> I was indeed very sorry to inform you in our cablegram of the 6th instant that the Chairman had died suddenly on the previous day . . . He was in the office on the 5th instant and although he seemed tired and had not been feeling too well, there was nothing to suggest the tragic end a few hours later.
>
> After a fairly heavy day in the City he attended in the evening a Meeting of the Central Committee of the Staines and District War Weapons week and after reading the financial report he collapsed and died almost immediately . . . Mr. Bolden had been keenly interested as Chairman of the War Weapons week for Laleham (the village where he lived) and had worked very hard to make it a success . . .
>
> . . . Of his many interests, I am sure the welfare of the Antofagasta Company always remained nearest to his heart. To me personally his death has been a shock, for I worked under him for 32 years . . . In recent years as you know he extended his activities, both business and social, and that and the strain of the conditions under which we have been living during the past two years no doubt had its effect. He died in harness and that is what I think he would have wished to do. [78]

Heskett replied:

> . . . He will be greatly missed, and long be remembered by us all as a gentleman of charming and dynamic personality, who played a great part in the development of the Antofagasta Railway and who always took a lively and sympathetic interest in the welfare of the staff . . . [79]

Bolden was sixty-seven when he died, having been appointed secretary of the FCAB at the age of thirty-three, a member of the board at forty-four, and managing director and chairman at the age of fifty-five. And his influence on company policy had been profound, particularly through his financial acumen. So long as he was in charge, and had the ear of the board, dividend distribution took second place to a deliberate strategy of keeping high reserves against contingencies, and his mastery of detail was generally enough to satisfy stockholders that that was the correct policy. Only in the later 1930s, when, as a result of the earlier economic crisis, dividends on preference and ordinary stock fell into arrear, was the slightest dissent expressed from the floor at annual general metings. It came primarily from one particular stockholder at the meeting on 15 June 1937, called to consider the results for 1936, and took the form of questions relating to Bolden's own remuneration, directors' fees and qualifications, attendance at board meetings and how long they lasted. Since notification of the questions had only been received the previous day, the matter was clearly out of order, but Bolden took the opportunity to make a spirited defence of company policy and progress in adverse times, and he carried the meeting with him. The aggrieved stockholder, however, kept up the attack through correspondence in the following year, arguing for part of the reserves to be distributed in order to pay off all arrears on the cumulative preference stock and a 1 per cent dividend on ordinary stock, at a cost of £389,000. Moreover, he proposed that, if that were not done, directors' fees should be cut by half until a dividend were paid on consolidated ordinary stock.

Again, Bolden was equal to the occasion, and he had a trump card in his hand. He pointed out that

> . . . during the last seven years the carry-forward has been reduced by £116,000, that is from what it was at the 1st January, 1931, and that in itself proves that over the period we have not kept back what has been available for distribution *when taking into account the basic idea of retaining the Company's financial position as sound as possible*. (Applause. Hear, hear.) *That idea includes having in mind our liabilities*, and the chief of these . . . is the maturity on the 1st January, 1940, that is, in only 18 months' time, of the £1,000,000 of 4½ per cent Debenture Stock repayable at 105 per cent. and £1,500,000 of 5 per cent. Debenture Stock repayable at 110 per cent., and who is to say what will be the condition of the financial world when we have to face that obligation? (Hear, hear.) As you see, the total cash involved is £2,700,000. I want to preserve the equity of this Company for the genuine Stockholder who has held his stock because of his knowledge of the past and his belief in the ultimate merits of the Company . . . Without our conservative finance, we should have had a moratorium on our Debenture Interest and a Committee managing the Company whose first and paramount duty would have been to the Debenture Holders . . . do not let us start now frittering away our reserves . . . in order to do something which the results of the past few years and of the year 1937 itself do not justify in any possible way. (Hear, hear.)[80]

As for directors' fees, he pointed out that they had been reduced by 10 per cent in 1931 and the cut not yet restored, that vacancies on the board had been deliverately left unfilled to save money, and that the present five directors had had to work very hard. He concluded:

> It is no sinecure which we have had and whilst any Stockholder of any Company not sufficiently acquainted with the facts might reflect on whether the fees of the Directors . . . were fair or otherwise, I am quite prepared to leave to my fellow Stockholders any such reflection in our own particular case (Applause) . . . [81]

When the offending resolution was put, it secured one vote, apart from the proposer and seconder, and was rejected by the meeting.

Perhaps Bolden's last great service to the company he had served so skilfully for so long was the settlement of the debenture question which he anounced at the last annual general meeting he chaired in June, 1940. The details of the transactions are somewhat tedious, and it may be sufficient to note the salient features. By the maturity date of the debenture stock, 1 January 1940, the whole of the 4½ per cent stock was redeemed at £105 per cent, and 60 per cent of the 5 per cent stock likewise at £110 per cent. The balance of 40 per cent of the latter stock to be redeemed was subject to postponement to 1 January 1943, and repayable on that date at a premium of 25 per cent, though the company had the option of redemption of that balance before the due date if that were practicable. The amount required by 1 January 1940, was some £2,200,000 and this was secured by the realization of the greater part of the company's investments in its subsidiary, the Andes Trust, and by the realization of other investments made by the FCAB as a reserve over the years. Apart from raising that large sum from its own resources, so prudently put aside in the past, the FCAB also reduced by some £100,000 a year the annual interest charge on debenture stocks. The liquidation of most of the debenture stock and the satisfactory arrangements made for redeeming the rest by 1943 were not only a personal triumph for Bolden and his board but also, indeed, final fitting testimony of the sound financial policies he had persistently pursued, even during the years of adversity.

Meanwhile, the war went on, and particularly after the entry of the United States and Japan into the conflict made it a global struggle, local management had another preoccupation – security against sabotage. Though Chile did not sever her diplomatic relations with the Axis until early 1943 and, in fact, maintained her neutrality for another two years, the country's long and largely indefensible coastline and the comparative weakness of her forces, did raise fears of exposure to sudden attack, particularly by the Japanese navy. With her minerals, and those of

Bolivia, becoming of growing importance to the Allied war effort, it seemed only prudent to prepare for that contingency and also to take on board the possible sabotage of vital installations by national sympathizers with the fascist cause. The FCAB's properties – railway lines, water tanks and pipes, engineering workshops, and so on – could have been singularly vulnerable had such a situation arisen and, while in the event it did not, proper precautions seemed reasonable. Moreover, that was precisely the view of both Washington and Santiago. Though President Ríos, for internal political reasons, could not break Chile's relations with Germany, Italy and Japan before 1943 – as recommended by the Conference of Inter-American States at Rio in April 1942 – his government recognized Chile's dependence on the USA, and was quite willing to grant limited co-operation for Chile's defence, such as allowing American shore-batteries on Chilean soil. In the north, Antofagasta assumed new importance for America's conduct of the war in the Pacific and for Allied shipping in the southern seas, and an eye-witness account of part of that story by an employee of the FCAB is worth quoting here:

> A few weeks after Pearl Harbour [writes George Craig, then Assistant Resident Engineer] early in 1942, the population of the town were taken by surprise when, overnight, a detachment of American Marines (32 strong) under the command of two officers, landed in the town. They immediately set up two six-inch gun batteries on elevated ground, one at each end of the town, and protected by anti-aircraft defences ... At the same time, the American Navy set up a large organization, staffed by their own Naval personnel, from which they controlled and directed all Allied shipping in the South Pacific – many ships were actually routed through Antofagasta which became a very busy port indeed ...[82]

The British government also was conscious of the world-wide nature of the war and the need to safeguard raw material supplies. Under the aegis of the body known as British Security Co-ordination, two employees of the FCAB, Craig himself and Deputy Manager Wells, were flown to a special camp in Canada at the beginning of August 1942, for six weeks intensive training in anti-sabotage measures and, while Heskett, already short-staffed, thought that might be inconvenient, he approved: 'in view of the great importance which the military authorities apparently attach to this mission, I feel that we should do everything possible to fall in with their wishes'.[83] Back in Antofagasta, it fell largely to Wells and Craig to implement what they had learned for the protection of the company's property, and that objective was reinforced in mid-September by the visit to Antofagasta of 'A gentleman named Mr E.R. Lingeman ... introduced to us by the British Consul as having been named Chief Security Officer for Peru, Bolivia and including the Antofagasta Railway in the North of Chile'.[84]

As a result of these events, measures were taken to strengthen the protection of what, after inspection, were felt to be the most vulnerable installations, such as bridges at San Pedro, Conchi and Calama, and water tanks and reservoirs at Antofagasta. By arrangement with the local Colonel of Carabineros, uniformed members of that force were permanently stationed at these points, but only after the Minister of Interior had issued the appropriate decree and the company agreed to pay two-thirds of the policemen's wages as well as living allowances, and provide accommodation and furniture at the particular points to be guarded. The management also increased the number of its own watchmen, instituted a system of gate passes, and enrolled a corps of mobile guards to patrol its property. Special lights were installed, fences were erected where necessary, for example, around the electric power and water condensing plants at Mejillones, and additional telephone lines installed. All this was in early 1943, but in March of that year Heskett reported that:

> We have also arranged with the military authorities to send 30 soldiers, 3 non-commissioned officers and one lieutenant, equipped with rifles and machine-guns, to Mejillones, for the protection of the Company's property ... principally the Workshops and Power and Water Plants ... Antofagasta has not been declared an Emergency Zone, and it has been somewhat difficult to obtain troops for Mejillones; but as Tocopilla was declared an Emergency Zone, we have repeatedly put forward the argument to the military authorities that it was little use protecting the Power Plant of the Chile Exploration Company at Tocopilla, if no military protection was given to our Workshops at Mejillones where our locomotives and wagons are repaired.
>
> It has given us great satisfaction that we have now been assigned such a valuable force for the protection of our Works at Mejillones ...[85]

The logic was inescapable: if the power plant of the Chilex at Tocopilla was vital for production of copper at Chuquicamata, no less critical were the FCAB's rolling stock and lines to get the mineral to the coast.

All this cost money, and in August Heskett reckoned the total bill at nearly $200,000 (about £20,000) for the six months to the end of June. He also stated that:

> The work of organizing and maintaining the necessary supervision has not always been easy, as we were confronted with the idea among certain senior members of the staff that the measures were quite unnecessary, as nothing would ever happen here. However, we have convinced them of the foolishness of such an idea.[86]

That view was shared by the British War Cabinet which, through Mr Duff Cooper, thanked the FCAB for its efforts, while urging it not to relax its vigilance. By mid-1944, however, the tide of war having turned,

Heskett felt that the company's own watchmen could, under inspection, maintain that vigilance without Chilean troops and police, whose services were then dispensed with, with grateful thanks. And a year later, with the end of the war in Europe, the threat, whether or not more apparent than real, was thought to have passed, and the number of watchmen was reduced.

Yet, if war brought to the FCAB additional preoccupations, those which it had in peace were more than enough. In Chile, until the late 1950s, when corrective measures were taken, inflation pursued a relentless course, as the following table shows:

Table 12. Inflation in Chile, 1940–1955, percentage increase by year

Year	Per Cent	Year	Per Cent
1940	10	1949	21
1941	23	1950	17
1942	26	1951	23
1943	8	1952	12
1944	15	1953	56
1945	8	1954	71
1946	30	1955	84
1947	23		
1948	17		

Source: Albert O. Hirschman, *Journeys Toward Progress: Studies of Economic Policy-Making in Latin America*, New York, 1963, p.160.

The causes of inflation are highly controversial, of course, but the consequences are clear enough. In Chile, though the years of war were years of economic expansion, through the demand for its minerals and by the import-substitution industrialization which war induced, rising costs were quite inevitable, and for employers this meant both more labour unrest as workers sought to keep abreast of the cost of living, and also as business sought to redress the balance through higher charges for goods and services. In this context, a foreign company, such as the FCAB, however long it had been in the country, was still a foreign company, and had to face particular problems related to that fact.

For the FCAB, in the post-war period, however, it was not so much its operations in Chile which were affected by the factors so far spelled out as those in Bolivia, where the particular circumstances of history and economy alike led to a very different outcome.

Notes

1. John Reese Stevenson, *The Chilean Popular Front*, Greenwood Press, 1942, Westport, Conn., p.89. For a more detailed economic analysis, see P.T. Ellsworth, *Chile: an economy in transition, loc. cit., passim.*
2. General manager to secretary, Antofagasta, 10 August 1934. Letter No. 474.
3. General manager to managing director, Antofagasta, 28 April 1933. Private. Official.
4. *Idem.* to *idem.*, Antofagasta, 6 June 1935. Private. Official.
5. *Idem.* to *idem.*, Antofagasta, 26 July 1935. Private. Official.
6. *FCAB, Report of Annual General Meeting*, 9 June 1936. p.7.
7. Extracts from Chilean Manager's Report Dated Antofagasta, 19 March, 1937. pp.18–19.
8. *Ibid.*, Antofagasta, 10 March 1938. p.19.
9. *FCAB, Report of Annual General Meeting*, 13 June 1939. p.7.
10. Extracts from Chilean Manager's Report Dated Antofagasta, 4th April, 1941. pp.7–8.
11. *Ibid.*, p.8.
12. *Ibid.*
13. Managing director to general manager, Chile, London, 3 December 1936. Private. Official. Airmail.
14. General manager to managing director, Antofagasta, 30 April 1937. Private. Official.
15. *Idem.* to *Idem.*, Antofagasta, 30 April 1937. Private. Official.
16. *Ibid.*
17. General manager to managing director, Santiago, 10 June 1937.
18. *Ibid.*
19. *Ibid.*
20. General manager to managing director, Santiago, 22 June 1937.
21. *Idem.* to *idem.*, Antofagasta, 13 August 1937. Private. Official.
22. Deputy general manager to managing director, Antofagasta, 8 October 1937. Private. Official.
23. *Idem.* to *idem.*, 3 November 1937.
24. *Idem.* to *idem.*, Antofagasta, 11 December 1937. Private. Official.
25. *Ibid.*
26. Deputy general manager to managing director, Antofagasta, 16 December 1937. Private. Official.

27. Secretary to general manager at Antofagasta, 5 March 1945. My emphasis.
28. Alan Angell, *Politics and the Labour Movement in Chile*, Oxford University Press 1972, p.54.
29. Deputy general manager to managing director, Antofagasta, 6 March 1936. Private. Official.
30. *Ibid.*
31. Deputy general manager to managing director, Antofagasta, 20 March 1936. Private. Official.
32. General manager to managing director, Antofagasta, 18 March 1936. Private. Official.
33. *Ibid.*
34. *Ibid.*
35. General manager to managing director, Antofagasta, 8 April 1938. Private. Official.
36. *Idem.* to *idem.*, Antofagasta, 8 May 1939. Private. Official.
37. *Idem* to *idem.*, same date. Separate.
38. *Ibid.*
39. General manager to managing director, Antofagasta, 27 May 1939. Private. Official.
40. *Idem.* to *idem.*, Antofagasta, 5 August 1939. Private. Official.
41. *Idem* to *idem.*, Antofagasta, 5 September 1939. Private. Official.
42. *Ibid.*
43. General manager to managing director, Antofagasta, 18 October 1939. Private. Official.
44. *Ibid.*
45. General manager to managing director, Antofagasta, 30 July 1938. Private. Official.
46. *Ibid.*
47. General manager to managing director, Antofagasta, 2 December 1938. Private. Official.
48. *Idem.* to *idem.*, Antofagasta, 14 July 1938. Private.
49. *Idem* to secretary, Antofagasta, 11 December 1936. Letter No. 633. The 'Lavaderos de Oro' (Gold Placer Washings) were instituted by the Socialist Republic of Dávila in 1932 to provide relief work for unemployed miners. In 1932, with exchange control, certain imports were only allowed at a much higher rate of exchange than the official rate. Presumably, they included golf clubs.
50. General manager to secretary, Antofagasta, 8 April 1938. Letter No. 738.
51. *Idem.* to *idem.*, Antofagasta, 9 February 1939. Letter No. 797.
52. *Idem.* to *idem.*, Antofagasta, 16 November 1938. Letter No. 779. My emphasis.
53. *FCAB, Report of Meeting*, 19 November 1956. p.15
54. *FCAB Annual Report for 1941: Abridged Extracts from the Chilian Manager's Report Dated Antofagasta, 10 April 1942.* p.5.
55. General manager to secretary, Antofagasta, 14 November 1941. Private. Official.

56. General manager to managing director, Antofagasta, 20 December 1941. Private. Official.
57. *Ibid.*
58. General manager to managing director. Santiago, 17 March 1942. Private. Official. For the question of the Longitudinal Railway, dating back to 1927, see above, pp.
59. Deputy general manager to managing director, Antofagasta, 6 February 1942. Private. Official.
60. *Idem.* to *idem.*, Antofagasta, 27 February 1942. Private. Official.
61. See ref. No. 58.
62. General manager to managing director, Antofagasta, 25 June 1942. Private. Official. My emphasis.
63. *Idem.* to *idem.*, Antofagasta, 3 September 1942. Private. Official. The Ministry of Public Works and Communications had replaced the old Ministry of Fomento in a reorganization and re-naming of ministries at the end of August 1942. See Luis Valencia Avaria, *Anales de la República*, 2nd ed., Santiago, 1986, p.610, n.146. Schnake kept his ministerial post.
64. General manager to managing director, Antofagasta, 8 September 1942. Private. Official.
65. *Idem.* to *idem.*, Antofagasta, 3 September 1942. Private. Official.
66. *Idem.* to *idem.*, Antofagasta, 23 September 1942. Private. Official.
67. *Idem.* to *idem.*, Antofagasta, 26 March 1943. Private. Confidential.
68. *Extracts from Chilean manager's report, dated Antofagasta, 5 April 1935* p.20.
69. General manager to managing director, Antofagasta, 22 November 1939. Private. Official. In his reply, Bolden commented that '... increased wages are not always an unmitigated blessing ... local newspapers refer to the increasing drunkenness among the workpeople ... and we gather the Government were introducing measures to reduce the supply of alcohol.' Managing director to Chilean manager, London, 5 January 1940.
70. General manager to managing director, Antofagasta, 10 October 1940. Private. Official.
71. Managing director to Chilean manager, London, 21 June 1940. Private. Official.
72. General manager to secretary, Antofagasta, 2 May 1941. Letter No. 948.
73. *Idem.* to *idem.*, Antofagasta, 29 October 1942. Letter No. 1018.
74. Secretary to general manager, London, 7 January 1943. No. 817. My emphasis.
75. Managing director to Chilean general manager, London, 6 October 1939. Private. Official. cf. above, p.105–7 for those regulations.
76. Secretary to Chilean general manager, London, 28 November 1940. No. 745.
77. *Idem.* to *idem.*, London, 12 November 1942. Letter No. 810.
78. *Idem.* to *idem.*, London, 19 June 1941. Private. Official.
79. General Manager to Secretary, Antofagasta, 10 June 1941. Private. Official. See also *The Woking Herald and Staines and Egham News*, 13 June 1941, for useful accounts of Bolden's life and work, and of his well-attended funeral.

80. *FCAB, report of meeting, 14 June 1938*, pp. 16–17. My emphasis.
81. *Ibid.*, p.17
82. Personal communication. George Craig to the author, September 1986.
83. General manager to managing director, Antofagasta, 29 July 1942. Private. Official.
84. *Idem.* to *idem.*, Antofagasta, 15 September 1942. Private. Confidential.
85. *Idem.* to *idem.*, Antofagasta, 6 March 1943. Private. Confidential.
86. *Idem.* to *idem.*, Antofagasta, 31 August 1943. Private. Confidential.

7
THE NEW COMPLEXITIES 1935–1973: Part 2

The Bolivian dimension: military socialism, revolution, nationalization, 1935–1967

In Bolivia, as in so many other ways, the Chaco War was a watershed for the military, and the 'generation gap' it opened up between the discredited higher commanders and more junior officers, who had direct experience of fighting alongside illiterate conscripts from all over Bolivia, had striking political consequences. As part of a widespread questioning about Bolivian society and government and why the country had lost the war, such officers became critical of the old order and were determined to change at least part of it under military tutelage.

In May 1936, Colonels David Toro and Germán Busch – powerful figures in the officer corps – carried out a bloodless coup, removing the civilian president Tejado Sorzano from office, and proclaiming their intention to lead a national renaissance through what they called 'military socialism'. Toro was president for only a year but his government created Bolivia's first Ministry of Labour and appointed a printing worker and prominent political activist to run it. The same government in March 1937, annulled the concessions (awarded in 1920–21) of the Standard Oil Company of Bolivia, a subsidiary of the giant parent company of New Jersey. This nationalization, demanded by Busch among others, was the culmination of a protracted series of disputes between the company and successive Bolivian governments which had, however, done little to satisfy nationalist aspirations. But, despite such expressions of military socialism, Toro, an inveterate intriguer, was suspected by Busch of moving to the right, and the latter, a Chaco War hero and commander-in-chief of the army, forced Toro out in July 1937, assumed power himself and announced a more reformist programme.

In the two years he held office, Busch presided over the writing of a new Bolivian constitution, notable for its emphasis on the limitation of property rights, including those of the church, and on the social responsibilities of the state in health, education and welfare. Its thrust was that economic liberalism and the neutral role of the state were no longer sufficient in tackling Bolivia's social and economic problems. After assuming dictatorial powers in April 1939, Busch promulgated Bolivia's first national labour code, a very detailed charter of workers' rights which, though subsequently as much honoured in the breach as in the observance, was to prove of lasting importance in Bolivian labour history. Finally, he also challenged the enormous power of the tin barons, the Patiños, Hochschilds and Aramayos, who had dominated national politics for the previous two decades. First, he encouraged the unionization of the tin workers; second, he established the state-owned Banco Minero as a financing and selling agent for the small and medium-size tin firms, and finally but most significantly, in June 1939, he not only refused to abolish the special taxes and exchange requirements laid on the tin exporters during the Chaco War but also issued a draconian decree, ordering them to turn over to the Banco Central 100 per cent of their foreign exchange earnings and obtain from the bank such letters of exchange as they required for purchases abroad and the payment of debts and dividends. Failure to comply would mean that export permits for minerals would not be given, and resistance in the form of inspired interruption of production would be judged high treason, carrying the death penalty. (In fact, Busch went so far in June as to have Mauricio Hochschild, who was a naturalized Argentine citizen, arrested for opposition and actually got his ministers to sign a death warrant, only to drop the case in the face of fierce opposition, not least from foreign diplomatic representatives.)

Within two months, however, Busch, who had not built up a political party of his own, and whose visionary energy was not always shared by those around him, had become a lonely man. On 23 August 1939, he committed suicide – some still say he was murdered – leaving behind a reputation as a genuine reformer frustrated by the Bolivian oligarchies, political and economic. To his followers and, in fact, to many of the left-wing parties which had sprung up in the period, his personal history was symbolic, a kind of mirror-image of the realities of the national situation.

Military socialism ended with his death and both the interim military government which took over and its successor, that of General Enrique Peñaranda, elected in 1940, were of conservative stamp. Yet the period had stimulated the forces for radical change in Bolivia and nothing would be quite the same again. Among the minority parties which emerged shortly afterwards, the Nationalist Revolutionary Movement (MNR), founded in 1941, was to prove the most important. Its future leaders, Victor Paz Estenssoro and Hernán Siles, had both been elected to Congress in 1939, but the ideology of their group was initially mildly reformist rather than revolutionary and it relied on middle-class support. What helped to change its character was the wave of popular protest which followed what became known as the Catavi massacre in December 1942.

The background to this tragic event was somewhat complex but its main outlines can be simply stated. Apart from the emergence of a multiplicity of non-traditional parties in the post-Busch years – mostly of a socialist hue – the period also saw a marked increase in labour organization and activity. In politics, in the congressional elections of May 1942, the parties of the left received over 23,000 votes and those of the right some 14,000, giving the former control of the legislature. On the labour front, in protest against what were often intolerable working conditions, the tin workers had begun to organize themselves on a district basis, resorting increasingly to strike action. This reached its peak in the latter months of 1942, despite the penal legislation of the Peñaranda government against such action, but, whereas the government reacted moderately to miners' demands at Oruro and Potosí, it took a firm line with the 9,000 workers at Patiño's mines at Catavi, sending troops under the command of Colonel Cuenca to keep order. Armed, as he thought, with the power of the law, Cuenca violently broke up a peaceful demonstration on 13 December. A second clash on 21 December saw troops open fire, killing thirty-five miners, and when, later that same day, women and children joined their menfolk in a demonstration against brutality and for negotiations, indiscriminate firing left several hundred dead. Government attempts to suppress the news failed completely: it came under fierce attack in Congress, amid demands for a full investigation, while throughout the country the Catavi massacre became the key event in fomenting working-class unity and revolutionary consciousness.

The issue smouldered on throughout 1943 until, on the anniversary of the massacre, a group of junior officers led by Major Gualberto Villaroel and in alliance with the MNR staged a successful coup to overthrow Peñaranda and establish a governing military junta. Though the new governing coalition proved unstable, it had some achievements to its credit. One was its encouragement of further unionization among the miners under the charismatic leadership of Juan Lechín; another, the first really serious attempt to discuss at national level the problems of Bolivia's majority, the peasant Indian population. In the short run, the first was the more significant in that Lechín's creation, the Federation of Mining Workers (FSTMB), gave its political allegiance to the MNR, giving the party much more of a working-class outlook and socialist ideology.

As for the government, it became increasingly unpopular as its response to opposition, particularly demonstrations, became increasingly barbaric. In November 1944, after an abortive and easily-suppressed attempted coup in Oruro, several leading political figures were indiscriminately seized and secretly executed. Torture and brutality condoned by government became commonplace. Moreover, though its reforms were more often rhetoric than reality, they frightened the powerful landowners and the tin interests; and the politicians, whether left or right, became fearful for their own lives. Rising anti-government sentiment fuelled by a teachers' strike in June-July 1946 finally culminated in a popular uprising on 14 July: with his military colleagues unwilling to come to his aid, Villaroel was isolated, a mob stormed the presidential palace in La Paz, threw him from a balcony and hanged him from a lamp-post.

During the next six years, Bolivia had makeshift coalition government under three effete presidents, dependent on a spiritually bankrupt oligarchy, an increasingly brutal army, and unstable combinations of unpopular parties. The MNR leadership was frequently exiled but, in clandestinely, built up its strength among the middle and working classes, not least the miners, whose growing militancy was put down with the utmost severity. In the words of a leading authority:

> Thus events were rapidly moving toward the definitive confrontation between the middle-class radical leadership of the MNR, united with the worker masses, and the oligarchy and its military dependencies, a confrontation which eventually led to full-scale revolution . . . [1]

In the presidential election of 1951, the MNR candidate, Paz Estenssoro, though in exile, won a landslide victory as did his vice-presidential candidate, Hernán Siles, in a separate election. At this juncture, and with the connivance of the then-civilian president, the army intervened again, on the pretext that the MNR was in league with the communists: the elections were annulled and General Hugo Ballivián took command. Thwarted in its attempts to come to power through elections and faced with an obdurate military government which had, however, itself lost the support of some key commanders, the MNR – now, far and away, the most powerful and popular party – turned to revolution. It began on 9 April 1952 and was over in three days as armed civilians and workers quickly took La Paz and, assisted by the defection from the army of many officers who fled into exile, forced the rest of the troops to surrender. 600 lives were lost but there would have been many more if the regime had not disintegrated from within, and if it had had any popular support. Paz assumed the presidency for a four-year term but events had forced the pace for the MNR which moved rapidly to implement a truly revolutionary programme.

If the seeds of radical political change in Bolivia were sown in the aftermath of the Chaco War, they were fertilized by the economic circumstances of the country after that conflict. The war itself had been a costly business, and the historic indebtedness inherited by government was compounded by the additional burdens of paying for it and for the reconstruction of the economy when the war was over. Unable to meet its obligations through regular and sustainable income, the government resorted to heavy deficit financing, while the post-war demand for goods and services boosted imports, and fuelled inflation. Thus, whereas during the war itself inflation averaged about 16½ per cent a year, between 1936 and 1939 the annual average rise in the cost of living was over 50 per cent. Its vertiginous acceleration thereafter is indicated in the following table:

Table 13. Inflation in Bolivia 1938–1952 (index. 1938 = 100)

Year	Cost of living index
1939	140.7
1940	164.3
1941	221.8
1942	287.1
1943	311.3
1944	335.1
1945	361.2
1946	418.2
1947	493.7
1948	510.6
1949	561.3
1950	762.1
1951	967.2
1952	1,170.3

Source: Comisión Económica para América Latina, *El desarrollo económico de Bolivia*, Mexico, 1958, p. 298. Cited in Klein, *Parties and political change, loc. cit.*, p.387.

Another economic characteristic of the immediate post-Chaco years was a shortage of skilled labour at a time when the economy was expanding. Apart from actual losses in manpower in the war itself, and the uprooting through conscription of thousands of individuals who did not subsequently return home, the recovery of the mining industry and the growth of industrial output created a competitive labour situation which, together with the benevolent attitude towards organized labour of the military socialist governments, fostered both union growth and workers' demands. To appease the latter in an inflationary context, the government – as in Chile – increasingly intervened in matters of wages and salaries, periodically raising them by decree, and in a wide variety of other matters such as working hours and pensions, all of which affected costs. The later 1930s were thus years of growing labour unrest as workers put increasing pressure on governments and managements alike. And, again as in Chile, managements sought compensation for increased labour costs through higher prices for what they provided.

Annual reports of the general manager of the Bolivian section of the FCAB's lines and of the lines leased from the Bolivia Railway Company eloquently record that cycle and the other economic factors to which reference has been made, though a few selective examples from a long catalogue must suffice. In his report on 1937, Pickwoad referred to the 'constant demands for increased wages and other concessions . . . put forward by the men on account of the high cost of living' and he continued:

> In the early part of the year there was a great shortage of labour in the mines, where better conditions as regards wages, supply of provisions, etc. were offered, and consequently many labourers from the Permanent Way gangs and also skilled workmen from the Shops left us . . .
>
> In my last report, I advised you of the Decree fixing a sliding scale of bonuses with a maximum of 120%, and that I had been able to arrange with the Government that, so far as the Railway was concerned, a maximum of 80% would apply. Continual claims, however, were made by the men . . . and finally the Government obliged us to pay the full bonuses as decreed by the law of 27th June, 1936.
>
> On the 9th March, 1937, another Decree was issued, granting further bonuses . . . This Decree also definitely fixed an 8-hour day for all employees and workmen . . . payment being made for all overtime worked.
>
> Towards the end of July, further demands were made and the men threatened to strike, but an arrangement was come to . . . giving further concessions to the men, including . . . a reduction in the price of articles of first necessity sold from our Provision Stores; the payment of overtime at double rates on the basis of salary plus bonuses, and an increased grant in respect of midwives attending confinements. Notwithstanding these concessions, a Decree was issued on the 11th August, obliging the Company to sell provisions . . . at 30% below cost. An increase in tariffs was granted to compensate us in part for the extra expense incurred . . . [2]

More was to follow: at the end of October, under strike threat, more demands were made, and direct negotiation failed, so the Minister of Labour, as arbitrator, awarded the men 30 per cent of the all-round increase they had demanded. This time, in compensation, the company was awarded freedom from customs duties on imported coal and petroleum.

There was less labour trouble in 1938 than in 1937, and the company was able to convince its staff that their petition in September for an increase of 40 per cent in salaries and 70 per cent in wages was impossible to meet, particularly because it had been obliged by decree to give increases of 10 per cent and 20 per cent in June. But, in July 1939, in what by now was the norm in such matters, 'very substantial increases in salaries and wages' were awarded through arbitration, and they were followed in October by a government decree to the same effect, the company receiving partial compensation by both further customs exemptions and higher tariffs on local currency items. In 1940, however, the usual course of events took a rather different turn, and Pickwoad found himself in the same boat as Heskett had in Chile, when it came to compensatory tariffs. His report is worth quoting at some length to illustrate how tortuous the process could be.

> In August . . . [he wrote] the Railway Federation made demands for general increases in salaries and wages of from 20% to 50% for employees and 30% to 60% for workmen. As the financial situation of the Company did not allow of such an extra expenditure, the demands were refused. Subsequently, arbitration was started, but before this was finished the men went on strike, at mid-night on the 22nd October. The Government declared the strike illegal and ordered the men to return to work within six hours. No notice was taken of this order and the strike continued until the morning of the 28th October. The Company was subsequently forced to give general increases in salaries and wages representing some 57% of the original demands . . . and with the formal promise of the Government that our tariffs would be increased to cover our losses through the strike and the amount represented by the increased salaries and wages.
>
> After some delay, the Government finally decreed a general increase in our tariffs, as a result of our presenting figures to prove our case, and after these figures had been checked by the "Dirección General de Ferrocarriles". The Supreme Resolution to this effect was issued on the 27th December, but unfortunately, as a result of a parliamentary complaint, the Government suspended their authority on the 31st idem. A Government Commission was subsequently formed to go into the whole question . . . In conversation with the President and Ministers of State, we were advised that the increases would be put into force so soon as the Commission's report was received . . . Congress should go into recess on the 30th April, and everything will be done to obtain formal approval to the increases already authorized by the Government . . . [3]

In fact, however, though the records do not reveal the intervention of a Bolivian equivalent of Señor Mujica in the analogous Chilean story, it was not until 5 December 1941 – well over a year since the trouble started – that the authorized tariff increases came into effect: 50 per cent on passenger fares, 35 per cent on luggage and general goods and 15 per cent on articles of first necessity.

The pattern thus established persisted, though it was more pronounced under governments which were broadly sympathetic to the workers, such as that of Villaroel, than under those which were frankly hostile, such as Peñaranda's and the conservative regimes which preceded the revolution of 1952. Nevertheless, even the latter felt obliged to decree wage increases, special bonuses and so on, in the light of the inflationary spiral and of the growing organization and militancy of the working classes. This was particularly the case with the miners, on whose labour the national economy virtually depended, though they themselves were no less dependent on the widely-fluctuating fortunes of Bolivian minerals in world markets, and notably tin which, by 1941, had come to represent almost 80 per cent of Bolivia's total exports by value.

After the Chaco War but before the Second World War, Bolivian exports of tin failed consistently to meet the quota allocated to the country under the international control scheme, partly owing to the shortage of labour, and partly owing to marked price fluctuations. But, as with Chilean copper, the outbreak of the European war in late 1939 saw the beginnings of a marked recovery in world demand, prices and Bolivian output. During the war years, quotas were raised for Bolivia to over 100 per cent of the 1929 standard figure, and greater stability of demand and supply was obtained from various agreements between Bolivian producers and foreign buyers. Thus, for example, as from 1 July 1940, a five-year contract between the American Metals Reserve Company – for 18,000 tonnes of fine tin a year for the USA – and the Hochschild, Aramayo and Banco Minero interests came into force. Similarly, the British government reached agreement with the Patiño interests, which then represented nearly 50 per cent of total Bolivian exports, to take the bulk of its production of high grade tin. Through such developments, exports of Bolivian tin during the war years attained levels not recorded since the peak year of 1929, as the following table shows:

Table 14. Bolivian exports of fine tin (metric tons) 1939–1945

Year	Tonnes
1939	27,648
1940	38,531
1941	42,740
1942	38,899
1943	40,959
1944	39,341
1945	43,147

Source: FCAB, Annual Reports of General Manager, Bolivian Section, 1940–1946

This recovery in tin which the war had boosted could also be exemplified with regard to other Bolivian minerals – wolfram, antimony, zinc and silver of both high and low grades. So far as a major carrier such as the FCAB was concerned, increases in such 'down traffic' also applied to the traditional 'up traffic' of such commodities as foodstuffs, fuel and mining machinery, not to mention the higher passenger movement over the lines it owned and leased which war-time stimulation of the economy encouraged. Though it would be too tedious to itemize all the traffic in statistical form and the different proportions of income and expenditure for the company which each commodity represented, it may be useful to tabulate the overall financial results for these years (cf. tables 6 and 7, p. 182–83)

Table 15. FCAB results (Bolivian section only). 1936–1945

Year	Gross Receipts	Working Expenses	Net Receipts
1936	230,249	145,643	84,606
1937	180,680	157,651	23,029
1938	168,494	148,846	19,648
1939	173,964	148,255	25,709
1940	237,483	184,582	52,901
1941	275,875	219,868	56,007
1942	431,061	270,172	70,889
1943	489,391	347,919	141,472
1944	456,756	377,923	78,833
1945	485,199	380,795	104,404

Source: FCAB, Annual Reports. 1937–1946

Table 16. Bolivia Railway company Results (leased lines). 1936–1945

Year	Gross Receipts	Working Expenses	Surplus	Rentals	Net Profit/Loss
	£	£	£	£	£
1936	317,071	163,308	153,763	126,829	26,935
1937	248,907	185,000	63,907	99,563	– 35,656
1938	224,628	174,306	50,323	89,851	– 39,529
1939	239,255	183,703	55,322	95,610	– 40,288
1940	301,147	222,104	86,043	123,259	– 37,216
1941	332,731	267,494	65,237	133,092	– 67,856
1942	392,178	311,212	80,967	156,871	– 74,905
1943	558,518	400,192	158,326	223,407	– 65,081
1944	532,496	461,043	71,452	212,998	–141,545
1945	633,131	481,982	151,149	253,252	–102,103

Source: FCAB, Annual Reports, 1937–1946

While the tables are a somewhat crude indicator of the profitability of the Bolivian lines of the FCAB in the period, they do reflect the impact of the war-time boom in increases in gross receipts and working expenses, particularly during the last three years of the war. Naturally, rising expenses are themselves partly a reflection of increased traffic, but they also mirror that element in costs attributable to rising salaries and wages, only partially offset by surcharges on tariffs. What they do not show from year to year are such variable factors as costs of renewals and repairs and, above all, widely fluctuating exchange rates of the boliviano to the pound sterling, the sums tabulated being, in part, conversions of local currency figures to sterling at the particular exchange rate then ruling. Though the Bolivian Exchange Control Commission, which fixed the rates periodically, and in some years changed them frequently, was abolished in August 1937, its functions were assumed by the Control Section of the Finance Ministry, all transactions being conducted through the banks. Broadly speaking, all imports and remittances were strictly controlled, needing official authorization, and much of the time of general managers in Bolivia was taken up with such matters.

A comparison of the two tables brings out very clearly, however, that, while the lines owned directly by the FCAB in Bolivia continued to work at a profit, despite all the difficulties, those it leased as the Bolivia Railway Company showed increasing working losses from 1937. This is largely attributable to the sizeable deductions from working surpluses to meet the financial obligations assumed by the FCAB in the reorganization of the Bolivia Railway Company in the late 1920s and early 1930s (see above, pp. 173–74) but it also reflected losses on exchange, the rising labour costs on the leased lines and the plain fact that those lines were increasingly expensive to run, given the terrain they covered and the climatic conditions under which they operated. Thus, because of exceptionally heavy rains in the regions served by the Oruro-Cochabamba line in the Bolivian 'winter' of 1943–44, that line was virtually closed for about ten weeks, and for over a week in the following year for the same reason. And, for all the lines in Bolivia, while the hazards of weather – and the cost of repairs – were a frequent preoccupation of management, human error, no less unpredictable, seems to have been a much more significant factor than in Chile in running up repair bills, as the following selected examples illustrate.

> *24th October, Alto Station*: Train No. 4 composed of two leading and two trailing engines and 15 vehicles.
>
> Owing to the points being wrongly set, the train entered a siding instead of continuing on the main line, with the result that a serious collision occurred with a convoy of loaded vehicles . . . When the train arrived the pointsman was not at his post and the station master had not revised the

entrance points as was his duty. Both men were subsequently transferred to stations of less importance ...[4]

7th October: The driver of cargo train No. 811, seeing that the distribution valve rings of the air brake equipment of his engine had fractured, warned the conductor of the train in Sevaruyo Station to be ready to apply the hand brakes in order to control the convoy in case of need. The conductor, however, instead of attending to his duty, rode in an empty covered goods wagon together with the brakesman, with the result that the speed of the train was not controlled and it entered Huari Station when travelling at some 50 kilms (sic) per hour. A collision took place with train No. 812, which was then entering a siding, as a result of which engine No. 404 and four goods vehicles were damaged ...[5]

Such were the day-to-day matters concerning management in Bolivia. But behind them were the long-term political, economic and social factors to which reference has been made, and which, in the post-war period, were accentuated. It was a period of growing labour unrest, in which the FCAB was increasingly caught up, as managers' reports devoted more and more space to wage demands and settlements, to surcharges on the company's tariffs in compensation, and to the necessary, often long-drawn out, negotiations with both unions and governments on such issues. For the FCAB as a whole, profitability was maintained – and, indeed, boosted in certain years such as the early 1950s when demand for minerals was high because of the Korean War – but this came from the Bolivian section of the main line almost entirely: the leased lines continued to work at a growing loss which was only offset in the overall accounts by the interest received by the FCAB from its holding of the Bolivia Railway Company Series 'B' Bonds (see above, pp. 175–76). By the mid-1950s, income from that source, however, was less than half the loss sustained in working that company's lines. And by that time also the FCAB's own lines in Bolivia were running into quite unprecedented difficulties, largely a consequence of the revolution of 1952.

Under the first Paz Estenssoro government (1952–56), an entirely new political and economic order was created in Bolivia, though the account here is necessarily brief. First, the system of land tenure was thoroughly reformed by decrees which, in effect, destroyed the great estates, returned the land to the Indian peasantry and released them from the more than feudal burdens of service which they had endured for centuries. Secondly, the holdings of the powerful tin barons – the Patiños, Aramayos and Hochschilds, who represented then about 80 per cent of the entire tin-mining sector – were nationalized under a new state agency, COMIBOL. The literacy qualification for voting in elections was abolished as was, at least for a time, the army, and civilian, worker and peasant militias were organized in its place. Politically, the revolution gave enormous power to the workers, particularly to the highly organized tin-miners who, under the umbrella of the nationwide Confederation of Bolivian Workers (COB), used that power to secure four ministerial posts in the first revolutionary government.

This was a profound political and social revolution, but it entailed enormous economic cost. First, the already acute inflationary situation spiralled almost out of control; second, food supplies to the cities fell dramatically as the now land-owning peasantry consumed more of what it produced, and, third, by this time, partly because of previous under-investment, the tin industry had become inefficient and high cost, unable to produce at prices competitive in world markets. In such circumstances – and, again, to cut a long story short – the government turned to the United States for a massive programme of economic assistance. This was forthcoming but at the political cost, in the long run, of a split in the political leadership and the cooling of revolutionary fervour. Meanwhile, in the aftermath of the revolution, companies such as the FCAB had to cope with the quite new circumstances it had created. One of these was the labour situation.

In his report on 1952, the general manager, now T.V. Woods, stated:

> The policy of this Government is, of course, to gain the support of the labour classes in order to establish itself securely in office, and, therefore, whether in the interests of the country or not, a request from labour is rarely refused ... [6]

His own experience of that fact came in the (northern) summer of that year. In July, the Railway Federation submitted to the management a series of 'fantastic' demands, including an increase of 80 per cent in salaries and wages. Protracted, but futile, direct negotiations were followed by the intervention of the Ministry of Labour but that, too, failed to secure a settlement, and the issues went, according to law, to arbitration. It took management a week to prepare its case but, in the event, when judgement was given on 12 September, it granted increases of 40 per cent, retroactive to 1 August. Woods reported:

> To cover this additional disbursement, however, we were able to obtain an increase of 18% in our tariffs. As was vigorously pointed out, this was insufficient to cover us, but in spite of our representations the Government was not prepared to assist us further, and we eventually had to accept this increase under protest ... [7]

Woods had, in fact, some sympathy with the men in the light of the vertiginous rise in the cost of living, but hitherto authorized surcharges on tariffs to offset in part higher wages had been much more generous. Moreover, not long afterwards, various obligatory decrees added substantially to labour costs as they imposed higher overtime pay, increased rates for night work and feast days, raised house and family allowances and also introduced a new levy of 10 per cent on basic pay for those workers employed in frontier zones, covering, so far as the FCAB was concerned, Río Mulato/Uyuni, Uyuni/Atocha and Uyuni/Ollagüe. Woods spelled out the implications of all this in listing the average annual wages of different types of staff at the end of December 1951, and the end of December 1952, quoting the sterling equivalent of bolivianos at the exchange rates then ruling but omitting the special addition for workers in frontier zones. His list is worth citing:

	1951	**1952**
Ganger	525	756
Labourer	300	443
Engine driver	1,379	2,182
Fitter	864	1,260
Brakesman	600	832
Traffic clerk, stations	905	1,244
Traffic clerk, head office	1,007	1,415

In the frontier zones, the 10 per cent special allowance ranged from an additional £68 for engine drivers to £24 for a station traffic clerk.

At the end of 1952, the FCAB in Bolivia had 31 contract staff and 3,446 local staff on its books: hence, while it is very difficult, if not impossible, to calculate precisely the increased cost of salaries and wages for 1952 over 1951, these figures suggest that it must have been considerable. Such a situation was tolerable so long as traffic income covered costs and, indeed, made a profit to give shareholders a reasonable return on their risk investment. Thus, in 1953, salary and wage increases for the FCAB – both negotiated and decree – were offset almost entirely by a massive authorized increase of 115 per cent in tariff surcharges, but in 1954 it was a very different picture. In January, the Minister of Labour announced that a cost of living allowance for employees, decreed two years before, would be consolidated into salaries and wages, thus obliging employers to pay social benefits on the extra amount. In April the government decreed a general 30 per cent increase on all salaries and wages, which the company felt it could not afford without compensation. Woods wrote:

> After protracted negotiations it was possible for the Company to obtain compensation for these extra costs, but only in the form of a subvention which complicated considerably our accountancy and, in any case, proved finally to be inadequate to cover all our needs. This deficit is now the subject

> of negotiation between the Company, the Ministry of Public Works and the Dirección General de Ferrocarriles ...[8]

The government subvention was supposed to apply until an agreed tariff structure was effected but, in fact, to the end of 1955 it was not forthcoming and by that time the government owed the company over 101 million bolivianos on that account alone. Other events in 1954 added another sentence to the writing on the wall:

> At a Railwaymen's Congress held in the month of August [Woods reported] a Resolution was passed that Workmen's Control should be established in the Company, and although it was possible subsequently to obtain the written assurance of the President of the Republic that no such measure was to be applied to our Company, nevertheless it soon became only too obvious that it was to be the policy of the Bolivian Workmen's Central Organization, backed by the Confederation [the COB] and the Federation of Railway Syndicates, to take every opportunity to force this issue upon us ...[9]

It was a prophetic statement, and subsequent events were to prove that for a private company economic constraints and political pressure were a powerful combination. Moreover, and much more than in Chile, the mood of the men employed by the FCAB had changed. Before 1952, their militancy had largely been confined to questions of working conditions and wages and, indeed, they had often openly sided with management in pressing the government to grant surcharges on tariffs to cover their claims as well as refusing to take part in sympathetic strikes with other workers. That loyalty had now been eroded in the new national situation, and Woods' commentary on 1955 became commonplace:

> During the year under review [he wrote] indiscipline among our Bolivian staff reached unprecedented proportions. In spite of the fact that they received increases in salaries, wages and social benefits as from 1st April, 1955, they were insatiable in their demands for further concessions. Their attitude ... was autocratic in the extreme and invariably bordered on the insolent, since they simultaneously threatened to strike if those demands were not complied with by a certain date ...
>
> From the middle of the year onwards, there appeared to be established among the men, an organized system of making trouble for our Contract Staff, for on more than one occasion, members of the latter were placed in invidious situations on account of insubordination and indiscipline of their local employees. On such occasions, our only recourse was to take the matter up with Her Majesty's Ambassador, requesting him to advise the Government Ministers of the position and request that the Syndicates be called to order. Unfortunately, however, this approach had very little effect, as it would apapear that the Central Workmen's Organization and the Syndicates had more power than the Ministers themselves ...[10]

The overall effect of all these factors affecting the company's interests is reflected in the following tables (cf. Tables 15 and 16, p. 252)

Table 17. FCAB results (Bolivian section only). 1946–1955

Year	Gross Receipts	Working Expenses	Net Receipts
	£	£	£
1946	535,280	400,929	134,351
1947	732,074	516,498	215,576
1948	912,307	649,899	262,408
1949	1,230,847	875,531	335,316
1950	1,331,271	939,244	392,028
1951	2,200,409	1,357,850	842,559
1952	2,575,000	2,033,102	541,898
1953	2,070,255	1,560,487	509,768
1954	1,738,806	1,610,706	128,100
1955	4,225,588	3,952,619	272,969

Source: FCAB, Annual Reports, 1947–1956

Table 18. Bolivia Railway Company results (leased lines). 1946–1955

Year	Gross Receipts	Working Expenses	Surplus	Rentals	Net Profit/Loss
	£	£	£	£	£
1946	715,558	506,161	209,396	286,223	–76,826
1947	874,977	602,400	272,576	349,991	–77,414
1948	958,820	752,464	206,357	383,528	–177,171
1949	1,383,296	1,011,231	372,065	553,319	–181,253
1950	1,512,786	1,092,101	420,686	605,115	–184,429
1951	2,306,074	1,538,353	767,720	922,429	–154,709
1952	2,431,818	2,023,525	408,293	972,727	–564,434
1953	1,869,920	1,558,406	311,514	748,578	–437,064
1954	2,428,690	1,934,979	493,711	973,001	–479,290
1955	6,570,724	5,360,112	1,210,617	1,061,684	+148,933

Source: FCAB, Annual Reports, 1947–1956

The improved results on the FCAB Bolivian Section for 1951–53 reflect the traffic boom due to the Korean War, though the figures for 1955 distort the general downward trend of losses on the leased lines, partly because of one-off increases in income through greater traffic to and from the burgeoning Bolivian oil-fields using the Cochabamba line, and partly through a windfall income tax rebate to the Bolivia Railway Company (over £875,000) by the US Treasury.

But the long-term trends were inescapable as Woods pointed out in 1957 in the context of the economic stabilization plan of President Hernán Siles who succeeded Paz Estenssoro in August, 1956:

> ... it was generally agreed that he was taking upon himself a most complex and difficult task, which essentially, must envisage sweeping adjustments to Bolivia's economy. Prior to his election, a Commission was formed to study the most practical manner in which Bolivian currency could be stabilised ... but, during this time, inflation increased to such an extent that, although the official rate for Bolivian currency was still Bs.190 to the dollar, the unofficial rate reached the unprecedented figure in October of over Bs.12,000 to the dollar. ... on the 16th December, the stabilised dollar rate was quoted at Bs.7,700. Equitable (so the Government maintain) compensation for the resultant increase in the cost of living was granted to all ... workers throughout the country and this Company received what then appeared to be an adequate increase in tariffs ... However, it rapidly became obvious, during the earlier months of the current year, that this was not the case – due chiefly to three factors, (1) a decrease in tonnages and passenger traffic greater than had been allowed for, (2) an increase in local prices considerably in excess of the margin allowed for ... and (3) the fact that even immediately after the introduction of the Stabilisation Plan, the Bolivian peso was well above the Bs.7,000 to the dollar rate on the basis of which our compensation had been calculated. In fact, it stands at Bs.8,700 at the time of writing. Our situation, in consequence ... is unsatisfactory in spite of all possible efforts to cut down costs and reduce expenditure to a minimum ...[11]

The situation deteriorated rapidly in 1957, owing to a combination of adverse factors. A recession in world metal markets reduced the tonnage carried for Bolivian producers, with a consequent marked fall in up-traffic and number of passengers; having taken on additional workers in the better conditions of 1956, the company now found that, by law, it was unable to dismiss superfluous hands, about one-quarter of its over 4,000 men; the price of Bolivian oil, fixed in December 1956, greatly in excess of world prices, meant, in effect, that the FCAB was subsidizing the national oil company through its purchases; and rampant inflation, pushing up local costs, continued unabated despite the stabilization plan. Though that plan included a government refusal to decree general increases in wages – as well as in tariff surcharges – substantial increases in family allowance were introduced, and labour unrest continued. Meanwhile, the company's costs for the provision of free medical attention and children's education rose inexorably. Behind all these issues was the exchange problem: whereas for most of 1956 the exchange rate stood at Bs.538 to the £, the average for 1957 was Bs.23,000, and, while this made comparison of working results over the two years somewhat difficult, the general manager calculated that profits on the main lines had fallen from about £417,000 in 1956 to £140,000 in 1957, while on the leased lines the deficit rose from some £129,000 to almost £538,000 over the same period.

In the light of this drastic situation, throughout 1957 representations were made to the Bolivian government on all the factors affecting the company's opoerations, including, indeed, direct correspondence between the managing director, R.H. Dobson, and President Siles himself. What the company sought was spelled out by the chairman, H.C. Drayton, at the AGM of the FCAB in November, 1958, in commenting on the directors' report for 1957, but also pointing out that there had been no improvement in the current year:

> To keep the railway running [he said] it is essential that we be allowed to apply ordinary commercial remedies, namely (1) the elimination of redundant staff, (2) increase in tariffs to enable us to cover operating expenses, (3) relief from onerous medical services ... [12]

But, in the ruling political and economic environment in Bolivia, the government was in a cleft stick: Siles, backed by the US administration, which had poured billions of dollars in aid into the country, walked the tightrope of his stabilization plan, while the powerful unions continually pushed for higher wages which would certainly wreck it. Consequently, when it came to dealing with the FCAB, delaying tactics looked like good policy. Though, in 1957, after long negotiations, agreement was reached for a revision of the rental arrangements on the leased lines, whereby in place of the 40 per cent of gross receipts payable to the government, an annual sterling rental of £350,000 or 40 per cent of gross receipts, whichever was the lesser, the government stalled on the major issues facing the company, setting up a commission of enquiry whose labours were inevitably protracted. And, as it happened, they were overtaken by events.

Crisis point came in 1958. When the results for that year were collated for the directors' report, presented in November 1959, they showed, *inter alia*, that the loss on working the Bolivia Railway Company's lines totalled over £400,000, that on the company's own lines in that country was approximately £100,000, and that the ratio of expenditure to gross receipts was only fractionally below 100 per cent. No interest was receivable for 1958 on the company's holding of over £4 million BRC 5 per cent mortgage and collateral trust income bonds, series B, compared with income of over £200,000 from that source the previous year. The reasons for this extremely serious financial situation lay in the combination of the cost factors to which reference has been made and the unwillingness or inability of the Bolivian government to do anything about them. Summing up the situation towards the end of 1959, Drayton succinctly spelled out the facts:

> ... Our traffics in Bolivia had fallen by 40 per cent. Inflation and depreciation of exchange had increased the cost of stores and other commodities. Wages had inceased but our tariffs remained frozen at the

1956 level. The Company, moreover, was denied its right to introduce economies by the dismissal of superfluous employees and workmen and the reduction of uneconomic train services. It was also unable to obtain relief from the onerous burden of providing an increasingly expensive medical service for its employees and workmen and their families. Furthermore, the powerful Railway Unions were out of hand to such an extent that effective control and management were being destroyed . . . [13]

These arguments he had put in a long letter to President Siles in September, 1958, adding the following firm statement:

> The foregoing unusual and inequitable factors are responsible for the position of the Company, which has invested so many million pounds in your great Country and is losing money in operating the railways from which the Country benefits. We are now compelled to request Your Excellency to immediately concede the steps necessary to put the Company on to an efficient and economic basis or otherwise to define the policy of Your Excellency's Government with respect to the present alarming situation . . . [14]

To press these arguments home, Dobson flew to Bolivia in November 1958, but a visit intended to last a few weeks was extended into March 1959. By this time the board in London had seized the bull by the horns, informing the Bolivian government, stockholders of the FCAB and the general public through a press release that, from mid-February, 1959, it would no longer be able to finance the operation of the railways it ran in Bolivia.

Dobson took with him a proposal from the board, subject to the necessary agreement of debenture and stock-holders, to sell the railways to the Bolivian government on generous terms, in instalments spread over twenty-five years, with nothing payable in the first year, and this was coupled with an offer to run the lines for government account while the government studied the matter. Consequently, the government set up a new commission to look at the issue but with considerable latitude to write its report: meanwhile, it preserved a stony silence on all the other questions the FCAB had raised. It did, however, issue a decree that, given the company's stance, the Government Railway Department would take over the running of the lines and, if they ran at a loss, it would be charged to the FCAB itself. Naturally, this was immediately rejected.

The commission's report was dated 31 August 1959, though it was weeks later that it was communicated to the company. It was a curious mixture of recognition of the economic facts with strident tones of 'economic nationalism', as the following extracts illustrate:

> The excessive desire for profit and the uncontrolled greed of the concessionaires put a brake on the economic development of Bolivia, in the

same way that its progress and growth are today impeded through the Trade Union Movement venturing into fields not strictly within its jurisdiction.

In the first case, the productivity of the Nation was exploited by Capital. In the second, reduced productivity is hindering development and having a prejudicial effect on the general welfare of the Country ...

In effect any solution which might be arrived at would be based on a readjustment of tariffs, as those ruling at present are not high enough to cover the direct cost of the railways ... Of course, as regards the raising of tariffs there exists a definite ceiling ... in any event, the users will have to bear the brunt of this unavoidable re-adjustment ... Neither private management nor a State administration can achieve positive results in the railway industry, unless it subordinates its fares to costs.

Definite solutions are now incumbent on the National Government, through its Legislative and Executive Departments, and it is to the consideration of these two Authorities that the Commission submits the results of its investigation.[15]

Those 'results', however, were singularly vague on concrete proposals for the future of the lines, and, as an exercise in passing the buck, the commission's report would take some beating. Its treatment of past history was clinically dissected in an internal memorandum of the FCAB, undated and unattributed, but probably the work of its secretary, N.L. Weatherall. No matter who wrote it, the author had some trenchant comments to make:

Capital can be obtained for investment only if there is prospect of a reasonable return on the money. Investors in the Bolivian railways have done very badly indeed. On the other hand, the railways were built and a regular and efficient service provided which had an untold effect on the economic development of the country, until conditions in Bolivia and the ever increasing losses made it necessary to call a halt ...

One would think, from the Commision's report, that the Company was able to do what it liked in complete disregard of Bolivian law. All of the Company's concessions and contracts were entered into freely by the Governments of the time and there is no reason to doubt their legality and validity. Nor can there be any doubt that they had been to the advantage of the country. If anyone has the right to complain it is the Company's stockholders, who have done very badly out of their investment ...[16]

The final balance-sheet on that argument and the views of the commission cannot, even now – thirty years later – be drawn up. But, in the circumstances of the time, decisions had to be made. In November 1960, on the initiative of the Bolivian government, negotiations began between its specially-appointed commission and the FCAB's representatives to resolve the railway's problems. But these were long drawn out, and it was only:

> Under date of 29th March, 1962 [that] an Agreement was signed under which the Bolivian Government agreed to purchase the Company's railway properties in Bolivia and those of its American subsidiary, The Bolivia Railway Company, on terms and conditions and for amounts which are to be studied within a period of not more than two years by a Mixed Commission. Those properties therefore passed into the possession of the Bolivian State as from 30th March, 1962. The Company also agreed to manage those lines, for a period of two years, as Managing Agents of, and for account of, the Bolivian Government . . . [17]

Nationalization was a very long and painful process. The two-year period of FCAB management was extended for a further six months, to the end of October 1964, and negotiations for an agreed compensation of £2,524,277 to the company were not consummated until December 1967. Over sixty years had gone by since the original Speyer contract, establishing the Bolivia Railway Company, and the FCAB's involvement with it. And almost eighty years had passed from the time that the then-newly registered Antofagasta (Chili) and Bolivia Railway Company had begun, with President Aniceto Arce and the Huanchaca Mining Company of Bolivia, to build a railway network to link that country and its mineral exports to the wider world. It was the end of an epoch.

The Chilean experience: 1945–1973

The history of the FCAB in Chile in the post-war period reveals no event strictly comparable to the eventual nationalization of its lines in Bolivia in the 1960s, though from time to time the notion of the state taking over its network did, in fact, surface, notably under the Popular Unity government of the early 1970s. But nothing came of it. Throughout the period, under a succession of presidencies of markedly different personalities and political persuasion, the chief preoccupations of chairmen and boards in London and local management on the ground were what might be termed the 'normal' ones of running a large-scale business efficiently and profitably in whatever circumstances ruled. Consequently, much of the story of the senior staff in Antofagasta has a somewhat familiar ring as they wrestled with problems of industrial relations, traffics and tariffs, maintenance and renewals, the promotion of a favourable public image, in short, the gamut of activities and attitudes associated with running a public company in a foreign environment. This did not mean, however, that suitable opportunities to embark on new ventures were not pursued, as the story of the Salta Railway illustrates.

The idea of linking the Chilean port of Antofagasta to the north-western Argentine town of Salta, and hence, through the Argentine rail network, to Buenos Aires and the Atlantic has a long and chequered history, though only the salient features concern us here. But, certainly, from the first decade of the century and particularly from the Chilean presidency of Pedro Montt (cf. above, p. 55), the building of that trans-Andean line had been a topic of interest from time to time to different Chilean and Argentine governments and, indeed, in April 1922, an agreement, known as the Barros Jarpa-Noel Convenio, was signed to affirm both countries' intention to pursue the work. This began on the Argentine side of the frontier as early as 1911, and by 1928 about one-third of the line from Salta was in operation, reaching San Antonio de los Cobres. But work was then suspended for ten years, for financial and other reasons, and it took another ten, to early 1948, before the line reached Socompa on the Chilean frontier, some 570 kilometres from Salta.

It was a similar story of stop and go on the Chilean side, though there the FCAB had a direct interest. In the first place, it already owned a line running from the station of O'Higgins (on the main line to La Paz) to the now-defunct nitrate *oficina* of Augusta Victoria, about one-third of the way to Socompa, and that was the route for the Salta Railway recommended in the early 1920s by a Chilean engineer, Gabriel Quiroz. Second, in 1930 the Chilean government of Carlos Ibáñez had commissioned the FCAB to look at the route again since the proposals of Quiroz, including 4,000 metres of tunnels, seemed too expensive, and it fell to A.H. Street, Assistant Resident Engineer of the company, to come up with alternatives. Though his detailed suggestions were not, in fact, carried through, his basic plan was adopted by the Chilean government, and work was resumed in 1933 on the line from Augusta Victoria to Socompa. But, under private contractors in that post-depression period, progress was halting, since government funds were somewhat intermittent: it was 1940 before the line reached Imilac (74 milometres from Antofagasta) and 1948 before it got to Socompa (332 kilometres). Throughout the construction period, the FCAB, under contract to the State Railways, provided much material, such as 65 lb rails to replace the 36 lb rails on the original line from O'Higgins to Augusta Victoria. The third factor in the FCAB's involvement was purely economic, and it chimed with the assumptions of successive Chilean governments that the Salta Railway, when completed, would prove its worth as agricultural produce and cattle from north-west Argentina would be carried west to the Pacific, and Chilean nitrate would go the other way to fertilize the land that produced them. Since it already owned a third of the line in its own right, the FCAB was in a strong position to bargain with the Chilean government about traffic on all of it. Furthermore, although the line from Augusta Victoria to Socompa was built by the state and belonged to it, the Chilean government was quite unable to run and maintain it, and it had to turn to the FCAB for rolling stock and services through a series of temporary agreements as the line was extended. The nearer the line got to the frontier, however, the more obvious it became that a more permanent arrangement should be made.

Various possibilities were canvassed in late 1947 and early 1948, one of which was not particularly welcomed by the FCAB. At the end of November 1947, the then Minister of Public Works and Ways of Communication, Señor Ernesto Merino Segura, paid an official visit to Antofagasta in order to inspect the line and works to Socompa. He and his wife were accommodated in the company's Administration House during their stay, and a special train was placed at their disposal for the inspection of the Salta line.

> During the journey [reported the General Manager, by then W. Wells] I had several conversations with the Minister, in the course of which he explained that the ultimate object of the Government was to take over all the private railways in Chili, but naturally he knew this could not be done in the near future, and he stated that what the Government most desired was to acquire the line between O'Higgins and Augusta Victoria, either by private purchase of expropriation ...
>
> Señor Merino told me that he would prefer to deal direct with the Company with the object of purchasing the line rather than to resort to expropriation ...[18]

At the same time, the minister made it very clear that this was a long-term objective, since the money for purchase was not then available, and he obviously made this ploy to make his other requests more plausible. First, he enquired whether the company could sell some of its heavier locos to the government for use on the Salta line, and then asked what terms the FCAB would accept for operating the state portion of it on government account. Wells pointed out that, in fact, the company had already allocated larger locos to that line, and was using 'some very old and uneconomical units on our main line' as a result, so there were simply no spare engines to be sold. On the second point, he temporized, saying that much work still needed to be done on the Chilean sector, and he simply had insufficient knowledge of the likely traffic to be able to answer the question. And there the matter rested while, in consulation with London and after a good deal of paperwork, involving speculation on the likely numbers of cattle to be carried from Salta, the appropriate tariffs to be applied for, and other relevant matters, he prepared a proposal for the FCAB to work the Salta railway for the Chilean government. He also estimated that a reasonable purchase price for the company's own line from O'Higgins to Augusta Victoria would be almost £800,000, should that proposal be pushed. For the government at that time, this was simply out of the question on financial grounds, and the alternative of expropriation – always more apparent than real – was surrounded with legal difficulties in view of existing railway laws. That issue was quietly dropped, and both sides concentrated on the fine points of an agreement which would make the FCAB the operating agent for the Chilean government for the whole of the Chilean sector of the Salta line. It was a long and tedious business, and the final contract was not signed and approved until the end of May 1948, though the minister himself had re-visited the north in January to drive the last spike home at Socompa. By the agreement, to operate for five years in the first instance, and renewable for a similar period, unless either side gave a year's notice to terminate it, the FCAB undertook to run the line on an agreed tariff structure and to maintain it on the account of government, to supply rolling stock and other equipment for a reasonable payment, and in addition to receiving the profits, if any, on traffic both ways between O'Higgins and Augusta Victoria, to receive an agency fee of 3 per cent on any excess over 800,000 pesos a month earned by traffic on the state portion of the line.

Despite its very complex nature, it seemed to both Wells and the board in London a reasonable deal when it was finally made. But it was not quite as simple as that. When the state line was taken over for running, it was found to be far from perfect, as a leading company engineer recalls:

> The condition of the line [writes George Craig] in 1948 was most unsatisfactory, the construction being far from complete and the general condition of the track very much below reasonable operating standards. From Augusta Victoria to Kilometre 40 the work carried out by private Contractors was reasonably good, but from this point to the frontier (Socompa) where the work had been carried out gradually under fiscal administration, the standard of work was appalling. Many cuttings were too narrow and constructed without regard to the correct slope (angle of repose) for the material through which they passed, resulting in continual falls of rock and volcanic ash. Embankments were to narrow, many with long depressions where settlement had taken place. Long stretches of track were unballasted . . . The telephone line was in an appalling condition. Wires were of mixed gauge material, and the route in many sections did not follow the track but lay in places up to eleven kilometres distance from the line. Long stretches of the permanent way had been laid with badly worn used rails, several thousand light rail spikes required to be changed (and) switches relaid . . . and there were numerous other defects . . . [19]

Indeed, somewhat before the agreement was signed, sealed and delivered, Wells himself was writing in a similar vein:

> In the hurry to carry out the rail laying [he wrote in December, 1947] the Government engineers had to use very light spikes, and as it was obviously necessary to change these as soon as possible, we have been doing this at the rate of 5,000 spikes per month . . .

> The Government also had to use some very old and much worn rails bought from the United States, some of which were manufactured in 1898 . . .[20]

Nor was this all. Though part of the agreement stipulated that the FCAB take over the fiscal line in working order, and the minister had frequently avowed that so it would, just over a month after it came into effect, Wells reported that:

> It now appears . . . that the funds allotted for New Works to be carried out by the Ministry of Public Works have been greatly reduced, with the result that there is nothing available for the Salta Railway . . .
>
> There is no doubt that several installations, such as the erection of oil and water tanks at Imilac, Monturaqui and Socompa, and housing accommodation at Imilac and Socompa are most urgently required, and until these works have been completed we shall always be faced with considerable difficulty in our efforts to operate the line efficiently . . .[21]

With this unhappy news, Wells also forwarded to London an official request from the Director of the Railway Department, Señor Leopoldo Guillén, for a loan of 6 million pesos from the FCAB to finance the completion of the works, a proposal he strongly supported in the interests of good public relations and urgent technical necessity. Though the board at first demurred it was persuaded by its general manager and by his cogent arguments that much of the material could be supplied from stores at a good rate of return, that interest would be paid on the loan, that the principal would be redeemed by the end of 1949 and, above all, that the company's relations would be enhanced by the transaction:

> Our relations with Señor Guillén [Wells argued] and his immediate superior, Señor Oscar Tenham, as well as with the Minister of Public Works, are of a most friendly nature, and while I am sure they would not fail to appreciate the reasons for our inability to provide financial assistance for improving the working of the Chilean Section of the Salta Railway, nevertheless a refusal on our part at a time when public interest, particularly in the North is fixed on the Salta/Antofagasta line, would prejudice the Railway Company both locally and in Santiago . . .[22]

So, the loan was made, the deficiencies on the line corrected by FCAB personnel, and much good will resulted. When the first five years of the agreement were over, it had proved sufficiently workable, and modestly profitable to the FCAB, and was renewed for a further period. By the end of that time, however, in 1958, it had become obvious that, taking the best years' working with the worst, the Salta Railway had fallen far short of what its protagonists from the 1920s had expected of it. By the late 1950s, its economic justification and, indeed, potential had been seriously undermined by the development of road transport between north-west

Argentina and desert Chile, as a highly experienced transport engineer points out:

> Modern trucks [says George Craig] can negotiate steeper grades (with shorter point-to-point distances), motorized traffic averts switching and trans-shipment to different destinations, and it can transport loads smaller than full rail waggon loads. Considering all these points, a truck saves on that essential element, time, which is so important for avoiding spoilage, especially in transporting fresh food products. Passenger trains from Salta to Antofagasta take 44 hours, whereas a motor truck in 1962 could negotiate the same distance in 18 hours . . . in years to come we must expect new highways to be built. There can be no future for the Salta Railway and there must be considerable loss in maintaining and operating it. The only solution is to lift it.[23]

However depressing that conclusion, it had the ring of truth, and in this context it is interesting to note that when in the late 1940s, the Chilean Ministry of Public Works put up an alternative to engaging the FCAB as agent to run the line, namely to charge the State Railways to undertake that task, all the reputable Chilean railway engineers in that department advised against so onerous and expensive an undertaking. For the FCAB, those lessons were learned the hard way.

Other lessons from the Chilean experience had already been well learned but the problems which taught them seemed endemic. One of the most persistent in the post-war period was inflation, and its impact on profits and on labour and public relations was a constant preoccupation. Clearly, it would be tedious – even if space allowed – to retail here, chapter and verse, the vicissitudes of the Chilean economy in the period as successive governments grappled with the problem with varying degrees of commitment and success. But, from the point of view of employers, national and foreign alike, certain features of working costs, notably of labour, merit comment, however brief. It has already been remarked that from the 1920s onwards, white-collar workers secured a privileged position compared with blue-collar workers in the Chilean system, not least through government-inspired legislation. By the 1950s, the practice of setting the living wage in the light of the previous year's inflation had become the norm for such *empleados* and, though that right had not yet been established for *obreros*, at least by law, in practice prudent employers tended to compensate the latter in the same way, either to head off labour trouble or to settle it when it occurred. The most difficult times for employers were naturally the periods of high inflation, as at the beginning and middle of the 1950s. Thus, in 1951, the *empleados* of the FCAB – in common with many other workers – protested against what they regarded as an insufficient increase in the *sueldo vital*, which was fixed by government committees at the regional level. Strike action, from 14 February to 5 March, finally resulted in a more favourable settlement, the *sueldo vital* being increased from 4,176 pesos to 4,678 pesos a year, but only after the *obreros* also struck in sympathy. Subsequently, the latter settled their own wage claim for 1951 by the normal method of direct negotiation with management, and without recourse to strike action. As already noted in addition, management's riposte to cover these increased costs was to petition government for tariff increases on traffics, and the following tables graphically illustrate the pattern of which the events of 1951 were simply an example.

Table 19. Sueldo vital for Antofagasta, 1950–1959

Year	Chilean pesos	% increase on previous year
1950	3,600	17%
1951	4,678	30%
1952	6,610	41%
1953	8,300	26%
1954	11,620	40%
1955	18,500	59%
1956	27,103	47%
1957	35,277	30%
1958	42,332	20%
1959	57,870	37%

Source: FCAB, General Managers' Annual Reports, Chilean Section, 1951–1960.

Table 20. Tariff increases granted by Chilean government to Chilean section, FCAB

Year	Month	% increase on previous rate
1950	July	33%
1951	February	23%
1952	March	15%
	November	23%
1953	April	11%
	November	10%
1954	May	35%
1955	April	40%
1956	February	60%
1957	August	35%
1958	March	28%

Source: FCAB, General Managers' Annual Reports, Chilean Section, 1951–1959.

Despite its name, the *sueldo vital* was not, of course, a living wage but an obligatory amount as part of salaries and wages fixed on employers by authority in the light of increases in the cost of living. The greater proportion of emoluments was negotiated annually directly between employers and workers – both *empleados* and *obreros* – through the latter's representatives and management. Nevertheless, it had considerable symbolic value in influencing the levels of overall pay, and rarely, if ever, were wage and salary increases, for whatever period, settled at a lower percentage increase than the *sueldo vital*. In soliciting compensatory increases in tariffs, the FCAB, like all employers, took both factors into account, as well as the obligatory increases under the social laws – on pensions, severance pay, housing allowances, medical provision, and so on – which higher salaries and wages entailed. Hence, however crude, the above tables are a reasonable reflection of the impact of inflation on labour costs, though the following figures of actual payments, while making the same point, are, perhaps, no less relevant to the basic arguments.

Table 21. Average earnings (including overtime) of Chilean staff of the FCAB in selected years

Staff category	1950	1954	1959
	(Annual payments in Chilean pesos)		
Labourer	45,126	136,495	681,000
Ganger	34,002	109,592	522,240
Engine driver*	89,403	232,279	1,254,480
Fitter	43,757	126,976	813,560
Brakesman	43,854	127,653	763,080
Traffic clerk*	54,247	170,576	848,640

**Empleados*. The rest are classified as *obreros*.

Source: FCAB, General Managers' Annual Reports, Chilean Section.

Over the same period, compulsory contributions under the social laws for each hand increased as follows:

Table 22. Costs additional to earnings under social laws

Staff category	1950	1954	1959
	(Annual payments in Chilean pesos)		
Labourer	2,775	32,690	224,730
Ganger	2,091	26,247	172,330
Engine Driver	31,183	84,083	493,380
Fitter	2,691	30,409	202,470
Brakesman	2,697	30,572	251,810
Traffic clerk	18,921	61,714	333,770

Source: as in Table 21.

Although the non-expatriate staff were paid in local currency, and the FCAB thus benefited from exchange depreciation, sterling costs continued to rise, while the company's profitability turned from year to year on the volume of traffic carried and the value it represented according to permitted tariffs. These, of course, were unpredictable, as was overall government economic policy. On the wages front, for example, after the somewhat effete government of Carlos Ibáñez (1952–58) and its failure to control inflation, that of Jorge Alessandri (1958–64) tried to stabilize the economy, in part by ending, in 1957, automatic wage increases for *empleados* tied to the cost of living, and regulating by law what those increases should be for both *empleados* and *obreros*. Thus, by Law 12861 in 1958, both categories of worker were awarded increases of 20 per cent on basic pay, and 28 per cent by Law 13305 a year later. To that extent, government intervention eroded the distinction between *empleados* and *obreros*, without, however, affecting the privileges of the former under the social laws. But, towards the end of 1961, after, perhaps, the most serious attempt to combat runaway inflation since the war and before the 1970s, the breakdown of stabilization was signalled by Law 14688 which restored the automatic readjustment of salaries and wages in line with the previous year's inflation as reflected in the *sueldo vital*. This *reajuste*, as it was called, obviously fell behind actual living conditions and, meanwhile, employers were faced increasingly with staff demands for rises in anticipation of what government might decide. For the FCAB in that situation, what government might allow it to charge in increased costs for services rendered was a critical financial pivot on which its continued viability turned, given its commitments to stockholders of different kinds, the need to hold reserves against contingencies, tax liabilities both at home and abroad and the always uncertain income from its separate corporate investment. Events in 1965 will serve to illustrate the problems.

Coming to the presidency in 1964 with an overwhelming popular vote, Eduardo Frei and his Christian Democratic government received another vote of confidence in the Congressional elections of 1965, when his party won control of the lower House of Congress. Backed by this mandate, he pursued his 'revolution in liberty', an ambitious attempt at radical social and economic reform within the Chilean democratic and pluralistic framework. Among its key components were not only long-overdue agrarian changes to break up the great estates and the 'Chileanization' of copper through the state acquiring a half-share in the *Gran Minería*, but also a frontal assault on inflation, universally seen as the most pernicious economic evil. Part of the programme to tackle it was to hold the *reajuste* at exactly the inflation rate for 1964, i.e., 38.4 per cent, while, at the same time, limiting compensatory price increases to around 25 per cent. Since, in the less-regulated atmosphere of 1964, the FCAB had been able to raise wages and salaries for *obreros* and *empleados* by 50 per cent and 55 per cent respectively, and get a compensatory tariff not far out of line at 45 per cent, the new dispensation was a shock to staff and management alike. The result for the company was its most serious labour dispute of the 1960s when, negotiations on rates for 1965 having begun in January and got nowhere by the end of March, all the Chilean staff came out on strike on 27 March and stayed out until 20 April. From the staff point of view, its grievance was as much against the government as it was against the company: for the FCAB, the problem was that of keeping in line as much as possible with government intentions on wage rates while knowing that those intentions on tariffs were far below both customary levels and also what it had asked for, namely a 40 per cent increase. A limit of around 25 per cent – which is what in 1965 State Railways were allowed to charge – would be way out of line with a minimum rise in salaries and wages of over 38 per cent. In his annual statement in 1964, the Chairman, H.C. Drayton, put his finger on the point:

> The matter of tariff increases [he said] is always a difficult one for the Board and Management. On the one hand, we have to keep our rates as low as is commercially possible in order to remain competitive with other forms of transport and – where traffic to and from Bolivia is concerned – with lines serving other ports of entry. On the other hand, when you have a depreciating exchange, continually rising prices and consequent demands for increased salaries and wages it is necessary to obtain some increase in rates to cover the excess costs which cannot be met by operating economies . . .[24]

In the event, the strike of 1965 was settled through arbitration, after the intendant had played a prominent part in engineering it but the award, announced on 19 June, while sticking to the government norm of an increase of 38.4 per cent for all, implied for the company an overall rise of 45.8 per cent because of the additional charges under the social laws. What this actually meant in costs Drayton subsequently spelled out:

> In 1965 [he reported] our salaries and wages bill for all staff in Chile amounted in terms of sterling to £692,015 or say 31 per cent of our total operating expenses. To this has to be added the cost of the payments and contributions under the labour laws currently in force, such as legal bonuses, reserve for indemnities for years of service, family and house allowances, health and accident insurance, etc. These in 1965 totalled £637,084 or another 29 per cent of the operating expenses.
>
> With labour costs of this magnitude our Management is constantly on the watch for means of introducing economies. A temporary prohibition on the dismissal of staff was in force to the end of 1965, so that freedom of action in effecting economies through the dismissal of surplus staff or of taking

disciplininary action in the case of unsatisfactory employees was severely restricted. It has to be reported with regret that these temporary regulations became a permanent part of the Chilean labour code by a law passed in April, 1966. Legislation of this kind makes it increasingly difficult to maintain acceptable standards of work and economical operation . . .[25]

To both board and local management, it might well have seemed that the ghost of Banquo or, at any rate, Bolivia, was about to reappear.

Apart from these unexpected additional costs, the FCAB had already embarked on a major programme of modernization – the complete change-over from steam to diesel-electric traction on the Chilean lines. This had been started in 1957, extended to the Antofagasta-Calama section in 1961 and, after the necessary experimentation at the higher altitudes of the trans-Andean crossing into Bolivia, carried through completely by May 1965. This was an expensive business but, more than most public or private enterprises, a railway off the track of technological advance runs the risk of being shunted into a derelict siding. It was not a risk the company in Chile was prepared to run, despite its other difficulties. Competition from road transport had already undermined its position in Bolivia in the 1950s, and threatened to do so in Chile in the 1960s – as, indeed, it had already done, but failed, in the early 1930s – and it had to be met. Yet, government and labour apart, so far as the FCAB was *directly* concerned, its traffic was ultimately dependent on others. Thus, in 1965, a 36-day strike at Chuquicamata by copper-workers cut production to its lowest level since 1960, and traffic on the line was inevitably affected, as, indeed, it was also by 'the frequent strikes and stoppages in the Antofagasta Port, where, in addition, work-to-rule tactics were continually adopted'.[26]

However brief and selective this summary of some events in 1965 which impinged on the company's fortunes, that year illustrates the complexities of operating the business in a period of much political, economic and social change in the host country. While Frei's government stood for one kind of continuity in its commitment to a democratic system, it also reflected that persistent, if intermittent, trend in Chilean public life from the 1920s – the expansion of the role and influence of the state in economic affairs. At the same time, however, the 'revolution in liberty', strongly backed by the US administration and its 'Alliance for Progress', sought to avoid fundamental social upheaval of the Bolivian kind through progressive and necessary reform. It was frustrated in the end by many factors: deep divisions about its nature and direction within the dominant party itself; obstruction in the Senate by an often unholy alliance between the impatient parties of the left and the uncompromising parties of the right; and, not least, the bane of all reforming governments, the creation of expectations that practically could not be fulfilled. Such disappointments overshadowed the government's achievements, notably in education, housing and, in part, agrarian reform, as well as the 'Chileanization' of copper, a key step towards the state fully taking over that critical natural resource.

Against that background of change and hope in Chile which marked the second quinquennium of the 1960s, the FCAB did reasonably well, and throughout the period was able to pay a dividend on the 5 per cent cumulative preference stock in every year. The dividend on consolidated ordinary stock, however, fell gradually from 5 per cent in 1966 and 1967, to 4 per cent in 1968, 3¾ per cent in 1969, and 1 per cent in 1970. Profitability was maintained in the early years through good traffics, reasonable salary and wage settlements (without recourse to arbitration) and compensatory tariffs not far out of line with those agreements. A major set-back in the underlying financial strength of the company, however, occurred during 1968, when the agreement painfully negotiated with the Bolivian government for compensation for the nationalization of the lines in Bolivia fell through. By the agreement of 22 December 1967, the company was to receive over £2,500,000 from the government, payable over twenty-five years, but less than three months later, on the government's stated unwillingness to commit the country to annual payments over such a period, the company reluctantly agreed to accept a single cash payment of just over £800,000, 'which, although most inadequate compared with the book value of the assets taken over, was the best that could be obtained'.[27] In all the circumstances, it probably was, though it meant writing off over £6,000,000 against reserves and provision for renewals, the whole of the company's 5 per cent (Bolivia) debenture stock held by the Andes Trust Ltd. being redeemed at its original cost of some £1,400,000 in November 1968.

However, 1970 was to prove a critical year for the FCAB in Chile in the modern phase of its history, as, indeed, that year was a turning-point for the republic itself. In the presidential election of September, Dr Salvador Allende, standard-bearer of a heterogeneous collection of marxist parties – the communists, socialists and left-wing radicals in particular – won on a minority vote over the Christian Democrat, Radomiro Tomic, and the right-wing candidate, the ageing Jorge Alessandri, beating the latter into second place by a mere 39,000 votes in an electorate of over 3,500,000. His Popular Unity coalition came into office, after his confirmation by Congress, on a sweeping platform for fundamental change in most aspects of the national life, including total nationalization of copper and the banking system, a rapid speeding-up of agrarian reform, massive expansion of social services such as housing, health and education, with central planning and control as hallmarks of the new economic and social structure. Rhetoric apart – though that was considerable – this internal programme looked very much like an accentuation of reformist policies adumbrated before, though promises of a radical redistribution of income frightened the upper classes, and Allende's victory caused a run on the banks and the temporary suspension of share dealings. Panic passed, however, but uncertainty remained and, in fact, increased as the government began to implement its programme by somewhat unorthodox means. Faced with an opposition majority in Congress, the government by-passed the legislature: to nationalize the banks, for example, instead of sending a bill to Congress, where resistance, dilution and delay would certainly have ensued, the government simply bought majority shareholdings through the CORFO. Other commanding heights of the economy such as monopolistic enterprizes in consumer goods, were scaled by the resurrection of a long-forgotten but unrepealed law of the 'Socialist Republic' of 1932, authorizing government to take over businesses 'failing to supply the people'. The powerful levers of exchange and commodity control reinforced these weapons against the private sector though with some areas, notably the *Gran Minería* of copper, there was little public or political dissent, and complete nationalization was effected in 1971. While, increasingly, the government came under attack as much for its methods as for its motives, it succumbed to internal dissensions within Popular Unity at the political level, and felt strong pressure from the left outside politics (such as the Movement of the Revolutionary Left – MIR) which fomented illegal seizures of land and factories to make radical change more rapid.

At the same time, through wage increases and price controls, a sizeable redistribution of income took place: this naturally led to a higher pattern of working-class spending and consumption which, while initially lowering unemployment as consumer-goods industries took up unused capacity to meet demand, helped to fuel inflation. In the longer run, for private industry, government pricing policies, exchange regulations, increasing control over imports of necessary goods and equipment – apart from the threat of nationalization of government or crude take-over by such as the MIR – created a complete lack of confidence, and investment in future capacity virtually stopped. To cut a long and controversial story short, by mid-1972 politics was moving to the streets; basic commodities, including foostuffs (affected by the disruption on the land), were in short supply; strikes by the self-employed, such as truck-drivers, and privileged workers, such as copper miners, were becoming commonplace, and a deepening sense of crisis took hold. It was fuelled on the extreme right by the emergence of terrorist groups which knew no other way to combat the left except violence of its own. Nor can there now be any doubt of the contributory role in the breakdown played by covert agencies of the USA through their financial support of anti-government strikes or of the pressures on the Allende government by official American attitudes on international issues of credit and finance. Though these were much less the causes than ancillary factors in the dénouement, they undoubtedly played a part.

Finally, however, and again to be brief, in a concerted move, on 11 September 1973, the Chilean armed forces overthrew the Popular Unity goverment and Allende died in the presidential palace. A ruling junta of service chiefs, presided over by the Commander-in-Chief of the Army, General Augusto Pinochet Ugarte, took over the government, to inaugurate a phase in Chilean history which, in the policies pursued and the changes wrought, has been no less controversial than its predecessor. This period lies largely outside the scope of this narrative but the story of the FCAB in the early 1970s provides, in many ways, a fitting final chapter to the history of a company which for almost a century met and overcame a series of challenges and was then faced with what was, perhaps, the most critical of them all.

Almost exactly two weeks after the Chilean electorate had put into power the country's first marxist president, stockholders of the FCAB received from the secretary, J.F. Sharp, the customary papers for the AGM to consider the results for 1969 on 13 October: they were, whether deliberately or not, despatched, in fact, on Chilean Independence Day, 18 September, and they included the usual statement by the board's then-chairman, W.T. Caulfield. Remarking, *inter alia*, that 'our operation in Chile throughout 1969 continued relatively smoothly', he went on:

> I am sorry to say, however, that the prospects for the current year are not encouraging. As compared with the 29.8 per cent increase which we obtained for application to our escudo tariffs for 1970 in order to counteract the inflation which took place in 1969, we had after much hard bargaining to concede an increase in salaries and wages of 35 per cent . . . Meanwhile, the devaluation of the escudo has continued at an even faster rate and for the first six months it was 17.4 per cent as compared with the 16.7 per cent during the similar period in 1969. But the principal cause of our poor results so far in the current year has been the reduction in the amount of copper from the Chuquicamata Mine carried by our Railway, this having been 23,000 tons lower for the first six months . . . there has also been a reduction of 19,000 tons in our traffic to Chuquicamata. The main factors for (*sic*) this have been stoppages of work at the mine and in the Port of Antofagasta and smelting difficulties in the plant . . . I hope to give you more encouraging news . . . at our Annual General Meeting . . . [28]

But, at the meeting itself, that promissory note could not be redeemed. Though copper shipments had begun to improve from July and 'the shortfall in freight in the first six months could be made up during the second', this was only 'provided the new strike at the mine does not last too long'. Moreover, the chairman said:

> There has also been an unfortunate but not altogether unexpected reduction in traffic to Bolivia. Although Down traffic, principally minerals, has been about the same as in 1969, the political unrest and the economic difficulties which that country has been experiencing since September last year (1969) have severely restricted imports. In consequence, the Up traffic to Bolivia looks like being between 15% and 20% lower.
>
> Traffic within Chile (other than that to and from Chuquicamata) has also fallen off . . . In the meantime, costs – principally salaries, wages and social benefits – have kept on going up . . . because of these factors the prospects for the current year cannot be described as anything but gloomy . . . [29]

Nor was the gloom lightened by the news that, following investigation of the company's books for the 1960s by the Chilean tax authorities, government claims for £300,000 of unpaid imposts had been met in 1969, but those for over £1,400,000 for later years were still *sub judice*. It was a large contingency but, in that context, it should be noted that throughout its history, the FCAB had stuck closely to Chilean law, and had retained, at considerable cost, prominent Chilean legal advisers to ensure that it did. More often than not, when understanding broke down it was the law which was the ass.

The prognosis for 1970 proved, unfortunately, correct. The strike at Chuquicamata, to which the chairman had referred, lasted three weeks, and the curtailment of traffic in copper, combined with the other adverse factors he had mentioned, resulted in a combined profit for 1970 of only just over £4,000. Dividends could only be paid by drawing on balances accumulated over previous years, leaving a carry-forward of almost £669,000. Whether that would be enough to back up expected income in operations, and meet all obligations, only time would tell. Meanwhile, in Chile, the marxist government of Popular Unity had come to power, and it certainly intended to use it.

According to Caulfield, in October 1970, the FCAB was not listed among the government's prime targets for nationalization but whether it would or could be taken over in one form of another – and a voluntary, negotiated purchase had been contemplated by the board – remained an open question: as he put it in reply to a shareholder:

> This is something which has been on our minds for a long time past and it is always very near the surface. We are sitting on the sidelines waiting for an indication of what we might do and we have got our ears to the ground all the time one hundred per cent. I cannot possibly make any prophesies or forecasts because I do not know and I do not think anybody knows but we are all lined up so we can catch any ball which may emerge from the scrum so to speak . . . [30]

The ball, so to speak, came out of the scrum in mid-February 1971, when according to the General Manager in Antofagasta, Emilio J. Barrie

Mackenzie the Sub-Secretary of the Transport Ministry, Señor Hernán Morales, wrote to the President of the Employees' Syndicate of the FCAB, asking for

> ... the nomination of a union representative to represent the workers of the FCAB on a commission which is to be set up to consider the "nationalisation or purchase by the State", of the FCAB.
>
> This Commission [Barrie went on] will be set up by Supreme Decree, and will have five members, one appointed by the Sub-Secretary of Transport, three related to the State Railways, and one nominated by our unions, as above.
>
> As you will see the Company itself is not represented on the Commission, nor have we been officially advised as yet, of its constitution ...[31]

This information, it is interesting to note, was passed to the general manager by the President of the Employees' Syndicate: that union wished to have nothing whatever to do with the State Railways and, indeed, publicly disowned one of its own committee members, Luís Franco, for speaking on the local radio and making statements to the local press in favour of the proposed commission. But the news simply re-inforced what the board had foreseen, or, at least, thought possible when its chairman addressed the AGM in 1970. In fact, shortly after that event, the managing director, James A. Blair (who had succeeded the long-serving F.R. Hancock on his retirement at the end of 1969 after fifty-two years with the company – the last few years successively as secretary, and eventually managing director) paid a visit to Chile precisely to find out, if he could, what the new government's intentions were. He had a very busy time in numerous meetings, including two with the new Sub-Secretary of Transport who assured him that, while nationalization of the FCAB was, indeed, in the programme, many other matters, such as the state's take-over of copper mining, took precedence and the FCAB should continue its services and improve them if possible. This, Blair subsequently recorded, 'we undertook to do *within the limits of the financial resources available to us, and in his turn the Subsecretary undertook in the Government's name, to see that we were provided with those resources*'.[32] In his letter reporting on this understanding and what had subsequently happened to it, Blair spelled out the facts of his company's financial position and what was meant by adequate resources. He pointed out that about 55 per cent of the FCAB's business was at tariff rates expressed in either dollars or sterling, these being for traffic to and from Bolivia and for the carriage of Chilean copper. The other 45 per cent of the business was on tariff rates in escudos, and it was a long-established practice for the company to apply anually for increases in those rates at least by the same percentage as the rise in the cost-of-living index in the previous year. No such increases, however, had been requested for many years in foreign currency tariffs since their sterling worth had remained unchanged and the escudo equivalent had been regularly increased by the steady annual devaluation of the escudo by 25 per cent to 30 per cent. In other words, the company's income in terms of escudos had been broadly sufficient to cover continually rising costs. In accordance with well-established policy, therefore, an application to raise escudo tariffs by 36 per cent for 1971 had been made at the end of 1970, 33 per cent on the expected cost-of-living increase that year, and 3 per cent as compensation for the fall in traffic already mentioned. It was not then thought necessary to apply also for an increase in foreign currency tariffs, although the exchange rate had not changed for six months and the new government had declared its intention to keep it fixed. Meanwhile, and again confirming to routine practice, at the end of 1970, Barrie had embarked on the usual round of negotiations with the unions to fix wage and salary rates for the coming year, anticipating, no doubt, that the normal *reajuste* or just over 30 per cent would be agreed.

Unfortunately, however, after long discussions, involving also the Subsecretary of Transport's office, Barrie was obliged to concede a 50 per cent increase for 1971 but only did so after the Railway Department had promised to support the claim for a 36 per cent rise in escudo tariffs and, moreover, to try to obtain for the company a 23 per cent increase in foreign currency tariffs, without which, it was reckoned, it might face a loss on Chilean opoerations of the equivalent of some £100,000 after tax unless, of course, traffic improved considerably over 1970, and there were no signs whatever of that. The 36 per cent increase was, in fact, approved but when it came to the 23 per cent the Chilean Ministry of Foreign Affairs objected to its application to the Bolivian traffic, some 60 per cent of total foreign currency business. Taking that blow into account, as well as the failure of copper traffic to recover – largely because of labour troubles at the mines – by the end of March, Blair was counting the total loss on all operations at the equivalent of £165,000. As he put it: 'This is a most serious situation because if we accept it, it will mean remitting money to Chile from our reserves to cover our operating expenses'.[33] Nor was this all: apart from the news of the setting-up of the government commission to look into the question of state acquisition of the railway, from 1 January 1971, payment of salaries in any other currency than escudos was prohibited, except by special permission. At that time, the FCAB had twenty-three senior members of staff, mostly expatriates, on its books, and they had been customarily paid largely in sterling. As a result of the new measure, seven resigned by the end of April, 7 more expressed the intention to do so at a later date, and the others remained undecided but clearly disturbed. The only good this ill wind blew was a policy decision to replace those leaving with well-qualified Chileans.

Faced with the prospect of continuing and unsustainable losses, the board had reached the conclusion by the early (northern) summer of 1971 that its best policy would be to negotiate with government for the state to take over its business. But from the time the first approaches were made in May to the very end of the Allende period, the government was in no hurry to do so, though discussions continued on-and-off, mostly on the initiatives of the company. A new government commission was set up to pursue the matter, and perfunctorily went about its task, and verbal promises to assist the company financially were not translated into reality. In the middle of May 1972, the chairman was writing as follows:

> To say that we are living from hand-to-mouth is to put it mildly, and in order to keep afloat at all we are being obliged to remit back to Chile all and more than we are receiving from there in foreign currency freights . . . we have just decided to pass for the second time in six months the half-yearly dividend on our 5% Cumulative Preference Stock . . . We have an intolerable situation where the chief U.K. investment in Chile . . . is not being permitted to operate with even a minimum return on its capital, while the decision of the Chilean Government ultimately to take over the Railway is being continually postponed . . . [34]

These strong opinions were to be reflected in the results for 1972 which showed a consolidated loss of over £400,000, leaving a carry-forward of only £213,000 to 1973. By the end of the year arrears on dividends on the 5 per cent cumulative preference stock had stretched to eighteen months and, of course, no dividend had been paid on the ordinary stock since 1970.

For management both at home and abroad, the Allende years were years of trials and tribulations. Blair himself paid frequent visits to Chile, many of them in fruitless pursuit of the company's policies, while staff resident there experienced the labour troubles, the mounting inflation and the growing sense of political and economic crisis. The very full reports of General Manager Barrie in Antofagasta provide a vivid commentary on the period, notably on the frequent strikes in the copper mines, notably after nationalization in July 1971, and on the disruptions of supplies caused both by the fall in national production of foodstuffs and by strikes of transport personnel in opposition to the government. The following examples must suffice.

> The shortage in supplies for the housewife [he wrote in July 1972] which have been intermittently affecting first some products and then others have lately become more frequent.
>
> For the last four or five days, for instance, there has been no beef, lamb or pork. According to the paper, 1200 chickens were received yesterday, but as you can imagine, this is a drop in the ocean for a town of this size.

At the same time, fish and sea-food were practically unobtainable, what with rough seas, and the Feast of San Pedro Pescador.

Groceries are also in short and intermittent supply, including such staples as spaghetti, beans, lentils, jam, butter, sausage meat, etc.

I was even without my usual porridge . . .![35]

Price increases. As you will see from the several enclosed cuttings from the local Mercurio, price increases for all products of prime necessity, as well as household articles, textiles, wool, thread, television sets, automobiles etc., were published in the Diario oficial of the 18th instant.

The price of bread increased by almost 98%, powdered milk by 300%. The choice cuts of meat are simply out of reach, even for those of ample means . . . and the prices for medium and inferior quality cuts are also quite high . . .[36]

On Monday all shops opened and were invaded by anxious shoppers. Clothes and shoes continue to be very scarce. As regards foodstuffs, butter and poultry were announced for today, and a possible solution to the shortage of flour was announced for next week, as bread continues to be scarce.

Last week . . . the scarcity of food had reached serious proportions. Amongst the products virtually unobtainable were the following: rice, sugar, butter, tea, powder milk, flour, beans, maize, canned fruit, brooms, lavatory paper etc.

Other products available could only be bought in limited quantities, by queueing up, or at exorbitant prices in the street markets, such as potatoes, onions etc., if you could find them, as usually they were sold immediately they were offered to the public . . .[37]

If, indeed, as Caulfield had put it, the company was living 'from hand to mouth', so were its staff in Antofagasta, and suffering much more severely.

The early 1970s, then, were years of great uncertainty and acute anxiety for the company. Yet, it survived and, though somewhat fortuitously, preserved its identity. But whether it would be able to do so for the rest of the decade would become a matter of conjecture.

Notes

1. Klein, *Parties and Political Change in Bolivia*, p. 391.
2. General manager, Bolivian section, to chairman, La Paz, 31 March 1938.
3. *Idem*. to *idem*., La Paz, 7 May 1941.
4. *Idem*. to *idem*., La Paz, 27 April 1944. (Annual Report for 1943)
5. *Idem*. to *idem*., La Paz, 27 April 1945. (Annual Report for 1944)
6. General manager, Bolivian Branch, to chairman, La Paz, 10 July 1953.
7. *Ibid*
8. General manager, Bolivian Branch, to chairman, La Paz, 10 September 1955.
9. *Ibid*.
10. General manager, Bolivian Section, to chairman La Paz, 21 November 1956.
11. *Idem*. to *idem*., La Paz, not dated, 1957. (Annual Report for 1956).
12. *FCAB, Report of Meeting*, 17 November 1958, p.18.
13. *FCAB, Report of Meeting*, 24 November 1959, p.15.
14. Chairman to HE Señor Dr Don Hernán Siles Zuazo, London, 12 September 1958. Copy. General Letter Book, No.8, ff.364–70.
15. Republic of Bolivia, National Commission of Investigation of the Antofagasta to Bolivia Railway (F.C.A.B.) and the Bolivia Railway. (B.R.C.) Typescript translation, dated La Paz, 31 August 1959, FCAB. Archive.
16. The Antofagasta (Chili) & Bolivia Railway Company Ltd., Answers to Points Raised in the Report of the Government Commission, undated typescript FCAB Archive.
17. *FCAB, Report of Meeting*, 17 September 1962, p.4.
18. General manager to managing director, Antofagasta, 28 November 1947. Confidential, No. 9.
19. Personal communication, George Craig to author, September 1986.
20. General manager to managing director, Antofagasta, 7 December 1947. Confidential No.10.
21. *Idem*. to *idem*., Antofagasta, 2 July 1948. Confidential No.30.
22. *Idem* to *idem*., Antofagasta, 20 August 1948. Confidential No.34.
23. Personal communication, George Craig to author, September 1986.
24. FCAB, *Annual Report for 1964,* 20 September 1965, p.17. The reference to Bolivia relates to increasing competition from the Chilean port of Arica,

the coastal terminus of the La Paz-Arica line, and the Peruvian port of Matarani, modernized in the 1950s and 1960s, to replace Mollendo, further south. See Fifer, *Bolivia; Land, Location and Politics*, *loc.cit.*, pp.82–88.

25. *FCAB, Annual Report for 1965,* 23 August 1966, pp.18–19.
26. *Ibid.*, p.19.
27. *FCAB, Annual Report for 1967*, 21 August 1968. p.13.
28. *FCAB, Annual Report for 1969*, 8 September 1970. p.15. The escudo, the standard rate of the Chilean currency, had replaced the old peso in the monetary reforms of Jorge Alessandri in 1959 (1 escudo = 1,000 old pesos). The non Spanish-speaking reader may wish to know that 'escudo' means 'shield', and 'peso', 'weight', but, whatever the name of the currency, inflation persisted.
29. *FCAB, Report of Proceedings at 82nd AGM*, 13 October 1970, pp.4–5 Typescript, FCAB Archive.
30. *Ibid.*, p.6.
31. General manager to managing director, Antofagasta, 5 March 1971. Confidential. No. 1285.
32. James A. Blair to the Hon. H.A.A. Hankey, London, 30 March 1971. Copy. General Letter Book No.19, ff.517–20. My emphasis. Henry Hankey was then Assistant Under-Secretary of State at the Foreign and Commonwealth Office.
33. *Ibid.*
34. W.T. Caulfield to the Hon. H.A.A. Hankey, London, 15 May 1972. Copy. General Letter Book No. 21, ff.123–25.
35. General manager to managing director, Antofagasta, 5 July 1972. Confidential No. 1404.
36. *Idem* to *idem*., Antofagasta, 23 August 1972. Confidential No. 1416.
37. *Idem* to *idem*., Antofagasta, 8 November 1972. Confidential No. 1437.

EPILOGUE: ENDS AND BEGINNINGS, 1973–1988

The early 1970s were difficult years for both FCAB's management team in Chile and the board and London office staff in Finsbury Circus.

As political and economic crisis increased its grip on Allende's Chile, the railway's traffics and revenues were badly affected by the sharply deteriorating climate in industrial relations. Repeated strikes and stoppages at the huge mining complex of Chuquicamata had serious consequences for the railway, not least because of the close links between the *sindicatos* of the copper miners and those of the FCAB rail workers at Calama, Antofagasta and Mejillones.

Seen from London, the Allende period was one when wage and salary rates were increased by government decree, while tariffs were either frozen or reduced. The resulting losses had to be made up from the company's inadequate reserves.

At the same time the existing controls on foreign exchange were being progressively tightened resulting in the mass resignation and exodus during 1971–72 of all foreign employed staff – mostly British – after payments to them in foreign currency were suddenly disallowed.

The exodus of senior staff was considered a serious blow at first but, in fact, the entry of Chilean nationals to work alongside the remaining Anglo-Chileans turned out very well. For many years the board had been informed that qualified Chileans would not leave the comforts of Santiago to work in the arid North and that the salaries being offered by FCAB were certainly insufficient to tempt them away from the big mining companies. However, the advice from successive general managers turned out to be mistaken and it proved possible to recruit suitable staff. Thus, the Chileanisation of the railway had begun by courtesy of a Central Bank edict.

During this time the financial situation was steadily worsening and the group's portfolio of stocks and shares and its cash reserves which were held by the Andes Trust were falling on a monthly basis and not being replenished from Chilean remittances. By the middle of 1973 the funds available in the Andes Trust were practically exhausted.

Tentative negotiations to reach an agreement as to the railway's future had begun in 1971 in Chile between the Ministry of Transport and the local manager, supported by frequent visits from the managing director and other board members from London. Both sides were negotiating against a background of economic chaos and political instability, and little or no progress was made although the board had decided as early as mid-1971 that the logical solution to the railway's problems was to negotiate a sale to the government. The military coup in September of that year, while bringing no instant panacea for the severe economic problems facing the company in its now run-down condition, did at least remove the question mark over its future. The Military Junta swiftly indicated that it wished the railway to remain in the hands of British shareholders, partly no doubt so it should continue as a neutral buffer between itself and the Bolivian generals with their long-held aspirations for a corridor to the Pacific. The Bolivian card had come into play to the company's advantage once again.

The years between 1974 and 1978 were as difficult for the railway as for Chile itself. Recovery from the ruins left by Chile's marxist experiment proved long and painful. Doing business with the Junta was not easy either. FCAB's management, now all Chilean, immediately became involved in almost continuous negotiations with the authorities to obtain authorizations to raise freight rates and water tariffs to economic levels, acquire foreign exchange permits to pay for essential imported materials (many items were no longer manufactured locally), and to re-capture traditional freight which had been directed away from the railway.

During the next two to three years the economic situation began to show signs of improvement, and in 1976 the FCAB finally agreed to invest about £1m. under the Decree-Law No. 600 which had been introduced back in 1974 to stimulate investment in the country. Only when the agreed amount had been invested in Chile could profits be remitted overseas. Part of the £1m. investment was satisfied by the purchase of a new diesel-electric locomotive, which seemed a good omen to everyone in the company.

In May 1977 control of the company changed hands in London. Two financial groups acquired the controlling stake then held by Estates House Investment Trust which had acquired it over a period of many years. Not surprisingly, some board and managerial changes followed and some feathers were ruffled, but this had now become normal practice after City take-overs. One of the groups was LET Investments (formerly

Lisbon Electric Tramways), an investment company owned by Mr. Jacob Rothschild's family interests, and the other was Deltec Panamerica S.A., an investment company with particular interests in Latin America and represented by the Marquess of Douro. Both had experience in turning round financial and industrial companies which were basically sound but lacked direction and the Antofagasta Railway was a classic example. Both investors also brought a much needed injection of entrepreneurial skills. These attributes were the 'shot in the arm' and the 'breath of fresh air' that the railway so badly needed. Board decisions were now taken quickly where necessary and data obtained to establish how and where costs could be reduced and revenue increased.

At the same time a small capital investment programme was initiated and more modern budgeting and reporting systems were introduced. This was achieved in the short space of two years. The stock market however must also have sensed that something had stirred as the Antofagasta share price doubled during the L.E.T./Deltec period of tenure although no dividends had been paid on the ordinary stock since the 1 per cent payment in respect of the year 1970, while the arrears on the preference stock had been reduced by just one half-year.

In late 1979 control of the company was acquired by Turismo e Inmobiliaria Bío-Bío S.A. a Chilean company owned by Mr Andrónico Luksic, a prominent Chilean industrialist who was born and brought up in the city of Antofagasta. Following the takeover, the previous chairman, Mr G.S. Stone and his deputy Lord Douro resigned in February 1980 and Viscount Montgomery of Alamein was appointed chairman. Lord Montgomery had known Mr Luksic during a period when they were both working in Antofagasta. Lord Montgomery was to remain as chairman for some three years and was to steer the company through a difficult transitional period.

There was record copper traffic in 1979 but the overall result for that year was a small loss of £28,470 mainly because most petroleum products moved to road transport.

During the first part of 1980 the Luksic group began evaluating all aspects of the company's operations prior to establishing their own management team. A vigorous cost-cutting programme was initiated and the cost of severance payments for the 350 employees who were made redundant largely contributed to a group loss before taxation of £766,086. This was to be the last recorded loss. Notwithstanding this, 1980 marked the emergence of a re-vitalized company, which became apparent later – in 1981 – when a group profit before taxation of £3.8m. was recorded. Another 387 employees were made redundant during that year. The payment of an extra half-year's dividend finally eliminated the arrears on the preference stock, clearing the way for payment of ordinary dividends which had been non-existent since 1971.

1981 was a crucial year which included the transfer of the railway workshops from Mejillones to Antofagasta, thus saving a round trip of some 140 kilometres for every locomotive and wagon in need of maintenance and repair. The transfer also produced a dramatic economy in the labour force as the five hundred or so men in Mejillones (with between a thousand and fifteen hundred dependants) eventually reduced to today's figure of only thirty, a very small number even allowing for the considerable contracting out of works traditionally carried out in the shops and the effects of the modernization programme. During the year a mixed road/rail passenger service was introduced. The new service reduced the journey time for passengers and saved the expense of running passenger trains from Antofagasta to Calama, a distance of 240 kilometres. Further important events during 1981 were the purchase and delivery of new wagons for the first time in over forty years, the appointment of worldwide freight agents, and the purchase of equity stakes in the George A. Fuller Company, a leading construction company in the United States and in Banco O'Higgins, one of the largest Chilean commercial banks. Finally, towards the end of the year a proposal was put forward to form a mirror-image holding company under a Scheme of Arrangement. This was duly approved on 24 May 1982 and Antofagasta Holdings PLC came into existence. Following completion of the reorganization in July 1982, Lord Montgomery resigned and Mr Luksic assumed the role of executive chairman.

1982 was a difficult year as the recession took hold worldwide with especially serious economic consequences in Chile. The peso was devalued by 47 per cent and the majority of banks in the private sector including Banco O'Higgins were subject to some form of government intervention. Group turnover slumped from around £15m. to £10.9m. and net profit from £3.4m. to £0.8m., still a creditable result considering the difficulties facing the country. Dividends were resumed after eleven years and long-suffering shareholders received a special interim dividend of 7p and a final of 3p per £1 unit of ordinary stock – a just reward for their patience and faith in the company.

Although world economic conditions improved only marginally during 1983 the company did better. Turnover increased from £10.9m. to nearly £15m. and net profit jumped from £780,000 to £3.3m. Further investments in strategic companies were made signalling the start of a programme to diversify the company's interests away from the railway. In January 1984 a 30 per cent stake was acquired in Madeco, the largest copper wire and tube manufacturer in the country. At the same time the interest in George A. Fuller was sold profitably and a 40 per cent interest was purchased in the Carolina de Michilla copper mine in Northern Chile.

The results for 1984 were better than for 1983 and Chile recorded the best economic growth of any Latin American country. Turnover increased from £14.8m. to £16m. and net profit was £4m. against £3.3m. Cash balances had now built up to over £9m. which demonstrated the company's increasing strength.

It now appeared that the company was well under way and this was confirmed by the 1985 results with a net profit of £7m. against £4m. Funds had by this stage grown sufficiently to enable capital expenditure to be increased. A comprehensive rail-welding programme was started after engineering studies had demonstrated that this would defer the necessity for large scale purchase of new rail. In addition the railway was able to purchase a hundred 43-ton hopper wagons with a view to adapting them for the transport of copper cathodes, an increasingly important type of freight for the railway. It was also decided to re-value certain assets such as track and freehold land in Antofagasta, most of which had been acquired in the 1890s. Dividends for 1985 had risen to 27.5p against 20p in 1984 and on this high note Mr Gonzalo Menéndez D., who had been general manager since 1980, relinquished his position and was appointed to the board of Antofagasta Holdings. Mr Menéndez's five-year stint in the North as one of the chief architects of the railway's recovery and success had been fully recognized.

In January 1986 control was acquired from Atlantic Richfield Company of Anaconda South America, which included among its assets one of the world's largest porphyry copper deposits, known as Los Pelambres. This underlined the direction the group was taking towards natural resources. The splendid timing of these mining property purchases by the group was only to be fully appreciated over the next two to three years. Further important investments were made in the mining and forestry sectors and although copper prices had declined by about 5 per cent to an average of 62 US cents per pound, the group still proceeded with the acquisition of a further 16 per cent stake in Carolina de Michilla, giving it control. A gold mining property at Punitaqui situated some 300 kilometres north of Santiago was also added to the group's mining interests, and a rights issue raising a total of £5,025,000 was successfully concluded.

As a first step into the forestry sector (fast becoming one of Chile's major exporters) the group took an option in December 1986 to invest in Forestal Colcura S.A. following a rights issue which Colcura planned for April 1987. Colcura's forests consisted of 15,000 hectares of mainly eucalyptus hardwood, a fast-growing species in high demand. The investment was to be financed totally in Chilean pesos.

The financial results for 1986 were again most satisfactory and were helped by improvement in the Chilean economy. The net profit, which included a bigger contribution from Madeco, was £8.25m. against £7m. and shareholders benefited by increased dividends.

The year 1987 was dominated by a resurgence in the copper price to an average of 81 US cents. This obviously benefited both the Chilean economy and the interests of the group as a whole although the increase came as something of a surprise to the industry. The copper price and good performances from the investments, particularly Michilla, resulted in net profits after taxation increasing from £8.2m. to £11.8m. Transradio Chilena S.A. (V.T.R.), 25 per cent of which had been acquired in 1985, itself acquired the Chilean interests of ITT Central American Cables and Radio Inc., thus increasing its market share. Total dividends increased by 17 per cent and prospects for 1988 appeared to be very favourable and turned out even better than expected.

The centenary year of 1988 also proved to be the group's *annus mirabilis*. The average copper price rose from 81 US cents to $1.18 per pound fully justifying the copper interests purchased in earlier years. In addition, the Chilean rate of inflation dropped from 21.5 per cent to 11 per cent. These factors helped to produce a group profit after tax of £20m. as compared with £11.8m. The group's 52 per cent interest in Forestal Colcura, acquired in April 1987, was sold to Shell Chile in April 1988 and resulted in an extraordinary profit of £12.9m. which boosted net profits for the year to £28.9m. Profits from the Michilla mine benefiting from higher copper prices were £11.4m. compared to £3.2m. Shareholders received a total dividend of 13p, an increase of 30 per cent over 1987 and saw that the market value of the group's investment in Madeco, purchased in 1983 for £1.6m., had increased to £15.8m. by the year end, while at the same date bank balances in sterling and dollars had reached £19m.

* * *

As the railway moves into its second century it continues to be a major factor in the economic life of the regions it traverses and remains a striking example of man's conquest of nature. Its fortunes still turn on the vagaries which have surrounded it from the beginning – policies of governments, fluctuations of supply and demand in the commodities it carries, problems of climatic conditions, the challenge of competition and the continued public acceptance of its purpose and performance.

The railway is now only a part of the assets of the group but, as in the first hundred years, adaptability will be vital for future success. The group's continuing ability to overcome the difficulties which have surrounded it from earliest days, will depend both upon Mr Andrónico Luksic's unique vision and extraordinary ability to translate vision into reality, and the dedication of everybody connected with the company.

APPENDIX I

The material for Appendix I was supplied by Mel Turner and Ray Ellis, and was edited by Mike Swift.

LOCOMOTIVE LISTS

The following conventional abbreviations are used to indicate locomotive builders:

AE	Avonside Engine Co. Ltd., Bristol, England
Alco C	American Locomotive Co., Cooke Works, Schenectady, N.Y., U.S.A.
Alco R	American Locomotive Co., Rogers Works, Paterson, NJ, U.S.A.
BLW	Baldwin Locomotive Works, Philadelphia, Pa., USA
BP	Beyer Peacock & Co. Ltd., Manchester, England
Cail	S.A. des anciens Establissements Cail, Paris, France
Dav	Davenport Locomotive Works, Davenport, Ia., USA
FCAB	FCAB, Mejillones Works, Chile
GM-EMD	General Motors Corporation, Electro-Motive Division, La Grange, Ill., USA
HC	Hudswell Clarke & Co. Ltd., Leeds, England
HE	Hunslet Engine Co. Ltd., Leeds, England
Hen	Henschel & Sohn, Cassel, Germany
HL	R. & W. Hawthorn, Leslie & Co. Ltd., Newcastle-upon-Tyne, England
K	Kitson & Co. Ltd., Leeds, England
Lima	Lima Locomotive Works Inc., Lima, Oh., U.S.A.
NBL	North British Locomotive Co. Ltd., Glasgow, Scotland
OK	Orenstein & Koppel A.G., Berlin-Drewitz, Germany
Rogers	Rogers Locomotive Co., Peterson, N.J., U.S.A.
RS	Robert Stephenson & Co., Newcastle-upon-Tyne, England
SS	Sharp Stewart & Co. Ltd., Manchester, England
VF	Vulcan Foundry Ltd., Newton-le-Willows, England
YE	Yorkshire Engine Co. Ltd., Sheffield, England

ANTOFAGASTA (CHILI) AND BOLIVIA RAILWAY CO. LTD.

1. Old Numbering Series for 2ft 6in gauge locos from 1876 to 1908

This period covers the two constituent companies:
Compñía de Salitres y Ferrocarriles de Antofagasta (1876 to 1887) and the
Compañía Huanchaca de Bolivia (1887 to 1903) until the general renumbering programme in 1908.

The majority of early locomotives were named, but at times these were changed. There is also some doubt about the authenticity of certain names and when they were carried. To keep the lists within a reasonable length the names have, therefore, been omitted.

1.1 Compañía de Salitres y Ferrocarril de Antofagasta

Original Numbers	*1908 Numbers*	*Type*	*Builder*	*Works Numbers*	*Year Built*	*Remarks*
1 – 12	–	4-6-0	RS	2291 – 2302	1876	
13 – 14	–	0-6-2T	AE	1182 – 1183	1877	
15	1	0-6-2T	AE	1195	1877	
16	–	0-6-2T	AE	1196	1877	
17	2	2-6-2T	SS	3032	1882	Rebuilt as 0-6-2T prior to 1912
18 – 19	–	4-2-4-2T	RS	2449 – 2450	1884	Webb compounds rebuilt to 4-6-0s at an unknown date.

1.2 Companía de Huanchaca de Bolivia

Railway officially known as Empresa del Ferrocarril a Antofagasta de Bolivia after purchase by the above company in 1887

20	33	2-4-2	BLW	8215	1886	This loco was converted to metre gauge at a date unknown, renumbered 351, and noted as such on the FC Bolivia by B. Fawcett in 1939
21	42	2-4-2	Rogers	3713	1887	
22	See note	0-4-4T	Rogers	3709	1887	Inspection coupé disposed of prior to 1912. Shown in Diagram Book *c*.1908 numbered 31 and in a photo taken 10/1903 numbered 33. Rebuilt to a conventional tank engine prior to 1912.
23 – 25	–	4-6-0	RS	2622 – 2624	1887	
26 – 29	–	4-6-0	RS	2633 – 2636	1888	

Railway sold to the Antofagasta (Chili) and Bolivia Railway Co. Ltd. on 28/11/1888, after which the Huanchaca Company leased the line for a period of 15 years, terminating on 31/12/1903. During this time the Huanchaca Co. used several different business names when purchasing locomotives.

Original Numbers	*1908 Numbers*	*Type*	*Builder*	*Works Numbers*	*Year Built*	*Remarks*
30	71	2-6-0TT	BLW	9846	1889	Reported Scr. in 1916 report.
31	72	2-6-0TT	BLW	9852	1889	
32	82	2-6-0TT	BLW	9855	1889	
33	83	2-6-0TT	BLW	9864	1889	
34	84	2-6-0TT	BLW	9859	1889	Converted to metre gauge in 1917. Out of service by 1925.
35	95	2-8-0TT	BLW	9773	1889	Scr. in 1916 report.
36	3	0-6-2ST	BLW	9770	1889	
37	81	2-6-0TT	BLW	10469	1889	
38 – 39	77/76	2-6-0TT	BLW	10470 – 10471	1889	
40	–	2-4-2	BLW	10942	1890	
41 – 42	34-35	2-4-2	BLW	10943 – 10944	1890	
43	73	2-6-0TT	BLW	10984	1890	
44	74	2-6-0TT	BLW	10988	1890	
45	75	2-6-0TT	BLW	10997	1890	Scr. in 1917 report.
46	–	0-6-2ST	BLW	10998	1890	‘Sold’ to Huanchaca Co. *c*.1892 for use on the FC Uyuni-Pulacayo and possibly initially used on construction of the line.

46(2nd)	see No. 51 below and notes					
47	4	0-6-2ST	BLW	10995	1890	
48	78	2-6-0TT	BLW	11426	1890	
49	79	2-6-0TT	BLW	11436	1890	
50	80	4-6-0TT	BLW	11437	1890	Listed in BLW data as 2-6-0TT but p.81 of *The Locomotives that Baldwin Built* by Fred Westing (1966) illustrates an unlettered 4-6-OST&T for the FCAB and company diagram book records it as a 4-6-0TT.
51	7	0-6-2ST	BLW	12752	1890	Renumbered 2nd. 46 – see notes below.
52	8	0-6-2ST	BLW	12753	1892	Renumbered 2nd. 51 – see notes below.
53	9	0-6-2ST	BLW	12754	1892	Renumbered 2nd. 52 – see notes below.
53(2nd)	96	2-8-0	BLW	12635	1892	
54	97	2-8-0	BLW	12633	1892	
55	98	2-8-0	BLW	12667	1892	

There is some confusion with the running numbers in this section as BLW numerical registers record 52-62 with higher running numbers than shown. About 1892, when 46 went to the Huanchaca Co., a new Baldwin No. 51 was renumbered 46 to fill this gap and the other engines delivered at this time were renumbered accordingly. It appears that Baldwin were not notified of this change, and as a result allocated higher running numbers to the later locos. It is unclear from available information whether these were given their correct numbers on arrival in Chile though this seems possible. To confuse the issue, it had long been assumed that the running numbers were sequential with the Baldwin construction numbers, i.e. 46 = 10995 and 47 = 10998. However, this does not appear to have been the case. The information on the renumbering of 51 to 46 is confirmed by the company's diagram book from the period 1908 – 1930. They had a curious habit in the pre-1912 period of using running numbers in lieu of builders' numbers, so the solution had to be found using names and dates. An early Livesey & Henderson list (the company's consulting engineers) confirms 47 as 10995, and a 1955 visit by a party of enthusiasts to Huanchaca confirmed that a loco numbered 46 was still in service. Two separate Baldwin lists give conflicting information, but both confirm that the unit transferred carried the same name but quote different builder's numbers.

Original Numbers	*1908 Numbers*	*Type*	*Builder*	*Works Numbers*	*Year Built*	*Remarks*
56 – 57	10 – 11	0-6-2ST	BLW	14220 – 14221	1895	
58 – 60	92 – 94	2-8-0	BLW	14461 – 14463	1895	58 unserviceable in 1937 report.
61 – 62	43 – 44	4-4-0	BLW	14464 – 14465	1895	Both scr. in 1915 report.
63	91	4-8-0	Cail	2466	1898	Shown in some lists as 4-6-2: company diagram shows 4-8-0 is correct.
64 – 65	99 – 100	2-8-0	BLW	17461 – 17462	1900	65 scr. in 1917 report.
66	–	2-8-0	Rogers	5544	1900	Retained by the Huanchaca Co. in 1903.
67 – 70	101 – 104	2-8-0	BLW	18388 – 18391	1900	101 scr. in 1917 report.
71 – 74	105 – 108	2-8-0	BLW	19437 – 19440	1901	108 last loco ordered by the Huanchaca Co.

1.3 Ferrocarril Uyuni – Pulacayo

After termination of its lease in 1903, the Huanchaca Mining Co. continued to operate its line from Uyuni to Pulacayo and Huanchaca. The line remained 2ft 6in gauge and continued to operate well into the 1970s under the above name. With two exceptions previously mentioned and shown below, the number of locos retained by the Huanchaca Co. to work this line has not so far been found. The rest of the locos shown below were direct purchases by the company and were not numbered in the main line register.

1(?)	2-6-0	BLW	12363	1892	Ordered for the Pacamayo & Huanchaca Railway.
2 – 3	0-4-0ST	BLW	12404 – 12405	1892	
?	0-6-0ST	BLW	13997	1894	
4	0-4-0ST	BLW	14301	1895	Baldwin records list: 'Huanchaca Co. – Corp. Minera de Bolivia No. 4' Observed in 1955 with plate: No. 1 PLAYA BLANCA
5	2-6-0	HL	2947	1912	Observed in 1955 – rebuilt from FCAB 165. This would have required a drastic boiler shortening, more likely a new, shorter boiler was supplied.

Original Numbers	*1908 Numbers*	*Type*	*Builder*	*Works Numbers*	*Year Built*	*Remarks*
12		4-6-0	HE	?	?	Observed in 1955 – this is one of the well-known ex-WDLR Hunslet 4-6-0Ts rebuilt into a tender engine.
46		0-6-2ST	BLW	10998	1890	Main line loco retained by the Huanchaca Co. Named UNION. Observed in 1955 with same number confirming no renumbering took place.
66		2-8-0	Rogers	5544	1900	Main line loco retained by the Huanchaca Co.

The identity of No.12 is not confirmed. A total of five former WDLR 4-6-0Ts went to Chile, all to the order of Beverly Pearce & Partners. None had seen active service in the war, having been built by Hunslet in 1919 and regauged from 60cm to 2ft 6in prior to despatch to Chile. HE numbers 1367 (WDLR 3251) and 1374 (3258) were despatched in March 1920 to Antofagasta; 1357 (3241) in April 1920 to Antofagasta, and 1359 (3243) and 1368 (3252) to Iquique, also in April 1920. It is possible that all of the Antofagasta locos may have ended up here.

The authors of Appendix I are aware that this list of locos which operated here may be incomplete and would welcome further information.

1.4 Ferrcarril de Antofagasta a Bolivia

75 – 78	109 – 112	2-8-2	HE	888 – 891	1906	75/78 sold to Boquete Nitrate Co. prior to 1912. 76-77 unserviceable in 1917 report.
1 – 3	12 – 14	0-6-4T	HE	878 – 880	1905	
4 – 12	15 – 20	0-6-4T	HE	907 – 912	1906	5/7/8/11 to Aguas Blancas Railway as 506-509 after 1908.
79	113	2-8-0	BLW	27995	1906	
80 – 81	114-115	2-8-0	BLW	28029 – 28030	1906	
82 – 83	116-117	2-8-0	BLW	28276 – 28277	1906	
84	118	2-8-0	BLW	28282	1906	
55 – 56	5 – 6	0-6-2T	HC	782 – 783	1906	
119-128	119 – 128	2-8-2	HL	2674 – 2683	1907	
129 – 138	129 – 138	2-8-2	HE	922 – 931	1907	
139 – 140	139 – 140	2-8-2	HC	787 – 788	1907	
45 – 50	45 – 50	2-8-0	Alco C	44617 – 44622	1908	
139 – 140	139 – 140	2-8-2	HC	787 – 788	1907	
63 – 70	63 – 70	2-8-0	Alco C	44623 – 44630	1908	69 scr. in 1916 report.
85 – 90	85 – 90	2-8-0	Alco C	44631 – 44636	1908	
36	36	2-6 + 6-4T	K	4534	1908	Meyer type.
21 – 26	21 – 26	0-6-4T	HE	945 – 950	1907	
141 – 150	141 – 150	2-8-0	HE	958 – 967	1908	

1.5 Ferrocarril Caleta Coloso a Aguas Blancas

Formed in 1898 and opened in 1902 to service the nitrate pampa south of the FCAB main line. Taken over by the *Compania Ferrocarril de Aguas Blancas,* which was wholly owned by the FCAB in 1909, and thereafter was operated as a branch of the FCAB, connection having been made with the FCAB soon after 1909. Engines allocated to the line were renumbered in the 500 series, probably when they were taken into FCAB stock on 24/3/1909.

Original Numbers	*1908 Numbers*	*Type*	*Builder*	*Works Numbers*	*Year Built*	*Remarks*
1	513	0-6-2ST	FCAB	–	1902	
2 – 3	514 – 515	2-8-0	Rogers	5701 – 5702	1902	
4	524	2-8-0	BLW	24444	1904	
5	503	0-6-0T	Hen	6489	1903	
6	504	0-6-0T	Hen	7491	1906	
7	–	0-6-0T	Hen	6490	1903	Sold in 1911
8 – 9	511 – 512	0-6-2ST	Rogers	6270 – 6271	1905	
10	516	2-8-0	Alco R	38445	1905	
11	519	2-8-0	Hen	7551	1906	
12	520	2-8-0	Hen	7753	1906	
13 – 14	517 – 518	2-8-0	Alco R	41115 – 4116	1906	
15	521	2-8-0	Hen	7754	1906	
16	–	0-6-2T	Hen	7550	1906	
17	–	0-6-0T	Hen	7549	1906	
18 – 19	–	0-6-2T	Hen	7958 – 7959	1907	
20	–	0-6-0T	Hen	7960	1907	Sold in 1911
21	–	0-4-0T	Hen	7995	1907	

22	–	0-4-4-0TG	Lima	1677	1906	Shay – see note below.
23 – 24	522 – 523	2-8-0	Hen	8355 – 8356	1908	
25 – 26	–	0-6-2T	Hen	7930 – 7931	1908	
27	–	0-4-2T	?		1907	Not positively identified; supplied through the agency of A. Krupp.

Not positively identified, only shown in lists as Shay, number, name and built 1907. This loco is probably 2ft 6in gauge No. 4 built for American Smelters Securities Co., Santa Barbara, Chil, desp. 12/4/1906 and is the only Shay in Koch's list around this date. Possibly bought or taken over in 1907.

2. Antofagasta (Chili) and Bolivia Railway Co. Ltd. Post 1908 numbers for 2 ft 6 in gauge locos.

This list also includes the 500 series locos allocated to the Aguas Blancas Railway. Locos built after 1908 did not carry names, though it is likely some earlier locos continued to carry their names after 1908. M = indicates that the loco was converted to metre gauge in 1926–1928, or earlier if a date is quoted.

1		0-6-2T	AE	1195	1877	
2		0-6-2T	SS	3032	1882	Rebuilt from 2-6-2T prior to 1912.
3		0-6-2ST	BLW	9770	1889	Disposed of prior to 1912.
4		0-6-2ST	BLW	10995	1890	Disposed of prior to 1912.
5 – 6	M	0-6-2T	HC	782 – 783	1906	
7		0-6-2ST	BLW	12752	1892	
8 – 9		0-6-2ST	BLW	12753 – 12754	1892	Disposed of prior to 1912.
10 – 11		0-6-2ST	BLW	14220 – 14221	1895	
12 – 14	M	0-6-4T	HE	878 – 880	1905	12 converted to 0-6-0T – see footnote.
15	M	0-6-4T	HE	907	1906	see footnote.

16 – 19		0-6-4T	HE	908 – 911	1906	Sold to Aguas Blancas Railway after 1908 as Nos. 506 – 509.
20	M	0-6-4T	HE	912	1906	see footnote.
21 – 26	M	0-6-4T	HE	945 – 950	1907	see footnote.
27 – 32	M	2-8-4T	K	4843 – 4848	1912	
33		2-4-2	BLW	8215	1886	
34 – 35		2-4-2	BLW	10943 – 1944	1890	Disposed of prior to 1912.
36		2-6 + 6-4TT	K	4534	1908	Meyer type. Renumbered 38 in 1914 to make way for metre gauge 4-6-2s. Scr. in 1929.
37		2-6 + 6-2T	K	4841	1912	Meyer type. Out of service by 1928.
42		2-4-2	Rogers	3713	1887	Disposed of prior to 1912
43 – 44		4-4-0	BLW	14464 – 14465	1895	Scr. in 1916 report.
45 – 50	2-8-0	Alco C	44617 – 44622	1908		
51 – 62		4-6-0	RS	?	?	Remaining units from 1876 and 1887 – 1888 batches, individual numbers unknown. Disposed of prior to 1912.
63 – 70		2-8-0	Alco C	44623 – 44630	1908	
71 – 72		2-6-0TT	BLW	9846/9852	1889	71 scr. in 1916 report
73 – 74		2-6-0TT	BLW	10984/10988	1890	

75		2-6-0TT	BLW	10997	1890	
76 – 77		2-6-0TT	BLW	10471/10470	1889	
78 – 79		2-6-0TT	BLW	11426/11436	1890	
80		4-6-0TT	BLW	11437	1890	
81		2-6-0TT	BLW	10469	1889	
82 – 83		2-6-0TT	BLW	9855/9864	1889	
84	M	2-6-0TT	BLW	9859	1889	Converted to metre gauge 1917. Out of service by 1925.
85 – 90		2-8-0	Alco C	44631 – 44636	1908	
91		4-8-0	Cail	2466	1898	
92 – 94		2-8-0	BLW	14461 – 14463	1895	
95		2-8-0TT	BLW	9773	1889	Scr. in 1916 report.
96		2-8-0	BLW	12635	1892	Scr. in 1917 report.
97 – 98		2-8-0	BLW	12633/12667	1892	
99 – 100		2-8-0	BLW	17461 – 17462	1900	100 scr. in 1917 report.
101 – 104		2-8-0	BLW	18388 – 18391	1900	
105 – 108		2-8-0	BLW	19437 – 19440	1901	
109 – 112		2-8-2	HE	888 – 891	1906	109/112 sold to Boquete Nitrate Co. prior to 1912. 110 – 111 unserviceable in 1917 report.
113		2-8-0	BLW	27995	1906	
114 – 115		2-8-0	BLW	28029 – 28030	1906	
116 – 117		2-8-0	BLW	28276 – 28277	1906	
118		2-8-0	BLW	28282	1906	

Original Numbers	*1908 Numbers*	*Type*	*Builder*	*Works Numbers*	*Year Built*	*Remarks*
119 – 128		2-8-2	HL	2674 – 2683	1907	Rebuilt to 2-8-0s in 1918 – 1922. Five locos rebuilt and renumbered 525 – 9 after 1928. Remainder withdrawn by 1928.
129 – 138		2-8-2	HE	922 – 931	1901	All converted to 2-8-0s in 1918-1922. One loco rebuilt and renumbered 530 after 1928. Remainder withdrawn by 1928.
139 – 140	M	2-8-2	HC	787 – 788	1907	Rebuilt as 2-8-0s in 1918-1922.
141 – 150	M	2-8-0	HE	958 – 966	1908	149 scr. after accident 4/11/1913.
151 – 152	M	2-8-0	HE	1066 – 1067	1911	
153 – 160	M	2-8-0	NBL	19428 – 19435	1911	
161 – 170	M	2-8-2	HL	2943 – 2952	1912	168 converted to 2-8-2T in 1922 and renumbered 1.
171 – 180	M	2-8-2	Hen	11891 – 11900	1913	
501		0-4-0T	Hen	7995	1907	
502	renumbered from 504 below					
503		0-6-0T	Hen	6489	1903	
504		0-6-0T	Hen	7491	1906	renumbered 502.
505	see note below					
506 – 509		0-6-4T	HE	908 – 911	1907	Ex 16 – 19.

510	see note below					
511 – 512		0-6-2ST	Rogers	6270 – 6271	1905	
513		0-6-2ST	FCAB	–	1902	
514 – 515		2-8-0	Rogers	5701 – 5702	1902	
516		2-8-0	Alco R	38445	1905	
517 – 518		2-8-0	Alco R	41115 – 41116	1906	
519		2-8-0	Hen	7551	1906	
520 – 521		2-8-0	Hen	7753 – 7754	1906	
522 – 523		2-8-0	Hen	8355 – 8356	1908	
524		2-8-0	BLW	24444	1904	
525 – 529		2-8-0	HL	(2674 – 2683)	1907	Ex 119 – 128 series.
530		2-8-0	HE	(922 – 931)	1901	Ex 129 – 138 series.

At an unknown date there was a major renumbering of 500 series locos to consolidate this group of numbers after some locos had been scrapped. Complete details are known only for 504 to 502, and 525 – 529 to 519 – 523. It is likely that the main line Hawthorn Leslie and Hunslet locos were stored in 1928 and later cannibalized to keep the Aguas Blancas 2-8-0s going. By this time both the Rogers 2-8-0s and Henschel 2-8-0s had been withdrawn.

Hunslet 0-6-4Ts: after 1908, but prior to the 1920s, a number of these were converted to 0-6-2Ts and 0-6-0Ts. There is an official photograph taken at the FCAB Shops showing 12 extensively rebuilt as an 0-6-0T, and later loco lists record at least six 0-6-2Ts, but details of which were converted (other than these mentioned), to what wheel arrangement, and at what date have not yet been established from available records.

ANTOFAGASTA (CHILI) AND BOLIVIA RAILWAY CO. LTD

3. Old Numbering Series for metre gauge locos from 1906 to 1928

This list covers all the metre gauge locos built prior to 1928 as well as some 2ft 6in gauge locos converted to metre gauge prior to 1928, when there was a general renumbering.

3.1 Bolivia Railway Co.

In 1909 the FCAB took over the lease of this railway from Speyer & Co., New York. The Bolivian section locos were lettered FCB but numbered in the main FCAB list. These locos are listed as built for the Bolivian National Railways and were initially numbered accordingly.

Original Numbers	*1928 Numbers*	*Type*	*Builder*	*Works Numbers*	*Year Built*	*Remarks*
1 – 4	401 – 404	2-8-0	Alco R	41130 – 41133	1906	
5 – 8	405 – 408	2-8-0	Alco R	44424 – 44427	1909	

3.2 FCAB Locos built up to the 1928 Renumbering

601 – 602	409 – 410	2-8-2	K	4860 – 4861	1912	
101 – 102	411 – 412	2-8-4T	HE	1102 – 1103	1912	Supplied lettered FCB.
51 – 56	451 – 456	0-6-2 + 0-6-2TT	BP	5617 – 5622	1913	Meyer type, designed to operate cab-leading. Supplied lettered FCB.
33 – 36	333 – 336	4-6-2	Hen	12478 – 12751	1914	
57 – 60	357 – 360	2-8-0	Hen	12544 – 12547	1914	
61 – 65	361 – 365	2-8-0	Hen	18305 – 18309	1922	
33 – 52	33 – 52	2-8-4T	NBL	29562 – 29576	1927	
84	–	2-6-0	BLW	9859	1889	Converted from 2ft 6in gauge in 1917. Out of service by 1925.
181 – 182	366 – 367	2-8-0	Hen	18310 – 18311	1922	Renumbered 66 – 67

3.3 Chilian Northern Railway Co. Ltd

In 1919 the FCAB took over the operation of the CNRCo. They inherited a batch of locos which had previously been the property of the Chilean Longitudinal Railway, some of which were probably used during construction. New locos were ordered for the line by the FCAB and, although numbered in the FCAB 9XX series, were lettered FCNC.

Original Numbers	*Second Numbers*	*Type*	*Builder*	*Works Numbers*	*Year Built*	
1 – 2	901 – 902	0-6-4T	HE	1062 – 1063	1911	These locos were named. Series renumbered 901 – 904
3 – 4	903 – 904	0-6-4T	HE	1065/1078	1911	but whether in original number order is not certain. Some were later fitted with tenders to become 0-6-4TT. 3 – 4 later became Ferrocarril del Estado (Chilian State Railways) Nos. 3060 – 3061.

5 – 8	1005 – 1008	2-6-0	Hen	10702 – 10705	1911	
9 – 20	1009 – 1020	2-6-0	Hen	10969 – 10980	1911	
21 – 32	1021 – 1032	2-6-0	OK	5201 – 5212	1912	
33 – 38	1033 – 1038	0-6-0T	OK	5461 – 5466	1912	
		2-6-0	Hen	10706 – 10710	1911	Built for the Chilian Longitudinal Railway as part of
		2-6-0	Hen	11080 – 11084	1912	the Henschel batch shown above but not taken into FCAB stock.
910 – 911		2-8-2	NBL	23298 – 23299	1925	Ordered by the FCAB, numbered in the FCAB series,
912	914	2-8-2	BP	6414 – 6416	1928	but lettered FCNC.
915 – 916	2-8-2	YE	2554 – 2555	1955		

4. FCAB Locos from 1928

This list includes all metre gauge locos from 1928. Included are those renumbered and converted from 2ft 6in gauge, indicated*. The Bolivian section of the FCAB was nationalized in 1962 to become the Empresa Nacional de Ferrocarriles Bolivia (ENFFCC, now ENFE) and a number of locos were renumbered into the ENFFCC/ENFE list as shown.

Original Numbers	*ENFFCC/ ENFE Numbers*	*Type*	*Builder*	*Works Numbers*	*Year Built*	*Remarks*
*1		2-8-2T	HL	2950	1912	Converted from 2-8-2 in 1922.
*5		0-6-2T	HC	782	1906	Sold to Soc. Fabrica de Cemento, El Melan, 3/1938.
*6		0-6-2T	HC	783	1906	Last rebuilt in 1954.
*12 – 14		0-6-4T	HE	878 – 880	1905	See footnote to list 2. 12 rebuilt as 0-6-0T.
*15		0-6-4T	HE	907	1906	see footnote to list 2.
*20		0-6-4T	HE	912	1906	see footnote to list 2.
*21 – 26		0-6-2T	HE	945 – 950	1907	Converted from 0-6-4T. 21 & 25 sold to contractor in Arica **c**.1962 and still in existence.
*27 – 28	553 – 554	2-8-4T	K	4843 – 4844	1912	
*29 – 30		2-8-4T	K	4845 – 4846	1912	Sold to Taltal Railway.
*31 – 32		2-8-4T	K	4847 – 4848	1912	
33 – 52		2-8-4T	NBL	29562 – 29576	1927	

*139 – 140		2-8-0	HC	787 – 788	1907	139 scr. in 1960, 140 stored in 1960.
*141 – 148		2-8-0	HE	958 – 965	1908	
*150		2-8-0	HE	966	1908	
*151 – 152		2-8-0	HE	1066 – 1067	1911	
*153 – 160		2-8-0	NBL	19428 – 19435	1911	157 sold to Taltal Railway.
*161 – 167		2-8-2	HL	2943 – 2949	1912	
*169 – 170		2-8-2	HL	2951 – 2952	1912	
*171 – 180		2-8-2	Hen	11891 – 11900	1913	
181 – 183		4-8-2T	HL	3743 – 3745	1929	
201 – 206	821 – 822 (202/206)	4-8-2	VF	6170-6175	1954	
333	756	4-6-2	Hen	12748	1914	Orig. numbered 33.
334 – 336	751 – 753	4-6-2	Hen	12749 – 12751	1914	Orig. numbered 34-36.
337 – 338	754 – 755	4-6-2	Hen	21213 – 21214	1928	Orig. numbered 37-38.

Original Numbers	*1908 Numbers*	*Type*	*Builder*	*Works Numbers*	*Year Built*	*Remarks*
341 – 346	811 – 816	4-8-2	VF	6176 – 6181	1954	
347 – 348	817 – 818	4-8-2	VF	6166 – 6167	1954	
349 – 350	819 – 820	4-8-2	VF	6169/6168	1954	
*351		2-4-2	BLW	8251	1886	Orig. numbered 33.
357 – 360	614 – 617	2-8-0	Hen	12544 – 12547	1914	Orig. numbered 57 – 60.
361 – 367		2-8-0	Hen	18305 – 18311	1921	Orig. numbered 61 – 65 and 181 – 182.
390	909	4-8-2 + 2-8-4T	BP	6524	1928	Beyer Garratt. Orig. numbered G1.
391 – 392	901 – 902	4-8-2 + 2-8-4T	BP	6525 – 6526	1928	Beyer Garratts. Orig. numbered G2 – G3.
393 – 398	903 – 908	4-8-2 + 2-8-4T	BP	7420 – 7425	1950	Beyer Garratts.
401 – 404	606 – 609	2-8-0	Alco R	41130 – 41133	1906	

405 – 408	610 – 613	2-8-0	Alco R	44424 – 44427	1909	
409 – 410		2-8-2	K	4860 – 4861	1912	
411 – 412	551 – 552	2-8-4T	HE	1102 – 1103	1912	
451 – 456		0-6-2 + -6-2TT	BP	5617 – 5622	1913	Meyer type.

During the Second World War two Argentinian metre gauge railways loaned Beyer Garratts to the FCAB: Buenos Aires Midland Railway: 1 loco from 101 – 102 4-6-2 + 2-6-4T BP 6570 – 6571 1929 work on the Uyuni-Oruro section.
Cordoba Central Railway: 3 locos from 1511 – 1520 4-8-2 + 2-8-4T Beyer Peacock BP 6550 – 6559 1929. These were almost identical to the FCAB Garratts, but were coal fired whereas the FCAB locos were oil fired.

The following are shown in the Henschell works list as supplied to the FCAB. Whether they were actually for the FCAB, one of its subsidiaries, or a mining company, is not known:

0-6-2T	Hen	21014	1928
0-6-2T	Hen	21280	1929

5. FCAB Diesel Locos

Running Numbers	*Type*	*HP*	*Model*	*Builder*	*Works Numbers*	*Year Built*	*In Service*	*Remarks*
600	B-B	380HP	44 ton	Dav	3046	1948	1958	Ex American Railroad of Puerto Rico, 601.
601 – 603	B-B	380HP	44 ton	Dav	3050 – 3052	1948	1965	Ex American Railroad of Puerto Rico, 605 – 607. 603 rebuilt 1980 with 500-460 h.p. engine.
950 – 952	B-B	890HP	GA8	GM-EMD	28546 – 28548	1964	1965	
953	B-B	1000HP	GA18	GM-EMD	34117	1969	1969	
954	A1A-A1A	1000HP	G18U	GM-EMD	758010 – 1	1976	1977	
1400 – 1405	C-C	1310HP	GR12U	GM-EMD	26607 – 26612	1961	1961	

1406 – 1409	C-C	1310HP	GR12UD	GM-EMD	28549 – 28552	1964	1964	
1410	C-C	1500HP	G22CU	GM-EMD	34118	1969	1969	
1411	C-C	1500HP	G22CU	GM-EMD	37423	1971	–	Sold to CODELCO (Chilian State Copper Mines) as their number 94 without having worked on FCAB.
1411 (2nd)	C-C	1310HP	GR12U	GM-EMD	26905	1961	1962	Ex FCE (Chilian State Railways) Dt13.014, previously numbered Dt 12.014.
1412	C-C	1310HP	GR12U	GM-EMD	26908	1961	1962	Ex FCE (Chilian State Railways) Dt 13.017, previously numbered Dt. 12.017.

APPENDIX 2

Copy of Agreement with George William Craig

An Agreement made the nineteenth day of June, one thousand nine hundred and twenty-five BETWEEN THE ANTOFAGASTA (CHILI) AND BOLIVIA RAILWAY COMPANY LIMITED, having its Registered Offices at No. 1, Broad Street Place, in the City of London (hereinafter called "the Company"), of the one part, and George William Craig of 13, Over Street, Brighton, Sussex of the other part.

The said George William Craig shall be and he is hereby engaged in the service of the said Company, on the following conditions, viz.:—

1. He shall proceed to Antofagasta at such time and in such manner as shall be required by the Directors of the said Company, and shall reside at Antofagasta or other points on the Company's line as may be determined by the Company's representative in

2. He shall faithfully and diligently employ himself in the service of the Company for the term of three years from the date of his arrival in Antofagasta as an Assistant Engineer Draughtsman at that place or elsewhere on the Company's line in Chili or Bolivia as he may be directed. He shall devote his whole time and attention to the service of the Company and he shall submit to such rules, regulations and arrangements as are in force in the Company's service or which may from time to time be made or imposed by the said Directors or their representative in Antofagasta, and he shall use his best exertions to promote the Company's interest in every way in his power.

3. He shall not directly or indirectly be engaged in any other service or business.

4. He shall pay due and becoming respect to the Civil and Religious Institutions and customs of the place he may be residing in,

abstaining from all interference therewith, nor in any way interfere or take part in the political affairs of the Country.

5. In view of the circumstances of his employment he undertakes that without the previous consent of the Directors or their representative in Antofagasta he will not marry within a period of three years from the date of his arrival in Antofagasta. Failure to comply with this undertaking shall be good ground for the Company to terminate this Agreement under Clause 8(A) hereof.

6. The Company shall pay to the said George William Craig a salary at the rate of Three hundred pounds sterling per annum payable in equal monthly payments, the said salary to commence from the date of his arrival in Antofagasta. The Company will also pay him his reasonable expenses when travelling on the Company's business.

7. The Company shall provide him with a second-class passage to Antofagasta, and the sum of Twenty-two pounds, ten shillings sterling as an allowance and to cover expenses on the voyage, and on the expiration of this Agreement, unless the same is determined under Sub-section (B) of Clause 8 hereof, with a second-class passage back to England, and the sum of Ten pounds sterling for his expenses during the voyage, provided that he returns to England within a period of three months after such determination.

8. The Company may determine this Agreement at any time during the said term of three years (A) on giving to the said George William Craig three months' previous notice in writing, or on paying to him three months' salary in lieu of notice; (B) if the said George William Craig shall misconduct or misbehave himself, or shall wilfully, and after warning, disobey the orders, regulations or instructions of the General manager or his representative, then the Board of Directors or their representative may determine this Agreement without notice, and in such event the said George William Craig shall have no claim against the Company in any respect.

9. If the Medical Adviser for the time being of the Company shall at any time certify in writing that the said George William Craig is incapable of performing his duty from illness or accident, and not likely to recover, then the representative of the Directors in Antofagasta may dissolve this Agreement, and, provided such illness or accident was not caused by any misconduct on his part, the Directors, in such case, will defray the passage home, and the sum of Ten pounds sterling for expenses, as provided for in Clause 7 hereof.

10. This Agreement, unless previously determined in manner aforesaid, shall remain in force after the expiration of the said term of three years until determined by either party by three months' previous notice in writing to the other in manner hereinbefore provided.

11. This Agreement shall have the same force and effect in Chili and Bolivia in respect of the laws of Chili and Bolivia as if the same had been made and concluded in either of those Countries.

As WITNESS the hands of the said George William Craig and of one of the Directors and the Secretary of the Company, the day and year first above written.

Signed by the said

GEORGE WILLIAM CRAIG. ______________________

in the presence of

Witness ______________

Address ______________

Occupation ______________

For and on behalf of
ANTOFAGASTA (CHILI) & BOLIVIA RAILWAY COMPANY LIMITED,

______________________ Director.

______________________ Secretary.

To be filled in by employee.
Name and Address in the United Kingdom of next-of-kin or other person to whom communications are to be sent during absence of employee abroad.

Name ______________

Address ______________

APPENDIX 3

NOTE ON SOURCES

Andrew Barnard

The principal sources used in the writing of this work were the following materials from the FCAB Archive, currently housed at the company's London office.

1. *Correspondence between the general managers of the Chilean Section, Antofagasta, and the company secretaries, managing directors and chairmen based in London.* There are over a hundred volumes in this series which covers the years 1904 to 1982. Inward and outward bound letters are grouped together throughout the series but there were some changes in the numbering of volumes and the classification of letters which are perhaps worthy of note since they give rise to apparent inconsistencies of annotation in the footnotes. Briefly, prior to 1948, the volumes were not numbered, except for the years between 1914 and 1920, and letters classified as 'Private Official' or 'Private Confidential' were not numbered until after June 1945 and both these classifications were replaced by a single new numbered class, 'Confidential', in October 1947. While the volumes began to be numbered again after 1948, their numbers have not generally been cited in this work since date, classification and provenance are sufficient to locate the whereabouts of any letter in the Archive.

The correspondence in this series consists of frequent and detailed reports on all aspects of the company's business and the responses and instructions from the London office. As such, it provides the richest source of information on the day-to-day running of the company and on the attitudes and concerns of the company's chief officers both in London and in Chile.

Over the years, there have been changes in the nature of the correspondence between London and Antofagasta, a reflection of both the ease or otherwise of communication and of the demands of the managing director in London. Undoubtedly the heyday of the formal and detailed communication was between the wars, particularly when A.W. Bolden was in charge of the London office in his various capacities. During the Second World War, letters became relatively brief and infrequent and, while there was something of a return to the lengthier report and instruction during the 1950s, the overall tendency was towards increasing conciseness. By the 1970s, written communications had become very brief indeed and by the 1980s the advent of new communication technology and the transfer of ownership and effective management to Chile in 1982 had obviated the need for lengthy reports and instructions.

It should, perhaps, be noted here that while the record of FCAB activities in Chile since 1904 has survived more or less intact, the same cannot be said of the Bolivian side of the enterprise. Some years after nationalization, the correspondence between London and La Paz dealing with the company's activities in Bolivia up to that point was destroyed. Thus, while there are a few volumes of correspondence dealing with company matters in the post-nationalization era, little evidence survives from the earlier period apart from account books, the printed annual reports of the Bolivia Railway Company and the FCAB, and such information as found its way into the Chilean series, general letter books and board minute books.

2. *General letter books*. This series commenced in 1948 and there are currently twenty-three numbered volumes, covering the years 1949 to 1979. Consisting of copies of letters sent by the London office to a variety of correspondents ranging from school children and members of the public to FCAB directors and Foreign Office officials, it is very much a miscellaneous collection of letters. However, it is useful for giving another perspective on the work and concerns of the London office, and for the evidence it provides of efforts made to protect company interests in matters ranging from tariff negotiations with Bolivian tin magnates to formal contacts with the British Foreign Office at moments of crisis when nationalization threatened in Bolivia and seemed to threaten in Chile.

3. *Annual account books, 1904–1969*. This series comprises detailed annual accounts together with reports by the local auditors and by the FCAB's chief accountants. They also contain copies of the annual reports prepared by the two general managers in Antofagasta and La Paz and which gave a comprehensive account of the activities and experience of the railway in both countries. The annual reports from the general manager, La Paz, are particularly valuable since they are the main surviving record of the FCAB's activities in Bolivia from the 1910s to the 1950s.

4. *Reports of directors and statements of accounts, 1904 to present*. These include the reports which the directors present to the shareholders each year and a record of the chairman's statement to the annual general

meeting together with the responses, if any, of the shareholders. From 1904, when the FCAB took over direct management of its lines, this information was published in pamphlet form, and verbatim reports of the annual general meetings also appeared in *The Times*. While the Second World War saw an end to that last practice, the information continued to be published in pamphlet form after the war although, as elsewhere, the tendency was towards increasing brevity. Since much of the information contained in the directors's reports was taken directly from the annual reports of the general managers, the series is mainly useful for its record of the annual general meetings and for the statements made by the chairmen on those occasions.

5. *Minutes of the FCAB board, 1888–1982.* Forty-three volumes. This series contains the minutes from the first board meeting in November 1888 until November 1982, when the seat of the company was formally transferred to Chile. It was chiefly useful in tracing developments prior to the FCAB's assumption of direct management in 1904.

6. *Card index of contract staff.* Contains details of employment of most contract staff who served the company in Chile and Bolivia from 1904 until the early 1970s. It also includes cards for some Chilean legal and medical experts employed by the company.

7. *Other materials.* While the FCAB Archive has been, by far, the most important resource for this book, where appropriate reference has also been made to the local press in Chile, in particular, to *El Mercurio* of Antofagasta. Some biographical information on the FCAB directors was also culled from local British newspapers such as *The South Wales Daily Star* and the *The Surrey Herald* although national newspapers, and notably *The Times,* and the standard works of biographical reference were the more usual sources of such information.

SELECT BIBLIOGRAPHY

AHUMADA MANCHOT, María T, CONTADOR VARAS, Adolfo, DURAN DIAZ, Guadalupe and STRAVROS BRACAMONTE, Jorge, *Antofagasta: repertorio del patrimonio histórico más representativo de la ciudad, 1866–1930,* Universidad del Norte, 1982.

ALBERT, Bill, *South America and the First World War. The impact of the war on Brazil, Argentina, Peru and Chile*, CUP, 1988.

ANDERSON SMITH, W., *Temperate Chile: A Progressive Spain*, London, 1899.

ANGELL, Alan, *Politics and the Labour Movement in Chile*, OUP, London, 1972.

ARAMAYO AVILA, Césareo, *Ferrocarriles Bolivianos: pasado, presente, futuro*. Imprenta Nacional, La Paz, 1959.

BERMUDEZ MIRAL, Oscar, 'Las oficinas salitreras adyacentes a la linea del ferrocarril de Antofagasta a Bolivia', *Boletín de la Asociación de Geógrafos de Chile*, No.3, 1967.

BLAKEMORE, Harold., 'Chile', in Harold Blakemore and Clifford T. Smith (eds.), *Latin America: Geographical Perspectives*, 2nd ed., Methuen, London, 1983, pp.457–531.

– 'Chile from the War of the Pacific to the World Depression, 1880–1930', in Leslie Bethell (ed.), *The Cambridge History of Latin America*, Vol. V, CUP, 1986, pp.449–551.

– *British Nitrates and Chilean Politics, 1886–1896: Balmaceda and North,* Athlone Press, London, 1974.

– 'Chile: the critical jucture?', in *The Yearbook of World Affairs*, Stevens & Sons, London, 1973, pp.39–61.

BONILLA, Heraclio, 'Peru and Bolivia from Independence to the War of the Pacific', in Leslie Bethell (ed.), *The Cambridge History of Latin America*, Vol. III, CUP, 1985.

BOWMAN, Isaiah, *Desert Trails of Atacama*, New York, 1924.

BRADY, G.S. and LONG, W.R., *Railways of South America, Part III – Chile*, Bureau of Foreign and Domestic Commerce, Washington D.C., 1930.

CARPENTER, Frank G., *South America: Social, Industrial and Political*, New York, 1900.

CASTEDO, Leopoldo, *Resumen de la Historia de Chile, 1891–1925*, Santiago, 1982.
COLLIER, Simon, 'Chile from Independence to the War of the Pacific', in Leslie Bethell (ed.), *The Cambridge History of Latin America*, Vol. III, CUP, 1985.
COUYOUMDJIAN, J.R., *Chile y Gran Bretana durante la guerra mundial y la postguerra, 1914–1921*, Santiago, 1986.
CURTIS, W.E., *Capitals of Spanish America*, New York, 1888.
DE SHAZO, Peter, *Urban Workers and Labor Unions in Chile, 1902–1927*, University of Wisconsin Press, Madison, 1983.
DRAKE, Paul W., *Socialism and Populism in Chile, 1932–1952*, University of Illinois Press, Urbana, 1978.
ELLSWORTH, P.T., *Chile: an Economy in Transition*, Macmillan, New York, 1945.
ENOCK, C.R., *The Republics of Central and South America*, London, 1922.
FAWCETT, Brian, *Railways of the Andes*, Allen & Unwin, London, 1963.
FIFER, J. Valerie, *Bolivia: Land, Location and Politics since 1825*, CUP, 1972.
FRANCIS, Michael J., *The Limits of Hegemony: United States Relations with Argentina and Chile during World War II*, Notre-Dame-London: University of Notre Dame Press, 1977.
GEDDES, Charles F., *Patiño: the Tin King*, Robert Hale, London, 1972.
GIL, Federico., *The Political System of Chile*, Houghton, Mifflin Co., Boston, 1966.
HIRSCHMAN, Albert O., 'Inflation in Chile', in *Journeys Towards Progress: Studies of Economic Policy-Making in Latin America*, The Twentieth Century Fund, 1963, New York, pp.161–223.
JOSLIN, David, *A Century of Banking in Latin America: Bank of London & South America Limited, 1862–1962*, OUP, London, 1963.
KLEIN, Herbert S., *Parties and Political Change in Bolivia, 1880–1952*, CUP, 1969.
– 'The Creation of the Patiño Tin Empire', *Inter-American Economic Affairs*, Vol.XIX, No.2, Autumn, 1965.
– 'David Toro and the Establishment of "Military Socialism" in Bolivia', *Hispanic American Historical Review*, Vol.XIV, No.1, February, 1965.
– 'German Busch and the Era of 'Military Socialism" in Bolivia' *Hispanic American Historical Review*, Vol.XLVII, No.2, May, 1967.
LEWIS, Colin M., *British Railways in Argentina, 1857–1914*, Athlone Press, London, 1983.
LORA, Guillermo, *A History of the Bolivian Labour Movement* (edited and abridged by Laurence Whitehead and translated from the Spanish by Christine Whitehead) CUP, 1977.

MAITLAND, Francis J.G., *Chile: its land and people,* London, 1914.
MARCOSSON, Isaac F., *Anaconda*, Dodd, Mead & Co., New York, 1957.
MESA-LAGO, Carmelo, *Social Security in Latin America: Pressure Groups, Stratification, and Inequality*, University of Pittsburgh Press, Pittsburgh, 1978, pp.22–69.
MILLER, Rory, 'Transferring Techniques: Railway Building and Management on the West Coast of South America', in Rory Miller and Henry Finch, *Technology Transfer and Economic Development in Latin America, 1850–1930*, University of Liverpool: Institute of Latin American Studies, Working Paper No.7, 1986.
MITRE Antonio, 'The Economic and Social Structure of Silver Mining in XIX Century Bolivia', Unpub. Ph.D. thesis, Columbia University, 1977.
MONTEON, Michael, *Chile in the Nitrate Era: the Evolution of Economic Dependence, 1880–1930,* University of Wisconsin Press, Madison, 1982.
NUNN, Frederick M., *Chilean Politics, 1920–1931. The Honorable Mission of the Armed Forces*, University of New Mexico Press, Albuquerque, 1970.
O'BRIEN, Thomas F., 'The Antofagasta Company: a Case Study of Peripheral Capitalism', *Hispanic American Historical Review*, Vol.60, No.1, Feb., 1980.
O'REARDON OVERBECK, Alicia, *Living High or at home in the High Andes*, London, 1935.
PENTLAND, J.P., *Report on Bolivia, 1827.* (edited and with an introduction by J. Valerie Fifer) Royal Historical Society, *Camden Miscellany*, XXV, London, 1974.
PIZARRO, Crisóstomo, *La Huelga Obrera en Chile, 1890–1970*, Ediciones SUR, Santiago, 1986.
RAVEST MORA, Manuel, *La Compañia Salitera y la Ocupación de Antofagasta, 1878–1879*, Santiago, 1983.
RECABARREN, Floreal, OBILINOVIC, Antonio, and PANADES, Juan, *Coloso: una aventura histórica*, Universidad de Antofagasta, 1983.
REYNOLDS, Clark Winton, 'Development Problems of an Export Economy: the Case of Chile and Copper' in Markos Mamalakis and Clark Winton Reynolds, *Essays on the Chilean Economy*, Richard D. Irwin Inc., Homewood Ill., 1965, pp. 203–357.
RUDOLPH, W.E., *Vanishing Trails of Atacama*, New York, 1963.
STEVENSON, J.R., *The Chilean Popular Front*, Greenwood Press, Westport, Conn., 1942.
SUTULOV, A. (ed.), *El Cobre chileno*, Santiago de Chile: Corporación del Cobre, 1975.
TITUS, A., *Monografía de los Ferrocarriles Particulares de Chile*, Valparaiso, 1910.

VIDAL CASTILLO, Marta Isabel, 'Estudio del Desarrollo de las Actividades del Ferrocarril de Antofagasta a Bolivia (1915–1924), Basada Preferentemente en el Análisis del Servicio de Transporte', Unpublished Memoria, Universidad del Norte, 1982.

ZONDAG, Cornelius H., *The Bolivian Economy 1952–1965. The Revolution and its Aftermath*, Praeger, New York, 1966.

INDEX